THE

ANALOGY OF RELIGION,

TO THE

Constitution and Course of Nature.

TO WHICH ARE ADDED

TWO BRIEF DISSERTATIONS:

I. ON PERSONAL IDENTITY.—II. ON THE NATURE OF VIRTUE.

BY

JOSEPH BUTLER, D.C.L.

Ejus [Analogiæ] hæc vis est, ut id quod dubium est ad aliquid simile, de quo non quæritur referat ut incerta certis probet.—QUINTIL. l. i. c. 6.

WITH

AN INTRODUCTION, NOTES, CONSPECTUS, AND AMPLE INDEX,

BY

HOWARD MALCOM, D.D.
PRESIDENT OF THE UNIVERSITY, LEWISBURG, PENNSYLVANIA.

SEVENTEENTH EDITION.

PHILADELPHIA:
J. B. LIPPINCOTT & CO.
1873.

Entered according to Act of Congress, in the year 1857, by
J. B. LIPPINCOTT & CO.
in the Clerk's Office of the District Court of the United States in and for the Eastern District of Pennsylvania.

CONTENTS.

PAGE

EDITOR'S INTRODUCTION 5

" PREFACE 19

" CONSPECTUS 21

AUTHOR'S ADVERTISEMENT 66

" INTRODUCTION 67

PART I.

OF NATURAL RELIGION.

CHAP. I.—A Future Life 77

CHAP. II.—The Government of God by Rewards and Punishments 95

CHAP. III.—The Moral Government of God 105

CHAP. IV.—Probation, as implying Trial, Difficulties, and Danger 128

CHAP. V.—Probation, as intended for Moral Discipline and Improvement. 136

CHAP. VI.—The Opinion of Necessity, considered as influencing Practice. 157

CHAP. VII.—The Government of God, considered as a Scheme or Constitution, imperfectly comprehended 171

CONCLUSION 180

PART II.

OF REVEALED RELIGION.

PAGE
CHAP. I.—The Importance of Christianity 186

CHAP. II.—The supposed Presumption against a Revelation, considered as miraculous 202

CHAP. III.—Our Incapacity of judging, what were to be expected in a Revelation; and the Credibility, from Analogy, that it must contain things appearing liable to Objections 209

CHAP. IV.—Christianity, considered as a Scheme or Constitution, imperfectly comprehended 223

CHAP. V.—The Particular System of Christianity; the Appointment of a Mediator, and the Redemption of the World by him 230

CHAP. VI.—Want of Universality in Revelation; and of the supposed Deficiency in the Proof of it 247

CHAP. VII.—The Particular Evidence for Christianity 263

CHAP. VIII.—Objections against arguing from the Analogy of Nature to Religion 296

CONCLUSION 306

DISSERTATIONS.

DISSERTATION I.—Personal Identity 317

DISSERTATION II.—The Nature of Virtue 324

INDEX TO PART I 333

INDEX TO PART II 343

Editor's Introduction.

Joseph Butler was born at Wantage, England, May 18th, 1692, the youngest of eight children. The biographies of that day were few and meagre; and in few cases is this so much to be regretted as in Butler's. It would have been both interesting and profitable to trace the development and occupations of one of the mightiest of human minds. But no cotemporary gathered up the incidents of his life, and now all efforts to elicit them have been without success.

His father was a prosperous dry-goods merchant, who, at the time of his son's birth, had retired from business with a competency, and resided in a suburban mansion called "The Priory," still in existence.

Being a non-conformist, he educated Joseph at a "dissenting" academy at Gloucester, under Samuel Jones, a gentleman of great ability, and a skilful instructor, who raised up some of the greatest men of their day.*

It was while a member of this academy, and about the age of twenty-one, that Butler disclosed to the world his wonderful power of abstract reasoning, in his famous correspondence with Samuel Clarke, in relation to that eminent author's "*Demonstration of the Being and Attributes of God.*" This correspondence is now generally inserted at the end of that work.

Mr. Butler having deliberately adopted Episcopal views, and resolved to unite himself with the Established Church, his father, with praiseworthy liberality, sent him to Oxford, where he entered Oriel College, March, 1714. Of his college life there is no account; nor of the time and place of his ordination. He removed to London in 1718, on receiving the appointment of "Preacher at the Rolls." His famous Fifteen Sermons were preached in that chapel, and published before resigning the place, with a dedication to Sir Joseph Jekyl, "as a parting mark of gratitude for the favors received during his connection with that learned society."

---

* Among these were *Jones*, author of the admirable Treatise on the Canon of the New Testament: *Lardner*, *Maddox*, *Chandler*, Archbishop *Secker*, &c.

One of Butler's warmest college friends was Edward Talbot second son of a clergyman who afterwards became Bishop of Durham. This admirable young man died of smallpox; in his last hours recommending Butler to his father's patronage; and scarcely had that gentleman attained the see of Durham, before he gave Mr. B. the living of Haughton, from whence he transferred him, in 1725, to the richer benefice of Stanhope.

On receiving this honorable and lucrative appointment, he resigned the Lectureship at the Rolls, and in the autumn of 1726 retired to his beautiful residence at Stanhope. Here, without a family to occupy his time, he devoted himself to his great work, the Analogy: using horseback exercise, seeing little company, living abstemiously and caring for his flock.

Seven years thus rolled away; when to draw him from what seemed to his friends too great retirement and application, Lord-Chancellor Talbot made him his chaplain, and afterwards, in 1736, gave him a prebend's stall in Rochester. In 1736, Butler being now forty-four, Caroline, consort of George II., appointed him "Clerk of the Closet," an office which merely required his attendance at the Queen's apartments every evening, from seven to nine.

Being now in London, convenient to the press, and enjoying both leisure and competency, he published his immortal ANALOGY—the cherished work of his life. The Queen was delighted with the book, and made herself master of its glorious array of reasoning. But she died the same year, and he lost not only a patroness, but a friend. He returned to his benefice at Stanhope, the income of which had been held during his residence in London.

On her death-bed, the Queen had urged her husband to promote her honored chaplain to a bishopric; and next year, the see of Norwich becoming vacant, the Bishop of Bristol was translated to it, and the see of Bristol given to Butler. Bristol was the poorest bishopric in England, its emoluments being but $2,000 per annum; less than those of the rectorship of Stanhope. Butler distinctly disclosed his disappointment in his letter to the minister Walpole, accepting the position; and declared that he did not think it "very suitable to the condition of his fortune, nor answerable to the recommendation with which he was honored." The king was not displeased at this candor, and in 1740 improved his income by giving him, in addition to his bishopric, the profitable and influential office of Dean of St. Paul's. Butler, who had retained the living of Stannope along with his bishopric, now resigned that rectorship. "The rich revenues," says Professor Fitzgerald, "of the Deanery of St. Paul, enabled him to gratify his taste at Bristol." He expended about $25,000 in improving and beautifying the episcopal residence and gardens. He fostered useful charities, and employed his wealth for others rather than for himself.

In 1750, upon the death of Dr. Edward Chandler, Bishop of Durham, Butler was promoted to that see, the most honorable and lucrative in England. He had before been offered the Primacy, on the death of Archbishop Potter, but declined it, with the remark that "it was too late for him to try to support a falling church." On assuming his diocese at Durham, Butler delivered and published his famous Charge to the Clergy, upon "The Use and Importance of External Religion." He was at once assailed vigorously, in pamphlets and papers, by Archdeacon Blackburn, the Rev. T. Lindsay, and others, on the charge of Popery; an imputation which is still sometimes cast upon him, and which finds some slender support in his setting up a marble cross over the communion-table at Bristol. That he never was a Papist, is now so evident, that we can account for the imputation only by the strong jealousy of the Romish Church then prevalent.

Butler now became still more munificent. His private charities were exceedingly generous, and his public ones seemed sometimes to border on extravagance. He gave $2,000 a year to the county hospital, and often gave away thousands of dollars at a time. But though quite lavish in buildings and ornaments, as well as in benevolence, he was remarkably frugal in his personal expenses. It is said of him, by Rev. John Newton, that on one occasion, when a distinguished visitor dined with him by appointment, the provision consisted of a single joint of meat, and a pudding. The bishop remarked to his guest on that occasion, that he "had long been disgusted with the fashionable expense of time and money in entertainments, and was determined that it should receive no countenance from his example."

Of his amusements we know little except that he took much horseback exercise, and often employed his secretary, Mr. Emms, to play for him on the organ.

Butler held the see of Durham less than two years. Symptoms of general physical decay betrayed themselves about the time of his promotion, and in spite of all that skill and affection could prompt, he sunk to rest June 16th, 1752, aged sixty. He was never married

A considerable number of his sermons and charges have been printed, but are too philosophical to be generally read. His great work is the Analogy, published in 1736, and from that day read and admired by every highly-cultivated mind. He was induced to write by a state of things very remarkable in the history of religion. Debauchery and infidelity were almost universal, not in any one class of society but in all. England had reached the culminating point of irreligion, and the firm re-establishment of Episcopacy had as yet done nothing to mend the nation's morals. Piety was deemed a mark of ignorance and vulgarity, and multitudes of those who professed it were persecuted to dungeons and death.

Infidel writers, warmed into life by court corruption, became more numerous and audacious than ever before. Their methods of attacking Christianity were various; but the most successful then, as always, was to impugn certain doctrines and declarations of the Sacred Scriptures, as irrational, and hence reject the whole. They generally admitted the Being and perfection of God, and extolled the sufficiency of natural religion; but denied any revelation, or any necessity for one. The verdict of the world was that the Bible is not authentic, that man is not accountable, nor even probably immortal, that God neither rewards nor punishes, and that present indulgence, as far as our nature admits, is both wise and safe.

Bishop Downam,* one of the most learned of the clergy, in the early part of the seventeenth century writes thus: "In these times, if a man do but labor to keep a good conscience, though he meddle not with matters of state, if he make conscience of swearing, sanctify the Sabbath, frequent sermons, or abstain from the common corruptions of the times, he shall straightway be condemned for a puritan, and be less favored than either a carnal gospeller, or a close Papist."

It was considered settled, especially in polite circles, that Christianity, after so long a prevalence, had been found out to be an imposture. The clergy, as a body, did nothing to dispel this moral gloom, but rather increased it by their violent and scandalous conduct. In the sad language of Bishop Warburton, "Religion had lost its hold on the minds of the people." He adds with great point, "Though a *rule of right* may direct the philosopher to a principle of

* Sermon at Spittle, on Abraham's trial

action; and the *point of honor* may keep up the thing called manners, among gentlemen: yet nothing but *religion* can ever fix a sober standard of behavior among the common people." Even the universities were on the side of irreligion; for professorships, as well as pulpits, were given to men, not for positive worth and fitness, but for possessing qualities then most in vogue with those who held the appointing power. Such were the trying times which had driven our pilgrim fathers to seek a home amid the wilds of an unexplored continent, and to face the dangers of sea and savage.

It must ever be regarded as among the highest instances of God's bringing good out of evil, that this outrageous rampancy of infidelity brought out a host of champions for the truth of His word; who boldly met the odium of discipleship, and waged battle in such style that the Deistical controversy was settled forever. Never was a dispute more determined on both sides, and never was victory more complete. Literary infidelity not only recoiled, but was routed; and can never again prevail. Henceforth, no *scholar* will ever treat the evidences of Christianity as a subject of ridicule or contempt.

When we contrast the stupendous learning, and powerful logic, of the Christian writers of that century, with the superficial and almost contemptible productions of the writers against whom they contended, we are tempted to wonder why such power should be requisite to overthrow such weakness. But we must remember, that frail logic and shallow considerations, will persuade men to indulge their vices; while the soundest reasonings and the most impressive inducements, with difficulty lead them to self-restraint and true holiness.

The infidel writers of that day have sunk into such oblivion that their works are now seldom found but in great libraries; and even well-educated persons scarcely know more of them than their names. Yet so perfectly did their principles accord with the temper of the times and the universal depravity of the carnal heart, that they enjoyed the highest popularity with all classes. Forever honored be the names of that noble band, who, in face of such odds, established the authority of the Bible, and left the advocates of atheism and immorality without a lurking-place.* In this noble cohort Butler

* Among them were CUDWORTH, born 1617; "Intel. Syst. of the Universe:" BOYLE, 1626; "Things above Reason:" STILLINGFLEET, 1635; "Letters to a Deist:" Sir I. NEWTON, 1642; "Observations on Prophecy:" LESLIE, 1650; "Short Method with Deists:" LOWTH, 1661, Vindic. of the Divine Author

stands conspicuous: and to him, I think, more than to all the others, is to be attributed the sudden and total overthrow of infidelity, when it was in its glory.

As a metaphysician, few have equalled him. What he added to the science, has ever since remained a part of it, which can be said of scarcely another. He advanced more that was new, fortified old positions more ably, and applied speculation to religion more usefully than any before him. Our language furnishes no profounder thinking. Merely to understand him is an honorable distinction, and requires no small previous training of the power of attention. As a polemic, he is keen, sagacious, candid, patient, persevering, calm, inventive, and profound: every page indicates that repose of mind, which belongs only to true greatness, combined with a full knowledge of the subject. So far as I am able to judge, he never presses a consideration beyond its just limits, and seldom introduces an illustration which has not the force of an argument. Fallacies he seems to abolish at a touch.

The Analogy employed much of his life. It was begun in his twentieth year, but was not published till he was forty-five. Such a mode of writing never makes large books, for the matter, constantly revised, becomes constantly condensed. The Analogy is so condensed, as that to make a satisfactory synopsis is scarcely practicable. Hence, though my Conspectus and notes have aided my pupils to understand and remember the argument, they do not in any measure obviate the necessity of studying the book itself. If they do not increase the number of those who shall studiously peruse the book itself, my aim and expectations will be disappointed.

To this work no reply has ever been attempted! Extensive as is its diffusion, and great as is its acknowledged influence, infidelity has had the highest inducements to attempt to set it aside. Written for a present purpose, and most signally accomplishing it, it is yet so written as to endure, in full value, through all coming time. It is

---

of the Bible: KING, 1669; "Origin of Evil:" SAM. CLARK, 1675; "Evidences of Nat. and Rev. Religion:" WATERLAND, 1683; "Scripture Vindicated:" LARDNER, 1684; "Credibility of Gospel History:" LELAND, 1691; "View of Deistical Writers," and "Advantage and Necessity of Rev.:" CHANDLER, 1693; 'Definition of Christianity," on "Prophecy," &c.: WARBURTON, 1698; "Divine Leg. of Moses;" Bishop NEWTON, 1704; "On the Prophecies:" WATSON, 1737; "Apology for Christianity," (against Gibbon,) and also "Apology for the Bible," (against Paine.)

undoubtedly "the most original and the most profound work extant, in any language, on the philosophy of religion,"* "the most argumentative and philosophical defence of Christianity ever submitted to the world."†

Writers in defence of Christianity had, before Butler, amply discussed the several departments of evidences; but still there remained objections. The structure of the globe, the course of nature, the organization of animals, &c. were affirmed to contradict revelation. Its doctrines and duties, moreover, were pronounced inconsistent with sound reason. Butler repeats none of the old arguments, but confines himself to the showing that the declarations of revelation are in perfect harmony with facts seen daily in the world, and which all admit. That the world might not have been ordered and governed otherwise, he does not choose to dispute. Taking things as they are, and closely studying the connection between one thing and another, we ought to inquire what course of action on our part, will conform to the needs of such a nature and such circumstances. Our bodies are constructed of parts, all adapted to each other, and also to one general end. So too, our souls. And the two together have relations and adaptations, which may, to some extent at least, indicate what is designed to be the *general* end of our existence. If Christianity befits these several parts of our mixed nature and their obvious uses, then there is nothing incongruous between the two; and no objections against Christianity can be drawn from the course of nature. On the contrary, all seems to be governed as the gospel declares it is, and shows that the Author of man and the Author of the Bible is the same. This is still more impressive when we consider that we have a *moral faculty;* for it is the very object and business of this faculty to deal with right and wrong, good and evil; the facts and magnitudes of which are obvious in the course of nature. If Christianity does, in an especial manner, *befit* this faculty, if it is adapted to promote our general rectitude and happiness, and if it contains no principle which is not discernible in the government of the visible world, then there is no discrepancy between Christianity and Providence.

This is Butler's position. He confines himself to proving such an analogy between revelation and the daily course of things, as that nothing known in the universe can be offered in disproof of Chris-

* McIntosh: "Progress of Ethical Philosophy."

† Brougham: "Disc. on Nat. Theology."

tianity. The mode of warfare was new. Without professing to prove Christianity to be true, he demonstrates that it cannot be proved to be false; and that if it be even probable, the rejection of it is a gross folly and a tremendous hazard. Every objection against it he proves to be equally forcible against facts which constantly occur, and which all admit, though none profess to understand. Thus leaving the ramparts of the church to be guarded by the mighty men who had valiantly maintained its defence, he quietly walked out into the camp of the enemy, and spiked every gun!

It has been said that the whole argument of the "Analogy" seems to be built on Ecclesiasticus xlii. 24: "All things are double, one against the other, and God hath made nothing imperfect." If it be so, it involves no disparagement to have received thus the seminal idea of this immortal work. Who else has so gloriously discerned and expanded the profound philosophy of the son of Sirac? Others have uttered sentiments which seem to involve the whole exposition of Butler. Origen affirms that "he who believes the Scripture to have proceeded from Him who is the Author of nature, may well expect to find the same sort of difficulties in it, as are found in nature." Shall we assign to Origen the whole credit of the "Analogy"? As well might we bestow all our admiration for the delightful papers of Addison, in the Spectator, to the classical authors from whom he selected appropriate mottoes! By such a rule, the entire merit of this most Christian work of Butler should be attributed to the pagan Quintilian, from whom he derives the motto which so appropriately graces his title-page.

A rapid sketch of the outline of the argument will aid the student at his outset. He begins by taking for granted the existence of an intelligent Author and Governor of the universe. Then, from the conditions and changes observed in the visible world, he argues the folly of objecting to revelation on account of doctrines which do but declare the same general laws and the same principles of government. That there is this harmony, he proves; and hence the probability that the same sort of government will prevail hereafter, which prevails now. He demonstrates that man is under exactly such a probation in this world, and as to this world, as revelation affirms him to be under, as to the next; and that embarrassments produced by the doctrine of necessity, involve nature no less than religion. He then evinces the need that man should be placed in a state of training and trial, if he is ever to be qualified for better conditions; and that this world, as now governed, is exactly adapted to give that training, and to produce such a character as will insure happiness under any possible contingencies. This is the argument of Part I.

Proceeding to examine Christianity, he discusses its importance, its proofs, the unavoidableness of its containing strange things, the absurdity of expecting fully to comprehend its statements, and the abundance of its evidence for candid minds, though they are not, and ought not to be, irresistible. He answers not only the objections to Christianity, but the objections against its proofs; which he shows are very different things. Though he keeps rigidly to the refutation of objections, and nowhere meddles with the direct evidence of Christianity, yet, by removing every objection, he does in fact confirm its claims. This clearing away of objections, *after* the usual proofs are presented, crowns and completes the evidence. Thus the ultimate result of a study of his book is not only negative but positive; and such has been its effect on every candid and competent student.

We should remember that we have no right to require the removal of objections, and that therefore the whole of Butler's work is in fact supererogatory; a concession and kindness to such as have doubts, either honest or captious. Our only rightful demand of Christianity is for *credentials.* It presents these in its nature, its miracles, its prophecies, its propagation, its influence, and its success. If these are competent, we should bow to its teachings. To suppose that we are capable of judging of the *propriety* of all God's law, or even to understand his reasons for it, if they were disclosed, is absurd.

It is true we naturally presume that a revelation in words, and a revelation by natural objects and the visible order of things, would coincide; but to find out the fact or the extent of such coincidence, is not our first business. We are to weigh the *testimony* in favor of religion, embrace it, if sufficient, and attribute the obscurity of any part, to our present want of capacity. The solution of difficulties serves to *confirm* our faith in Christianity, but has no place in our *ground of reception:* and we have no right to wait for such solution, however painful and embarrassing may be the difficulties.

Another, and perhaps even more important, use of the "Analogy," is to dissipate the prejudices and objections to Christianity which prevent a candid study of its evidences. These prepossess and poison the mind, and obstruct or abate the force of the best arguments. Few, if any, after a careful examination of the positive evidences of Christianity, conclude them to be inadequate. But many are they, who having heard objections which their scanty learning does not enable them to answer, and their no less scanty interest in the subject does not induce them to examine, or which their inclinations lead them to cherish, cast it all aside. In this way they relieve themselves from the labor of investigation, as well as their compunctions of conscience; while they indulge both their love of sin and pride of singularity.

An instance of the use of this book to such a mind, we have in the case of Chalmers. He had read, when a young man, several infidel productions. Their semblance of logic and learning, and supercilious confidence of style, disposed him to regard all religion as mere superstition. His mind was poisoned. Accustomed as he had been to the positive and precise reasonings of mathematics, he could not find similar proofs for Christianity. But he was induced, by some friends, to study Butler's Analogy. This, as he expresses it, took Christianity "out of the class of unlikelihoods." It brought him to the investigation, as if the evidence was neither plus nor minus. He examined the evidences as he would have done a declaration that Cicero weighed just one hundred and fifty pounds; open to the smallest proof or presumption on the positive side of the question. Delivered from prejudice, not only against Christianity but against its proofs, he soon saw the madness of deism, and immovably accepted the word of God, though he did not, at that time, feel its transforming power on his own heart. Long afterwards he writes, "I cannot render sufficient homage to the argument, which first, addressing itself to the *subject-matter* of Christianity, relieves it of all disproof, and pronounces it worthy of a trial; and then, addressing itself to the evidence of Christianity, relieves it of all objections, and makes good, to that evidence, all the entireness and efficiency which natively belong to it." Years afterwards he said, "Butler made me a Christian." That it did far more for him than to effect his change of sentiment, that it continued to be a light in his firmament, is touchingly told in the Preface of his Bridgewater Treatise, where he says, "I have derived greater aid from the views and reasonings of Butler, than I have been able to find, besides, in the whole range of our extant authorship."

To the sincere believer in the word of God the study of Butler is of great use. Doubts are among Satan's tried weapons, and often haunt the holiest, especially if of a contemplative turn. They see goodness oppressed, and vice rampant; the world ruled by wicked men, and truth making its way with difficulty. Their hearts are traitorous, their surroundings full of temptation, and the direct evidence of Christianity they may never have studied. To such the analogical argument comes with full power, meets a candid examination, and prevails.

To no Christian is this book so useful as the minister. He is constantly confronted by the difficulties which Butler so triumphantly handles. Here he is furnished, not only with a shield to protect his own mind from subtle darts, but a sword to demolish the cavil, and defend the system of which he is a public teacher.

To *all* persons this book is of great value. We arrive at certainty in but few of our decisions, and are often obliged, even in matters of great moment, to act on probability. Thus we employ precautions when an evil is not certain to occur. If the evil would be very serious, we adopt the precaution, when there is but little probability, or perhaps a bare possibility, of its occurrence. Now, Butler has shown that if the proofs of revelation were weak, nay, if it had absolutely no proof, nay further, if on fair examination there appeared not even a probability of its truth, still there would remain a *possibility*, and this alone, considering the tremendous issues at stake, should make every man a Christian. This argument cannot be applied to Mahometanism or any other religion, because against those much may be advanced as *disproof*. Our author, having shown the utter absence of disproof, shuts us up to the reception of Christianity, were its truth barely possible.

There have not been wanting persons to disparage the "Analogy," because it affords, as they say, no *direct* proof of revelation. As well might we demand a discussion of chemistry in a work on astronomy. Scores of writers *prove* Christianity, and here we have one to relieve us from the difficulties which beset it, and objections which still remain. There is an aspect in which the Analogy may be said to contribute the best of proof. What can go further towards establishing a point, than to demonstrate that there is no proof of the contrary? What can show the fallacy of a set of objections, more than to prove that they might be urged with no less force against the obvious course of nature? This use of analogy is conformable to the severest logic, and though offering no pretence of positive argument, goes far towards establishing full conviction. "The probabilities," says STEWART, "resulting from a concurrence of different analogies, may rise so high as to produce an effect on the belief scarcely dis tinguishable from moral certainty."

When it is considered that Butler's argument is wholly in addition to the cumulative mass of direct and almost irresistible evidence, and removes even the objections which attend the subject, we see the rejection of Christianity to be inexpressibly rash and absurd. We see the skeptic condemned at his own bar, for acting in the most momentous of all possible concerns, in a manner the very opposite of that which he calls sensible and prudent in his ordinary affairs. The "Analogy" establishes, beyond cavil, strong *presumptions* that Christianity is true, aside from all inspection of its proofs. The man, therefore, who really understands this book, and refuses to be a Christian, is led by his lusts and not his reason.

Some admirers of this book have lamented as a defect, its want of evangelical tincture, and its exclusive reference to natural things. To me, this is a prime recommendation. Were it otherwise, the reasoning would be in a circle. The very structure of the argument demands that it should avoid quotations from the Bible.

It must be admitted, however, that some expressions, taken just as they stand, without qualification by the current of the argument, tend to lead astray. For instance, "There is nothing in the human mind contrary to virtue." "Men's happiness and virtue are left to themselves." "Religion requires nothing which we are not well able to perform." "Our repentance is accepted, to eternal life." "Our relations to God are made known by reason." Such expressions are not to be taken alone, but as explained by the general drift of sentiment and doctrine. No one can be familiar with his works, without finding the fullest evidence that Christianity was to Butler infinitely more than a creed or a ritual. Nor should we forget that such expressions are not to be interpreted by the tenor of the "Analogy" only, but by that of his whole 'Works.'

Even if it be judged that he everywhere fails to express himself in such phrase as we usually call evangelical, it should be remembered that he was a Church-of-England man, at a time when there was a powerful reaction against the evangelism of the Puritans, and when a real lack of emotional piety was general in his church.

That he did not enjoy in his last illness, which extended over a long period, that sustaining sense of the love of Christ which hearty Christians generally feel, is certain. A friend, trying to relieve his depression, reminded him of his excellent life, and especially his wide liberalities. He immediately replied, "I am but a steward! All is His, intrusted to me, to promote his glory and the good of mankind; how can I know that I have not abused the trust? I reflect on all these things, and they fill my soul with terror by the feeling of responsibility they awaken."

On another occasion, his chaplain sought to soothe his troubled spirit by referring to the extensive influence of his *Analogy* in reclaiming skeptics. His reply was, "I *began* the Analogy with a view to the glory of God; but as I proceeded, visions of the fame it might bring me mingled themselves with my motives, and all was polluted and made sinful! The book may be a blessing to others, but it weighs like lead on my soul." "Admit all this," tenderly replied the chaplain; "yet has not Jesus said, 'Whosoever cometh unto me shall in no wise be cast out'?" Instantly the Bishop raised himself in the bed, exclaiming, "How wonderful that the force of this passage never struck me before! 'Whosoever,'—*all*, ALL! 'In no wise,'—no amount of sin can prevent acceptance! Christ's righteousness will hide the iniquities of *all* who accept his offer of mercy!"

From that time, for weeks, Butler spoke to all who approached him, of a *full* and *free* salvation. He died triumphantly repeating this passage.

If all that is said of the lack of evangelical sentiment in Butler or his book be conceded, it certainly cannot impair either the value of the analogical argument, or the force of our author's use of it.

Various circumstances conspire to make the study of "The Analogy" difficult. The nature of the reasoning—the conciseness, and often obscurity of the style—the dislocation of parts by frequent digressions—the arrest of a close course of reasoning to answer objections—and the abstruseness of the subject itself—combine to make the full comprehension of its import difficult. Mackintosh says, "No thinker so great, was ever so bad a writer." But this, like some other objections of Sir James, is stated too strongly. The language is good, sinewy Saxon, and will endure when much that is now called fine writing, will seem grotesque. Still it is possible to write philosophy in better phrase, as has been shown by at least two great men, Berkeley and Stewart. Had Butler but possessed the glowing style of Berkeley, or the smooth, graceful, and transparent diction of Dugald Stewart, his work, instead of serving only for close thinkers, or a college text-book, would have been read by all classes, and banished that vulgar infidelity which flippant writers still disseminate. That it is thus restricted in its influence is a misfortune to the world. But he wrote for a class, and did his work completely. Literary infidelity was conquered. Vulgar, ignorant, licentious infidelity, will always exist, and is even now deplorably prevalent. Both Europe and America contain conceited and malignant ignoramuses, who by their sneers, their cavils, and their audacity, make havoc of souls. Of these, Tom Paine is a type, whose book, the contempt of cultivated minds, continues to be sold and read. For this class of persons, "Baxter's Call," or "Alleine's Alarm," are far more suitable than treatises on the evidences of Christianity, or even Butler's Analogy.

Editor's Preface.

THE text is the result of a careful collation of the various principal editions. Occasionally solecisms are corrected, and a word transposed or put in italics, when a sentence could thus be made perspicuous. The author had a fashion of beginning a large proportion of his sentences with "and," "but," "now," "indeed," "however," &c., which often served to perplex, and in such cases they have been omitted. Long paragraphs, comprehending different topics, have been so divided as to correspond with the true analysis; which will greatly assist the student in detecting the successive stages of the argument. Special pains has been taken to correct and improve the punctuation. Hundreds of sentences have thus been rendered more perspicuous, and many which were obscure, have been made lucid. In no respect was Butler's style, as printed, so defective.

The Conspectus is made much ampler than any other, for this reason: that students are apt to content themselves with such help instead of mastering the full discussion by the author. In the present case they cannot so do, for such is the fulness of the Conspectus, that if they master this, they have mastered the subject itself in full.

Notes by the present editor are distinguished from those of the author by being enclosed in brackets. They are designed to open out further views, to elucidate the text, to facilitate extended researches, and to suggest topics for conversation in the class-room.

The Index has cost far more labor than would be supposed, and may not be of much benefit to the undergraduate. Its advantages will not be small to him in after life when he desires to recur to particular topics. The general scholar will find it enable him to make use of the book for occasional reference. Without it the work is not complete for the class-room, still less for the library.

That students of the Analogy need help, is confessed; and all attempts to furnish it have been kindly received. As is remarked by Bishop Wilson, "His argument, clear and convincing as it is to a prepared mind, is not obvious to the young reader, whose experience of life being small, and his habits of reflection feeble, has not the furniture necessary for comprehending, at first, the thoughts and conclusions of such a mind. The style is too close, too negligent, too obscure, to be suitable for the young."

If it be asked why, with several existing helps to the study of the Analogy, I offer another, I frankly reply, because I have found none of them satisfactory, either to the public or to myself.

Some teachers prefer their text-books to be accompanied by a set of questions. Such will find in this edition all they desire. They have only to enunciate each sentence of the Conspectus in the interrogative form, and they will have every possible question prepared to their hand.

Conspectus of the Author's Introduction.

I. *What is probable evidence?*

1. It differs from demonstration in that it admits of degrees; of all degrees.

1.) One probability does not beget assurance.

2.) But the slightest presumption makes a probability,

3.) The repetition of it may make certainty.

2. What constitutes probability is *likeness;* in regard to the event itself, or its kind of evidences, or its circumstances.

1.) This daily affords presumptions, evidence, or conviction: according as it is occasional, common, or constant.

2.) Measures our hopes and fears.

3.) Regulates our expectations as to men's conduct.

4.) Enables us to judge of character from conduct.

3. It is an imperfect mode of judging, and adapted to beings of limited capacities.

4. Where better evidence cannot be had, it constitutes moral obligation, even though great doubts remain.

1.) We are as much bound to do what, on the whole, *appears* to be best, as if we *knew* it to be so.

2.) In questions of great moment, it is reasonable to act when the favorable chances are no greater than the unfavorable.

3.) There are numberless cases in which a man would be thought distracted if he did not act, and that earnestly, where the chances of success were *greatly against* him.

II. *The use and application of probabilities.*

Shall not go further into the *nature* of probable evidence, nor inquire *why* likeness begets presumption and conviction; nor how far analogical reasoning can be reduced to a *system;* but shall only show how just and conclusive this mode of reasoning is.

1. In determining our judgments and practice.

1.) There may be cases in which its value is doubtful.

2.) There may be seeming analogies, which are not really such.

3.) But as a mode of argument, it is perfectly just and conclusive.

2. In noting correspondencies between the different parts of God's government.

1.) We may expect to find the same sort of difficulties in the Bible, as we do in Nature.
2.) To deny the Bible to be of God, because of these difficulties, requires us to deny that the world was made by him.
3.) If there be a likeness between revelation and the system of nature, it affords a presumption that both have the same author.
4.) To reason on the construction and government of the world, without settling foundation-principles, is mere hypothesis.
5.) To apply principles which are certain, to cases which are not applicable, is no better.
6.) But to join abstract reasonings to the observation of facts, and argue, from known present things, to what is likely or credible, must be right.
7.) We cannot avoid acting thus, if we act at all.

3. In its application to religion, revealed, as well as natural. This is the use which will be made of analogy in the following work. In so using it,

1.) It will be taken for proved that there is an intelligent Creator and Ruler.
—There are no presumptions *against* this, prior to proof.
—There are proofs:—from analogy, reason, tradition, &c.
—The fact is not denied by the generality of skeptics.
2.) No regard will be paid to those who idly speculate as to how the world *might* have been made and governed.
—Such prating would amount to this:
- All creatures should have been made at first as happy as they could be.
- Nothing of hazard should be put upon them.
- Should have been *secured* in their happiness.
- All punishments avoided.

—It is a sufficient reply to such talk that mankind have not faculties for such speculations.
3.) We are, to some extent, judges as to *ends;* and may conclude that Nature and Providence are designed to produce virtue and happiness; but of the *means* of producing these in the highest degree, we are not competent judges.
—We know not the extent of the universe;
—Nor even how one person can best be brought to perfection.
—We are not often competent to judge of the conduct of each other.
—As to God, we may presume that order will prevail in his universe; but are no judges of his modes for accomplishing this end.
4.) Instead of vainly, and perhaps sinfully, imagining schemes for God's conduct, we must *study what is.*
—Discovering general laws.
—Comparing the known course of things with what revelation teaches us to expect.

III. *The force of this use of Analogy.*

1. Sometimes is practically equivalent to proof.
2. Confirms what is otherwise proved.

3. Shows that the system of revelation is no more open to ridicule, than the system of nature.
4. Answers almost all objections against religion.
5. To a great extent answers objections against the *proofs* of religion.

IV. *General scope of the book.*

1. The divine government is considered, as containing in it,
Chap. 1. Man's future existence.
" 2. In a state of reward or punishment.
" 3. This according to our behavior.
" 4. Our present life probationary.
" 5. And also disciplinary.
" 6. Notwithstanding the doctrine of necessity.
" 7. Or any apparent want of wisdom or goodness.
2. Revealed religion is considered,
Chap. 1. As important.
" 2. As proved by miracles.
" 3. As containing strange things.
" 4. As a scheme imperfectly comprehended.
" 5. As carried on by a mediator.
" 6. As having such an amount of evidence as God saw fit to give
" 7. As having sufficient and full evidence.

Conspectus of the Analogy.

PART I.

CHAPTER I.

A FUTURE LIFE.

Will not discuss the subject of identity; but will consider what analogy suggests from changes which do not destroy; and thus see whether it is not *probable* that we shall live hereafter.

I. *The probabilities that we shall survive death.*

1. It is a law of nature that creatures should exist in different stages, and in various degrees of perfection.
—Worms turn into flies.
—Eggs are hatched into birds.
—Our own present state is as different from our state in the womb, as two states of the same being can be.

—That we shall hereafter exist in a state as different from the present as the present is from our state in the womb, is according to analogy.

2. We now have capacities for happiness, action, misery, &c., and there is always a probability that things will continue as they are, except when experience gives us reason to think they will be altered. This is a general law; and is our *only* natural reason for expecting the continuance of any thing.

3. There is no reason to apprehend that death will destroy us.

If there was, it would arise from the nature of death; or from the analogy of nature.

1.) Not from the nature of death.

—We know not what death is.

—But only *some* of its *effects*.

—These effects do not imply the destruction of the living agent.

—We know little of what the *exercise* of our powers depends upon; and nothing of what *the powers* themselves depend on.

—We may be unable to *exercise* our powers, and yet not lose them—*e.g.* sleep, swoon.

2.) Not from analogy.

—Reason shows no connection between death and our destruction.

—We have no faculties by which to trace any being beyond it.

—The possession of living powers, up to the very moment when our faculties cease to be able to trace them, is a probability of their continuing.

—We have already survived wonderful changes.

—To live after death is analogous to the course of nature.

II. *Presumptions against a future life.*

1. That death *destroys* us.

Ans. 1. This is an assumption that we are compound and material beings, and hence discerptible; which is not true.

1.) Consciousness is a single, indivisible power, and of course the subject of it must be.

2.) The material body is not ourself.

3.) We can easily conceive of our having more limbs, or of a different kind, or of having more or fewer senses, or of having no bodies at all, or of hereafter animating these same bodies, remodelled.

4.) The dissolution of a succession of new and strange bodies, would have no tendency to destroy *us*.

Ans. 2. Though the absolute simplicity of the living being cannot be proved by *experiment*, yet facts lead us so to conclude. We lose limbs, &c. Our bodies were once *very* small, but we might, then, have lost part of them. There is a constant destruction and renewal going on.

1.) Thus we see that no certain *bulk* is necessary to our existence, and unless it were proved that there is, and that it is larger than an indissoluble atom, there is no reason to presume that death destroys us, even if we are discerptible.

2.) The living agent is not an *internal material organism*, which dies with the body. Because

—Our only ground for this presumption is our relation to other systems of matter. But we see these are not necessary to us.

—It will not do to say that lost portions of the body were not *essential*—who is to determine?

—The relation between the living agent, and the most essential parts of the body, is only one by which they mutually affect each other.

3.) If we regard our body as made up of organs of sense, we come to the same result.

—We see with the eyes, just as we do with glasses. The eye is not a *recipient*, any more than a telescope.

—It is not pretended that vision, hearing, &c. can be traced clear up to the percipient; but so far as we *can* trace perceptions, *the organ* does not perceive.

—In dreams we perceive without organs.

—When we lose a limb we do not lose the *directing power;* we could move a new one, if it could be made, or a wooden one. But the limb cut off has no power of moving.

—Thus, our loss of the *organs* of perception and motion, not being the destruction of the power, there is no ground to think that the destruction of other organs or instruments would destroy *us*.

Objection. These observations apply equally to brutes.

Ans. 1. Be it so. Perhaps they are immortal:—may hereafter improve: we know not what latent powers they may have.

1.) The human being at one period looks as little likely to make great intellectual attainments; for a long time he has capacities for virtue and religion, but cannot use them.

2.) Many persons go out of the world who never became able to exercise these capacities; *e.g.* infants.

Ans. 2. If brutes were immortal, it does not prove them to be *moral agents.*

1.) It may be necessary, for aught we know, that there should be living creatures not moral agents, nor rational.

2.) All difficulties as to what would become of them, are founded in our ignorance.

2. That our souls, though not material, so depend upon the bodily structure, that we cannot survive its destruction.

Ans. 1. Reason, memory, &c. *do not* depend on the body, as perceptions by the senses do. Death may destroy those *instruments,* and yet not destroy the *powers* of reflection.

Ans. 2. Human beings exist, here, in two very different states, each having its own laws: sensation and reflection. By the first we feel; by the second we reason and will.

1.) Nothing which we know to be destroyed at death, is necessary to reflecting on ideas formerly received.

2.) Though the senses act like scaffolds, or levers, to *bring in* ideas, yet when once in, we can reflect, &c. without their aid.

Ans. 3. There are diseases which prove fatal, &c., yet do not, in any part of their course, *impair* the intellect; and this indicates that they do not *destroy* it.

1.) In the diseases alluded to, persons have their reflective power, in full, the very moment before death.

2.) Now, why should a disease, at a certain degree, utterly destroy powers which were not even affected by it, up to that point?

3. That death at least *suspends* our reflective powers, or interrupts our continuing to exist in the like state of reflection which we do now.

Ans. There appears so little connection between our powers of sensation and our powers of reflection that we cannot presume that what might *destroy the former,* could even *suspend the latter.*

1.) We daily see reason, memory, &c. exercised without any assistance, that we know of, from our bodies.

2.) Seeing them in lively exercise to the last, we must infer that death is not a discontinuance of their exercise, nor of the enjoyments and sufferings of such exercise.

3.) Our posthumous life may be but a going on, with additions. Like the change at our birth—which produced not a suspension of the faculties we had before, nor a *total* change in our state of life; but a continuance of both, with great alterations.

4.) Death may but at once put us into a *higher* state of life, as our birth did; our relation to bodily organs may be the only hinderance to our entering a higher condition of the reflective powers.

5.) Were we even sure that death would suspend our intellectual powers, it would not furnish even the lowest probability that it would destroy them.

Objec. From the analogy of plants.

Ans. This furnishes poets with apt illustrations of our frailty, but affords no proper analogy. Plants are destitute of perception and action, and this is the very matter in question.

REMARKS.

1. It has been shown, that confining ourselves to what we know, we see no probability of ever ceasing to be:—it cannot be concluded from the reason of the thing:—nor from the analogy of nature.

2. We are therefore to go upon the belief of a future existence.

3. Our going into *new scenes* and conditions, is just as natural as our coming into the world.

4. Our condition may naturally be a social one.

5. The advantages of it may naturally be bestowed, according to some fixed law, in proportion to one's degrees in virtue.

1.) Perhaps not so much as now *by society;* but by God's more immediate action.

2.) Yet this will be no less *natural, i.e.* stated, fixed, or settled.

3.) Our notions of what is natural, are enlarged by greater knowledge of God and his works.

4.) There may be some beings in the world, to whom the whole of Christianity is as natural as the visible course of nature seems to us.

6. These probabilities of a future life, though they do not satisfy curiosity, answer all the purposes of religion, as well as demonstration.

1.) Even a demonstration of a future state, would not demonstrate religion, but would be reconcilable with atheism.

2.) But as religion implies a future state, any presumption against such a state, would be a presumption against religion.
3.) The foregoing observations remove all presumptions of that sort, and prove to a great probability, a fundamental doctrine of religion.

CHAPTER II.

THE GOVERNMENT OF GOD BY REWARDS AND PUNISHMENTS.

THE question of a future life is rendered momentous by our capacity for happiness and misery.

Especially if that happiness or misery depends on our present conduct.

We should feel the deepest solicitude on this subject.

And that if there were no proof of a future life and interest, other than the probabilities just discussed.

I. *In the present world our pleasures and pains are, to a great extent, in our own power.*

1. We see them to be consequences of our actions.
2. And we can *foresee* these consequences.
3. Our desires are not gratified, without the right kind of exertion.
4. By prudence we may enjoy life; rashness, or even neglect may make us miserable.
5. Why this is so is another matter.
   1.) It may be impossible to be otherwise.
   2.) Or it may be best on the whole.
   3.) Or God's plan may be to make only the good happy.
   4.) Or the whole plan may be incomprehensible to us.

Objec. It may be said "this is only the course of nature."

Ans. It is granted: but

1. The course of nature is but the will of God. We admit that God is the natural governor of the world: and must not turn round and deny it because his government is *uniform.*
2. Our natural foresight of the consequences of actions, is his appointment.
3. The consequences themselves, are his appointment.
4. Our ability to foresee these consequences, is God's *instruction* how we are to act.

Objec. By this reasoning we are instructed to gratify our appetites, and such gratification is our reward for so doing.

Ans. Certainly not. Foreseen pleasures and pains are proper motives to action *in general;* but we may, in particular cases, damage ourselves by indulgence. Our eyes are made to see with, but not to look at every thing:—for instance the sun.

It follows, from what has been said, that

II. *We are, now, actually under God's government, in the strictest sense.*

1. Admitting that there is a God, it is not so much a matter of speculation, as of experience, that he governs us.

2. The annexing of pleasures and pains to certain actions, and giving notice of them, is the very essence of government.
3. Whether by direct acts upon us, or by contriving a general plan, does not affect the argument.
1.) If magistrates could make laws which should *execute themselves*, their government would be far more perfect than it is.
2.) God's making fire burn us, is as much an instance of government, as if he *directly inflicted* the burn, whenever we touched fire.
4. Hence the analogy of nature shows nothing to render incredible the Bible doctrine of God's rewarding or punishing according to our actions.

Additional remarks on Punishment.

As men object chiefly to future punishment, it is proper to show further that the course of administration, as to *present* punishment, is analogous to what religion teaches as to *the future.*

Indeed they add credibility to it.

And ought to raise the most serious apprehension.

I. *Circumstances to be observed touching present punishments.*

1. They often follow acts which produce present pleasure or advantage.
2. The sufferings often far exceed the pleasure or advantage.
3. They often follow remotely.
4. After long delay they often come suddenly.
5. As those remote effects are not certainly foreseen, they may not be thought of at the time; or if so, there is a hope of escaping.
6. There are opportunities of advantage, which if neglected do not recur.
7. Though, in some cases, men who have sinned up to a certain point, may retrieve their affairs, yet in many cases, reformation is of no avail.
8. Inconsiderateness is often as disastrous as wilful wrong-doing.
9. As some punishments by civil government, are capital, so are some natural punishments.
1.) Seem intended to remove the offender out of the way.
2.) Or as an example to others.

II. *These things are not accidental, but proceed from fixed laws.*

1. They are matters of daily experience.
2. Proceed from the general laws, by which the world is governed.

III. *They so closely resemble what religion teaches, as to future punishment, that both might be expressed in the same words.*

e.g. Proverbs, ch. i.

The analogy sufficiently answers all objections against the Scripture doctrine of future punishment, such as
1.) That our frailty or temptations annihilate the guilt of vice.
2.) Or the objection from necessity.
3.) Or that the Almighty cannot be contradicted.
4.) Or that he cannot be offended.

REMARKS.

1. Such reflections are terrific, but ought to be stated and considered.
2. Disregard of a hereafter cannot be justified by any thing short of a *demonstration* of atheism. Even skeptical doctrines afford no justification.
3. There is no pretence of reason for presuming that the licentious will not find it better for them that they had never been born.

CHAPTER III.

MORAL GOVERNMENT OF GOD.

As the structure of the world shows *intelligence*, so the mode of distributing pleasure and pain, shows government. That is, God's *natural* government, such as a king exercises over his subjects.

But this does not, at first sight, determine what is the *moral character* of such government.

I. *What is a moral or righteous government?*

1. Not mere rewarding and punishing.
2. But doing this according to character.
3. The perfection of moral government is doing this *exactly.*

Objec. God is simply and absolutely benevolent.

Ans. Benevolence, infinite in degree, would dispose him to produce the greatest possible happiness, regardless of behaviour. This would rob God of other attributes; and should not be asserted unless it can be proved. And whether it can be proved is not the point now in hand.

The question is not whether there may not be, in the universe, beings to whom he manifests absolute benevolence, which might not be incompatible with justice; but whether he treats *us* so.

4. It must be owned to be vastly difficult, in such a disordered world, to estimate with exactness the overplus of happiness on the side of virtue: and there may be exceptions to the rule. But it is far from being doubtful that *on the whole,* virtue is happier than vice, in this world.

II. *The beginnings of a righteous administration, are seen in nature.*

1. It has been proved (ch. ii.) that God *governs:* and it is reasonable to suppose that he would govern *righteously.*
   1.) Any other rule of government would be harder to account for.
   2.) The Bible doctrine that hereafter the good shall be happy, and the wicked miserable, is no more than an expectation that a method of government, now begun, shall be carried on.
2. The opposite consequences of prudence and rashness, show a right constitution of nature; and our ability to foresee and control these consequences, shows that we are under moral law.
3. God has so constructed society that vice, to a great degree, is actually punished by it.
   1.) Without this, society could not exist.

2.) This is God's government, through society; and is as *natural*, as society.
3.) Since the course of things is God's appointment, men are unavoidably accountable for their behaviour.

Objec. Society often punishes good actions, and rewards wickedness.

Ans. 1. This is not *necessary*, and consequently not natural.
2. Good actions are never punished by society *as good*, but because considered bad.

4. By the course of nature, virtue is rewarded, and vice punished, *as such*, which proves a moral government; as will be seen if we rightly distinguish between actions and their qualities.

1.) An action may produce present gratification though it be wrong: in which case the gratification is in the act, not the morality of it: in other cases the enjoyment consists wholly in the quality of virtuousness.
2.) Vice is naturally attended with uneasiness, apprehension, vexation, remorse, &c.
—This is a very different feeling from that produced by mere misfortune.
—Men comfort themselves under misfortune, that it was not their own fault.
3.) Honest and good men are befriended *as such*.
4.) Injuries are resented as implying fault; and good offices are regarded with gratitude on account of the *intention*, even when they fail to benefit us.
—This is seen in family government, where children are punished for falsehood, fretfulness, &c., though no one is hurt.
—And also in civil government, where the absence or presence of ill intention goes far in determining the penalty of wrong-doing.
5.) The whole course of the world, in all ages and relations, turns much upon approbation and disapprobation.
6.) The very fact of our having a moral nature, is a proof of our being under God's moral government.
—We are placed in a condition which unavoidably operates on our moral nature.
—Hence it arises that reward to virtue and reprobation of vice, as such, is a *rule*, never inverted. If it be thought that there are instances to the contrary, (which is not so,) they are evidently monstrous.
—The *degree* in which virtue and vice receive proper returns, is not the question now, but only the thing itself, in some degree.
7.) It is admitted that virtue sometimes suffers, and vice prospers; but this is *disorder*, and not the order of nature.
8.) It follows, that we have in the government of the world, a declaration from God, for virtue and against vice. So far as a man is true to virtue, is he on the side of the divine administration. Such a man must have a *sense of security*, and a hope of *something better*.

5. This hope is confirmed by observing that virtue has necessary tendencies beyond their present effects.

1.) These are very obvious with regard to individuals.
2.) Are as real, though not so patent, in regard to society.
—The power of a society under the direction of virtue, tends to prevail over power not so directed, just as power under direction of reason, tends to prevail over brute force.

—As this may not be conceded, we will notice how the case stands, as to reason:
- Length of time, and proper opportunity, are necessary for reason to triumph over brutes.
- Rational beings, disunited, envious, unjust, and treacherous, may be overcome by brutes, uniting themselves by instinct: but this would be an inverted order of things.

—A like tendency has virtue to produce superiority.
- By making the good of society, the object of every member of it.
- By making every one industrious in his own sphere.
- By uniting all in one bond of veracity and justice.

3.) If the part of God's government which we see, and the part we do not see, make up one scheme, then we see a *tendency* in virtue to superiority.

4.) But to *produce* that superiority there must be
—A force proportioned to the obstacles.
—Sufficient lapse of time.
—A fair field of trial; such as extent of time, adequate occasions, and opportunities for the virtuous to unite.

5.) These things are denied to virtue in this life, so that its tendencies, though real, are *hindered*.

6.) But it may have all requisite advantages hereafter.
—Eternity will be lasting enough.
—Good men will unite; as they cannot do now, scattered over the earth, and ignorant of one another.
—Other orders of virtuous beings will join; for the very nature of virtue is a bond of union.

7.) The tendency of such an order of things, so far as seen by vicious beings in any part of the universe, would be to the amendment of all who were capable of it, and their recovery to virtue.

8.) All this goes to show that the hinderances to virtue are contingent, and that its beneficial tendencies are God's declarations in its favor.

9.) If the preceding considerations are thought to be too speculative, we may easily come to the same result by reflecting on the supremacy which any earthly nation would attain, by entire virtue for many ages.

REMARKS.

Consider now the general system of religion. The government of the world is one; it is moral; virtue shall in the end prevail over wickedness; and to see the importance and fitness of such an arrangement we have only to consider what would be the state of things, if vice had these advantages, or virtue the contrary.

Objec. Why may not things be now going on in other worlds, and continue always to go on in this world, in the same mixed and disordered state as at present?

Ans. We are not proving that God's moral government is *perfect*, or the truth of religion, but only seeing what there is in the course of nature, to confirm it, supposing it to be known. Were there nothing to judge by, but the present distribution of pleasure and pain, we should have no ground to conclude that hereafter we should be rewarded or punished exactly according to our deserts. But even then there would be no indication that vice is better than virtue. Still the preceding observations *confirm* the doctrine of future retribution; for,

1.) They show that the Author of nature is not indifferent to virtue and vice.
2.) That future distributive justice would differ not in *kind*, but in degree only, from God's present government. It would be the *effect*, towards which we see the *tendency*.
3.) That higher rewards and punishments *may be* hereafter.
4.) That we should *expect* it to be so; because the tendencies of vice and virtue are immutable, while the hinderances are only artificial.

SUMMARY.

[This enumerates the steps of the argument, in the foregoing chapter, in as condensed a form as possible.]

CHAPTER IV.

OF A STATE OF PROBATION.

THE doctrine of probation comprehends several particulars. But the most common notion is that our future interests are *depending;* and depending on *ourselves.* And that we have *opportunities* for both good and bad conduct, and *temptations* to each.

This is not exactly the same as our being under moral government; for it implies allurement to evil, and difficulties in being good.

Hence needs to be considered by itself.

Doctrine. THE NATURAL GOVERNMENT OF GOD, IN THIS WORLD, PUTS US ON TRIAL AS TO THE THINGS OF THIS WORLD; AND SO IMPLIES, WHAT RELIGION TEACHES, THAT HIS MORAL GOVERNMENT PUTS US ON TRIAL AS TO A FUTURE WORLD.

I. *So far as we are tempted to do what will damage our future temporal interests, so far we are under probation as to those interests.*

1. The annexing of pleasures and pains to actions, as good or bad, and enabling us to foresee their effect, implies that our interests, in part at least, depend on ourselves.
2. We often *blame* ourselves and others for evils, as resulting from misconduct.
3. It is very certain that we often miss possible good, and incur evils, not for want of knowing better, but through our *fault.*
4. Every one speaks of the hazards of young persons, from other causes than ignorance.

II. *These natural or temporal trials are analogous to our moral and religious trial.*

1. In both cases, what constitutes the trial, is either in our circumstances or in our nature.

1.) Some would do right but for violent or extraordinary temptations.

2.) Others will *seek* evil, and go out of their way after wicked indulgence, when there are no external temptations.

3.) But even those who err through temptation, must have that within which makes them *susceptible* of temptation.

4.) So that we are in a like state of probation with respect to both present and future interests.

2. If we proceed to observe how mankind behave in both capacities, we see the same analogy.

1.) Some scarcely look beyond the present gratification.

2.) Some are driven by their passions against their better judgment and feeble resolutions.

3.) Some shamelessly go on in open vice.

4.) Some persist in wrong-doing, even under strong apprehensions of future misery.

3. The analogy is no less plain in regard to the influence of others upon us.

1.) Bad example.

2.) Wrong education.

3.) Corruptions of religion.

4.) General prevalence of mistakes as to true happiness.

4. In both cases negligence and folly bring difficulty as well as vice.

III. *The disadvantages we labor under from our fallen and disordered state, are the same, in relation to both earthly and future interests.*

This disadvantage affords no ground of complaint; for,

1. We *may* manage to pass our days in comfort and peace.

2. And so may we obtain the security and comfort of religion.

3. We might as well complain that we are not a higher order of beings.

REMARKS.

1. It is thus proved that the state of trial, which religion says we are in, is credible; for it exactly corresponds to what we see.

1.) If from birth till death we were in a constant security of enjoyment, without care or correctness, it would be a presumption against religion.

2.) It might, if we had no experience, be urged that an infinitely good Being would not expose us to the hazard of misery. This is indeed a difficulty, and must remain so; but still the course of nature is as it is.

3.) The miseries which we bring on ourselves are no more unavoidable than our deportment.

2. It has been proved that we are in danger of miscarrying as to our interests, both present and future.

3. The sum of the whole is, that as we do not have present enjoyments and honors forced upon us, in spite of misconduct, so this *may* be the case, as to that chief and final good which religion proposes.

CHAPTER V.

PROBATION INTENDED FOR MORAL DISCIPLINE AND IMPROVEMENT.

WHY we should be placed in the condition spoken of in the last chapter, is a question which cannot be answered. It may be that we could not understand, if told. And if we could, it might injure us to know, just now. It certainly is consistent with God's righteous government.

Religion tells us that we are so placed in order to become qualified for a better state.

This, though a very partial answer to the inquiry *why* we are so placed, answers an infinitely more important question,—viz.: *What is our business here?*

I. *We are placed in this state of trial, for our improvement in virtue, as the requisite qualification for future security and happiness.*

1. Every creature is designed for a particular way of life.

1.) Happiness depends on the congruity between a creature's nature and its circumstances.

2.) Man's character might be so changed as to make him *incapable* of happiness on earth.

3.) Or he might be placed, without changing his nature, in a world where he must be wretched, for want of the proper objects to answer to his desires.

4.) So that without determining what is the future condition of good men, we know there must be necessary *qualifications* to make us capable of enjoying it.

2. Human beings are so constituted as to become fit for new and different conditions.

1.) We not only acquire ideas, but store them up.

2.) We can become more expert in any kind of action.

3.) And can make settled alterations in our tempers.

4.) We can form *habits*—both bodily and mental.

As these operate in producing radical changes in human character, we will look for a moment at the process.

—Neither perceptions, nor knowledge, are habits; though necessary to *forming* them.

—There are habits of perception, however, and habits of action: the former are passive, the latter active.

—Habits of body are produced by external acts, and habits of mind by the exertion of principles; *i.e.* carrying them out.

—Resolutions to do well are acts, and may *help* towards forming good habits. But *mere* theorizing, and forming pictures in the mind, not only do not help, but may harden the mind to a contrary course.

—Passive impressions, by repetition grow weaker. Thus familiarity with danger lessens fear

—Hence active habits may be formed and strengthened, by acting according to certain motives or excitements, which grow less sensibly felt and less and less felt, as the habit strengthens.

. Thus the sight of distress excites the passive emotion of pity, and the active principle of benevolence. But inquiring out cases of distress in order to relieve them, causes diminished sensitiveness at the sight of misery, and stronger benevolence and aptitude in relieving it.

. So admonition, experience, and example, if acted upon, produce good; if not, harden.

5.) The formation of a habit may be imperceptible and even inexplicable, but the thing itself is matter of certain experience.

6.) A habit once formed, the action becomes easy and often pleasurable: opposite inclinations grow weaker: difficulties less: and occasions more frequent.

7.) Thus, a new character, in several respects, is formed.

3. We should not have these capacities for improvement and for the reconstruction of character, if it were not necessary.

1.) They are necessary, even as to this life.

—We are not qualified, at first, for mature life: understanding and strength come gradually.

—If we had them in full, at birth, we should at first be distracted and bewildered, and our faculties would be of no use previous to experience. Ignorant of any employment, we could not provide for ourselves.

—So that man is an unformed, unfinished creature, even as to this world, till he *acquire* knowledge, experience, and habits.

2.) Provision is made for our acquiring, in youth, the requisite qualities for manhood.

—Children *learn*, from their very birth,

. The nature and use of objects.

. The subordinations of domestic life.

. The rules of life.

—Some of this learning is acquired so insensibly, as to seem like instinct; but some requires great care and labor, and the doing of things we are averse to.

—According as we act during this formative period, is our character formed; and our capacity for various stations in society determined.

—Early opportunities lost, cannot be recovered.

3.) Our state of discipline throughout this life, for another, is exactly of the same kind: and comprehended under one general law.

—If we could not see how the present discipline fitted us for a higher life, it would be no objection.

. We do not know how food, sleep, &c. enlarges the child's body; nor would we expect such a result, prior to experience.

. Nor do children understand the need of exercise, temperance, restraint, &c.

—We thus see a general analogy of Providence indicating that the present life is preparatory.

4. If virtue is a necessary qualification for future happiness, then we see our need of the moral culture of our present state.

1.) Analogy indicates that our future state will be social.

—Nature furnishes no shadow of unreasonableness in the Scripture doctrine that this future community will be under the more immediate government of God.

—Nor the least proof that its members will not require the exercise of veracity, justice, &c. towards each other; and that character which *results* from the practice of such virtues.

—Certainly the universe is under moral government; and a virtuous character must, in some way, be a condition of happiness in that state.

2.) We are deficient, and in danger of deviating from what is right.

—We have desires for outward objects.

—The times, degrees, &c. of gratifying these desires, are, of right, subject to the control of the moral principle.

—But that principle neither excites them, nor prevents their being excited.

—They may exist, when they cannot be lawfully gratified, or gratified at all.

—When the desire exists, and the gratification is unlawful, we are tempted.

3.) The only security is the principle within.

—The strengthening of this lessens the danger.

—It may be strengthened, by discipline and exercise.

- Noting examples.
- Attending to the right, and not to preference.
- Considering our true interests.

—When improved, it becomes, in proportion to its strength, our security from the dangers of natural propensions.

—Virtue, become habitual by discipline, is improved virtue; and improved virtue must produce increased happiness, if the government of the world is moral.

4.) Even creatures made upright may fall.

—The fall of an upright being, is not accounted for by the nature of liberty; for that would only be saying that an event happened because it might happen.

—But from the very nature of propensions.

—A finitely perfect being would have propensions corresponding to its surroundings; its understanding; and its moral sense; and all these in due proportions.

—Such a being would have propensions, though the object might not be present, or the indulgence might be contrary to its moral sense; and this would have some tendency, however small, to induce gratification.

—The tendency would be increased by the frequency of occasions; and yet more by the least indulgence, even in thought; till, under peculiar conjunctures, it would become effect.

—The first transgression might so utterly disorder the constitution, and change the proportions of forces, as to lead to a repetition of irregularities; and hence to the construction of bad habits, and a depraved character.

5.) On the contrary, a finitely perfect being may attain higher virtue, and more security, by obeying the moral principle.
—For the danger would lessen, by the increased submissiveness of propensions.
—The moral principle would gain force by exercise.

6.) Thus vice is not only criminal, but degrading; and virtue is not only right, but improving.
—The degree of improvement may be such that the danger of sinning may be almost infinitely lessened.
—Yet the security may always be the habits formed in a state of discipline; making such a state altogether fit and necessary.

7.) This course of reasoning is vastly stronger when applied to fallen and corrupt creatures.
—The upright need improvement; the fallen must be renewed.
—Discipline is expedient for the one; necessary for the other; and of a severer sort.

II. *The present world is peculiarly fit for such discipline as we need.*

1. Surrounding evils tend to produce moderation, practical knowledge, &c. very different from a mere speculative knowledge of our liability to vice and misery.
2. Our experience in this world, with right views and practice, may leave eternal impressions for good.
3. Every act of self-government in the exercise of virtue, must, from the very make of our nature, form habits of virtue, and a more intense virtuous principle.
4. Resolute and persevering resistance to particular and violent temptations, is a *continued* act of virtue, and that in a *higher degree* than if the seduction were transient and weak.
5. Self-denial is not essential to virtue, but is almost essential to discipline and improvement.
   1.) Because actions materially virtuous, which have no difficulty, but agree with our inclinations, may be done merely from inclination, and so not be *really* virtuous.
   2.) But when they are done in face of danger and difficulty, virtuousness is increased, and confirmed into a habit.

Objec. 1. As our intellectual or physical powers may be overtasked, so may our moral.

Ans. This may be so in exceptional cases, but it does not confute the argument. In general, it holds good. All that is intended to be proved is, that this world is *intended* to be a state of improvement, and is *fitted* for it.
   1.) Some sciences which of themselves are highly improving, require a trying measure of attention, which some will not submit to.
   2.) It is admitted that this world disciplines many to vice: but this viciousness of many is the very thing which makes the world a virtuous discipline to good men. The *whole end* in placing mankind as they

are we know not; but these things are evident—the virtues of some are exercised:—and so exercised as to be improved: and improved beyond what they would be in a perfectly virtuous community.

3.) That all, or even the generality, do not improve, is no proof that their improvement was not *intended*. Of seeds and animals not one in a million comes to perfection; yet such as do, evidently answer an end for which they were designed. The *appearance of waste* in regard to seeds, &c. is just as unaccountable, as the ruin of moral agents.

Objec. 2. Rectitude arising from hope and fear, is only the discipline of self-love.

Ans. Obedience *is* obedience, though prompted by hope or fear: and a *course* of such obedience, forms a habit of it: and distinct habits of various virtues, by repressing inclination whenever justice, veracity, &c. require.

Beside, veracity, justice, regard to God's authority, and self-interest, are coincident; and each, separately, a just principle. To begin a good life from either of them, and persist, produces that very character which corresponds to our relations to God, and secures happiness.

Objec. 3. The virtues requisite for a state of afflictions, and produced by it, are not wanted to qualify us for a state of happiness.

Ans. Such is not the verdict of experience. Passive submission is essential to right character. Prosperity itself begets extravagant desires; and imagination may produce as much discontent as actual condition. Hence, though we may not need *patience* in heaven, we shall need that *temper* which is formed by patience.

Self-love would always coincide with God's commands, when our interest was rightly understood; but it is liable to error. Therefore, HABITS of resignation are necessary, for *all* creatures; and the proper discipline for resignation is affliction.

Objec. 4. The trouble and danger of such discipline, might have been avoided by making us at once, what we are intended to become.

Ans. What we are to be, is the effect of what we are to do. God's natural government is arranged not to save us from trouble or danger, but to enable and incline us to go through them. It is as natural for us to seek means to obtain things, as it is to seek the things; and in worldly things we are left to our choice, whether to improve our powers and so better our condition, or to neglect improvement and so go without the advantage.

Analogy, therefore, makes the same arrangement credible, as to a future state.

III. *This state of discipline may be necessary for the display of character.*

1. Not to the all-knowing Being, but to his creation, or part of it, and in many ways which we know not.
2. It may be a *means* in disposing of men according to character.
3. And of showing creation that they are so disposed of.
4. Such display of character certainly contributes, largely, to the general course of things considered in this chapter.

CHAPTER VI.

OF NECESSITY AS INFLUENCING CONDUCT.

FATALISTS have no right to object to Christianity, for they of course hold the doctrine to be compatible with what they see in nature.

The question is, whether it be not equally compatible with what Christianity teaches.

To argue on the supposition of so great an absurdity as necessity, is puzzling; and the obscurity and puzzle of the argument must therefore be excused.

I. *Necessity does not destroy the proof of an intelligent Author and Governor of the world.*

1. It does not exclude design and deliberation.

1.) This is matter of actual experience and consciousness.

—Necessity does not account for the *existence* of any thing, but is only a *circumstance* relating to its origin. Instance the case of a house: the fatalist admits that it had a builder, and the only question would be, was he obliged to build it as he did?

2.) It is the same as to the construction of the world. To say it exists by necessity must mean it had a maker, who *acted* by necessity: for necessity is only an abstract notion, and can *do* nothing.

3.) We say God exists by necessity, because we intuitively discern that there must be an infinite Being, prior to all causes; but we cannot say that *every thing* so exists. The fact that many changes in nature are produced by man's contrivance is a proof of this.

4.) Thus though the fatalist does not choose to mean by necessity *an agent acting necessarily,* he is obliged to mean this.

5.) And it also follows that a thing's being done by necessity does not exclude *design.*

2. It does not exclude a belief that we are in a state of religion.

1.) Suppose a fatalist to educate a child on his own principles,—viz.: that he cannot do otherwise than he does; and is not subject to praise or blame.

(It might be asked, *would* he, if possessed of common sense, so educate his child?)

—The child would be delighted with his freedom; but would soon prove a pest, and go to destruction.

—He would meet with checks and rebuffs, which would teach him that he *was* accountable.

—He would, in the end, be convinced either that his doctrine was wrong, or that he had reasoned inconclusively upon it, and misapplied it.

2.) To apply fatalism to practice, in any other way, would be found equally fallacious: *e.g.* that he need not take care of his life.

3.) No such absurdity follows the doctrine of freedom.

—Reasoning on this ground is justified by all experience.

—The constitution of things is *as if* we were free.

4.) If the doctrine of necessity be true, and yet, when we *apply it* to life, always misleads us; how, then, can we be sure it would not mislead us with respect to future interests?

5.) It follows that if there are proofs of religion on the supposition of freedom, they are just as conclusive on the supposition of necessity.

3. It does not refute the notion that God has a will and a character.

1.) It does not hinder *us* from having a will and a character; from being cruel, or benevolent, or just, &c.

2.) If necessity be plead as the excuse for crime, it equally excuses the *punishment* of crime; for if it destroys the sin of the one, it destroys the sin of the other.

3.) The very assumption of injustice in punishing crime, shows that we cannot rid ourselves of the notion of justice and injustice.

Objec. If necessity be *reconcilable* with the character of God, as portrayed in Christianity, does it not destroy *the proof* that he has that character; and so destroy the proofs of religion?

Ans. No. Happiness and misery are not our fate, but the results of our conduct. God's government is that of a father and a magistrate; and his natural rule of government must be veracity and justice. We shall proceed to show that,

II. *Necessity does not destroy the proofs of religion.*

1. It is a plain fact that God rewards and punishes.

1.) He has given us a moral faculty, by which we discern between actions, and approve or disapprove, &c.

2.) This implies a *rule*, a peculiar *kind* of rule; *i.e.* one from which we cannot depart without being self-condemned.

3.) The dictates of our moral faculty are God's laws, with sanctions. It not only raises a sense of *duty*, but a sense of *security* in obeying, and danger in disobeying; and this is an explicit sanction.

4.) God's government must conform to the nature he has given us; and we must infer that in the upshot happiness will follow virtue, and misery vice.

5.) Hence religious worship is a duty, if only as a means of keeping up the sense of this government.

6.) No objection from necessity can lie against this course of proof.

—The conclusion is wholly and directly from facts; not from what might appear to us to be *fit*, but from what his actions tell us *he wills*.

2. Natural religion has external evidence which necessity, if true, does not affect.

1.) Suppose a person convinced of the truths of natural religion, but ignorant of history, and of the present state of mankind, he would inquire:

—How this religion came?

—How far the belief of it extended?

—If he found that some one had totally propounded it, as a deduction of reason, then, though its evidences from reason would not be impaired, its history would furnish no further proof.

2.) But such an one would find, on the contrary,
—That essentially it had been professed in all countries.
—And can be traced up through all ages.
—And was not *reasoned out*, but revealed.

3.) These things are of great weight.
—Showing natural religion to be conformed to the common sense of mankind.
—And either that it was revealed, or forces itself upon the mind.
—The rude state of the early ages leads to the belief of its being revealed, and such is the opinion of the learned.

3. Early pretences to revelation indicate some original real one from which they were copied.
—The history of revelation is as old as history itself.
—Such a fact is a proof of religion, against which there is no presumption.
—And indicates a revelation prior to the examination of the book said to contain it; and independent of all considerations of its being corrupted, or darkened by fables.

4. It is thus apparent that the *external* evidence of religion is considerable; and is not affected by the doctrine of necessity.

REMARKS.

1. The danger of taking custom, &c. for our moral rule.
1.) We are all liable to prejudice.
2.) Reason may be impaired, perverted, or disregarded.
3.) The matter in hand is of infinite moment.

2. The foregoing observations amount to practical proof.

Objec. Probabilities which cannot be confuted, may be overbalanced by greater probabilities: much more by demonstration. Now, as the doctrine of necessity must be true, it cannot be that God governs us as if we were free when he knows we are not.

Ans. This brings the matter to a point, and the answer is not to be evaded,—viz.: that the whole constitution and course of things shows this reasoning to be false, be the fallacy where it may.

The doctrine of freedom shows where,—viz.: in supposing ourselves necessary agents when in fact we are free.

Admitting the doctrine of necessity, the fallacy evidently lies in denying that necessary agents are accountable; for that they *are* rewarded and punished is undeniable.

CONCLUSION.—It follows that necessity, if true, neither proves that God will not make his creatures happy or miserable according to their conduct, nor destroys the proofs that he will do so. That is, necessity, practically, is false.

CHAPTER VII.

DIVINE GOVERNMENT A SCHEME IMPERFECTLY COMPREHENDED.

MORAL government, *as a fact*, has now been considered; it remains for us to remove objections against its *wisdom and goodness*. A thing being true does not prove it to be good.

In arguing as to its truth, analogy could only show it to be credible. But, if a moral government be admitted as a fact, analogy makes it credible that it is a scheme or system, and that man's comprehension of it is necessarily so limited, as to be inadequate to determine its injustice.

This we shall find to be the case.

Doctrine. ON THE SUPPOSITION THAT GOD EXERCISES MORAL GOVERNMENT, THE ANALOGY OF NATURE TEACHES THAT IT MUST BE A SCHEME, AND ONE QUITE BEYOND OUR COMPREHENSION.

I. *The ordering of nature is a scheme; and makes it credible by analogy, that moral government is a scheme.*

1. The parts curiously correspond to each other; individuals to individuals, species to species, events to events; and all these both immediate and remote.
2. This correspondence embraces all the past, and all the future; including all creatures, actions, and events.
   1.) There is no event, which does not depend for its occurrence on some further thing, unknown to us; we cannot give the whole account of any one thing.
   2.) Things apparently the most insignificant, seem to be necessary to others, of the greatest importance.
3. If such is God's natural government, it is credible that such is his moral government.
   1.) In fact they are so blended as to make one scheme.
   —One is subservient to the other, just as the vegetable kingdom subserves the animal, and our animal organization subserves our mental.
   —Every act of God seems to look beyond the occasion, and to have reference to a general plan.
   —There is evidently a previous adjustment.
   - The periods, &c. for trying men.
   - The instruments of justice.
   - The kinds of retribution.

   2.) The whole comprises a system, a very small part of which is known to us: therefore no objections against any part can be insisted on.
   3.) This ignorance is universally acknowledged, except in arguing against religion. That it ought to be a valid answer to objections against religion, we proceed to show.
   —Suppose it to be asserted that all evils might have been prevented by repeated interpositions; or that more good might have been so produced; which would be the utmost that could be said: still,
   —Our ignorance would vindicate religion from any objections arising from apparent disorders in the world.

—The government of the world might be *good*, even on those suppositions; for at most they could but suggest that it might be *better*.

—At any rate, they are mere assertions.

—Instances may be alleged, in things much less out of reach, of suppositions palpably impossible, which *all* do not see to be so: nor *any, at first sight*.

4.) It follows that our ignorance is a satisfactory answer to all objections against the divine government.

—An objection against an act of Providence, no way connected with any other thing, as being unjust, could not be answered by our ignorance.

—But when the objection is made against an act related to other and unknown acts, then our ignorance is a full answer.

—Some unknown relation, or unknown impossibility, may render the act not only good, but good in the highest degree.

II. *Consider some particular things, in the natural government of God, the like of which we may infer, by analogy, to be contained in his moral government.*

1. No ends are accomplished without means.

1.) Often, means very disagreeable bring the most desirable results.

2.) How means produce ends, is not learned by reason, but experience.

3.) In many cases, before experience, we should have expected contrary results.

4.) Hence we may infer that those things which are objected against God's moral government, produce good.

5.) It is evident that our not seeing *how* the means work good, or their seeming to have an opposite effect, offers no presumption against their fitness to work good.

6.) They may not only be fit, but the *only* means of ultimate good.

Objec. Though our capacity of vice and misery may promote virtue, and our suffering for sin be better than if we were restrained by force, yet it would have been better if evil had not entered the world.

Ans. It is granted that though sinful acts may produce benefits, to refrain from them would produce more. We have curative pains, yet pain is not better than health.

2. Natural government is carried on by general laws.

1.) Nature shows that this is best: all the good we enjoy is because there are general laws. They enable us to *forecast* for the procurement of good.

2.) It may not be possible, by general laws, to prevent all irregularities, or remedy them.

3.) Direct interpositions might perhaps remedy many disorders arising under them, but this would have bad effects.

—Encouraging improvidence.

—Leaving us no rule of life.

—Every interposition would have *distant* effects: so that we could not guess what would be the *whole* result.

• If it be replied that those distant effects might also be corrected by direct interpositions—this is only talking at random.

Objec. If we are so ignorant as this whole argument supposes, we are too ignorant to understand the proofs of religion.

Ans. 1. Total ignorance of a subject precludes argument, but partial ignorance does not. We may, in various degrees, know a man's character, and the way he is *likely* to pursue certain ends; and yet not know how he *ought* to act to gain those ends. In this case objections to his mode of pursuing ends may be answered by our ignorance, though that he *does* act in a certain manner is capable of proof. So we may have evidence of God's character and aims, and yet not be competent judges as to his measures. Our ignorance is a good answer to the difficulties of religion, but no objection to religion itself.

Ans. 2. If our ignorance did invalidate the proofs of religion, as well as the objections, yet is it undeniable that moral obligations remain unaffected by our ignorance of the consequences of obedience or violation. The consequences of vice and virtue may not be fully known, yet it is credible that they may be such as religion declares: and this credibility is an obligation, in point of prudence, to abstain from sin.

Ans. 3. Our answers to the objections against religion, are *not* equally valid against the proofs of it.

[Answers rehearsed.]

Ans. 4. Our answers, though they may be said to be based on our ignorance, are really not so, but on what analogy teaches *concerning* our ignorance,—viz.: that it renders us incompetent judges. They are based on experience, and what we *do know;* so that to credit religion is to trust to experience, and to disregard it is the contrary.

CONCLUSION.

1. The reasoning of the last chapter leads us to regard this life as part of a larger plan of things.

1.) Whether we are connected with the distant *parts* of the universe, is uncertain; but it is very clear we are connected, more or less, with present, past, and future.

2.) We are evidently in the midst of a scheme, not fixed but progressive; and one equally incomprehensible, whether we regard the present, past, or future.

2. This scheme contains as much that is wonderful as religion does: for it certainly would be as wonderful that all nature came into existence without a Creator, as that there should be a Creator: and as wonderful that the Creator should act without any rule or scheme, as that he should act with one; or that he should act by a bad rule, rather than a righteous one.

3. Our very nature compels us to believe that the will and character of the Author of nature, is just and good.

4. Whatever be his character, he formed the world as it is, and controls it as he does, and has assigned us our part and lot.

5. Irrational creatures act their part, and receive their lot, without reflection; but creatures endued with reason, can hardly avoid reflecting whither we go, and what is the scheme, in the midst of which we find ourselves.

[Here follows a recapitulation of the book.]

PART II.

CHAPTER I.

IMPORTANCE OF CHRISTIANITY.

EVERY one must admit that we *need* a revelation. Few, if any, could reason out a system, even of natural religion. If they could, there is no probability that they would. Such as might, would still feel the want of revelation. To say that Christianity is superfluous, is as wild as to say all are happy.

No exactness in attending to natural religion can make Christianity of small importance.

If Christianity be from God, we must obey, unless we know all his reasons for giving it: and also that those reasons no longer exist; at least in our case. This we cannot know.

The importance of Christianity appears if we regard it

I. *As a republication of natural religion.*

1. It gives the moral system of the universe.
   1.) Free from corruptions; teaching that
      —Jehovah created all things.
      — governs all things.
      —Virtue is his law.
      —Mankind will be judged according to character.
   2.) It publishes its facts authoritatively.
   3.) With vastly more clearness; *e.g.* the doctrines of a future state: danger of sin: efficacy of repentance.
   4.) With the advantage of a visible church, distinguished from the world by peculiar institutions.

Objec. The perversions of Christianity, and the little good it has done.

Ans. 1. Natural religion is no less perverted, and has done less good.
   2. The benefits of Christianity are *not* small.
   3. The evils ascribed to it, are not *its* effects. Things are to be judged by their genuine tendencies.
   4. The light of reason, no more than revelation forces acquiescence.

   5.) With the additional advantage that every Christian, is bound to instruct and persuade others.

II. *As containing truths not discoverable by natural reason.*

1. A mode of salvation for the ruined.
2. Duties unknown before.
3. Our relations to the Son and Holy Ghost.
   1.) Hence the form of baptism.
   2.) Pious regards to Christ, and the Holy Ghost, based on our relations to them.
4. The manner of external worship.

III. *The fearful hazard of neglecting Christianity.*

1. Those who think natural religion *sufficient*, must admit that Christianity is highly *important*.

2. Our relations to Christ being made known, our religious regard to him is an evident obligation.

3. These relations being real, there is no reason to think that our neglect of behaving suitably to them, will not be attended with the same kind of consequences as follow the neglect of duties made known by reason.

4. If we are corrupt and depraved, and so unfit for heaven, and if we need God's Holy Spirit to renew our nature, how can it be a slight thing whether we make use of the means for obtaining such assistance?

5. Thus, if Christianity be either true, or merely credible, it is most rash and presumptuous to treat it lightly.

REMARKS.

1. The distinction between positive and moral obligations.

1.) For moral precepts we can see *the reason:* for positive we cannot.

2.) Moral duties are such *prior* to command; positive duties are such *because* commanded.

3.) The manner in which a duty is made known, does not make it moral or positive.

2. The ground of regarding moral duties as superior to positive.

1.) Both have the nature of moral commands.

2.) If the two conflict, we must obey the moral.

—Positive institutions are *means* to moral ends.

—Ends are more excellent than means.

—Obedience to positive institutions, has no value but as proceeding from moral principle.

3.) Both moral and positive duties are *revealed*, and so are on a level; but the moral law is *also* interwoven with our very nature, and so its precepts must prevail when the two interfere.

3. There is less necessity for determining their relative authority, than some suppose.

1.) Though man is disposed to outward and ritual religion, nothing can give us acceptance with God, without moral virtue.

2.) Scripture always lays stress on moral duties.

3.) It is a great weakness, though very common, to make light of positive institutions, because less important than moral.

—We are bound to obey *all* God's commands.

—A precept, merely positive, admitted to be from God, creates moral obligation, in the strictest sense.

CONCLUSION.

This account of Christianity shows our great obligation to study the Scriptures.

CHAPTER II.

PRESUMPTIONS AGAINST A REVELATION, CONSIDERED AS MIRACULOUS.

HAVING shown the need of revelation, we now examine the presumptions against it.

The analogy of nature is generally supposed to afford presumptions against miracles.

They are deemed to require stronger evidence than other events.

I. *Analogy furnishes no presumptions against the general scheme of Christianity.*

1. It is no presumption against Christianity, that it is not the discovery of reason, or of experience.

2. Nor is it a presumption against Christianity, that it contains things *unlike* the apparent course of nature.

1.) We cannot suppose every thing, in the vast universe, to be just like what is the course of nature in this little world.

2.) Even within the present compass of our knowledge, we see many things greatly unlike.

3. If we choose to call what is unlike our known course of things, *miraculous*, still that does not make it *improbable.*

II. *There is no presumption against such a revelation, as we should now call miraculous, being made, at the beginning of the world.*

1. There was then *no* course of nature, as to this world.

2. Whether man *then* received a revelation involves a question not of miracles, but of *fact.*

3. Creation was a very different exertion of power from that which *rules* the world, now it *is* made.

4. Whether the power of forming *stopped* when man was made; or went on, and formed a religion for him, is merely a question as to the *degree* or *extent,* to which a power was exerted.

5. There is then no presumption from analogy against supposing man had a revelation when created.

6. All tradition and history teaches that he had, which amounts to a real and material proof.

III. *There is no presumption against miracles, or a miraculous revelation, after the course of nature was settled.*

1. Such a presumption, requires the adduction of some *parallel case.*

2. This would require us to know the history of some other world.

3. Even then, if drawn from only one other world, the presumption would be very precarious.

To be more particular,

1. There is a strong presumption against any truth till it is proved—which yet is overcome by almost any proof.

—Hence the question of a presumption against miracles, involves only the *degree* of presumption, (not whether the presumption is *peculiar* to miracles,) and whether that degree is such as to render them incredible.

2. If we *leave out religion*, we are in total darkness as to the cause or circumstances on which the course of nature depends.
   —Five or six thousand years may have given occasion and reasons for miraculous interpositions of Providence.
3. *Taking in religion*, there are distinct reasons for miracles; to afford additional instruction; to attest the truth of instruction.
4. Miracles must not be compared with common events, but with uncommon; earthquakes, pestilence, &c.

CONCLUSION.

1. There are no analogies to render miracles incredible.
2. On the contrary, we see good reasons for them.
3. There are no presumptions against them, *peculiar* to them, as distinguished from other unusual phenomena.

CHAPTER III.

OUR INCAPACITY OF JUDGING WHAT SHOULD BE EXPECTED IN A REVELATION FROM GOD.

Beside the objectors to the *evidences* of Christianity, there are many who object to its *nature*. They say it is not full enough: has in it foolish things: gives rise to superstition: subserves tyranny: is not universally known: not well arranged: figurative language, &c.

It is granted that if it contained *immoralities* or *contradictions* they would show it to be false. But other objections against religion, aside from objections against its evidences, are frivolous: as will now be shown.

Let the student look to the *force* of the proofs, rather than any *consequences* which may be drawn from them.

I. *The Scripture informs us of a scheme of government, in addition to the material laws of the world.*

1. If both these schemes, the physical and the moral, coincide and form one whole, then our inability to criticise the system of nature, renders it credible that we are incompetent to criticise the system of grace.
2. Nature shows many things we should not have expected, prior to experience.
3. Hence it is altogether likely it would be so in religion.
4. If a citizen is incompetent to judge of the propriety of the *general* laws of his government, he is equally incompetent to judge when and how far those laws should be suspended, or deviated from.

II. *We are no better judges of how revelation should be imparted.*

Whether to every man, or to some for others; or what mode or degree of proof should be given; or whether the knowledge should be given gradually or suddenly.

1. We are not able to judge how much new knowledge ought to be given by revelation.
2. Nor how far, nor in what way, God should qualify men to transmit any revelation he might make.
3. Nor whether the evidence should be certain, probable, or doubtful.
4. Nor whether all should have the same benefit from it.
5. Nor whether it should be in writing, or verbal. If it be said that if not in writing it would not have answered its purpose: I ask, what purpose? Who knows what purposes would best suit God's *general* government?
6. All which shows it to be absurd to object to particular things in revelation as unsuitable.

III. *Hence the only question, concerning the truth of revelation is, whether it* IS *a revelation.*

1. No obscurities, &c. could overthrow the authority of a revelation.
2. It can only be overthrown by nullifying the proofs.
3. Though the proofs could be shown to be less strong than is affirmed, it still should control our conduct.

IV. *Modes of arguing, which are perfectly just, in relation to other books, are not so as to the Bible.*

1. We are competent judges of common books, but not of Scripture.
2. Our only inquiry should be to find out the sense.
3. In other books, internal improbabilities weaken external proof; but in regard to revelation, we scarcely know what are improbabilities.
   1.) Those who judge the Scripture by preconceived expectations, will imagine they find improbabilities.
   2.) And so they would by thus judging in natural things.
      —It would seem very improbable, prior to experience, that man should be better able to determine the magnitudes and motions of heavenly bodies, than he is to determine the causes and cures of disease, which much more nearly concerns him.
      —Or that we should sometimes hit upon a thing in an instant, even when thinking of something else, which we had been vainly trying to discover for years.
      —Or that language should be so liable to abuse, that every man may be a deceiver.
      —Or that brute instinct should ever be superior to reason.

V. *Such observations apply to almost all objections to Christianity, as distinguished from objections against its evidence.*

For instance, the disorderly manner in which some, in the apostolic age, used their miraculous gifts.

1. This does not prove the acts *not* miraculous.

2. The person having any such gift, would have the same power over it which he would have over any other ability, and might pervert it.

3. To say why was he not also endued with prudence, to restrain its use, is but saying why did not God give a *higher degree* of miraculous endowment? As to which we are not competent judges.

4. God does not confer his *natural* gifts, (memory, eloquence, knowledge, &c.) only on those who are prudent and make the best use of them.

5. Nor is worldly instruction, by educators, commonly given in the happiest manner.

VI. *There is a resemblance between religion and nature in several other respects.*

1. In both, common and necessary things, are plain; but to "go on to perfection" in either, requires exact and laborious study.

2. The hinderances to both religious and physical knowledge, are the same in kind. A more perfect knowledge may be brought about,

1.) By the progress of learning and liberty.

2.) By students attending to intimations overlooked by the generality.

3. It is not wonderful that our knowledge of Bible truth should be small; for the natural world has laid open to inspection, for thousands of years, and yet only lately are any great discoveries made.

4. Perhaps these scientific discoveries, are to be the means of opening and ascertaining Bible truth.

Objec. The cases are not parallel; for natural knowledge is of no consequence, compared to spiritual.

Ans. 1. The cases *are* parallel; for natural knowledge is as important to our natural well-being, as spiritual knowledge is to our spiritual well-being.

Ans. 2. If the cases were not parallel, there are plenty of other analogies, which show that God does not dispense his gifts according to *our* notions of their value.

Objec. 2. If Christianity be intended for the recovery of men, why not sooner introduced, and more widely diffused?

Ans. The objection is just as strong against the natural sciences. Nay, if the light of nature and of revelation are both from the same source, we might *expect* that revelation would have been introduced and diffused just as it is.

1.) Remedies for disease are known but to a few, or not known at all, nor to any without care and study.

2.) When proposed by discoverers, they have been treated with derision, and the use rejected by thousands whom they might have cured.

3.) The best remedies have been used unskilfully, and so made to produce more disease.

4.) Their benefit may come very slowly.

5.) In some cases they may be wholly ineffectual.

6.) They may be so disagreeable that many will not submit to use them, even with the prospect of a cure.

7.) Sometimes the remedy may be entirely out of reach if we were ready to take it.

All this reasoning may be applied to Christianity.

VII. *Having obviated all objections to Christianity, from its containing things we should not have expected, we will now consider the objections against its morality.*

1. Reason may judge, as to whether revelation contains things contrary to justice, and wisdom, &c. as those attributes are taught by natural religion. But no such objections are advanced, except such as would equally condemn the constitution of nature.
2. There are indeed particular precepts, to particular persons, which *would* be immoral, but for the precept. The precept changes the nature of the action.
3. None are contrary to immutable morality. We are never commanded to cultivate the principles of ingratitude, treachery, &c.
4. God may command the taking of life or property because these are *his.*
5. The only real difficulty is, that such commands are liable to be perverted by the wicked to their own horrid purposes; and to mislead the weak. But such objections do not lie against revelation, as such, but against the very notion of *religion as a trial.*
6. The sum of the whole is, objections against the *scheme* of Christianity do not affect its truth; since there are no objections against its morality. Hence objections against it, aside from its evidences, are frivolous. Objections against the *evidence,* will be considered in a subsequent chapter, [*i.e.* ch. vii.]

CHAPTER IV.*

CHRISTIANITY A SCHEME IMPERFECTLY UNDERSTOOD.

In the last chapter it was shown that we might expect, beforehand, that a revelation would contain strange things, and things liable to great objections.

This abates the force of such objections, or rather precludes them.

But it may be said this does not show such objectionable things to be good, or credible.

It was a sufficient answer [ch. vii. part i.] to objections against the course of nature, that it was a *scheme,* imperfectly comprehended.

If Christianity be a scheme, the like objections admit of a like answer.

I. *Christianity is a scheme, beyond our comprehension.*

1. God's *general* plan is to conduct things *gradually,* so that, finally, every one shall receive what he deserves.
2. Christianity is a *particular* arrangement, under this general plan: is a part of it, and conduces to its completion.
3. It is itself a complicated and mysterious economy.
   1.) Its arrangements began from the fall of man.
   2.) Various dispensations, patriarchal, prophetic, &c. were preparatory to it.
   3.) At a certain juncture in the condition of the world Jesus Christ came.

---

* [In studying this chapter, let chap. vii. part i. be kept in view.]

4.) The mission of the Holy Ghost was part of this economy.
5.) Christ now presides over it, and will establish the church, judge the world, give up the kingdom, &c. &c.

4. Of course, we can comprehend but little of such a scheme.
5. We plainly see, from what is revealed, that there is very much unrevealed.
6. Thus it is evident that we are as little capable of judging as to the whole system of religion, as we are as to the whole system of nature.

II. *In both material and spiritual things, means are used to accomplish ends.*

1. Hence a thing may seem foolish to us, because we do not know its object and end.
2. Its seeming foolish to us, is no proof that it is so.

III. *Christianity is carried on by general laws, no less than nature.*

1. Why do we say there are *laws of nature?*
1.) We indeed know some such. But nothing of the laws of many things, *e.g.*
• Pestilence. • Storms. • Earthquakes. • Diversities of human powers. • Association of ideas.
2.) Hence we call many things *accidental,* which we know are not matters of chance, but are subject to general laws.
3.) It is a very little way that we can trace things to their general laws.
4.) We attribute many things to such laws, only by analogy.

2. Just for the same reasons, we say that miracles comport with God's *general laws of wisdom.* These laws may be unknown to us; but no more so than those by which some die as soon as born, or live to old age, or have superior understandings, &c.
3. We see no more reason to regard the frame and course of nature as a scheme, than we have to regard Christianity as such.
1.) If the first is a scheme, then Christianity, if true, would be *likely* to be a scheme.
2.) As Christianity is revealed but in part, and is an arrangement to accomplish ends, there would of course seem to us, in it, irregularities; just as we see in nature.
3.) Therefore objections against the one, are answered in the same manner as objections against the other.

Having, in a previous chapter, [ch. iii.,] answered objections to Christianity *as a matter of fact,* and in this, as a general question of *wisdom and goodness,* the next thing is to discuss *objections in particular.*

As one of these is directed against *the scheme,* as just now described, it will be considered here.

Objec. Christianity is a roundabout, and perplexed contrivance; just such as men, for want of understanding or power, are obliged to adopt, in their designs.

Ans. 1.) God uses just such complex arrangements in the natural world. The mystery is quite as great in nature as in grace.

2.) We do not know what are means, and what are ends.
3.) The natural world, and its government, are not fixed, but progressive.
4.) Great length of time is required in some changes; *e.g.* animals, vegetables, geological periods, &c.
5.) One state of life is a preparation and means for attaining another.
6.) Man is impatient, but Jehovah deliberate.

CHAPTER V.

OF A MEDIATOR, AND REDEMPTION BY HIM.

NOTHING in Christianity is so much objected to as the position assigned to Christ; yet nothing is more unjust. The whole world exhibits mediation.

I. *Our existence, and all its satisfactions, are by the medium of others.*

1. If so in the natural world, why not in the spiritual?
2. The objection therefore is not only against *Christ's* mediation, but *all* mediation.

II. *We cannot know all the ends for which God punishes, nor by whom he should punish.*

1. Future punishment may be as natural a sequence of sin, as a broken limb is of falling from a precipice.
2. This is not taking punishment out of the hands of God, and giving it to nature; it is only distinguishing ordinary events from miraculous.

III. *In natural providence, God has made provision that the bad consequences of actions do not always follow.*

1. We may say God could have prevented all evil. But we see he permits it, and has provided relief, and even sometimes perfect remedies for it.
1.) Thus the bad consequences of trifling on a precipice may be prevented by a friend, if we do not reject his assistance.
2.) We may ourselves do much towards preventing the bad consequences of our misdeeds.
3.) Still more if assisted.
2. It might have been perfectly just if it were not so; but that it is so, shows compassion, as distinguished from goodness.
3. The course of nature affords many instances of such compassion.
4. Thus analogy sanctions an arrangement, by which the ruinous consequences of vice or folly may be averted, at least in some cases.
5. If the consequences of rash and inconsiderate acts, which we scarcely call vicious, are often so serious, we may apprehend that the bad consequences will be greater, in proportion as the irregularity is greater.
6. A dissolute disregard to all religion, if there be a religion, is incomparably more reprehensible than the mere neglects, imprudencies, &c. of this life.
7. As the effects of worldly imprudence and vice are often misery, ruin, and even death, no one can say what may be the consequences of blasphemy, contempt of God, and final impenitence.

8. Nor can any one tell, how far the consequences of such great wickedness can possibly be prevented, consistently with the eternal rule of right.
9. Still there would, from analogy, be some hope of room for pardon.

IV. *There is no probability that any thing we could do alone, would entirely prevent the effects of our irregularities.*

1 We do not know all the reasons for punishment, nor why it should be fit to remit punishment.
2 Nor do we know all the consequences of vice, and so should not know how to prevent them.
3. Vice impairs men's abilities for helping themselves.
4. Misconduct makes assistance necessary, which otherwise would not have been. Why should not the same things be so, as to our future interests?
5. In temporal things, behaving well in time to come, does not repair old errors, why should it as to future things?
6. Were it so in *all cases* it would be contrary to all our notions of government.
7. It could not be determined in what degree, or in what cases, it would be so, even if we knew it might in *some* cases.
8 The efficacy of repentance, as urged in opposition to atonement, is contrary to the general sense of mankind; as shown by the prevalence of propitiatory sacrifices.

V. *In this state of apprehension, awakened by the light of nature, revelation comes in, and teaches positively, the possibility of pardon and safety.*

1. Confirms our fears as to the unprevented consequences of sin.
2. Declares the world to be in a state of ruin.
3. That repentance alone will not secure pardon.
4. That there is a mode of pardon, by interposition.
5. That God's moral government is compassionate, as well as his natural government.
6. That he has provided, by the interposition of a mediator, to save men.
7. All this seems to put man in a strange state of helpless degradation. But it is not Christianity which puts him so. All philosophy and history show man to be degraded and corrupt.

VI. *Scripture, in addition to confirming the dim testimony of the light of nature, reveals a Christ, as mediator and propitiatory sacrifice.*

1. He is "*that prophet.*"
   1.) Declared the will of God.
   2.) Published anew the law of nature.
   3.) Taught with authority.
   4.) Revealed the right manner of worship.
   5.) Revealed the exact use of repentance.
   6.) Revealed future rewards and punishments.
   7.) Set us a perfect example.

2. He has a *kingdom* which is not of this world.
   1.) Founded a church.
   2.) Governs it.
   3.) Of it, all who obey him are members.
   4.) Each of these shall live and reign with him forever.
3. He is a propitiatory *sacrifice*.
   1.) How his sacrifice becomes efficacious, we are not exactly told.
   2.) Conjectures may be absurd; at least cannot be certain.
   3.) If any complain for want of further instruction, let him produce his claim to it.
   4.) Some, because they cannot explain, leave it out of their creed; and regard Christ only as a teacher.
   5.) We had better accept the benefit, without disputing about how it was procured.

VII. *We are not judges, antecedent to revelation, whether a mediator was necessary, nor what should be the whole nature of his office.*

1. We know not how future punishment would have been inflicted.
2. Nor all the reasons why it would be necessary.
3. The satisfaction by Christ, does not represent God as indifferent whether he punishes the innocent or guilty.
   1.) We see, in this world, the innocent *forced* to suffer for the faults of the guilty.
   2.) But Christ suffered *voluntarily*.
4. Though, finally, every one shall receive according to his own deserts; yet, during the progress of God's scheme, *vicarious* sufferings may be necessary.
   1.) God commands us to assist others, though in many cases it costs us suffering and toil.
   2.) One person's sufferings often tend to relieve another.
5. Vicarious atonement for sinners, serves to vindicate the authority of God's laws, and to deter men from sin.
6. Objections to vicarious suffering are obviously not objections to Christianity, but to the whole course of nature.
7. The objection, therefore, amounts to nothing more than saying that a divine arrangement is not necessary, or fit, because the objector does not see it to be so; though he must own he is no judge, and *could* not understand why it should be necessary, if it were so!

VIII. *We have no reason to expect the same information touching God's conduct, as we have in relation to our own duty.*

1. God instructs us by experience.
2. This experience, though sufficient for *our* purposes, is an infinitely small part of his providence.
3. The things not understood involve God's appointment, and Christ's execution; but what *is required of us*, we are clearly informed.
4. Even the reasons for Christian precepts are made obvious.

CHAPTER VI.

SUPPOSED LACK OF PROOF OF REVELATION, AND ITS WANT OF UNIVERSALITY.

It has been thought to be a positive argument against revelation, that its evidences are not adequate, and that it is not universally known and believed.

But the argument amounts to just this, that God would not bestow on us any favor, except in such a mode and degree as we thought best, and did exactly the same for everybody else.

Such a notion, all analogy contradicts.

I. *Men act in their most important concerns on doubtful evidence.*

1. It is often absolutely *impossible* to say which of two modes of acting will give most pleasure or profit.
2. If it were possible, we cannot know what changes temper, satiety, ill health, &c. might produce, so as to destroy our pleasure.
3. We cannot foresee what accidents may cut it all off.
4. Strong objections and difficulties may attach to the course of action we adopt, which yet all would admit ought not to deter us.
5. We may, after all, be deceived by appearances, or by our passions, &c.
6. Men think it reasonable to engage in pursuit of advantage, even when the probabilities of success are *against* them.

II. *As to the light of Christianity not being universal.*

1. Temporal good is enjoyed in very different degrees even among creatures of the same species.
2. Yet it is certain that God governs.
3. We may prudently or imprudently use our good things.
4. The Jewish religion was not universal.
5. If it be *intended* that Christianity should be a small light, shining in a great and wide-spread darkness, it would be perfectly uniform with other parts of God's providence.
6. If some have Christianity so corrupted, and interpolated, as to cause thoughtful persons to doubt it, as is the case in some countries; and if, where it is the purest, some learn much less from it than they might, there are manifest parallels in God's natural dispensations.
7. No more is expected of any one, than is equitable under his circumstances.
8. Every one is bound to get rid of his ignorance, as far as he can, and to instruct his neighbor.
9. If revelation *were* universal, in extent and degree, different understandings, educations, tempers, length of lives, and outward advantages, would soon make the knowledge of it as different as it is at present.

III. *Practical reflections.*

First. That the evidence of religion is not such as *unavoidably* to convince all, may be part of our probation.

1. It gives scope for a wise or vicious use of our understanding. Just as is the case in common affairs.

2. Intellectual inattention to so serious a matter, is as immoral, as disobedience after conviction of the truth.

Secondly. If the evidence is really doubtful, it puts us on probation.

1. If a man were in doubt whether a certain person had done him the greatest favor, or whether his whole temporal interest depended on him, he ought not to regard that person as he would if there were *no* reason to think so.

2. So if there is only reason to apprehend that Christianity *may* be true, we are as much bound to *examine,* &c. as we would be bound to *obey,* if we *knew* it was true.

3. Considering the infinite importance of religion, there is not much difference as to what ought to be the mode of life of those who are convinced and those who doubt its truth. Their hopes and fears are the same in kind, though not in degree; and so their obligations are much the same.

4. Doubts presuppose *some* evidence, belief *more,* and certainty *more still.* Each state should influence our conduct, and does so, in common things.

5. It shows a mental defect not to see evidence unless it is glaring; and a corrupt heart not to be influenced by it unless overpowering.

Thirdly. Difficulties as to believing religion, are no more a ground of complaint, than difficulties in practising it.

1. They constitute a wholesome discipline.

1.) In allowing an unfair mind to deceive itself.

2.) In requiring belief and the practice of virtue under some uncertainties.

2. In the case of some minds, speculative difficulties as to the evidence of religion is the *principal* trial. A full conviction of its truth would *constrain* some to obedience.

Fourthly. The difficulties may be *in the objector* rather than in the religion.

1. Not sufficiently in earnest to be informed.

2. Secretly *wishes* religion not to be true.

3. Looks at objections rather than replies.

4. Treats the subject ludicrously.

Fifthly. The proof of Christianity is level to common men.

1. They are capable of being convinced of the existence of God, and of their moral accountability.

2. And they can understand the evidence of miracles, and the fulfilment of prophecy.

3. If they are capable of seeing the difficulty, they are capable of understanding the proof.

4. If they pick up objections from hearsay, and will not or cannot examine them thoroughly, they must remain ignorant, just as they do as to the sciences.

Objec. Our directions should be too plain to *admit* of doubt; like those of an earthly master.

Ans. The earthly master only wants his work done, and is careless as to the state of the heart; but as the whole of morality consists in the state of the heart, the cases are not parallel.

Finally. The credibility of our being in a state of probation is just as great as the credibility of there being any religion. Our probation may be whether we choose to inform ourselves as to our duty, and then whether we choose to do it.

Such is exactly the case as to temporal matters. To discern what is best often requires difficult consideration, and yet leaves doubts: and not reflecting carefully, or not acting even when there may be doubt, is often fatal.

CHAPTER VII.

POSITIVE EVIDENCES OF CHRISTIANITY.

HAVING considered the objections both to the general scheme of Christianity, and to particular doctrines in it, it only remains to consider the positive evidence of its truth; *i.e.* what analogy teaches with regard to that evidence.

There are many evidences of Christianity, beside those from miracles or prophecy, which are the principal; embracing a great variety of proofs, direct and collateral, and reaching through all past time. We shall now consider the proofs from MIRACLES and PROPHECY.

I. *Miracles.*

1. Bible history gives the same evidence for the miracles described, as for common events.

1.) The miracles are evidently not put in for ornament, as speeches are by historians and poets put into the mouths of heroes.

2.) The accounts of them have been quoted as genuine, by various writers, from that day to this.

3.) These accounts are confirmed by subsequent events; and the miracles alone, can account for those events.

4.) The only fair way of accounting for these statements, and their reception in the world, is that the things really happened.

5.) The statements should be admitted till disproved, even if doubtful.

2. Paul's Epistles have evidences of genuineness, beyond what can attach to mere history.

1.) *Additional.* His evidence is quite detached. He received the gospel not in common with the other apostles, but separately, and direct from Christ, *after* his ascension.

2.) *Peculiar.* He speaks of Christ's miracles and those of others *incidentally,* as familiar facts, fully believed by those to whom he wrote.

3. Christianity demands credence on the ground of its miracles, and was so received by great numbers, at the time and on the spot; which is the case with no other religion.

1.) Its first converts embraced it on this ground.

2.) It is not conceivable that they would have done so, at such fearful sacrifice, unless fully satisfied of the truth of these miracles.

3.) Such a profession and sacrifices furnish the same kind of evidence as if they had testified to the truth of the miracles in writing.

4.) It is real evidence, for they had full opportunity to inform themselves.

5.) It is a sort of evidence *distinct* from direct history, though of the same nature.

6.) Men are suspicious as well as credulous, and slow to believe *against their interests*, as these did.

4. It lies upon unbelievers to show why all this array of proof is to be rejected; but in such an important concern we shall proceed to notice some possible objections.

Objec. 1. Enthusiasts make similar sacrifices for idle follies.

Ans. 1. This objection ignores the distinction between opinions and facts. Suffering for an opinion is no proof of its truth; but in attestation of observed facts, it is proof.

2. Enthusiasm *weakens* testimony, it is true, even as to facts; and so does disease, *in particular instances.* But when great numbers, not weak, nor negligent, affirm that *they* saw and heard certain things, it is the fullest evidence.

3. To reject testimony on the ground of enthusiasm, requires that the things testified be *incredible;* which has not been shown, as to religion, but the contrary.

4. Religion is not the only thing in regard to which witnesses are liable to enthusiasm. In common matters, we *get at the truth* through witnesses, though influenced by party spirit, custom, humor, romance, &c. &c.

Objec. 2. Enthusiasm and knavery may have been combined in the apostles and first Christians.

Ans. Such a mixture is often seen, and is often reproved in Scripture; but not more in religious than in common affairs. Men in all matters deceive themselves and others, in every degree, yet human testimony is good ground of belief.

Objec. 3. Men have been deluded by false miracles.

Ans. Not oftener than by other pretences.

Objec. 4. Fabulous miracles have historical evidence.

Ans. 1. If this were equal to that for Scripture miracles, the evidence for the latter would not be *impaired.* The objection really amounts to this, that evidence proved not to be good, destroys evidence which is good and unconfuted! Or to this, that if two men, of equal reputation, testify, in *cases not related* to each other, and one is proved false, the other must not be believed!

2. Nothing can rebut testimony, but proof that the witness is incompetent, or misled.

3. Against all such objections must be set the fact that Christianity was too serious a matter to allow the first converts to be careless as to its evidence; and also that their religion forbid them to deceive others.

II *As to the evidence from prophecy.*

1. Obscurity as to *part* of a prophecy does not invalidate it, but is, as to us, as if that part were not written, or were lost. We may not see the whole prophecy fulfilled, and yet see enough fulfilled to perceive in it more than human foresight.

2. A *long series* of prophecies, all applicable to certain events, is proof that such events were intended. This answers the objection that *particular* prophecies were not intended to be applied as Christians apply them.

Mythological and satirical writings greatly resemble prophecy. Now we apply a parable, or fable, or satire, merely from seeing it *capable* of such application.

So if a long series of prophecies be *applicable* to the present state of the world, or to the coming of Christ, it is proof that they were so *intended*.

Besides, the ancient Jews, *before* Christ, applied the prophecies to him, just as Christians do now.

3. If it could be shown that the prophets did not understand their own predictions, or that their prophecies are capable of being applied to other events than those to which Christians apply them, it would not abate the force of the argument from prophecy, even with regard to those instances. For,

1.) To know the whole meaning of an author we must know the whole meaning of his book, but knowing the meaning of a book is not knowing the whole mind of the author.

2.) If the book is a *compilation*, the authors may have meanings deeper than the compiler saw. If the prophets spoke by inspiration, they are not the authors, but the writers of prophecy, and may not have known all that the Divine Spirit intended. But the fulfilment of the prophecy shows a foresight more than human.

REMARK.

This whole argument is just and real; but it is not expected that those will be satisfied who will not submit to the perplexity and labor of understanding it; or who have not modesty and fairness enough to allow an argument its due weight; or who wilfully discard the whole investigation.

We *now* proceed to THE GENERAL ARGUMENT embracing both direct and circumstantial evidence. A full discussion would require a volume, and cannot be expected here; but *something* should be said, especially as most questions of difficulty, in practical affairs, are settled by evidence arising from circumstances which confirm each other.

The thing asserted is that God has given us a revelation declaring himself to be a moral governor; stating his system of government; and disclosing a plan for the recovery of mankind out of sin, and raising them to perfect and final happiness.

I. *Consider this revelation as a history.*

1. It furnishes an account of the world, as God's world.

1.) God's providence, commands, promises, and threatenings.

2.) Distinguishes God from idols.

3.) Describes the condition of religion and of its professors, in a world considered as apostate and wicked.

4.) Political events are related as affecting religion, and not for their importance as mere political events.

5.) The history is continued by prophecy, to the end of the world.

2. It embraces a vast variety of other topics; natural and moral.

1.) Thus furnishing the largest scope for criticism.
2.) So that *doubts* of its truth confirm that truth, for in this enlightened age the claims of a book of such a nature could be easily and finally shown to be false, if they were so.
3.) None who believe in natural religion, hold that Christianity has been thus confuted.

3. It contains a minute account of God's selecting one nation for his peculiar people, and of his dealings with them.
1.) Interpositions in their behalf.
2.) Threats of dispersion, &c. if they rebelled.
3.) Promises of a Messiah as their prince; so clearly as to raise a general expectation, &c.
4.) Foretelling his rejection by them, and that he should be the Savior of the Gentiles.

4. Describes minutely the arrival of the Messiah, and his life and labors; and the result, in the establishment of a new religion.

II. *As to the authenticity of this history.*

Suppose a person ignorant of all history but the Bible, and not knowing even that to be true, were to inquire into its evidence of authenticity, he would find,

1. That natural religion owes its establishment to *the truths* contained in this book. This no more *disproves* natural religion, than our learning a proposition from Euclid, shows that the proposition was not true before Euclid.
2. The great antiquity of revelation.
3. That its chronology is not contradicted but confirmed by known facts.
4. That there is nothing in the history itself to awaken suspicion of its fidelity.
1.) Every thing said to be done in any age or country, is conformable to the manners of that age and country.
2.) The characters are all perfectly natural.
3.) All the domestic and political incidents are credible. Some of these, taken alone, seem strange to *some*, in *this* day; but not more so than things now occurring.
4.) Transcribers may have made errors, but these are not more numerous than in other ancient books; and none of them impair the narrative.
5. That profane authors confirm Scripture accounts.
6 That the credibility of the *general* history, confirms the accounts of the miracles, for they are all interwoven, and make but one statement.
7. That there certainly was and is such a people as the Jews; whose form of government was founded on these very books of Moses; and whose acknowledgment of the God of the Bible, kept them a distinct race.
8. That one Jesus, of Jewish extraction, arose at the time when the Jews expected a Messiah, was rejected by them, as was prophesied, and was received by the Gentiles, as was prophesied.
9. That the religion of this Jesus spread till it became the religion of the world, notwithstanding every sort of resistance; and has continued till now.

10. That the Jewish government was destroyed, and the people dispersed into all lands; and still for many centuries, continue to be a distinct race, professing the law of Moses. If this separateness be *accounted for*, in any way, it does not destroy the fact that it was *predicted*.

CONCLUSION.

1. Recapitulation of the preceding ten observations.
2. Add the fact that there are obvious appearances in the world, aside from the Jews, which correspond to prophetic history.
3. These appearances, compared with Bible history, and with each other, in *a joint view*, will appear to be of great weight, and would impress one who regarded them for the first time, more than they do us who have been familiar with them.
4. The preceding discussion, though not thorough, amounts to proof of something more than human in this matter.
   1.) The sufficiency of these proofs may be denied, but the *existence* of them cannot be.
   2.) The conformity of prophecies to events may be said to be accidental, but the *conformity itself* cannot be denied.
   3.) These collateral proofs may be pronounced fanciful, but it cannot be said they are *nothing*. Probabilities may not amount to demonstration, but they remain probabilities.
5. Those who will set down all seeming completions of prophecy, and judge of them by the common rules of evidence, will find that *together* they amount to strong proof. Because probable proofs, added together, not only increase evidence, but multiply it.
6. It is very well to observe objections; but it should be remembered that a mistake on one side is far more dangerous than a mistake on the other; and the safest conclusion is the best.
7. Religion, like other things, is to be judged by all the evidence taken together. Unless *all* its proofs be overthrown, it remains proved. If no proof singly were sufficient, the whole taken together might be.
8. It is much easier to start an objection, than to comprehend the united force of a whole argument.
9. Thus it appears that the positive evidence of revelation cannot be destroyed, though it should be lessened.

CHAPTER VIII.

OBJECTIONS AGAINST THE ANALOGICAL ARGUMENT.

If all made up their minds with proper care and candor, there would be no need of this chapter. But some do not try to understand what they condemn: and our mode of argument is open to objections, especially in the minds of those who judge without thinking. The chief objections will therefore be considered. They are these:—it does not solve difficulties in revelation to say that there are as great in natural religion:—it will not make men religious to show them that it is *as* important as worldly prudence, for showing that, does not make them prudent:—the justice of God in the system of religion, is not proved by showing it is as apparent as in his natural providence:—no reasoning from analogy can carry full conviction:—mankind will not renounce present pleasures, for a religion which is not free from doubt. To each of which a reply will now be given.

I. *As to requiring a solution of all difficulties*

1. This is but resolving to comprehend the nature of God, and the whole plan of his government throughout eternity.
2. It is always right to argue from what is known, to what is disputed. We are constantly so doing. The most eminent physician does not understand all diseases, yet we do not despise what he does know.
3. It is very important to find that objections against revelation are just as strong, not only against natural religion, but against the course of nature.

II. *As to men's having as little reason for worldly pursuits, as they have for being religious.*

1. If men can be convinced that they have as much reason to be religious as they have to practise worldly prudence, then *there is* a reason for being religious.
2. If religion proposes greater than worldly interests, and has the same reasons for belief, then it has proportionally a greater claim.
3. If religion being left doubtful, proves it to be false, then doubts as to the success of any worldly pursuit show it to be wrong. Yet we constantly act, even in the most important affairs, without *certainty* of being right.

III. *As to the justice and goodness of God in religion.*

1. Our business is not to vindicate God, but to learn our duty, governed as we are; which is a very different thing. It has been shown that if we knew all things, present, past, and future, and the relations of each thing to all other things, we might see to be just and good what now do not seem so: and it is probable we should.
2. We do not say that objections against God's justice and goodness are removed by showing the like objections against natural providence, but that they are not *conclusive*, because they apply equally to what we know to be facts.
3. The existence of objections does not destroy the evidence of facts. The fact for instance that God rewards and punishes, though men may think it unjust. Even necessity, plead for human acts, does no more to abolish justice than it does injustice.
4. Though the reasonableness of Christianity cannot be shown from analogy, the truth of it may. The truth of a fact may be proved without regard to its quality. The reasonableness of obeying Christianity is proved, if we barely prove Christianity itself to be possible.
5. Though analogy may not show Christian precepts to be good, it proves them to be credible.

IV. *The analogical argument does not remove doubt.*

1. What opinion does any man hold, about which there can be no doubt? Even the best way of preserving and enjoying this life, is not agreed upon. Whether our measures will accomplish our objects, is always uncertain; and still more whether the objects, if accomplished, will give us happiness. Yet men do not on this account refuse to make exertion.
2. This objection overlooks the very nature of religion. The embracing of it presupposes a certain degree of candor and integrity, to try which, and exercise, and improve it, is its intention. Just as warning a man of danger, presupposes a disposition to avoid danger.
3. Religion is a probation, and has evidence enough as such; and would not be such, if it compelled assent.
4. We never mean by sufficient evidence, such an amount as necessarily determines a man to act, but only such as will show an action to be prudent.

V. *As to the small influence of the analogical argument.*

1. As just observed, religion is a *test*, and an *exercise*, of character; and that some reject it is nothing to our purpose. We are inquiring not what sort of creature man is, but what he should be. This is each man's own concern.
2. Religion, as a probation, accomplishes its end, whether individuals believe or not.
3. Even this objection admits that religion has some weight, and of course it should have some influence; and if so, there is the same reason, though not so strong, for publishing it, that there would be, if it were likely to have greater influence.

FURTHER. It must be considered that the reasoning in this treatise is on the principles of other men, and arguments of the utmost importance are omitted, because not universally admitted. Thus as to Fatalism, and the abstract fitness or unfitness of actions. The general argument is just a question of fact, and is here so treated. Abstract truths are usually advanced as proof; but in this work, only *facts* are adduced. That the three angles of a triangle are equal to two right angles, is an abstract truth: but that they so appear to us, is only a matter of fact. That there is such a thing as abstract right and wrong, which determines the will of God in rewarding and punishing, is an assertion of an abstract truth, as well as a fact. Suppose God in this world rewarded and punished every man exactly as he obeyed or disobeyed his conscience, this would not be an abstract truth, but a fact. And if all acknowledged this as a fact, all would not see it to be right. If, instead of his doing it now, we say he will do it hereafter, this too is not an abstract truth, but a question of fact. This fact could be fully proved on the abstract principles of moral fitness; but without them, there has now been given a *conclusive practical proof;* which though it may be cavilled at, and shown not to amount to demonstration, cannot be answered.

Hence it may be said as to the force of this treatise,

1. To such as are convinced of the truth of revelation, as proved on the principles of liberty and moral fitness, it will furnish a full confirmation. To such as do not admit those principles it is an original proof.
2. Those who believe will find objections removed, and those who disbelieve will find they have no grounds for their scepticism; and a good deal beside.
3. Thus though some may think *too much* is here made of analogy, yet there can be no denying that the argument is *real.* It confirms *all facts* to which it can be applied; and of many is the only proof. It is strong on the side of religion, and ought to be regarded by such as prefer facts to abstract reasonings.

CONCLUSION.

Recapitulates the general structure and design of the argument, the classes of persons for whose benefit it is particularly adopted, and declares those who reject Christianity to be wholly without excuse.

Advertisement prefixed to the First Edition.

If the reader should here meet with any thing which he had not before attended to, it will not be in the observations upon the constitution and course of nature, these being all obvious, but in the application of them; in which, though there is nothing but what appears to me of some real weight, and therefore of great importance, yet he will observe several things, which will appear to him of very little, if he can think things to be of little importance, which are of any real weight at all, upon such a subject of religion. However, the proper force of the following treatise lies in the whole general analogy considered together.

It is come, I know not how to be taken for granted, by many persons, that Christianity is not so much as a subject of inquiry; but that it is, now at length, discovered to be fictitious. Accordingly they treat it, as if, in the present age, this were an agreed point among all people of discernment; and nothing remained, but to set it up as a principal subject of mirth and ridicule, as it were by way of reprisals, for its having so long interrupted the pleasures of the world. On the contrary, thus much at least, will be here found, not taken for granted but proved, that any reasonable man, who will thoroughly consider the matter, may be as much assured, as he is of his own being, that it is not so clear a case, that there is nothing in it. There is, I think, strong evidence of its truth; but it is certain no one can, upon principles of reason, be satisfied of the contrary. The practical consequence to be drawn from this, is not attended to by every one who is concerned in it.

May, 1736.

INTRODUCTION.

PROBABLE evidence is essentially distinguished from demonstrative by this, that it admits of degrees; and of all variety of them, from the highest moral certainty, to the very lowest presumption. We cannot indeed say a thing is probably true upon one very slight presumption for it; because, as there may be probabilities on both sides of a question, there may be some against it; and though there be not, yet a slight presumption does not beget that degree of conviction, which is implied in saying a thing is probably true. But that the slightest possible presumption is of the nature of a probability, appears from hence; that such low presumption, often repeated, will amount even to moral certainty. Thus a man's having observed the ebb and flow of the tide to-day, affords some sort of presumption, though the lowest imaginable, that it may happen again to-morrow: but the observation of this event for so many days, and months, and ages together, as it has been observed by mankind, gives us a full assurance that it will.

That which chiefly constitutes *probability* is expressed in the word *likely*, *i.e.* like some truth,[*] or true event; like it, in itself, in its evidence, in some (more or fewer) of its circumstances.[a] For when we determine a thing to be probably true, suppose that an event has or will come to pass, it is from the mind's remarking in it a likeness to some other event, which we have observed has come to pass. This observation forms, in numberless daily instances, a presumption, opinion, or full conviction, that such event has or will come to pass; according as the observation is, that the like event has sometimes, most commonly, or always, so

[*] Verisimile.

[a] [These three ways of being "like," are very distinct from each other. The first is equivalent to a logical induction. The second produces belief, because the same evidence made us believe in a similar case. The third is just an analogy, in the popular sense of the term.]

far as our observation reaches, come to pass at like distances of time, or place, or upon like occasions. Hence arises the belief, that a child, if it lives twenty years, will grow up to the stature and strength of a man; that food will contribute to the preservation of its life, and the want of it for such a number of days, be its certain destruction. So likewise the rule and measure of our hopes and fears concerning the success of our pursuits; our expectations that others will act so and so in such circumstances; and our judgment that such actions proceed from such principles; all these rely upon our having observed the like to what we hope, fear, expect, judge; I say, upon our having observed the like, either with respect to others or ourselves. Thus, the prince* who had always lived in a warm climate, naturally concluded in the way of analogy, that there was no such thing as water's becoming hard, because he had always observed it to be fluid and yielding. We, on the contrary, from analogy conclude, that there is no presumption at all against this: that it is supposable there may be frost in England any given day in January next; probable that there will on some day of the month; and that there is a moral certainty, *i.e.* ground for an expectation without any doubt of it, in some part or other of the winter.

Probable evidence, in its very nature, affords but an imperfect kind of information; and is to be considered as relative only to beings of limited capacities. For nothing which is the possible object of knowledge, whether past, present, or future, can be probable to an infinite intelligence; since it cannot but be discerned absolutely as it is in itself, certainly true, or certainly false. But to us, probability is the very guide of life.

From these things it follows, that in questions of difficulty, or such as are thought so, where more satisfactory evidence cannot be had, or is not seen; if the result of examination be, that there appears upon the whole, any even the lowest presumption on one side, and none on the other, or a greater presumption on one side, though in the lowest degree greater; this determines the question, even in matters of speculation. In matters of practice, it will lay us under an absolute and formal obligation, in point of prudence and of interest, to act upon that presumption or low probability, though it be so low as to leave the mind in very great

* The story is told by Mr. Locke in the Chapter of Probability.

doubt which is the truth. For surely a man is as really bound in prudence to do what upon the whole, according to the best of his judgment, appears to be for his happiness,[b] as what he certainly knows to be so.

Further, in questions of great consequence, a reasonable man will think it concerns him to remark lower probabilities and presumptions than these; such as amount to no more than showing one side of a question to be as supposable and credible as the other: nay, such even as but amount to much less than this. For numberless instances might be mentioned respecting the common pursuits of life, where a man would be thought, in a literal sense, distracted, who would not act, and with great application too, not only upon an even chance, but upon much less, and where the probability or chance was greatly against his succeeding.*

It is not my design to inquire further into the nature, the foundation, and measure of probability; or whence it proceeds that *likeness* should beget that presumption, opinion, and full conviction, which the human mind is formed to receive from it, and which it does necessarily produce in every one; or to guard against the errors, to which reasoning from analogy is liable. This belongs to the subject of Logic; and is a part of that subject which has not yet been thoroughly considered. Indeed I shall not take upon me to say, how far the extent, compass, and force, of analogical reasoning, can be reduced to general heads and rules; and the whole be formed into a system. But though so little in this way has been attempted by those who have treated of our intellectual powers, and the exercise of them; this does not hinder but that we may be, as we unquestionably are, assured, that analogy is of weight, in various degrees, towards determining our judgment and our practice. Nor does it in any wise cease to be of weight in those cases, because persons, either given to dispute, or who require things to be stated with greater exact-

[b] [This is good common sense, and men always act thus if prudent. But it is not enough thus to act in the matter of salvation. "He that *believeth* not shall be damned:" Mark xvi. 16. "He that *believeth* hath everlasting life:" John iii. 36. "With the heart man *believeth* unto righteousness:" Rom. x. 10. Belief is part of the sinner's *duty* in submitting himself to God; and not merely a question of prudence.]

* See Part II. chap. vi.

ness than our faculties appear to admit of in practical matters, may find other cases in which it is not easy to say, whether it be, or be not, of any weight; or instances of seeming analogies, which are really of none. It is enough to the present purpose to observe, that this general way of arguing is evidently natural, just, and conclusive. For there is no man can make a question but that the sun will rise to-morrow, and be seen, where it is seen at all, in the figure of a circle, and not in that of a square.

Hence, namely from analogical reasoning, Origen* has with singular sagacity observed, that "*he who believes the Scripture to have proceeded from him who is the Author of nature, may well expect to find the same sort of difficulties in it, as are found in the constitution of nature.*" And in a like way of reflection it may be added, that he who denies the Scripture to have been from God upon account of these difficulties, may, for the very same reason, deny the world to have been formed by him. On the other hand, if there be an analogy or likeness between that system of things and dispensation of Providence, which *revelation* informs us of, and that system of things and dispensation of Providence, which *experience* together with reason informs us of, *i.e.* the known course of nature; this is a presumption, that they have both the same author and cause; at least so far as to answer objections against the former's being from God, drawn from any thing which is analogical or similar to what is in the latter, which is acknowledged to be from him; for an Author of nature is here supposed.

Forming our notions of the constitution and government of the world upon reasoning, without foundation for the principles which we assume, whether from the attributes of God, or any thing else, is building a world upon hypothesis, like Des Cartes. Forming our notions upon reasoning from principles which are certain, but applied to cases to which we have no ground to apply them, (like those who explain the structure of the human body, and the nature of diseases and medicines, from mere mathematics,) is an error much akin to the former: since what is assumed in order to make the reasoning applicable, is Hypothesis. But it must be allowed just, to join abstract reasonings with the observation of facts, and argue from such facts as are known, to

* Philocal. p. 23, Ed. Cant.

others that are like them; from that part of the divine government over intelligent creatures which comes under our view, to that larger and more general government over them which is beyond it; and from what is present, to collect what is likely, credible, or not incredible, will be hereafter.

This method then of concluding and determining being practical, and what, if we will act at all, we cannot but act upon in the common pursuits of life; being evidently conclusive, in various degrees, proportionable to the degree and exactness of the whole analogy or likeness; and having so great authority for its introduction into the subject of religion, even revealed religion; my design is to apply it to that subject in general, both natural and revealed: taking for proved, that there is an intelligent Author of nature, and natural Governor of the world. For as there is no presumption against this prior to the proof of it: so it has been often proved with accumulated evidence; from this argument of analogy and final causes; from abstract reasonings; from the most ancient tradition and testimony; and from the general consent of mankind. Nor does it appear, so far as I can find, to be denied by the generality of those who profess themselves dissatisfied with the evidence of religion.

As there are some, who, instead of thus attending to what is in fact the constitution of nature, form their notions of God's government upon hypothesis: so there are others, who indulge themselves in vain and idle speculations, how the world might possibly have been framed otherwise than it is; and upon supposition that things might, in imagining that they should, have been disposed and carried on after a better model, than what appears in the present disposition and conduct of them.[c] Suppose now a person of such a turn of mind, to go on with his reveries, till he had at length fixed upon some particular plan of nature, as appearing to him the best.—One shall scarce be thought guilty of detraction against human understanding, if one should say, even beforehand, that the plan which this speculative person would fix upon, though he were the wisest of the sons of men, probably would not be the very best, even according to his own

c [Some of these speculations, carried to the full measure of absurdity and impiety, may be found in Bayle's great "Historical and Critical Dictionary." See as instances, the articles ORIGEN, MANICHÆUS, PAULICIANS.]

notions of *best;* whether he thought that to be so, which afforded occasions and motives for the exercise of the greatest virtue, or which was productive of the greatest happiness, or that these two were necessarily connected, and run up into one and the same plan.

It may not be amiss, once for all, to see what would be the amount of these emendations and imaginary improvements upon the system of nature, or how far they would mislead us. It seems there could be no stopping, till we came to some such conclusions as these: that all creatures should at first be made as perfect and as happy as they were capable of ever being: that nothing, surely, of hazard or danger should be put upon them to do; some indolent persons would perhaps think nothing at all: or certainly, that effectual care should be taken, that they should, whether necessarily or not, yet eventually and in fact, always do what was right and most conducive to happiness; which would be thought easy for infinite power to effect, either by not giving them any principles which would endanger their going wrong, or by laying the right motive of action in every instance before their minds in so strong a manner, as would never fail of inducing them to act conformably to it: and that the whole method of government by punishments should be rejected as absurd; as an awkward roundabout method of carrying things on; nay, as contrary to a principal purpose, for which it would be supposed creatures were made, namely, happiness.

Now, without considering what is to be said in particular to the several parts of this train of folly and extravagance, what has been above intimated, is a full direct general answer to it; namely, that we may see beforehand that we have not faculties for this kind of speculation. For though it be admitted that, from the first principles of our nature, we unavoidably judge or determine some ends to be absolutely in themselves preferable to others, and that the ends now mentioned, or if they run up into one, that this one is absolutely the best; and consequently that we must conclude the ultimate end designed, in the constitution of nature and conduct of Providence, is the most virtue and happiness possible; yet we are far from being able to judge what particular disposition of things would be most friendly and assistant to virtue; or what means might be absolutely necessary to produce the most happiness in a system of such extent as our own world may be, taking in all that is past and to come, though we should suppose it detached from the whole things. Indeed we are so far from being able to judge of this, that we are not judges what may be the necessary means of raising and conducting one per son to the highest perfection and happiness of his nature. Nay, even in the little affairs of the present life, we find men of different educations and ranks are not competent judges of the conduct of each other. Our whole nature leads us to ascribe all moral perfection to God, and to deny all imperfection of him. And this will forever be a practical proof of his moral character, to such as will consider what a practical proof is; because it is the voice of God speaking in us. Hence we conclude, that virtue must be the happiness, and vice the misery, of every creature; and that regularity and order and right cannot but prevail finally in a universe under his government. But we are in no sort judges, what are the necessary means of accomplishing this end.

Let us then, instead of that idle and not very innocent employment of forming imaginary models of a world, and schemes of governing it, turn our thoughts to what we experience to be the conduct of nature with respect to intelligent creatures; which may be resolved into general laws or rules of administration, in the same way as many of the laws of nature respecting inanimate matter may be collected from experiments. Let us compare the known constitution and course of things with what is said to be the moral system of nature; the acknowledged dispensations of Providence, or that government which we find ourselves under, with what religion teaches us to believe and expect; and see whether they are not analogous and of a piece. Upon such a comparison it will, I think, be found that they are very much so: that both may be traced up to the same general laws, and resolved into the same principles of divine conduct.

The analogy here proposed to be considered is of pretty large extent, and consists of several parts; in some more, in others less exact. In some few instances perhaps, it may amount to a real practical proof; in others not so. Yet in these it is a confirma tion of what is proved otherwise. It will undeniably show, what too many need to have shown them, that the system of religion, both natural and revealed, considered only as a system, and prior to the proof of it, is not a subject of ridicule, unless that of nature be so too. And it will afford an answer to almost all objections against the system both of natural and revealed religion; though not perhaps an answer in so great a degree, yet in a very considerable degree an answer to the objections against the evidence of it: for objections against a proof, and objections against what is said to be proved, the reader will observe are different things.

The divine government of the world, implied in the notion of religion in general and of Christianity, contains in it: that mankind is appointed to live in a future state;* that there every one shall be rewarded or punished;† rewarded or punished respectively for all that behaviour here, which we comprehend under the words, virtuous or vicious, morally good or evil:‡ that our present life is a probation, a state of trial,§ and of discipline,|| for that future one; notwithstanding the objections, which men may fancy they have, from notions of necessity, against there being any such moral plan as this at all;¶ and whatever objections may appear to lie against the wisdom and goodness of it, as it stands so imperfectly made known to us at present:** that this world being in a state of apostasy and wickedness, and consequently of ruin, and the sense both of their condition and duty being greatly corrupted amongst men, this gave occasion for an additional dispensation of Providence; of the utmost importance;†† proved by miracles;‡‡ but containing in it many things appearing to us strange, and not to have been expected;§§ a dispensation of Providence, which is a scheme or system of things;|||| carried on by the mediation of a divine person, the Messiah, in order to the recovery of the world;¶¶ yet not revealed to all men, nor proved with the strongest possible evidence to all those to whom it is revealed; but only to such a part of mankind, and with such particular evidence, as the wisdom of God thought fit.***

The design then of the following treatise will be to show, that the several parts principally objected against in this moral and Christian dispensation, including its scheme, its publication, and the proof which God has afforded us of its truth; that the par-

* Ch. i. † Ch. ii. ‡ Ch. iii. § Ch. iv. || Ch. v. ¶ Ch. vi.
** Ch. vii. †† Part II. Ch. i. ‡‡ Ch. ii. §§ Ch. iii. |||| Ch. iv.
¶¶ Ch. v *** Ch. vi. vii.

ticular parts principally objected against in this whole dispensation, are analogous to what is experienced in the constitution and course of nature or Providence; that the chief objections themselves which are alleged against the former, are no other than what may be alleged with like justness against the latter, where they are found in fact to be inconclusive; and that this argument from analogy is in general unanswerable, and undoubtedly of weight on the side of religion,* notwithstanding the objections which may seem to lie against it, and the real ground which there may be for difference of opinion, as to the particular degree of weight which is to be laid upon it. This is a general account of what may be looked for in the following treatise. I shall begin it with that which is the foundation of all our hopes and of all our fears; all our hopes and fears, which are of any consideration; I mean a future life.

* Ch. viii.

THE

ANALOGY OF RELIGION.

PART I.

Natural Religion.

CHAPTER I.

A FUTURE LIFE.[a]

STRANGE difficulties have been raised by some concerning personal identity, or the sameness of living agents, implied in the notion of our existing now and hereafter, or in any two succes

[a] [This chapter Dr. Chalmers regards as the least satisfactory in the book: not because lacking in just analogies, but because infected with the obscure metaphysics of that age. His reasoning, however, only serves to show that B. has perhaps made too much of the argument from the indivisibility of consciousness; and by no means that he does not fairly use it.

We certainly cannot object that the subject of identity is not made plain. Who has explained identity, or motion, or cohesion, or crystallization, or any thing? Locke goes squarely at the subject of personal identity, (see Essay, ch. 27,) but has rendered us small aid. His definition is, "Existence itself, which determines a being of any sort, to a particular time and place, incommunicable to two beings of the same kind." I had rather define it "the uninterrupted continuance of being." What ceases to exist, cannot again exist: for then it would exist after it had ceased to exist, and would have existed before it existed. Locke makes *consciousness* to constitute identity, and argues that a man and a person are not the same; and that hence if I kill a man, but was not conscious of what I did, or have utterly forgotten, I am not the same person. Watts shows up this notion of Locke very ludicrously.

Butler, in his "Dissertation," urges that consciousness *presupposes* identity, as knowledge presupposes truth. On Locke's theory, no person would have existed any earlier than the period to which his memory extends. We cannot suppose the soul made up of many consciousnesses, nor could memory, if material, spread itself over successive years of life.]

sive moments; which, whoever thinks it worth while, may see considered in the first dissertation at the end of this treatise. But without regard to any of them here, let us consider what the analogy of nature, and the several changes which we have undergone, and those which we know we may undergo without being destroyed, suggest, as to the effect which death may, or may not, have upon us; and whether it be not from thence probable, that we may survive this change, and exist in a future state of life and perception.

I. From our being born into the present world in the helpless imperfect state of infancy, and having arrived from thence to mature age, we find it to be a general law of nature in our own species, that the same creatures, the *same individuals*, should exist in degrees of life and perception, with capacities of action, of enjoyment and suffering, in one period of their being, greatly different from those appointed them in another period of it. In other creatures the same law holds. For the difference of their capacities and states of life at their birth (to go no higher) and in maturity; the change of worms into flies, and the vast enlargement of their locomotive powers by such change: and birds and insects bursting the shell of their habitation, and by this means entering into a new world, furnished with new accommodations for them, and finding a new sphere of action assigned them; these are instances of this general law of nature. Thus all the various and wonderful transformations of animals are to be taken into consideration here. The states of life in which we ourselves existed formerly, in the womb and in our infancy, are almost as different from our present in mature age, as it is possible to conceive any two states or degrees of life can be. Therefore that we are to exist hereafter, in a state as different (suppose) from our present, as this is from our former, is but according to the analogy of nature; according to a natural order or appointment of the very same kind, with what we have already experienced.

II. We know we are endued with capacities of action, of happiness and misery: for we are conscious of acting, of enjoying pleasure and suffering pain. Now that we have these powers and capacities before death, is a presumption that we shall retain them through and after death; indeed a probability of it abundantly sufficient to act upon, unless there be some positive reason to think that death is the destruction of those living powers: because there is in every case a probability, that all things will continue as we experience they are, in all respects, except those in which we have some reason to think they will be altered. This is that *kind** of presumption or probability from analogy, expressed in the very word *continuance*, which seems our only natural reason for believing the course of the world will continue to-morrow, as it has done so far as our experience or knowledge of history can carry us back. Nay, it seems our only reason for believing, that any one substance now existing will continue to exist a moment longer; the self-existent substance only excepted. Thus if men were assured that the unknown event, death, was not the destruction of our faculties of perception and of action, there would be no apprehension that any other power or event, unconnected with this of death, would destroy these faculties just at the instant of each creature's death; and therefore no doubt but that they would remain after it; which shows the high probability that our living powers will continue after death, unless there be some ground to think that death is their destruction.† For, if it would be in a manner certain that we should survive death,[b] provided it were certain that death would not be our destruction, it must be highly probable we shall survive

* I say *kind* of presumption or probability; for I do not mean to affirm that there is the same *degree* of conviction, that our living powers will continue after death, as there is, that our substances will.

† *Destruction of living powers*, is a manner of expression unavoidably ambiguous; and may signify either *the destruction of a living being, so as that the same living being shall be incapable of ever perceiving or acting again at all;* or *the destruction of those means and instruments by which it is capable of its present life, of its present state of perception and of action.* It is here used in the former sense. When it is used in the latter, the epithet *present* is added. The loss of a man's eye is a destruction of living powers in the latter sense. But we have no reason to think the destruction of living powers, in the former sense, to be possible. We have no more reason to think a being endued with living powers, ever loses them during its whole existence, than to believe that a stone ever acquires them.

[b] [The next paragraph indicates that Butler does not, as Chalmers thinks, consider this argument as "handing us over to an absolute demonstration." It just places all arguments for and against the soul's future life, in that balanced condition, which leaves us to learn the fact from revelation, free from presumptions *against* its truth. This view of the case entirely relieves the objection as to the future life of brutes; and shows how entirely we must rely on revelation, as to the future, both of man and beast.]

it, if there be no ground to think death will be our destruction.

Though I think it must be acknowledged, that prior to the natural and moral proofs of a future life commonly insisted upon, there would arise a general confused suspicion, that in the great shock and alteration which we shall undergo by death, we, *i.e.* our living powers, might be wholly destroyed; yet even prior to those proofs, there is really no particular distinct ground or reason for this apprehension at all, so far as I can find. If there be, it must arise either from *the reason of the thing*, or from *the analogy of nature.*

But we cannot argue from *the reason of the thing*, that death is the destruction of living agents, because we know not at all what death is in itself; but only some of its effects, such as the dissolution of flesh, skin, and bones. These effects do in no wise appear to imply the destruction of a living agent. Besides, as we are greatly in the dark, upon what the exercise of our living powers depends, so we are wholly ignorant what the powers themselves depend upon; the powers themselves as distinguished, not only from their actual exercise, but also from the present capacity of exercising them; and as opposed to their destruction: for sleep, or certainly a swoon, shows us, not only that these powers exist when they are not exercised, as the passive power of motion does in inanimate matter; but shows also that they exist, when there is no present capacity of exercising them: or that the capacities of exercising them for the present, as well as the actual exercise of them, may be suspended, and yet the powers themselves remain undestroyed. Since then we know not at all upon what the existence of our living powers depends, this shows further, there can no probability be collected from the reason of the thing, that death will be their destruction: because their existence may depend upon somewhat in no degree affected by death; upon somewhat quite out of the reach of this king of terrors. So that there is nothing more certain, than that *the reason of the thing* shows us no connection between death and the destruction of living agents.

Nor can we find any thing throughout the whole *analogy of nature* to afford us even the slightest presumption, that animals ever lose their living powers; much less if it were possible, that they lose them by death: for we have no faculties wherewith to trace any beyond or through it, so as to see what becomes of them. This event removes them from our view. It destroys the *sensible* proof, which we had before their death, of their being possessed of living powers, but does not appear to afford the least reason to believe that they are, then, or by that event, deprived of them.

Our knowing that they were possessed of these powers, up to the very period to which we have faculties capable of tracing them, is itself a probability of their retaining them beyond it. This is confirmed, and a sensible credibility is given to it, by observing the very great and astonishing changes which we have experienced; so great, that our existence in another state of life, of perception and of action, will be but according to a method of providential conduct, the like to which has been already exercised even with regard to ourselves; according to a course of nature, the like to which we have already gone through.

However, as one cannot but be greatly sensible, how difficult it is to silence imagination enough to make the voice of reason even distinctly heard in this case; as we are accustomed, from our youth up, to indulge that forward, delusive faculty, ever obtruding beyond its sphere; (of some assistance indeed to apprehension, but the author of all error,) as we plainly lose ourselves in gross and crude conceptions of things, taking for granted that we are acquainted with what indeed we are wholly ignorant of: it may be proper to consider the imaginary presumptions, that death will be our destruction, arising from these kinds of early and lasting prejudices; and to show how little they really amount to, even though we cannot wholly divest ourselves of them. And,

I. All presumption of death's being the destruction of living beings, must go upon supposition that they are compounded;[c] and

[c] [Dodwell had published a book, in which he argues that human souls are not *naturally* immortal, but become so, by the power of the Holy Ghost, in regeneration. Dr. Clarke replied. The controversy was continued by Collins. Dr. C. wrote four tracts on the subject.

These "presumptions" form the base of materialism, and hence the denial of a future state. Surely, thoughts and feelings, if material, have extension. But can any one conceive of love a foot long, or anger an inch thick? How superior to the gloomy mists of modern infidels have even pagans been! Cicero

F

so, discerptible. But since consciousness is a single and indivisible power, it should seem that the subject in which it resides must be so too. For were the motion of any particle of matter absolutely one and indivisible, so as that it should imply a contradiction to suppose part of this motion to exist, and part not to exist, *i.e.* part of this matter to move, and part to be at rest, then its power of motion would be indivisible; and so also would the subject in which the power inheres, namely, the particle of matter: for if this could be divided into two, one part might be moved and the other at rest, which is contrary to the supposition.

In like manner it has been argued,* and, for any thing appearing to the contrary, justly, that since the perception or consciousness, which we have of our own existence, is indivisible, so as that it is a contradiction to suppose one part of it should be here and the other there; the perceptive power, or the power of consciousness, is indivisible too: and consequently the subject in which it resides, *i.e.* the conscious being. Now, upon supposition that the living agent each man calls himself, is thus a single being, which there is at least no more difficulty in conceiving than in conceiving it to be a compound, and of which there is the proof now mentioned; it follows, that our organized bodies are no more ourselves or part of ourselves, than any other matter around us. And it is as easy to conceive, how matter, which is no part of ourselves, may be appropriated to us in the manner which our present bodies are; as how we can receive impressions from, and have power over, any matter. It is as easy to conceive, that we may exist out of bodies, as in them; and that we might have animated bodies of any other organs and senses wholly different from these now given us; and that we may hereafter animate these same or new bodies, variously modified and organized; as to conceive how

makes Cato say, "The soul is a simple, uncompounded substance, without parts or mixture: it cannot be divided, and so cannot perish." And in another place, "I never could believe that the soul lost its senses by escaping from senseless matter; or that such a release will not enlarge and improve its powers;" and again, "I am persuaded that I shall only begin truly to live, when I cease to live in this world." Xenophon reports Cyrus as saying, in his last moments, "O my sons! do not imagine that when death has taken me from you, I shall cease to exist."]

* See Dr. Clarke's Letter to Mr. Dodwell, and the defences of it.

we can animate such bodies as our present. And lastly, the dissolution of all these several organized bodies, supposing ourselves to have successively animated them, would have no more conceivable tendency to destroy the living beings ourselves, or deprive us of living faculties, the faculties of perception and of action, than the dissolution of any foreign matter, which we are capable of receiving impressions from, and making use of, for the common occasions of life.

II. The simplicity and absolute oneness of a living agent cannot, from the nature of the thing, be properly proved by experimental observations. But as these *fall in* with the supposition of its unity, so they plainly lead us to *conclude* certainly, that our gross organized bodies, with which we perceive objects of sense, and with which we act, are no part of ourselves; and therefore show us, that we have no reason to believe their destruction to be ours: even without determining whether our living substance be material or immaterial. For we see by experience, that men may lose their limbs, their organs of sense, and even the greatest part of these bodies, and yet remain the same living agents. Persons can trace up the existence of themselves to a time, when the bulk of their bodies was extremely small, in comparison of what it is in mature age: and we cannot but think, that they might *then* have lost a considerable part of that small body, and yet have remained the same living agents; as they may now lose great part of their present body, and remain so. And it is certain, that the bodies of all animals are in a constant flux,[d] from that never-ceasing attrition, which there is in every part of them. Now, things of this kind unavoidably teach us to distinguish, between these living agents ourselves, and large quantities of matter, in which we are very nearly interested; since these may be alienated, and actually are in a daily course of succession, and changing their owners; whilst we are assured, that each living agent re-

[d] [As every particle of our bodies is changed within seven years, an average life would take us through many such changes. If the mind changes with the body, it would be unjust for an old man to be made to suffer for the sins of his youth. To escape this, the materialist is driven to affirm that *the whole* is not altered, though every particle be changed.

This argument from the constant flux is irresistible. It proves our identity, and that matter and mind are not the same. Does it not also destroy all presumption that the Ego cannot exist without this particular body?]

mains one and the same permanent being.* And this general observation leads us on to the following ones.

First, That we have no way of determining by experience, what is the certain bulk of the living being each man calls himself: and yet, till it be determined that it is larger in bulk than the solid elementary particles of matter, which there is no ground to think any natural power can dissolve, there is no sort of reason to think death to be the dissolution of it, of the living being, even though it should not be absolutely indiscerptible.

Secondly, From our being so nearly related to and interested in certain systems of matter, (suppose our flesh and bones,) and afterwards ceasing to be at all related to them, the living agents, ourselves, remaining all this while undestroyed notwithstanding such alienation; and consequently these systems of matter not being ourselves, it follows further that we have no ground to conclude any other (suppose *internal*) *systems* of matter, to be the living agents ourselves; because we can have no ground to conclude this, but from our relation to and interest in such other systems of matter: and therefore we can have no reason to conclude what befalls those systems of matter at death, to be the destruction of the living agents. We have already several times over, lost a great part or perhaps the whole of our body, according to certain common established laws of nature, yet we remain the same living agents. When we shall lose as great a part, or the whole, by another common established law of nature, death, why may we not also remain the same? That the alienation has been gradual in one case, and in the other will be more at once, does not prove any thing to the contrary. We have passed undestroyed through those many and great revolutions of matter, so peculiarly appropriated to us ourselves; why should we imagine death will be so fatal to us? Nor can it be objected, that what is thus alienated or lost, is no part of our original solid body, but only adventitious matter. Because we may lose entire limbs, which must have contained many solid parts and vessels of the original body; or if this be not admitted, we have no proof, that any of these solid parts are dissolved or alienated by death. Though we are very nearly related to that extraneous or adventitious matter, whilst it continues united to and distending the several parts of

* See Dissertation I.

our solid body, yet after all, the relation a person bears to those parts of his body, to which he is most nearly related, amounts but to this, that the living agent, and those parts of the body, mutually affect each other.[e] The same thing, the same thing in kind though not in degree, may be said of *all foreign* matter, which gives us ideas, and over which we have any power. From these observations the whole ground of the imagination is removed, that the dissolution of any matter, is the destruction of a living agent, from the interest he once had in such matter.

Thirdly, If we consider our body somewhat more distinctly, as made up of organs and instruments of perception and of motion, it will bring us to the same conclusion. Thus the common optical experiments show, and even the observation how sight is assisted by glasses shows, that we see with our eyes in the same sense as we see with glasses. Nor is there any reason to believe, that we see with them in any other sense; any other, I mean, which would lead us to think the eye itself a percipient. The like is to be said of hearing; and our feeling distant solid matter by means of something in our hand, seems an instance of the like kind, as to the subject we are considering. All these are instances of foreign matter, or such as is no part of our body, being instrumental in preparing objects for, and conveying them to, the perceiving power, in a manner similar to the manner in which our organs of sense prepare and convey them. Both are in a like way instruments of our receiving such ideas from external objects, as the Author of nature appointed those external objects to be the occasions of exciting in us. Glasses are evident instances of this; namely of matter which is no part of our body, preparing objects for and conveying them towards the perceiving power, in like manner as our bodily organs do. And if we see with our eyes only in the same manner as we do with glasses, the like may justly be concluded, from analogy, of all our other senses. It is not intended, by any thing here said, to affirm, that the whole apparatus of vision, or of perception by

[e] [The mind affects the body, as much as the body does the mind. Love, anger, &c. quicken the circulation; fear checks it; terror may stop it altogether. Mania is as often produced by moral, as by physical causes, and hence of late moral means are resorted to for cure. The brain of a maniac, seldom shows, on dissection, any derangement. But this does not prove that there was no *functional* derangement.]

8

any other sense, can be traced through all its steps, quite up to the *living power* of seeing, or perceiving: but that so far as it can be traced by experimental observations, so far it appears, that our organs of sense prepare and convey objects, in order to their being perceived, in like manner as foreign matter does, without affording any shadow of appearance, that they themselves perceive. And that we have no reason to think our organs of sense percipients, is confirmed by instances of persons losing some of them, the living beings themselves, their former occupiers, remaining unimpaired. It is confirmed also by the experience of dreams; by which we find we are at present possessed of a latent, and what would be otherwise an unimagined unknown power of perceiving sensible objects, in as strong and lively a manner without our external organs of sense, as with them.

So also with regard to our power of moving, or directing motion by will and choice; upon the destruction of a limb, this active power evidently remains, unlessened; so that the living being, who has suffered this loss, would be capable of moving as before, if it had another limb to move with. It can walk by the help of an artificial leg. It can make use of a pole or a lever, to reach towards itself and to move things, beyond the length and the power of its arm; and this it does in the same manner as it reaches and moves, with its natural arm, things nearer and of less weight. Nor is there so much as any appearance of our limbs being endued with a power of moving or directing themselves; though they are adapted, like the several parts of a machine, to be the instruments of motion to each other; and some parts of the same limb, to be instruments of motion to the other parts.

Thus a man determines that he will look at an object through a microscope; or being lame, that he will walk to such a place with a staff, a week hence. His eyes and his feet no more determine in these cases, than the microscope and the staff. Nor is there any ground to think they any more put the determination in practice; or that his eyes are the seers, or his feet the movers, in any other sense than as the microscope and the staff are. Upon the whole, then, our organs of sense, and our limbs, are certainly *instruments*,[f] which the living persons ourselves

[f] ["S. What shall we say, then, of the shoemaker? That he cuts with his

make use of to perceive and move with: there is not any probability, that they are any more; nor consequently, that we have any other kind of relation to them, than what we have to any other foreign matter formed into instruments of perception and motion, suppose into a microscope or a staff; (I say any other kind of relation, for I am not speaking of the degree of it) nor consequently is there any probability, that the alienation or dissolution of these instruments, is the destruction of the perceiving and moving agent.

And thus our finding that the dissolution of matter, in which living beings were most nearly interested, is not their dissolution; and that the destruction of several of the organs and instruments of perception and of motion belonging to them, is not their destruction; shows demonstratively, that there is no ground to think that the dissolution of any other matter, or destruction of any other organs and instruments, will be the dissolution or destruction of living agents, from the like kind of relation. And we have no reason to think we stand in any other kind of relation to any thing which we find dissolved by death.

But it is said, these observations are equally applicable to brutes:[g] and it is thought an insuperable difficulty, that they

instrument only, or with his hands also? A. With his hands also. S. Does he use his eyes also, in making shoes? A. Yes. S. But are we agreed that he who uses, and what he uses, are different? A. Yes. S. The shoemaker, then, and harper, are different from the hands and eyes they use? A. It appears so. S. Does a man then *use* his whole body? A. Certainly. S. But he who uses, and that which he uses are different. A. Yes. S. A man then is something different from his own body." PLAT. ALCIBI. PRIM. p. 129, D. Stallb. Ed.

"It may easily be perceived that the *mind* both sees and hears, and not those parts which are, so to speak, windows of the mind." "Neither are we bodies; nor do I, while speaking this to thee, speak to thy body." "Whatever is done by thy mind, is done by thee." CICERO, Tusc. Disput. I. 20, 46 and 22, 52.

"The mind of each man is the man; not that figure which may be pointed out with the finger." CIC., de Rep. b. 6, s. 24.]

g [Butler's argument, if advanced for *proof* would prove too much, not only as to brutes but as to man; for it would prove prëexistence. And this is really the tenet, (*i.e.* transmigration,) of those who arrive at the doctrine of immortality only by philosophy. Philosophy cannot establish the doctrine of a future state, nor can it afford any presumptions *against* either a future or a preexistent state.

Nothing is gained by insisting that reason teaches the true doctrine of the soul; any more than there would be by insisting that by it we learned the doctrine of a trinity, or atonement. Philosophy does teach that He who can should be immortal, and by consequence capable of everlasting happiness. Now this manner of expression is both invidious and weak: but the thing intended by it, is really no difficulty at all, either in the way of natural or moral consideration. For 1, Suppose the invidious thing, designed in such a manner of expression, were really implied, as it is not in the least, in the natural immortality of brutes, namely, that they must arrive at great attainments, and become rational and moral agents; even this would be no difficulty, since we know not what latent powers and capacities they may be endued with. There was once, prior to experience, as great presumption against human creatures, as there is against the brute creatures, arriving at that degree of understanding, which we have in mature age. For we can trace up our own existence to the same original with theirs. We find it to be a general law of nature, that creatures endued with *capacities* of virtue and religion should be placed in a condition of being, in which they are altogether without *the use* of them, for a considerable length of their duration; as in infancy and childhood. And great part of the human species go out of the present world, before they come to the exercise of these capacities in *any* degree.

2. The natural immortality of brutes does not in the least imply, that they are endued with any latent capacities of a rational or *moral* nature. The economy of the universe might require, that there should be living creatures without any capacities of this kind. And all difficulties as to the manner how they are to be disposed of, are so apparently and wholly founded in our ignorance, that it is wonderful they should be insisted upon by any, but such as are weak enough to think they are acquainted with the whole system of things. There is then absolutely

create, under infinite diversity of forms, can *sustain* existence, in any mode he pleases.

The reader who chooses to look further into the discussion as to the immortality of brutes, will find it spread out in POLIGNAC's Anti-Lucretius, and still more in BAYLE's Dictionary, under the articles PEREIRA, and RORARIUS. The topic is also discussed in DES CARTES on the Passions: BAXTER on The Nature of the Soul: HUME's Essays, Essay 9: SEARCH's Light of Nature: CHEYNE's Philosophical Principles: WAGSTAFF on the Immortality of Brutes EDWARDS' Critical and Philosophical Exercitations: WATT's Essays, Essay 9· COLLIBER's Enquiry: LOCKE on the Understanding, b. 2, ch. IX. · DITTON on the Resurrection: WILLIS De Anima Brutæ.]

nothing at all in this objection, which is so rhetorically urged, against the greatest part of the natural proofs or presumptions of the immortality of human minds; I say the greatest part, for it is less applicable to the following observation, which is more peculiar to mankind.

III. As it is evident our *present* powers and capacities of reason, memory, and affection, do not depend upon our gross body in the manner in which perception by our organs of sense does; so they do not appear to depend upon it at all, in any such manner as to give ground to think, that the dissolution of this body will be the destruction of these our present powers of reflection, as it will of our powers of sensation; or to give ground to conclude, even that it will be so much as a suspension of the former.

Human creatures exist at present in two states of life and perception, greatly different from each other; each of which has its own peculiar laws, and its own peculiar enjoyments and sufferings. When any of our senses are affected, or appetites gratified with the objects of them, we may be said to exist or live in a state of sensation. When none of our senses are affected or appetites gratified, and yet we perceive, and reason, and act, we may be said to exist or live in a state of reflection. Now it is by no means certain, that any thing which is dissolved by death, is in any way necessary to the living being, in this its state of reflection, *after* ideas are gained. For, though, from our present constitution and condition of being, our external organs of sense are necessary for conveying in ideas to our reflecting powers, as carriages, and levers, and scaffolds are in architecture:[h] yet when these ideas are brought in, we are capable of reflecting in the most intense degree, and of enjoying the greatest pleasure, and feeling the greatest pain, by means of that reflection, without

[h] [It is as absurd to suppose that a brain thinks, as that an eye sees, or a finger feels. The eye no more sees, than the telescope or spectacles. If the *nerve* be paralyzed, there is no vision, though the eye be perfect. A few words spoken or read, may at once deprive of sight, or knock a person down.

The mind sometimes survives the body. Swift, utterly helpless from palsy, retained his faculties. In some, the body survives the mind. MORGAGNI, HALLER, BONNET, and others, have proved that there is no part of the brain, not even the pineal gland, which has not been found destroyed by disease, where there had been no hallucination of mind, nor any suspicion of such disease, during life.]

any assistance from our senses; and without any at all, which we know of, from that body which will be dissolved by death. It does not appear then, that the relation of this gross body to the reflecting being is, in any degree, necessary to thinking; to intellectual enjoyments or sufferings: nor, consequently, that the dissolution or alienation of the former by death, will be the destruction of those present powers, which render us capable of this state of reflection.

Further, there are instances of mortal diseases, which do not at all affect our present intellectual powers; and this affords a presumption, that those diseases will not destroy these present powers. Indeed, from the observations made above,* it appears, that there is no presumption, from their mutually affecting each other, that the dissolution of the body is the destruction of the living agent. By the same reasoning, it must appear too, that there is no presumption, from their mutually affecting each other, that the dissolution of the body is the destruction of our present reflecting powers: indeed instances of their not affecting each other, afford a presumption of the contrary. Instances of mortal diseases not impairing our present reflecting powers, evidently turn our thoughts even from imagining such diseases to be the destruction of them. Several things indeed greatly affect all our living powers, and at length suspend the exercise of them; as for instance drowsiness, increasing till it ends in sound sleep: and hence we might have imagined it would destroy them, till we found by experience the weakness of this way of judging. But in the diseases now mentioned, there is not so much as this shadow of probability, to lead us to any such conclusion, as to the reflecting powers which we have at present. For in those diseases, persons the moment before death appear to be in the highest vigor of life. They discover apprehension, memory, reason, all entire; the utmost force of affection; a sense of character, of shame and honor; and the highest mental enjoyments and sufferings, even to the last gasp. These surely prove even greater vigor of life than bodily strength does. Now what pretence is there for thinking, that a progressive disease when arrived to such a degree, I mean that degree which is mortal, will destroy those powers, which were not impaired, which were

* Pp. 84, 85.

not affected by it, during its whole progress quite up to that degree? And if death by diseases of this kind, is not the destruction of our present reflecting powers, it will scarce be thought that death by any other means is.

It is obvious that this general observation may be carried further. There appears to be so little connection between our bodily powers of sensation, and our present powers of reflection, that there is no reason to conclude, that death, which destroys the former, does so much as *suspend the exercise* of the latter, or interrupt our *continuing* to exist in the like state of reflection which we do now.[1] For suspension of reason, memory, and the affections which they excite, is no part of the idea of death, nor implied in our notion of it. Our daily experiencing these powers to be exercised, without any assistance, that we know of, from those bodies which will be dissolved by death; and our finding often, that the exercise of them is so lively to the last; afford a sensible apprehension, that death may not perhaps be so much as a discontinuance of the exercise of these powers, nor of the enjoyments and sufferings which it implies.* So that our posthumous life, whatever there may be in it additional to our present, may yet not be beginning entirely anew; but going on. Death may, in some sort and in some respects, answer to our birth; which is not a suspension of the faculties which we had before it, or a *total* change of the state of life in which we existed when in the womb; but a continuation of both, with such and such great alterations.

Nay, for aught we know of ourselves, of our present life and of death, death may immediately, in the natural course of

[1] [We are told by sceptics that "mind is the result of a curious and complicated organization." A mere jumble of words! But were the mind material, there is no evidence that death would destroy it: for we do not see that death has any power over matter. The body remains the very same as it does in a swoon, till *chemical* changes begin.]

* There are three distinct questions, relating to a future life, here considered: Whether death be the destruction of living agents; if not, Whether it be the destruction of their *present* powers of reflection, as it certainly is the destruction of their present powers of sensation; and if not, Whether it be the suspension, or discontinuance of the exercise of these present reflecting powers. Now, if there be no reason to believe the last, there will be, if that were possible, less for the next, and less still for the first.

things, put us into a higher and more enlarged state of life, as our birth does;* a state in which our capacities, and sphere of perception and of action, may be much greater than at present. For as our relation to our external organs of sense, renders us capable of existing in our present state of sensation; so it may be the only natural hinderance to our existing, immediately, and of course, in a *higher* state of reflection. The truth is, reason does not at all show us, in what state death naturally leaves us. But were we sure, that it would suspend all our perceptive and active powers; yet the suspension of a power and the destruction of it, are effects so totally different in kind, as we experience from sleep and a swoon, that we cannot in any wise argue from one to the other; or conclude even to the lowest degree of probability, that the same kind of force which is sufficient to suspend our faculties, though it be increased ever so much, will be sufficient to destroy them.[j]

These observations together may be sufficient to show, how little presumption there is, that death is the destruction of human creatures. However, there is the shadow of an analogy, which may lead us to imagine it,—viz.: the supposed likeness which is observed between the decay of vegetables, and of living creatures. This likeness is indeed sufficient to afford the poets very apt allusions to the flowers of the field, in their pictures of the frailty of our present life. But in reason, the analogy is so far from holding, that there appears no ground for the comparison, as to the present question; because one of the two subjects compared is wholly void of that, which is the principal and chief thing in the other, the power of perception and of action; which is the only thing we are inquiring about the continu-

* This, according to Strabo, was the opinion of the Brachmans, *νομίζειν μὲν γὰρ δὴ τὸν μὲν ἐνθάδε βίον, ὡς ἂν ἀκμὴν κυομένων εἶναι· τὸν δὲ θάνατον, γένεσιν εἰς τὸν ὄντως βίον, καὶ τὸν εὐδαίμονα τοῖς φιλοσοφήσασι·* Lib. xv. p. 1039, Ed. Amst. 1707. ["For they think that the present life is like that of those who are just ready to be born; and that death is a birth into the real life, and a happy one to those who have practised philosophy."] To which opinion perhaps Antoninus may allude in these words, *ὡς νῦν περιμένεις, πότε ἔμβρυον ἐκ τῆς γαστρὸς τῆς γυναικός σου ἐξέλθῃ, οὕτως ἐκδέχεσθαι, τὴν ὥραν ἐν ᾗ τὸ ψυχάριόν σου τοῦ ἐλύτρου τούτου ἐκπεσεῖται.* Lib. ix. c. 3. [As this last passage may, by some, be thought indelicate, it is left untranslated.]

j [The *increase* of a force in any direction, cannot of itself *change* that direction. An arrow shot from a bow, towards an object, does not aim at some other object, by being shot with more force.]

ance of. So that the destruction of a vegetable, is an event not similar or analogous to the destruction of a living agent.

If, as was above intimated, leaving off the delusive custom of substituting imagination in the room of experience, we would confine ourselves to what we do know and understand; if we would argue only from that, and from that form our expectations, it would appear at first sight, that as no probability of living beings ever ceasing to be so, can be concluded from the reason of the thing, so none can be collected from the analogy of nature; because we cannot trace any living beings beyond death. But as we are conscious that we are endued with capacities of perception and of action, and are living persons; what we are to go upon is, that we shall continue so, till we foresee some accident or event, which will endanger those capacitities, or be likely to destroy us: which death does in no wise appear to be.

Thus, when we go out of this world, we may pass into new scenes, and a new state of life and action, just as naturally as we came into the present. And this new state may naturally be a social one.[k] And the advantages of it, advantages of every kind, may naturally be bestowed, according to some fixed general laws of wisdom, upon every one in proportion to the degrees of his virtue. And though the advantages of that future natural state should not be bestowed, as these of the present in some measure are, by the will of the society; but entirely by his more immediate action, upon whom the whole frame of nature depends: yet this distribution may be just as natural, as their being distributed here by the instrumentality of men. Indeed, though one should allow any confused undetermined sense, which people please to put upon the word *natural*, it would be a shortness of thought scarce credible, to imagine, that no system or course of things can be so, but only what we see at present:* especially whilst the

[k] [Our nature will *always* be ours, or we should cease to be ourselves, and become something else. And this nature is *social*. Every one feels, at least sometimes, that he is not complete in himself for the production of happiness; and so looks round for that which may fit his wants, and supply what he cannot produce from within. Hence amusements, of a thousand kinds, are resorted to, and still more, society. Society is a want of the mind; as food is of the body. Society, such as perfectly suits our real nature, and calls out, in a right manner, its every attribute, would secure our perfect happiness. But such society must include God.]

* See Part II. chap. ii. and Part II. chap. iv.

probability of a future life, or the natural immortality of the soul, is admitted upon the evidence of reason; because this is really both admitting and denying at once, a state of being different from the present to be natural. But the only distinct meaning of that word is, *stated*, *fixed*, or *settled;* since what is natural as much requires and presupposes an intelligent agent to render it so, *i.e.* to effect it continually, or at stated times, as what is supernatural or miraculous does to effect it for once.

Hence it must follow, that persons' notion of what is natural, will be enlarged in proportion to their greater knowledge of the works of God, and the dispensations of his providence. Nor is there any absurdity in supposing, that there may be beings in the universe, whose capacities, and knowledge, and views, may be so extensive, as that the whole Christian dispensation may to them appear natural, *i.e.* analogous or conformable to God's dealings with other parts of his creation; as natural as the visible known course of things appears to us. For there seems scarce any other possible sense to be put upon the word, but that only in which it is here used; similar, stated, or uniform.

This credibility of a future life, which has been here insisted upon, how little soever it may satisfy our curiosity, seems to answer all the purposes of religion, in like manner as a demonstrative proof would. Indeed a proof, even a demonstrative one, of a future life, would not be a proof of religion. For, that we are to live hereafter, is just as reconcilable with the scheme of atheism, and as well to be accounted for by it, as that we are now alive is: and therefore nothing can be more absurd than to argue from that scheme, that there can be no future state. But as religion implies a future state, any presumption against such a state, is a presumption against religion. The foregoing observations remove all presumptions of that sort, and prove, to a very considerable degree of probability, one fundamental doctrine of religion; which, if believed, would greatly open and dispose the mind seriously to attend to the general evidence of the whole.

CHAPTER II.

THE GOVERNMENT OF GOD BY REWARDS AND PUNISHMENTS.

THAT which makes the question concerning a future life to be of so great importance to us, is our capacity of happiness and misery. And that which makes the consideration of it to be of so great importance to us, is the supposition of our happiness and misery hereafter depending upon our actions here. Indeed, without this, curiosity could not but sometimes bring a subject, in which we may be so highly interested, to our thoughts; especially upon the mortality of others, or the near prospect of our own. But reasonable men would not take any further thought about hereafter, than what should happen thus occasionally to rise in their minds, if it were certain that our future interest no way depended upon our present behavior; whereas, on the contrary, if there be ground, either from analogy or any thing else, to think it does, then there is reason also for the most active thought and solicitude, to secure that interest; to behave so as that we may escape that misery, and obtain that happiness, in another life, which we not only suppose ourselves capable of, but which we apprehend also is put in our own power. And whether there be ground for this last apprehension, certainly would deserve to be most seriously considered, were there no other proof of a future life and interest, than that presumptive one, which the foregoing observations amount to.

In the present state, all which we enjoy, and a great part of what we suffer, *is put in our own power*. Pleasure and pain are the consequences of our actions; and we are endued by the Author of our nature with capacities of foreseeing these consequences. We find by experience that he does not so much as preserve our lives, exclusive of our own care and attention, to provide ourselves with, and to make use of, that sustenance, by which he has appointed our lives shall be preserved; and without which, he has appointed, they shall not be preserved. In general we foresee, that the external things, which are the objects of our various passions, can neither be obtained nor enjoyed, without exerting ourselves in such and such manners: but by thus exerting ourselves, we obtain and enjoy these objects, in which our natural good consists; or by this means God gives us the possession and enjoyment of them. I know not, that we have any one kind or degree of enjoyment, but by the means of our own actions. By prudence and care, we may, for the most part, pass our days in tolerable ease and quiet: on the contrary, we may, by rashness, ungoverned passion, wilfulness, or even by negligence, make ourselves as miserable as ever we please. And many do please to make themselves extremely miserable, *i.e.* to do what they know beforehand will render them so. They follow those ways, the fruit of which they know, by instruction, example, and experience, will be disgrace, and poverty, and sickness, and untimely death. This every one observes to be the general course of things; though it is to be allowed, we cannot find by experience, that *all* our sufferings are owing to our own follies.

Why the Author of nature does not give his creatures promiscuously such and such perceptions, without regard to their behavior; why he does not make them happy without the instrumentality of their own actions, and prevent their bringing any sufferings upon themselves, is another matter.[a] Perhaps there may be some impossibilities in the nature of things, which we are unacquainted with.* Or less happiness, it may be, would upon the whole be produced by such a method of conduct, than is by the present. Or perhaps divine goodness, with which, if I mistake not, we make very free in our speculations, may not be a bare single disposition to produce happiness; but a disposition to make the good, the faithful, the honest, happy. Perhaps an infinitely perfect mind may be pleased with seeing his creatures behave suitably to the nature which he has given them; to the relations which he has placed them in to each other; and to that which they stand in to himself: that relation to himself, which, during their existence, is even necessary,[b] and which is the most

[a] [Objections and difficulties belong to all subjects, in *some* of their bearings. Ingenious and uncandid men may start others, which care and candor may remove. It is therefore no proof of weakness in a doctrine, that it is attacked with objections, both real and merely plausible. Error has been spread by two opposite means :—a dogmatic insisting on doubtful points, and an unteachable cavilling at certain truth.]

* Part I. chap. vii.

[b] [Our relation to God is "even necessary," because we are his creatures; so

important one of all: perhaps, I say, an infinitely perfect mind may be pleased with this moral piety of moral agents, in and for itself; as well as upon account of its being essentially conducive to the happiness of his creation. Or the whole end, for which God made, and thus governs the world, may be utterly beyond the reach of our faculties: there may be somewhat in it as impossible for us to have any conception of, as for a blind man to have a conception of colors. However this be, it is certain matter of universal experience, that the general method of divine administration is, forewarning us, or giving us capacities to foresee, with more or less clearness, that if we act so and so, we shall have such enjoyments, if so and so, such sufferings; and giving us those enjoyments, and making us feel those sufferings, in consequence of our actions.

"But all this is to be ascribed to the general course of nature." True. This is the very thing which I am observing. It is to be ascribed to the general course of nature: *i.e.* not surely to the words or ideas, *course of nature;* but to Him who appointed it, and put things into it; or to a course of operation, from its uniformity or constancy, called natural;* and which necessarily implies an operating agent. For when men find themselves necessitated to confess an Author of nature, or that God is the natural governor of the world, they must not deny this again, because his government is uniform. They must not deny that he does things at all, because he does them constantly,[c] because the effects of his acting are permanent, whether his acting be so or not; though there is no reason to think it is not. In short, every man, in every thing he does, naturally acts upon the forethought and apprehension of avoiding evil or obtaining good: and if the natural course of things be the appointment of God, and our natural faculties of knowledge and experience are given

that the relation must endure so long as we endure. But our relations to other creatures are contingent, and may be changed or abrogated.]

* Pp. 93, 94.

c ["The terms nature, and power of nature, and course of nature, are but empty words, and merely mean that a thing occurs usually or frequently. The raising of a human body out of the earth we call a miracle, the generation of one in the ordinary way we call natural, for no other reason than because one is usual the other unusual. Did men usually rise out of the earth like corn we should call that natural." Dr. CLARKE, Controv. with Leibnitz.]

us by him, then the good and bad consequences which follow our actions, are his appointment, and our foresight of those consequences, is a warning given us by him, how we are to act.

"Is the pleasure then, naturally accompanying every particular gratification of passion, intended to put us upon gratifying ourselves in every such particular instance, and as a reward to us for so doing?" No, certainly. Nor is it to be said, that our eyes were naturally intended to give us the sight of each particular object, to which they do or can extend; objects which are destructive of them, or which, for any other reason, it may become us to turn our eyes from. Yet there is no doubt, but that our eyes were intended for us to see with.[d] So neither is there any doubt, but that the foreseen pleasures and pains belonging to the passions, were intended, in general, to induce mankind to act in such and such manners.

From this general observation, obvious to every one, (that God has given us to understand, he has appointed satisfaction and delight to be the consequence of our acting in one manner, and pain and uneasiness of our acting in another, and of our not acting at all; and that we find these consequences, which we were beforehand informed of, uniformly to follow;) we may learn, that we are at present actually under his government in the strictest and most proper sense; in such a sense, as that he rewards and punishes us for our actions.

An Author of nature being supposed, it is not so much a deduction of reason, as a matter of experience, that we are thus under his government; under his government, in the same sense, as we are under the government of civil magistrates. Because the annexing of pleasure to some actions, and pain to others, in our power to do or forbear, and giving notice of this

[d] [That man consists of parts, is evident; and the use of each part, and of the whole man, is open to investigation. In examining any part we learn what it *is*, and what it is *to do: e.g.* the eye, the hand, the heart. So of mental faculties; memory is to preserve ideas, shame to deter us from things shameful, compassion to induce us to relieve distress. In observing our whole make, we may see an ultimate design,—viz.: not particular animal gratifications, but intellectual and moral improvement, and happiness by that means. If this be our end, it is our duty. To disregard it, must bring punishment: for shame, anguish, remorse, are by the laws of mind, the sequences of sin.

See LAW's Notes on King's Origin of Evil.]

appointment beforehand to those whom it concerns, is the proper formal notion of government.

Whether the pleasure or pain which thus follows upon our behavior, be owing to the Author of nature's acting upon us every moment which we feel it; or to his having at once contrived and executed his own part in the plan of the world; makes no alteration as to the matter before us. For if civil magistrates could make the sanctions of their laws take place, without interposing at all, after they had passed them; without a trial, and the formalities of an execution: if they were able to make their laws *execute themselves*, or every offender to execute them upon himself; we should be just in the same sense under their government then, as we are now; but in a much higher degree, and more perfect manner.

Vain is the ridicule, with which one foresees some persons will divert themselves, upon finding lesser pains considered as instances of divine punishment. There is no possibility of answering or evading the general thing here intended, without denying all final causes. For final causes being admitted, the pleasures and pains now mentioned must be admitted too as instances of them. And if they are; if God annexes delight to some actions, and uneasiness to others, with an apparent design to induce us to act so and so; then he not only dispenses happiness and misery, but also rewards and punishes actions. If, for example, the pain which we feel, upon doing what tends to the destruction of our bodies, suppose upon too near approaches to fire, or upon wounding ourselves, be appointed by the Author of nature to prevent our doing what thus tends to our destruction; this is altogether as much an instance of his punishing our actions, and consequently of our being under his government,[e] as declaring by a voice from heaven, that if we acted so, he would inflict such pain upon us; and inflicting it, whether it be greater or less.

Thus we find, that the true notion or conception of the Author

[e] [It is almost amazing that philosophy, because it discovers the laws of matter, should be placed in antagonism with the Bible which reveals a superintending Providence. The Bible itself teaches this very result of philosophy, —viz.: that the world is governed by *general laws*. See Prov. viii. 29: Job. xxxviii. 12, 24, 31, 33: Ps. cxix. 90, 91: Jer. xxxi. 35, and xxxiii. 25.]

of nature, is that of a master or governor, prior to the consideration of his moral attributes. The fact of our case, which we find by experience, is, that he actually exercises dominion or government over us at present, by rewarding and punishing us for our actions, in as strict and proper a sense of these words, and even in the same sense, as children, servants, subjects, are rewarded and punished by those who govern them.

Thus the whole analogy of nature, the whole present course of things, most fully shows, that there is nothing incredible in the general doctrine of religion, that God will reward and punish men for their actions hereafter: nothing incredible, I mean, arising out of the notion of rewarding and punishing. For the whole course of nature is a present instance of his exercising that government over us, which implies in it rewarding and punishing.

As divine *punishment* is what men chiefly object against, and are most unwilling to allow; it may be proper to mention some circumstances in the natural course of punishments at present, which are analogous to what religion teaches us concerning a future state of punishment; indeed so analogous, that as they add a further credibility to it, so they cannot but raise a most serious apprehension of it in those who will attend to them.

It has been now observed, that such and such miseries naturally follow such and such actions of imprudence and wilfulness, as well as actions more commonly and more distinctly considered as vicious; and that these consequences, when they may be foreseen, are properly natural punishments annexed to such actions. The general thing here insisted upon, is, not that we see a great deal of misery in the world, but a great deal which men bring upon themselves by their own behavior, which they might have foreseen and avoided. Now the circumstances of these natural punishments, particularly deserving our attention, are such as these. Oftentimes they follow, or are inflicted in consequence of, actions which procure many present advantages, and are accompanied with much present pleasure; for instance, sickness and untimely death are the consequence of intemperance, though accompanied with the highest mirth and jollity. These punishments are often much greater, than the advantages or pleasures obtained by the actions, of which they are the punishments or consequences. Though we may imagine a constitution of nature, in which these natural punishments, which are in fact to follow, would follow, immediately upon such actions being done, or very soon after; we find on the contrary in our world, that they are often delayed a great while, sometimes even till long after the actions occasioning them are forgot; so that the constitution of nature is such, that delay of punishment is no sort nor degree of presumption of final impunity. After such delay, these natural punishments or miseries often come, not by degrees, but suddenly, with violence, and at once; however, the chief misery often does. As certainty of such distant misery following such actions, is never afforded persons, so perhaps during the actions, they have seldom a distinct, full expectation of its following:* and many times the case is only thus, that they see in general, or may see, the credibility, that intemperance, suppose, will bring after it diseases; civil crimes, civil punishments; when yet the real probability often is, that they shall escape; but things notwithstanding take their destined course, and the misery inevitably follows at its appointed time, in very many of these cases. Thus also though youth may be alleged as an excuse for rashness and folly, as being naturally thoughtless, and not clearly foreseeing all the consequences of being untractable and profligate, this does not hinder, but that these consequences follow; and are grievously felt, throughout the whole course of mature life. Habits contracted even in that age, are often utter ruin: and men's success in the world, not only in the common sense of worldly success, but their real happiness and misery, depends, in a great degree, and in various ways, upon the manner in which they pass their youth; which consequences they for the most part neglect to consider, and perhaps seldom can properly be said to believe, beforehand. In numberless cases, the natural course of things affords us opportunities for procuring advantages to ourselves at certain times, which we cannot procure when we will; nor ever recall the opportunities, if we have neglected them. Indeed the general course of nature is an example of this. If, during the opportunity of youth, persons are indocile

* See Part II. chap. vi.

and self-willed, they inevitably suffer in their future life, for want of those acquirements, which they neglected the natural season of attaining. If the husbandman lets seedtime pass without sowing, the whole year is lost to him beyond recovery. Though after men have been guilty of folly and extravagance *up to a certain degree*, it is often in their power, to retrieve their affairs, to recover their health and character, at least in good measure; yet real reformation is in many cases, of no avail at all towards preventing the miseries, poverty, sickness, infamy, naturally annexed to folly and extravagance *exceeding that degree* There is a certain bound to imprudence and misbehavior, which being transgressed, there remains no place for repentance in the natural course of things. It is further very much to be remarked, that neglects from inconsiderateness, want of attention,* not looking about us to see what we have to do, are often attended with consequences altogether as dreadful, as any active misbehavior, from the most extravagant passion. And lastly, civil government being natural, the punishments of it are so too: and some of these punishments are capital; as the effects of a dissolute course of pleasure are often mortal. So that many natural punishments are final† to him who incurs them, if considered only in his temporal capacity; and seem inflicted by

* Part II. chap. vi.

† The general consideration of a future state of punishment, most evidently belongs to the subject of natural religion. But if any of these reflections should be thought to relate more peculiarly to this doctrine, as taught in Scripture, the reader is desired to observe, that Gentile writers, both moralists and poets, speak of the future punishment of the wicked, both as to the duration and degree of it, in a like manner of expression and of description, as the Scripture does. So that all which can positively be asserted to be matter of mere revelation, with regard to this doctrine, seems to be, that the great distinction between the righteous and the wicked, shall be made at the end of this world; that each shall *then* receive according to his deserts. Reason did, as it well might, conclude that it should, finally and upon the whole, be well with the righteous, and ill with the wicked: but it could not be determined upon any principles of reason, whether human creatures might not have been appointed to pass through other states of life and being, before that distributive justice should finally and effectually take place. Revelation teaches us, that the next state of things after the present is appointed for the execution of this justice; that it shall be no longer delayed; but *the mystery of God*, the great mystery of his suffering vice and confusion to prevail, *shall then be finished;* and he will *take to him his great power and will reign*, by rendering to every one according to his works.

natural appointment, either to remove the offender out of the way of being further mischievous, or as an example, though frequently a disregarded one, to those who are left behind.

These things are not what we call accidental, or to be met with only now and then; but they are things of every day's experience. They proceed from general laws, very general ones, by which God governs the world in the natural course of his providence.[f]

And they are so analogous, to what religion teaches us concerning the future punishment of the wicked, so much of a piece with it, that both would naturally be expressed in the very same words, and manner of description. In the book of *Proverbs*,* for instance, wisdom is introduced, as frequenting the most public places of resort, and as rejected when she offers herself as the natural appointed guide of human life. *How long*, speaking to those who are passing through it, *how long, ye simple ones, will ye love folly, and the scorners delight in their scorning, and fools hate knowledge? Turn ye at my reproof. Behold, I will pour out my spirit upon you, I will make known my words unto you.* But upon being neglected, *Because I have called, and ye refused, I have stretched out my hand, and no man regarded; but ye have set at nought all my counsel, and would none of my reproof: I also will laugh at your calamity, I will mock when your fear cometh; when your fear cometh as desolation, and your destruction cometh as a whirlwind; when distress and anguish come upon you. Then shall they call upon me, but I will not answer; they shall seek me early, but they shall not find me.* This passage, every one sees, is poetical, and some parts of it are highly figurative; but the meaning is obvious. And the thing intended is expressed more literally in the following words; *For that they hated knowledge, and did not choose the fear of the Lord——therefore shall they eat of the fruit of their own way, and be filled with their own devices. For the security of*

[f] [Our language furnishes no finer specimens of the argument analogical. Butler here seizes the very points, which are most plausible and most insisted on, as showing the harshness and unreasonableness of Christianity; and overthrows them at a stroke by simply directing attention to the same things, in the universally observed course of nature.]

* Chap. i.

the simple shall slay them, and the prosperity of fools shall destroy them. The whole passage is so equally applicable to what we experience in the present world, concerning the consequences of men's actions, and to what religion teaches us is to be expected in another, that it may be questioned which of the two was principally intended.

Indeed when one has been recollecting the proper proofs of a future state of rewards and punishments, nothing methinks can give one so sensible an apprehension of the latter, or representation of it to the mind, as observing, that after the many disregarded checks, admonitions, and warnings, which people meet with in the ways of vice and folly and extravagance, warnings from their very nature, from the examples of others, from the lesser inconveniences which they bring upon themselves, from the instructions of wise and virtuous men: after these have been long despised, scorned, ridiculed: after the chief bad consequences, temporal consequences, of their follies, have been delayed for a great while, at length they break in irresistibly, like an armed force: repentance is too late to relieve, and can serve only to aggravate their distress, the case is become desperate: and poverty and sickness, remorse and anguish, infamy and death, the effects of their own doings, overwhelm them beyond possibility of remedy or escape. This is an account of what is, in fact, the general constitution of nature.

It is not in any sort meant, that, according to what appears at present of the natural course of things, men are always uniformly punished in proportion to their misbehavior. But that there are very many instances of misbehavior punished in the several ways now mentioned, and very dreadful instances too; sufficient to show what the laws of the universe may admit, and, if thoroughly considered, sufficient fully to answer all objections against the credibility of a future state of punishments, from any imaginations, that the frailty of our nature and external temptations, almost annihilate the guilt of human vices: as well as objections of another sort; from necessity, from suppositions, that the will of an infinite Being cannot be contradicted, or that he must be incapable of offence and provocation.*

Reflections of this kind are not without their terrors to serious

* See chaps. iv. and vi.

persons, even the most free from enthusiasm, and of the greatest strength of mind; but it is fit that things be stated and considered as they really are. There is, in the present age, a certain fearlessness with regard to what may be hereafter under the government of God, which nothing but a universally acknowledged demonstration on the side of atheism can justify; and which makes it quite necessary, that men be reminded, and if possible made to feel, that there is no sort of ground for being thus presumptuous, even upon the most sceptical principles. For, may it not be said of any person upon his being born into the world, he may behave so as to be of no service to it, but by being made an example of the woeful effects of vice and folly? That he may, as any one may, if he will, incur an infamous execution from the hands of civil justice, or in some other course of extravagance shorten his days; or bring upon himself infamy and diseases worse than death? So that it had been better for him, even with regard to the present world, that he had never been born. And is there any pretence of reason for people to think themselves secure, and talk as if they had certain proof, that, let them act as licentiously as they will, there can be nothing analogous to this, with regard to a future and more general interest, under the providence and government of the same God?

CHAPTER III.[a]

THE MORAL GOVERNMENT OF GOD.

As the manifold appearances of design, and of final causes, in the constitution of the world, prove it to be the work of an intelligent mind, so the particular final causes of pleasure and pain distributed amongst his creatures, prove that they are under his

[a] [This chapter, more than any other, carries the force of positive argument. If in this world, we have *proofs* that God is a moral governor, then in order to evince that we shall be under moral government *hereafter*, we have only to supply an intermediate consideration,—viz.: that God, as such, must be unchangeable. The argument, as just remarked, assumes a substantive form, because admitted facts, as to this world, exhibiting the very *principles* on which God's government goes at present, compel us not only to *suppose* that the principles of God will remain, but to *believe* so.]

government; what may be called his natural government of creatures endued with sense and reason. This implies somewhat more than seems usually attended to, when we speak of God's natural government of the world. It implies government of the very same kind with that which a master exercises over his servants, or a civil magistrate over his subjects. These latter instances of final causes, as really prove an intelligent *Governor* of the world, in the sense now mentioned, and before* distinctly treated of; as any other instances of final causes prove an intelligent *Maker* of it.

But this alone does not appear at first sight to determine any thing certainly, concerning the moral character of the Author of nature, considered in this relation of governor; does not ascertain his government to be moral, or prove that he is the righteous Judge of the world. Moral government consists, not in barely rewarding and punishing men for their actions, which the most tyrannical may do, but in rewarding the righteous, and punishing the wicked: in rendering to men according to their actions, considered as good or evil. And the *perfection* of moral government consists in doing this, with regard to all intelligent creatures, in an exact proportion to their personal merits or demerits.

Some men seem to think the only character of the Author of nature to be that of simple absolute benevolence. This, considered as a principle of action and infinite in degree, is a disposition to produce the greatest possible happiness, without regard to persons' behavior, otherwise than as such regard would produce higher degrees of it. And supposing this to be the only character of God, veracity and justice in him would be nothing but benevolence conducted by wisdom. Surely this ought not to be asserted, unless it can be proved; for we should speak with cautious reverence upon such a subject. Whether it can be proved or no, is not the thing here to be inquired into; but whether in the constitution and conduct of the world, a righteous government be not discernibly planned out: which necessarily implies a righteous governor. There may possibly be in the creation beings, to whom the Author of nature manifests himself under this most amiable of all characters, this of infinite absolute benevolence; for it is the most amiable, supposing it not, as

* Chap. ii.

perhaps it is not, incompatible with justice; but he manifests himself to us under the character of a righteous governor. He may, consistently with this, be simply and absolutely benevolent, in the sense now explained: but he is (for he has given us a proof in the constitution and conduct of the world that he is) a governor over servants, as he rewards and punishes us for our actions. And in the constitution and conduct of it, he may also have given, besides the reason of the thing, and the natural presages of conscience, clear and distinct intimations, that his government is righteous or moral: clear to such as think the nature of it deserving their attention, and yet not to every careless person, who casts a transient reflection upon the subject.*

It is particularly to be observed, that the divine government, which we experience ourselves under in the present state, taken alone, is allowed not to be the perfection of moral government. Yet this by no means hinders, but that there may be *somewhat*, be it more or less, truly moral in it. A righteous government may plainly appear to be carried on to some degree, enough to give us the apprehension that it shall be completed, or carried on to that degree of perfection which religion teaches us it shall; but which cannot appear, till much more of the divine administration be seen, than can be seen in the present life. The design of this chapter is to inquire how far this is the case: how far, over and above the moral nature† which God has given us, and our natural notion of him as righteous governor of those his creatures, to whom he has given this nature;‡ I say how far besides this, the principles and beginnings of a moral government over the world may be discerned, notwithstanding and amidst all the confusion and disorder of it.

One might mention here, what has been often urged with

* The objections against religion, from the evidence of it not being universal, nor so strong as might possibly have been, may be urged against natural religion, as well as against revealed. And therefore the consideration of them belongs to the first part of this treatise, as well as the second. But as these objections are chiefly urged against revealed religion, I choose to consider them in the second part. And the answer to them there, ch. vi., as urged against Christianity, being almost equally applicable to them as urged against the religion of nature; to avoid repetition, the reader is referred to that chapter.

† Dissertation II.

‡ Chap. vi.

great force, that, in general, less uneasiness and more satisfaction, are the natural consequences* of a virtuous than of a vicious course of life, in the present state, as an instance of a moral government established in nature; an instance of it collected from experience and present matter of fact.[b] But it must be owned a thing of difficulty to weigh and balance pleasures and uneasinesses, each amongst themselves, and also against each other, so as to make an estimate with any exactness, of the overplus of happiness on the side of virtue. And it is not impossible, that, amidst the infinite disorders of the world, there may be exceptions to the happiness of virtue; even with regard to persons, whose course of life from their youth up has been blameless: and more with regard to those who have gone on for some time in the ways of vice, and have afterwards reformed. For suppose an instance of the latter case; a person with his passions inflamed, his natural faculty of self-government impaired by habits of indulgence, and with all his vices about him, like so many harpies, craving their accustomed gratification; who can say how long it might be, before such a person would find more satisfaction in the reasonableness and present good consequences of virtue, than difficulties and self-denial in the restraints of it? Experience also shows, that men can to a great degree, get over their sense of shame, so as that by professing themselves to be without prin-

* See Lord Shaftesbury's Inquiry concerning Virtue, Part II.

[b] [At the foundation of moral improvement, lies the conviction that what is right, is our happiness, no less than our duty. This again is based upon a conviction that God governs justly; and has all power over us for good or evil. As creation is full of the evidences of *design*, so is Providence. And as the human mind shows, in its structure, the most exquisite marks of design, so the government of mind shows a final object for all our faculties. Among the attributes of mind we observe, conspicuous, a disposition to seek ends, lay plans, and sacrifice present indulgence to future and greater good: and a facility in learning how to subordinate one thing to another, so as to secure success in our plans. This, with conscience to approve or disapprove our modes, constitutes an evident *adaptedness* to a moral government on the part of God; and would be worse than superfluous, if there be no such government. Every rule of action, deduced by reason from the light of nature, may fairly be regarded as God's law; and the inconveniences resulting from wrong actions, are God's retributions. These retributions, felt or observed, are divine teachings, saying, emphatically, if you act thus you shall receive thus. We do actually so judge, in relation to physics. Every rule of motion, distance, gravitation, heat, electricity, &c. &c., is received as God's law; and we would deem it insane to act in opposition.]

ciple, and avowing even direct villany, they can support themselves against the infamy of it. But as the ill actions of any one will probably be more talked of, and oftener thrown in his way, upon his reformation; so the infamy of them will be much more felt, after the natural sense of virtue and of honor is recovered. Uneasiness of this kind ought indeed to be put to the account of former vices: yet it will be said they are in part the consequences of reformation. Still I am far from allowing it doubtful, whether virtue, upon the whole, be happier than vice in the present world. If it were, yet the beginnings of a righteous administration may, beyond all question, be found in nature, if we will attentively inquire after them.[c]

I. In whatever manner the notion of God's moral government over the world might be treated, if it did not appear, whether he were in a proper sense our governor at all; yet when it is certain matter of experience, that he does manifest himself to us under the character of a governor in the sense explained,* it must deserve to be considered, whether there be not reason to apprehend, that he may be a righteous or moral governor. Since it appears to be fact, that God does govern mankind by the method of rewards and punishments, according to some settled rules of distribution; it is surely a question to be asked, what presumption is there against his *finally* rewarding and punishing them according to this particular rule, namely, as they act reasonably, or unreasonably, virtuously or viciously? Rendering men happy or miserable by this rule, certainly falls in, much more falls in, with our natural apprehensions and sense of things, than doing so by any other rule whatever; since rewarding and punishing actions by any other rule, would appear much harder to be accounted for, by minds formed as he has formed ours. Be the evidence of religion then more or less clear, the expectation which it raises in us, that the righteous shall, upon the whole, be happy, and the wicked miserable, cannot possibly be con-

[c] [Consult CAPP on the Gov. of God: TWISSE Vindiciæ Prov. Dei: WITTICHII Excrc. Theol.: DWIGHT'S Theol.: MARTINIUS de Gubernatione Mundi: LIEFCHILD on Providence: MORTON on do.: SHERLOCK on do.: RUTHERFORD on do.: and the Sermons of Thos. Leland, Porteus, Topping, Hunt, Davies, Horseley, South Wisheart, Seed, Collings, and Doddridge.]

* Chap. ii

sidered as absurd or chimerical; because it is no more than an expectation, that a method of government already begun, shall be carried on, the method of rewarding and punishing actions; and shall be carried on by a particular rule, which unavoidably appears to us at first sight more natural than any other, the rule which we call distributive justice. Nor,

II. Ought it to be entirely passed over, that tranquillity, satisfaction, and external advantages, being the natural consequences of prudent management of ourselves, and our affairs; and rashness, profligate negligence, and wilful folly, bringing after them many inconveniences and sufferings; these afford instances of a right constitution of nature, as the correction of children, for their own sakes, and by way of example, when they run into danger or hurt themselves, is a part of right education.[d] Thus, that God governs the world by general fixed laws, that he has endued us with capacities of reflecting upon this constitution of things, and foreseeing the good and bad consequences of behavior, plainly implies *some sort* of moral government; since from such a constitution of things it cannot but follow, that prudence and imprudence, which are of the nature of virtue and vice,* must be, as they are, respectively rewarded and punished.

III. From the natural course of things, vicious actions are, to a great degree, actually punished as mischievous to society; and besides punishment actually inflicted upon this account, there is also the fear and apprehension of it in those persons, whose crimes have rendered them obnoxious to it, in case of a discovery; this state of fear being often itself a very considerable punishment. The natural fear and apprehension of it too, which restrains from such crimes, is a declaration of nature against them. It is necessary to the very being of society, that vices, destructive of it, should be punished *as being so;* the vices of falsehood, injustice, cruelty: which punishment therefore is as natural as

[d] [In the structure of man, physical and mental, we find no contrivances for disease or pain, so that in general those who conform to the laws of their being, enjoy happiness; and suffering is chiefly the result of our own conduct. But, as without revelation we could only learn the evil of vice, by its effects, and would often learn it too late to retrieve our affairs, or our souls' peace, God has in mercy given forth his teachings, by which, *beforehand,* we may know the effects of actions.]

* See Dissertation II.

society, and so is an instance of a kind of moral government, naturally established, and actually taking place. And, since the certain natural course of things is the conduct of providence or the government of God, though carried on by the instrumentality of men, the observation here made amounts to this, that mankind find themselves placed by him in such circumstances, as that they are unavoidably accountable for their behavior; and are often punished, and sometimes rewarded, under his government, in the view of their being mischievous, or eminently beneficial to society.

If it be objected that good actions and such as are beneficial to society, are often punished, as in the case of persecution and in other cases; and that ill and mischievous actions are often rewarded:[e] it may be answered distinctly, first, that this is in no sort necessary, and consequently not natural in the sense in which it is necessary, and therefore natural, that ill or mischievous actions should be punished: and in the next place, that good actions are never punished, considered as beneficial to society, nor ill actions rewarded, under the view of their being hurtful to it. So that it stands good, without any thing on the side of vice to be set over against it, that the Author of nature has as truly directed, that vicious actions, considered as mischievous to society, should be punished, and put mankind under a *necessity* of thus punishing them, as he has directed and necessitated us to preserve our lives by food.

IV. In the natural course of things, virtue *as such* is actually rewarded, and vice *as such* punished: which seems to afford an instance or example, not only of government, but of moral government, begun and established; moral in the strictest sense, though not in that perfection of degree, which religion teaches us to expect. In order to see this more clearly, we must distinguish between *actions* themselves, and that *quality* ascribed to them, which we call virtuous or vicious.[f] The gratification itself

[e] [It was contended by MANDEVILLE in his "*Fable of the Bees*," that private vices, as luxury for instance, are often conducive to the well-being of society. This idea is fully refuted by WARBURTON, Divine Legation of Moses, b. 1: BERKELEY, Minute Philosopher, Dial. 2: and by BROWN, Characteristics, Ess 2.]

[f] [A strong illustration of this distinction is seen in the "delivering up" of our Savior to be crucified. As to the mere act of delivering up, we find it

of every natural passion, must be attended with delight; and acquisitions of fortune, however made, are acquisitions of the means or materials of enjoyment. An action then, by which any natural passion is gratified, or fortune acquired, procures delight or advantage; abstracted from all consideration of the morality of such action. Consequently, the pleasure or advantage in this case, is gained by the action itself, not by the morality, the virtuousness or viciousness of it; though it be perhaps virtuous or vicious.

To say that such an action or course of behavior, procured such pleasure or advantage, or brought on such inconvenience and pain, is quite a different thing from saying, that such good or bad effect was owing to the virtue or vice of such action or behavior. In one case, an action abstracted from all moral consideration, produced its effect: in the other case, for it will appear that there are such cases, the morality of the action under a moral consideration, *i.e.* the virtuousness or viciousness of it, produced the effect. Now I say virtue as such, naturally procures considerable advantages to the virtuous, and vice as such, naturally occasions great inconvenience and even misery to the vicious, in very many instances. The immediate effects of virtue and vice upon the mind and temper, are to be mentioned as instances of it. Vice as such is naturally attended with some sort of uneasiness, and not uncommonly, with great disturbance and apprehension. That inward feeling, which, respecting lesser matters and in familiar speech we call being vexed with oneself, and in matters of importance and in more serious language, remorse; is an uneasiness naturally arising from an action of a man's own, reflected upon by himself as wrong, unreasonable, faulty, *i.e.* vicious in greater or less degrees: and this manifestly is a different feeling from that uneasiness, which arises from a sense of mere loss or harm. What is more common, than to hear a man lamenting an accident or event, and adding—but

referred, **1.** To God the Father, John iii. 16: Acts ii. 23: Rom. viii. 32. **2.** To Christ himself, Eph. v. 2, and v. 25, &c. In this last passage it is literally *delivered himself*. **3.** To the Jewish rulers, Luke xx. 20: Mark xii. 12. **4.** To Pontius Pilate, Matt. xxvii. 26: Mark xv. 15: John xix. 6. **5.** To Judas, Matt. xxvi. 15: Zec. xi. 12.

As to the *mere act*, Judas and Pilate did just what God the Father, and our Lord Jesus did. But how infinitely unlike the *qualities* of the act!]

however he has the satisfaction that he cannot blame himself for it; or on the contrary, that he has the uneasiness of being sensible it was his own doing? Thus also the disturbance and fear, which often follow upon a man's having done an injury, arise from a sense of his being blameworthy; otherwise there would, in many cases, be no ground of disturbance, nor any reason to fear resentment or shame. On the other hand, inward security and peace, and a mind open to the several gratifications of life, are the natural attendants of innocence and virtue. To which must be added the complacency, satisfaction, and even joy of heart, which accompany the exercise, the real exercise of gratitude, friendship, benevolence.

And here, I think, ought to be mentioned the fears of future punishment, and peaceful hopes of a better life, in those who fully believe, or have any serious apprehension of religion: because these hopes and fears are present uneasiness and satisfaction to the mind, and cannot be got rid of by great part of the world, even by men who have thought most thoroughly upon the subject of religion. And no one can say, how considerable this uneasiness or satisfaction may be, or what upon the whole it may amount to.[g]

In the next place comes in the consideration, that all honest and good men are disposed to befriend honest good men as such, and to discountenance the vicious as such, and do so in some degree; indeed in a considerable degree: from which favor and discouragement cannot but arise considerable advantage and inconvenience. Though the generality of the world have little regard to the morality of their own actions, and may be supposed to have less to that of others, when they themselves are not concerned; yet let any one be known to be a man of virtue, somehow or other he will be favored and good offices will be done him, from regard to his character, without remote views, occasionally, and in some low degree, I think, by the generality of the world,

g ["When one supposes he is about to die, there comes over him a fear and anxiety about things in regard to which he felt none before. For the stories which are told about *Hades*, that such as have practised wrong, must there suffer punishment, although made light of for a while, these torment the soul lest they should be true. But he who is conscious of innocence, has a pleasant and good hope, which will support old age." PLATO, Respub. i. s. 5.]

as it happens to come in their way. Public honors too and advantages are the natural consequences, and sometimes at least, the consequences in fact, of virtuous actions; of eminent justice, fidelity, charity, love to our country, considered in the view of being virtuous. And sometimes even death itself, often infamy and external inconveniences, are the public consequences of vice as vice. For instance, the sense which mankind have of tyranny, injustice, oppression, additional to the mere feeling or fear of misery, has doubtless been instrumental in bringing about revolutions, which make a figure even in the history of the world. For it is plain, that men resent injuries as implying faultiness, and retaliate, not merely under the notion of having received harm, but of having received wrong; and they have this resentment in behalf of others, as well as of themselves. So likewise even the generality are, in some degree, grateful and disposed to return good offices, not merely because such a one has been the occasion of good to them, but under the view, that such good offices implied kind intention and good desert in the doer.

To all this may be added two or three particular things, which many persons will think frivolous; but to me nothing appears so, which at all comes in towards determining a question of such importance, as, whether there be or be not, a moral institution of government, in the strictest sense moral, *visibly* established and begun in nature. The particular things are these: That in domestic government, which is doubtless natural, children and others also are very generally punished for falsehood, injustice, and ill-behavior, as such, and rewarded for the contrary: which are instances of veracity and justice and right behavior, as such, naturally enforced by rewards and punishments, more or less considerable. That, though civil government be supposed to take cognizance of actions in no other view than as prejudicial to society, without respect to the immorality of them, yet as such actions are immoral, so the sense which men have of the immorality of them, very greatly contributes, in different ways, to bring offenders to justice. And that entire absence of all crime and guilt in the moral sense, when plainly appearing, will almost of course procure, and circumstances of aggravated guilt prevent, a remission of the penalties annexed to civil crimes, in many cases, though by no means in all.

Upon the whole then, besides the good and bad effects of virtue and vice upon men's own minds, the course of the world does, in some measure, turn upon the approbation and disapprobation of them as such, in others. The sense of well and ill doing, the presages of conscience, the love of good characters and dislike of bad ones, honor, shame, resentment, gratitude, all these, considered in themselves, and in their effects, do afford manifest real instances, of virtue as such naturally favored, and of vice as such discountenanced, more or less, in the daily course of human life; in every age, in every relation, in every general circumstance of it. That God has given us a moral nature,* may most justly be urged as a proof of our being under his moral government: but that he has placed us in a condition, which gives this nature, as one may speak, scope to operate, and in which it does unavoidably operate; *i.e.* influence mankind to act, so as thus to favor and reward virtue, and discountenance and punish vice, this is not the same, but a further additional proof of his moral government; for it is an instance of it. The first is a proof, that he will finally favor and support virtue effectually: the second is an example of his favoring and supporting it at present, in some degree.

If a more distinct inquiry be made, whence it arises, that virtue as such is often rewarded, and vice as such is punished, and this rule never inverted, it will be found to proceed, in part, immediately from the moral nature itself, which God has given us;[h] and also in part, from his having given us, together with

* See Dissertation II.

[h] [Aside from revelation, our ideas of the divine attributes must be derived from a knowledge of our own. Among these is our moral sense, which constrains us to consider right and wrong as an immutable distinction, and moral worth as our highest excellence. Hence we ascribe perfect virtue to God. It does not follow from such reasoning, that we form a Deity after our own conceptions, for it is but the argument *a fortiori*, "He that formed the eye, shall he not see? He that teacheth man knowledge, shall he not know?" Ps. xciv. 9. We do not conceive of a Deity who sees just as we do; but that *he sees*, for he makes sight. So we infer that he has moral attributes, because we have hem, from him.

This point is not sufficiently pressed upon infidels. They readily acknowledge God's physical attributes, because the argument is addressed to their *understanding*, but deny his moral ones, because their *hearts* are hardened through the deceitfulness of sin.]

this nature, so great a power over each other's happiness and misery. For, *first,* it is certain, that peace and delight, in some degree and upon some occasions, is the necessary and present effect of virtuous practice; an effect arising immediately from that constitution of our nature. We are *so made,* that well-doing as such, gives us satisfaction, at least in some instances; ill-doing as such, in none. And, *secondly,* from our moral nature, joined with God's having put our happiness and misery in many respects in each other's power, it cannot but be, that vice as such, some kinds and instances of it at least, will be infamous, and men will be disposed to punish it as in itself detestable; and the villain will by no means be able always to avoid feeling that infamy, any more than he will be able to escape this further punishment, which mankind will be disposed to inflict upon him, under the notion of his deserving it. But there can be nothing on the side of vice, to answer this; because there is nothing in the human mind contradictory, as the logicians speak, to virtue. For virtue consists in a regard to what is right and reasonable, as being so; in a regard to veracity, justice, charity, in themselves: and there is surely no such thing, as a like natural regard to falsehood, injustice, cruelty. If it be thought, that there are instances of an approbation of vice, as such, in itself, and for its own sake, (though it does not appear to me, that there is any such thing at all;) it is evidently monstrous: as much so, as the most acknowledged perversion of any passion whatever. Such instances of perversion then being left out, as merely imaginary, or at least unnatural; it must follow, from the frame of our nature, and from our condition, in the respects now described, that vice cannot at all be, and virtue cannot but be, favored as such by others, upon some occasions, and happy in itself, in some degree. For what is here insisted upon, is not the *degree* in which virtue and vice are thus distinguished, but only the thing itself, that they are so in some degree; though the whole good and bad effect of virtue and vice as such, is not inconsiderable in degree. But that they must be thus distinguished in some degree, is in a manner necessary: it is matter of fact of daily experience, even in the greatest confusion of human affairs.

It is not pretended but that, in the natural course of things, happiness and n isery appear to be distributed by other rules, than only the personal merit and demerit of characters. They may sometimes be distributed by way of mere discipline. There may be the wisest and best reasons, why the world should be governed by general laws, from whence such promiscuous distribution perhaps must follow; and also why our happiness and misery should be put in each other's power, in the degree which they are. And these things, as, in general, they contribute to the rewarding virtue and punishing vice, as such, so they often contribute also, not to the inversion of this, which is impossible, but to the rendering persons prosperous, though wicked; afflicted, though righteous; and, which is worse, to the *rewarding some actions*, though vicious, and *punishing other actions*, though virtuous.[1] But all this cannot drown the voice of nature in the conduct of Providence, plainly declaring itself for virtue, by way of distinction from vice, and preference to it. For our being so constituted as that virtue and vice are thus naturally favored and discountenanced, rewarded and punished, respectively as such, is an intuitive proof of the intent of nature, that it should be so; otherwise the constitution of our mind, from which it thus immediately and directly proceeds, would be absurd. But it cannot be said, because virtuous actions are sometimes punished, and vicious actions rewarded, that nature intended it. For, though this great disorder is brought about, as all actions are, by means of some natural passion; yet *this may be*, as it undoubtedly is, brought about by the perversion of such passion, implanted in us for other, and those very good purposes. And indeed these other and good purposes, even of every passion, may be clearly seen.

We have then a declaration, in some degree of present effect, from Him who is supreme in nature, which side he is of, or what part he takes; a declaration for virtue, and against vice. So far therefore as a man is true to virtue, to veracity and justice, to equity and charity, and the right of the case, in whatever he is concerned; so far he is on the side of the divine administration, and co-operates with it: and from hence, to such a man,

[1] [It is easy to see that the occasional disadvantages of virtue, are no less conducive to moral excellence, than its being generally advantageous. In view of its general advantages, we are virtuous with a proper and commanded view to our instinctive desire for happiness. In face of its disadvantages, we cultivate virtue for its own sake.]

arises naturally a secret satisfaction and sense of security, and implicit hope of somewhat further.

V. This hope is confirmed by the necessary tendencies of virtue, which, though not of present effect, yet are at present discernible in nature; and so afford an instance of somewhat moral in the essential constitution of it. There is, in the nature of things, a tendency in virtue and vice to produce the good and bad effects now mentioned, in a greater degree than they do in fact produce them. For instance; good and bad men would be much more rewarded and punished as such, were it not, that justice is often artificially eluded,[j] that characters are not known, and many, who would thus favor virtue and discourage vice, are hindered from doing so, by accidental causes. These tendencies of virtue and vice are obvious with regard to *individuals*. But it may require more particularly to be considered, that power in a *society*, by being under the direction of virtue, naturally increases, and has a necessary tendency to prevail over opposite power, not under the direction of it; in like manner, as power, by being under the direction of reason, increases, and has a tendency to prevail over brute force. There are several brute

[j] [The common remark, "virtue brings its own reward," is true only with qualifications. The apostles, as to *this* life, were the most miserable of men: (1 Cor. xv. 9.) Virtue does not *always* bring earthly rewards. The grand support of the good is drawn from considerations of that future state which the infidel denies. Observe, 1. We cannot suppose that God would so construct man, as that his principal comfort and reward for virtue, is a delusion. 2. Very good persons are often beset with painful doubts and fears, as to their future safety. Would God allow such doubts, if the expectation of future happiness were the *only* reward of virtue? 3. This reward, at best, is private; but for the encouragement of virtue, it must have *obvious* triumphs.

On the other hand, bad men grow callous to the rebukes of conscience, so that great sinners suffer less from remorse than small ones, and what is worse, owe their tranquillity to their guilt. Again, he who kills a good man, wholly *deprives* him of his only reward, if this life alone gives it. And the villain who kills himself, escapes his only punishment.

Virtuous persons, in the strong language of Robert Hall,* would be "the *only* persons who are wholly disappointed of their object; the only persons who (by a fatal and irreparable mistake), expecting an imaginary happiness in an imaginary world, lose their only opportunity of enjoying those present pleasures, of which others avail themselves; dooming themselves to grasp at shadows, while they neglect the substance, and harassed with a perpetual struggle against their natural propensities and passions, and all in vain!"]

* Sermon on the Vanity of Man

creatures of equal, and several of superior strength, to that of men; and possibly the sum of the whole strength of brutes may be greater than that of mankind; but reason gives us the advantage and superiority over them; and thus man is the acknowledged governing animal upon the earth. Nor is this superiority considered by any as accidental; but as what reason has a tendency, in the nature of the thing, to obtain. And yet perhaps difficulties may be raised about the meaning, as well as the truth, of the assertion, that virtue has the like tendency.

To obviate these difficulties, let us see more distinctly, how the case stands with regard to reason; which is so readily acknowledged to have this advantageous tendency. Suppose then two or three men, of the best and most improved understanding, in a desolate open plain, attacked by ten times the number of beasts of prey: would their reason secure them the victory in this unequal combat? Power then, though joined with reason, and under its direction, cannot be expected to prevail over opposite power, though merely brutal, unless the one bears some proportion to the other. Again: put the imaginary case, that rational and irrational creatures were of like external shape and manner: it is certain, before there were opportunities for the first to distinguish each other, to separate from their adversaries, and to form a union among themselves, they might be upon a level, or in several respects upon great disadvantage; though united they might be vastly superior: since union is of such efficacy, that ten men united, might be able to accomplish, what ten thousand of the same natural strength and understanding wholly ununited, could not. In this case, brute force might more than maintain its ground against reason, for want of union among the rational creatures. Or suppose a number of men to land upon an island inhabited only by wild beasts; men who, by the regulations of civil government, the inventions of art, and the experience of some years, could they be preserved so long, would be really sufficient to subdue the wild beasts, and to preserve themselves in security from them: yet a conjuncture of accidents might give such advantage to the irrational animals as they might at once overpower, and even extirpate, the rational ones. Length of time then, proper scope, and opportunities for reason to exert itself, may be absolutely necessary to its prevailing over brute force.

Further: there are many instances of brutes succeeding in attempts, which they could not have undertaken, had not their irrational nature rendered them incapable of foreseeing the danger of such attempt, or the fury of passion hindered their attending to it: and there are instances of reason and real prudence preventing men's undertaking what, it has appeared afterwards, they might have succeeded in by a lucky rashness. In certain conjunctures, ignorance and folly, weakness and discord, may have their advantages. So that rational animals have not *necessarily* the superiority over irrational ones; but, how improbable soever it may be, it is evidently possible, that in some globes the latter may be superior. And were the former wholly at variance and disunited, by false self-interest and envy, by treachery and injustice, and consequent rage and malice against each other, whilst the latter were firmly united among themselves by instinct, this might greatly contribute to the introducing such an inverted order of things. For every one would consider it as inverted: since reason has, in the nature of it, a tendency to prevail over brute force; notwithstanding the possibility it may not prevail, and the necessity, which there is, of many concurring circumstances to render it prevalent.

Now I say, virtue in a society has a like tendency to procure superiority and additional power: whether this power be considered as the means of security from opposite power, or of obtaining other advantages. It has this tendency, by rendering public good, an object and end, to every member of the society; by putting every one upon consideration and diligence, recollection and self-government, both in order to see what is the most effectual method, and also in order to perform their proper part, for obtaining and preserving it; by uniting a society within itself, and so increasing its strength; and, which is particularly to be mentioned, uniting it by means of veracity and justice. For as these last are principal bonds of union, so benevolence or public spirit, undirected, unrestrained by them, is, nobody knows what.

And suppose the invisible world, and the invisible dispensations of Providence, to be, in any sort, analogous to what appears: or that both together make up one uniform scheme, the two parts of which, the part which we see, and that which is beyond our observation, are analogous to each other: then, there must be a like natural tendency in the derived power, throughout the universe, under the direction of virtue, to prevail in general over that which is not under its direction; as there is in reason, derived reason in the universe, to prevail over brute force.

But then, in order to the prevalence of virtue, or that it may actually produce, what it has a tendency to produce; the *like concurrences are necessary*, as are, to the prevalence of reason. There must be some proportion, between the natural power or force which is, and that which is not, under the direction of virtue: there must be sufficient length of time; for the complete success of virtue, as of reason, cannot, from the nature of the thing, be otherwise than gradual: there must be, as one may speak, a fair field of trial, a stage large and extensive enough, proper occasions and opportunities, for the virtuous to join together, to exert themselves against lawless force, and to reap the fruit of their united labors. Now indeed it is to be hoped, that the disproportion between the good and bad, even here on earth, is not so great, but that the former have natural power sufficient to their prevailing to a considerable degree, if circumstances would permit this power to be united. For, much less, very much less, power under the direction of virtue, would prevail over much greater not under the direction of it.[k] However, good men over the face of the earth cannot unite; because, (among other reasons,) they cannot be sufficiently ascertained of each other's characters. And the known course of human things, the scene we are now passing through, particularly the shortness of life, denies to virtue its full scope in several other respects.

The natural tendency which we have been considering, though real, is *hindered* from being carried into effect in the present state: but these hinderances may be removed in a future one. Virtue, to borrow the Christian allusion, is militant here; and various untoward accidents contribute to its being often over-

[k] [Because, so soon as any community, or collection of persons, conclude a man to be wholly vicious in his course, and without any restraint of conscience, he is at once shorn of his influence, and will soon be stripped of all power of mischief. On the other hand, we see the might of virtue unarmed with power, in Luther, in Roger Williams, in Wm. Penn, and innumerable other instances.]

borne: but it may combat with greater advantage hereafter, and prevail completely, and enjoy its consequent rewards, in some future states. Neglected as it is, perhaps unknown, perhaps despised and oppressed here; there may be scenes in eternity, lasting enough, and in every other way adapted, to afford it a sufficient sphere of action; and a sufficient sphere for the natural consequences of it to follow in fact. If the soul be naturally immortal, and this state be a progress towards a future one, as childhood is towards mature age, good men may naturally unite, not only among themselves, but also with other orders of virtuous creatures, in that future state. For virtue, from the very nature of it, is a principle and bond of union, in some degree, among all who are endued with it, and known to each other; so as that by it, a good man cannot but recommend himself to the favor and protection of all virtuous beings, throughout the whole universe, who can be acquainted with his character, and can any way interpose in his behalf in any part of his duration.

One might add, that suppose all this advantageous tendency of virtue to become effect, among one or more orders of creatures, in any distant scenes and periods, and to be seen by any orders of vicious creatures, throughout the universal kingdom of God; this happy effect of virtue would have a tendency, by way of example, and possibly in other ways, to amend those of them who are capable of amendment, and of being recovered to a just sense of virtue. If our notions of the plan of Providence were enlarged in any sort proportionable to what late discoveries have enlarged our views with respect to the material world, representations of this kind would not appear absurd or extravagant. They are not to be taken as intended for a literal delineation of what is in fact the particular scheme of the universe, which cannot be known without revelation: for suppositions are not to be looked on as true, because not incredible: but they are mentioned to show, that our finding virtue to be hindered from procuring to itself such superiority and advantages, is no objection against its having, in the essential nature of the thing, a tendency to procure them. And the suppositions now mentioned do plainly show this: for they show, that these hinderances are so far from being necessary, that we ourselves can easily conceive, how they may be removed in future states, and full scope be granted to virtue

And all these advantageous tendencies of it are to be considered as declarations of God in its favor. This however is taking a pretty large compass: though it is certain, that, as the material world appears to be, in a manner, boundless and immense, there must be *some* scheme of Providence vast in proportion to it.

But let us return to the earth our habitation; and we shall see this happy tendency of virtue, by imagining an instance not so vast and remote: by supposing a kingdom or society of men upon it, perfectly virtuous, for a succession of many ages; to which, if you please, may be given a situation advantageous for universal monarchy. In such a state, there would be no such thing as faction: but men of the greatest capacity would of course, all along, have the chief direction of affairs willingly yielded to them; and they would share it among themselves without envy. Each of these would have the part assigned him, to which his genius was peculiarly adapted; and others, who had not any distinguished genius, would be safe, and think themselves very happy, by being under the protection and guidance of those who had. Public determinations would really be the result of the united wisdom of the community: and they would faithfully be executed, by the united strength of it. Some would contribute in a higher way, but all in some way, to the public prosperity: and in it, each would enjoy the fruits of his own virtue. And as injustice, whether by fraud or force, would be unknown among themselves, so they would be sufficiently secured from it in their neighbors. For cunning and false self-interest, confederacies in injustice, ever slight, and accompanied with faction and intestine treachery; these on one hand would be found mere childish folly and weakness, when set in opposition against wisdom, public spirit, union inviolable, and fidelity on the other: allowing both a sufficient length of years to try their force. Add the general influence, which such a kingdom would have over the face of the earth, by way of example particularly, and the reverence which would be paid it. It would plainly be superior to all others, and the world must gradually come under its empire; not by means of lawless violence; but partly by what must be allowed to be just conquest; and partly by other kingdoms submitting themselves voluntarily to it, throughout a course of ages, and claiming its protection, one after another, in successive exigencies. The head of it would be a universal monarch, in another sense than any mortal has yet been; and the Eastern style would be literally applicable to him, *that all people, nations, and languages should serve him.* And though indeed our knowledge of human nature, and the whole history of mankind, show the impossibility, without some miraculous interposition, that a number of men, here on earth, should unite in one society or government, in the fear of God and universal practice of virtue; and that such a government should continue so united for a succession of ages: yet admitting or supposing this, the effect would be as now drawn out. Thus for instance, the wonderful power and prosperity promised to the Jewish nation in the Scripture, would be, in a great measure, the consequence of what is predicted of them; that the *people should be all righteous, and inherit the land forever;** were we to understand the latter phrase of a long continuance only, sufficient to give things time to work. The predictions of this kind, for there are many of them, cannot come to pass, in the present known course of nature; but suppose them come to pass, and then, the dominion and preëminence promised must naturally follow, to a very considerable degree.

Consider now the general system of religion; that the government of the world is uniform, and one, and moral; that virtue and right shall finally have the advantage, and prevail over fraud and lawless force, over the deceits as well as the violence of wickedness, under the conduct of one supreme governor: and from the observations above made, it will appear that God has, by our reason, given us to see a peculiar connection in the several parts of this scheme, and a tendency towards the completion of it, arising out of the very nature of virtue: which tendency is to be considered as something moral in the essential constitution of things. If any one should think all this to be of little importance, I desire him to consider, what he would think, if vice had, essentially and in its nature, these advantageous tendencies; or if virtue had essentially the contrary ones.

It may be objected, that notwithstanding all these natural effects and natural tendencies of virtue, yet things may be now going on throughout the universe, and may go on hereafter, in the same mixed way as here at present upon earth: virtue some-

* Isa. lx. 21.

times prosperous, sometimes depressed; vice sometimes punished, sometimes successful.

The answer to which is, that it is not the purpose of this chapter, nor of this treatise, properly to prove God's perfect moral government over the world, or the truth of religion; but to observe what there is in the constitution and course of nature, to confirm the proper proof of it, supposed to be known: and that the weight of the foregoing observations to this purpose may be thus distinctly proved. Pleasure and pain are, to a certain degree, say to a very high degree, distributed among us without any apparent regard to the merit or demerit of characters. And were there nothing else concerning this matter discernible in the constitution and course of nature, there would be no ground from the constitution and course of nature, to hope or to fear that men would be rewarded or punished hereafter according to their deserts: which, however, it is to be remarked, implies, that even then there would be no ground from appearances to think, that vice upon the whole would have the advantage, rather than that virtue would. Thus the proof of a future state of retribution would rest upon the usual known arguments for it; which are I think plainly unanswerable; and would be so, though there were no additional confirmation of them from the things above insisted on. But these things are a very strong confirmation of them. For,

First, They show that the Author of nature is not indifferent to virtue and vice. They amount to a declaration, from him, determinate and not to be evaded, in favor of one, and against the other; such a declaration, as there is nothing to be set over against or answer, on the part of vice. So that were a man, laying aside the proper proof of religion, to determine from the course of nature only, whether it were most probable, that the righteous or the wicked would have the advantage in a future life; there can be no doubt, but that he would determine the probability to be, that the former would. The course of nature then, in the view of it now given, furnishes us with a real practical proof of the obligations of religion.

Secondly, When, conformably to what religion teaches us, God shall reward and punish virtue and vice as such, so as that every one shall, upon the whole, have his deserts; this distributive justice will not be a thing different in *kind*, but only in *degree*, from what we experience in his present government. It will be that in *effect*, towards which we now see a *tendency*. It will be no more than the *completion* of that moral government, the *principles and beginning* of which have been shown, beyond all dispute, discernible in the present constitution and course of nature.

Thirdly, As under the *natural* government of God, our experience of those kinds and degrees of happiness and misery, which we do experience at present, gives just ground to hope for, and to fear, higher degrees and other kinds of both in a future state, supposing a future state admitted: so under his *moral* government our experience, that virtue and vice are, in the manners above mentioned, actually rewarded and punished at present, in a certain degree, gives just ground to hope and to fear, that they *may be* rewarded and punished in a higher degree hereafter. It is acknowledged indeed that this alone is not sufficient ground to think, that they *actually will be* rewarded and punished in a higher degree, rather than in a lower: but then,

Lastly, There is sufficient ground to think so, from the good and bad tendencies of virtue and vice. For these tendencies are essential, and founded in the nature of things: whereas the hinderances to their becoming effect are, in numberless cases, not necessary, but artificial only. Now it may be much more strongly argued, that these tendencies, as well as the actual rewards and punishments, of virtue and vice, which arise directly out of the nature of things, will remain hereafter, than that the accidental hinderances of them will. And if these hinderances do not remain; those rewards and punishments cannot but be carried on much farther towards the perfection of moral government: *i.e.* the tendencies of virtue and vice will become effect; but when, or where, or in what particular way, cannot be known at all, but by revelation.

Upon the whole: there is a kind of moral government implied in God's natural government:* virtue and vice are naturally rewarded and punished as beneficial and mischievous to society;† and rewarded and punished directly as virtue and vice.‡ The notion of a moral scheme of government is not fictitious, but

* P. 109. † P. 110, &c. ‡ P. 111, &c

natural; for it is suggested to our thoughts by the constitution and course of nature: and the execution of this scheme is actually begun, in the instances here mentioned. And these things are to be considered as a declaration of the Author of nature, for virtue, and against vice: they give a credibility to the supposition of their being rewarded and punished hereafter; and also ground to hope and to fear, that they may be rewarded and punished in higher degrees than they are here. All this is confirmed, and the argument for religion, from the constitution and course of nature, is carried on farther, by observing, that there are natural tendencies, and, in innumerable cases, only artificial hinderances, to this moral scheme's being carried on much farther towards perfection, than it is at present.*

The notion then of a moral scheme of government, much more perfect than what is seen, is not a fictitious, but a natural notion; for it is suggested to our thoughts, by the essential tendencies of virtue and vice. These tendencies are to be considered as intimations, as implicit promises and threatenings, from the Author of nature, of much greater rewards and punishments to follow virtue and vice, than do at present. Indeed, every *natural* tendency, which is to continue, but which is hindered from becoming effect by only *accidental* causes, affords a presumption, that such tendency will, some time or other, become effect: a presumption proportionable in degree to the length of the duration, through which such tendency will continue. From these things together, arises a real presumption, that the moral scheme of government established in nature, shall be carried on much farther towards perfection hereafter; and, I think, a presumption that it will be absolutely completed. From these things, joined with the moral nature which God has given us, considered as given us by him, arises a practical proof† that it *will* be completed: a proof from fact; and therefore a distinct one from that which is deduced from the eternal and unalterable relations, the fitness and unfitness of actions.

* P. 118, &c.

† See this proof drawn out briefly, ch. vi.

CHAPTER IV.

PROBATION, AS IMPLYING TRIAL, DIFFICULTIES, AND DANGER.[a]

THE general doctrine of religion, that our present life is a tate of probation for a future one, comprehends under it several particular things, distinct from each other. The first and most common meaning of it seems to be, that our future interest is now depending, and depending upon ourselves; that we have scope and opportunities here, for that good and bad behavior, which God will reward and punish hereafter; together with temptations to one, as well as inducements of reason to the other. And this, in a great measure, is the same as saying, that we are under the moral government of God, and to give an account of our actions to him. For the notion of a future account and general righteous judgment, implies some sort of temptations to what is wrong: otherwise there would be no moral possibility of doing wrong, nor ground for judgment, or discrimination. But there is this difference, that the word *probation* is more distinctly and particularly expressive of allurements to wrong, or difficulties in adhering uniformly to what is right, and of the danger of miscarrying by such temptations, than the words *moral government.* A state of probation then, as thus particularly implying in it trial, difficulties, and danger, may require to be considered distinctly by itself.[b]

As the moral government of God, which religion teaches us,

[a] [This chapter is one of many attempts to account for the mixture of suffering and enjoyment in this world; and demands close examination both of its theory and its arguments. The student may consult, as he has opportunity, MUSÆI Disput.: HOLTZSFUSII Disp. de Lapsu Prim. Hominum: SELDEN de Laps. Angelorum: STAPFERI Inst.: WITSII Econom. Fœd.: BATE'S Harmony of the Divine Attrib.: CALCOTT on the Fall: SHUCKFORD on the Creation of Man: MANTON'S Sermons: SOUTH'S do.: TOPLADY'S do.: PEARSON on the Creed: LE CLERC'S Diss.: HENLY'S Dissert.: KENNICOTT on the Tree of Life: and FABRICIUS de Primo Peccato Angelorum Lapsorum.]

[b] [The *evils* of life, are not to be regarded as entering, necessarily, into God's plan of probation; and they are not here so presented. The Scriptures show that *all* suffering is either punitive, or castigatory. Man at first was to be tried by temptations, not by sufferings.]

implies that we are in a state of trial with regard to a future world, so also his natural government over us implies that we are in a state of trial, in the like sense, with regard to the present world. Natural government by rewards and punishments, as much implies natural trial, as moral government does moral trial. The natural government of God here meant,* consists in his annexing pleasure to some actions, and pain to others, which are in our power to do or forbear, and giving us notice of such appointment, beforehand. This necessarily implies, that he has made our happiness and misery, or our interest, to depend in part upon ourselves. So far as men have temptations to any course of action, which will probably occasion them greater temporal inconvenience and uneasiness, than satisfaction, so far their temporal interest is in danger from themselves; or they are in a state of trial with respect to it. Now people often blame others, and even themselves, for their misconduct in their temporal concerns. And we find many are greatly wanting to themselves, and miss that natural happiness, which they might have obtained in the present life: perhaps every one does in some degree. But many run themselves into great inconvenience, and into extreme distress and misery, not through incapacity of knowing better, and doing better, for themselves, which would be nothing to the present purpose, but through their own fault. These things necessarily imply temptation, and danger of miscarrying, in a greater or less degree, with respect to our worldly interest or happiness. Every one too, without having religion in his thoughts, speaks of the hazards which young people run, upon their setting out in the world: hazards from other causes, than merely their ignorance, and unavoidable accidents. And some courses of vice, at least, being contrary to men's worldly interest or good; temptations to these must at the same time be temptations to forego our present and our future interest.

Thus in our natural or temporal capacity, we are in a state of trial, *i.e.* of difficulty and danger, analogous, or like to our moral and religious trial. This will more distinctly appear to any one, who thinks it worth while, more distinctly, to consider, what it is which constitutes our trial in both capacities, and to observe, how mankind behave under it.

* Chap. ii.

That which constitutes this trial, in both these capacities, must be something either in our external circumstances, or in our nature. For, on the one hand, persons may be betrayed into wrong behavior upon surprise, or overcome upon any other very singular and extraordinary external occasions, who would, otherwise, have preserved their character of prudence and of virtue: in which cases, every one, in speaking of the wrong behavior of these persons, would impute it to such particular external circumstances. On the other hand, men who have contracted habits of vice and folly of any kind, or have some particular passions in excess, will seek opportunities, and, as it were, go out of their way, to gratify themselves in these respects, at the expense of their wisdom and their virtue; led to it, as every one would say, not by external temptations, but by such habits and passions. And the account of this last case is, that particular passions are no more coincident with prudence, or that reasonable self-love, the end of which is our worldly interest, than they are with the principle of virtue and religion; but often draw contrary ways to one, as well as to the other: and so such particular passions are as much temptations, to act imprudently with regard to our worldly interest, as to act viciously.* When we say, men are misled by external circumstances of temptation; it cannot but be understood, that there is somewhat within themselves, to render those circumstances temptations, or to render them susceptible of impressions from them. So when we say, they are misled by passions; it is always supposed, that there are occasions, circumstances, and objects, exciting these passions, and affording means for gratifying them. Therefore, temptations from within, and from without, coincide, and mutually imply each other. The several external objects of the appetites, passions, and affections, being present to the senses, or offering themselves to the mind, and so exciting emotions suitable to their nature; not only in cases where they can be gratified consistently with innocence and prudence, but also in cases where they cannot, and yet can be gratified imprudently and viciously: this as really puts them in danger of voluntarily foregoing their present interest or good, as their future; and as really renders self-denial necessary to secure

* See Sermons preached at the *Rolls*, 1726, 2d ed. p. 205, &c. Pref. p. 25, &c. Serm. p. 21, &c.

one, as the other: *i.e.* we are in a like state of trial with respect to both, by the very same passions, excited by the very same means.

Thus mankind having a temporal interest depending upon themselves, and a prudent course of behavior being necessary to secure it, passions inordinately excited, whether by means of example, or by any other external circumstance, towards such objects, at such times, or in such degrees, as that they cannot be gratified consistently with worldly prudence, are temptations; dangerous, and too often successful temptations, to forego a greater temporal good for a less; *i.e.* to forego what is, upon the whole, our temporal interest, for the sake of a present gratification. This is a description of our state of trial in our temporal capacity. Substitute now the word *future* for *temporal*, and *virtue* for *prudence;* and it will be just as proper a description of our state of trial in our religious capacity; so analogous are they to each other.[c]

If, from consideration of this our like state of trial in both capacities, we go on to observe farther, how mankind behave under it; we shall find there are some, who have so little sense of it, that they scarce look beyond the passing day: they are so taken up with present gratifications, as to have, in a manner, no feeling of consequences, no regard to their future ease or fortune in this life: any more than to their happiness in another. Some appear to be blinded and deceived by inordinate passion, in their worldly concerns, as much as in religion. Others are not deceived, but as it were forcibly carried away by the like passions, against their better judgment, and feeble resolutions too of acting better.[d] And there are men, and truly not a few, who shamelessly avow, not their interest, but their mere will and pleasure, to be their law of life: and who, in open defiance of every thing reasonable,

[c] ["If we persist in our objection, notwithstanding these analogies, then should we conclude, either that we are under the regimen of an unrighteous Deity, or that there is no Deity at all."—Dr. CHALMERS.]

[d] [Shall *we* be of such? Shall we forget or disregard the great fact that when death has transferred us to other conditions, we, our proper selves, will remain? No longer, indeed, united with flesh and blood, surrounded with houses, lands, business, or enjoyments, such as the present, *but still ourselves.* Still with wants to be supplied, desires to be gratified, and capacities to be employed and developed!]

will go on in a course of vicious extravagance, foreseeing, with no remorse and little fear, that it will be their temporal ruin; and some of them, under the apprehension of the consequences of wickedness in another state. To speak in the most moderate way, human creatures are not only continually liable to go wrong voluntarily, but we see likewise that they often actually do so, with respect to their temporal interests, as well as with respect to religion.

Thus our difficulties and dangers, or our trials in our temporal and our religious capacity, as they proceed from the same causes, and have the same effect upon men's behavior, are evidently analogous, and of the same kind.

It may be added, that the difficulties and dangers of miscarrying in our religious state of trial, are greatly increased, and one is ready to think, are in a manner wholly *made*, by the ill behavior of others; by a wrong education, wrong in a moral sense, sometimes positively vicious; by general bad example; by the dishonest artifices which are got into business of all kinds; and, in very many parts of the world, by religion's being corrupted into superstitions, which indulge men in their vices. In like manner, the difficulties of conducting ourselves prudently in respect to our present interest, and our danger of being led aside from pursuing it, are greatly increased, by a foolish education; and, after we come to mature age, by the extravagance and carelessness of others, with whom we have intercourse: and by mistaken notions, very generally prevalent, and taken up from common opinion, concerning temporal happiness, and wherein it consists.

Persons, by their own *negligence* and *folly* in temporal affairs, no less than by a course of vice, bring themselves into new difficulties, and, by habits of indulgence, become less qualified to go through them: and one irregularity after another, embarrasses things to such a degree, that they know not whereabout they are; and often makes the path of conduct so intricate and perplexed, that it is difficult to trace it out; difficult even to determine what is the prudent or the moral part. Thus, for instance, wrong behavior in one stage of life, youth; wrong, I mean considering ourselves only in our temporal capacity, without taking in religion; this, in several ways, increases the difficulties of right behavior in mature age; *i.e.* puts us into a more disadvantageous state of trial in our temporal capacity.

We are an inferior part of the creation of God. There are natural appearances of our being in a state of degradation.* We certainly are in a condition, which *does not seem*, by any means, the most advantageous we could imagine or desire, either in our natural or moral capacity, for securing either our present or future interest. However, this condition, low, and careful, and uncertain as it is, does not afford any just ground of complaint. For, as men *may* manage their temporal affairs with prudence, and so pass their days here on earth in tolerable ease and satisfaction, by a moderate degree of care: so likewise with regard to religion, there is no more required than what they are well able to do,[e] and what they must be greatly wanting to themselves, if they neglect. And for persons to have that put upon them, which they are well able to go through, and no more, we naturally consider as an equitable thing; supposing it done by proper authority. Nor have we any more reason to complain of it, with regard to the Author of nature, than of his not having given us advantages belonging to other orders of creatures.

[REMARKS.] The thing here insisted upon is, that the state of trial, which religion teaches us we are in, is rendered credible, by its being throughout uniform and of a piece with the general conduct of Providence towards us, in all other respects within the compass of our knowledge. Indeed if mankind, considered in their natural capacity, as inhabitants of this world only, found themselves, from their birth to their death, in a settled state of

* Part II. chap. v.

[e] [This is one of those passages, remarked on in our introduction, as a statement not properly explained or guarded. We cannot suppose the author, to have overlooked the great fact of man's fall and corruption. That the argument properly considered, stands good, is the verdict of such a man as CHALMERS. After speaking of human helplessness in matters of religion, he says, "There is nothing in this [helplessness] to break the analogies on which to found the negative vindication that forms the great and undoubted achievement of this volume. The analogy lies here:—that if a man wills to obtain prosperity in this life, he may, if observant of the rules which experience and wisdom prescribe, in general, make it good. And if he wills to attain blessedness in the next life, he shall, if observant of what religion prescribes, most certainly make it good; in conformity with the declaration, 'he that seeketh findeth.'"]

security and happiness, without any solicitude or thought of their own: or if they were in no danger of being brought into inconveniences and distress, by carelessness, or the folly of passion, through bad example, the treachery of others, or the deceitful appearances of things: were this our natural condition, then it might seem strange, and be some presumption against the truth of religion, that it represents our future and more general interest, as not secure *of course*, but as depending upon our behavior, and requiring recollection and self-government to obtain it. It *then* might be alleged, "What you say is our condition, in one respect, is not in any wise of a sort with what we find, by experience, is our condition in another. Our whole present interest is secured to our hands, without any solicitude of ours; and why should not our future interest, if we have any such, be so too?" But since, on the contrary, thought and consideration, the voluntary denying ourselves many things which we desire, and a course of behavior, far from being always agreeable to us, are absolutely necessary to our acting even a common decent, and common prudent part, so as to pass with any satisfaction through the *present* world, and be received upon any tolerable good terms in it: since this is the case, all presumption against self-denial and attention being necessary to secure our *higher* interest,[f] is removed.

Had we not experience, it might, perhaps speciously, be urged, that it is improbable any thing of hazard and danger should be put upon us by an infinite being; when every thing which has hazard and danger in our manner of conception, and will end in error, confusion, and misery, is already certain in his foreknowledge. Indeed, why any thing of hazard and danger should be put upon such frail creatures as we are, may well be thought a difficulty in speculation; and cannot but be so, till we know the whole, or at least much more of the case. But still the constitution of nature is as it is. Our happiness and misery are trusted to our conduct, and made to depend upon it. Somewhat, and, in many circumstances, a great deal too, is put upon us, either to

[f] [It comes to this:—good things, in this life, are not forced upon us; for we may refuse them, or turn any of them into evils. Nor are they offered for our mere acceptance: but only as the *results* of self-control and pains-taking So is it, as to heaven.]

do, or to suffer, as we choose. All the various miseries of life, which people bring upon themselves by negligence and folly, and might have avoided by proper care, are instances of this: which miseries are, beforehand, just as contingent and undetermined as conduct, and left to be determined by it.

These observations are an answer[g] to the objections against the credibility of a state of trial, as implying temptations, and real danger of miscarrying with regard to our general interest, under the moral government of God. And they show, that, if we are at all to be considered in such a capacity, and as having such an interest, the general analogy of Providence must lead us to apprehend ourselves in danger of miscarrying, in different degrees, as to this interest, by our neglecting to act the proper part belonging to us in that capacity. For we have a present interest under the government of God, which we experience here upon earth. This interest, as it is not forced upon us, so neither is it offered to our acceptance, but to our acquisition; and in such manner, as that we are in danger of missing it, by means of temptations to neglect, or act contrary to it; and without attention and self-denial, we must and do miss it. It is then perfectly credible, that this may be our case, with respect to that chief and final good, which religion proposes to us.

[g] [They *are* an answer, but a cavil remains,—viz.: "the difference between temporal and eternal things, is so vast that the cases are not analogous." Fairly considered, the cases are analogous, differing only in *degree*, and not at all in principle. What would be wrong on a great scale, is wrong on a small one.

Perhaps the analogy may be pressed further. As the happiness and life of some animals, may be sacrificed for the benefit of man, why may not the happiness and life of some men, be sacrificed for the good of innumerable beings of a higher order, who witness the affairs of this earth? It would but be securing "the greatest good of the greatest number." No analogies could *teach* this, for analogies of course teach nothing. But if the Scriptures contained this doctrine, immensely more repugnant than that which our author is here defending, would analogy offer repellant presumptions?]

CHAPTER V.

PROBATION, AS INTENDED FOR MORAL DISCIPLINE AND IMPROVEMENT.

FROM the consideration of our being in a probation-state, of so much difficulty and hazard, naturally arises the question, how we came to be placed in it? But such a general inquiry as this would be found involved in insuperable difficulties. For, though some of these difficulties would be lessened, by observing that all wickedness is voluntary, as is implied in its very notion; and that many of the miseries of life have apparent good effects: yet, when we consider other circumstances belonging to both, and what must be the consequence of the former in a life to come, it cannot but be acknowledged plain folly and presumption, to pretend to give an account of the *whole reasons* of this matter; the whole reasons of our being allotted a condition, out of which so much wickedness and misery, so circumstanced, would in fact arise. Whether it be not beyond our faculties, not only to find out, but even to understand; or, though we should be supposed capable of understanding it, yet, whether it would be of service or prejudice to us to be informed of it, is impossible to say. But as our present condition can in no wise be shown to be inconsistent with the perfect moral government of God: so religion teaches us we were placed in it, that we might qualify ourselves, by the practice of virtue, for another state which is to follow it. This, though but a partial answer, a very partial one indeed, to the inquiry now mentioned; is yet a more satisfactory answer to another, which is of real, and of the utmost importance to us to have answered,—viz.: What is our business here? The known end then, why we are placed in a state of so much affliction, hazard, and difficulty, is, our improvement in virtue and piety, as the requisite qualification for a future state of security and happiness.

The beginning of life, considered as an education for mature age in the present world, appears plainly, at first sight, analogous to this our trial for a future one: the former being in our temporal capacity, what the latter is in our religious capacity. Some observations common to both, and a more distinct consideration of each, will more distinctly show the extent and force of the analogy between them; and the credibility, which arises from hence, as well as from the nature of the thing, that the present life was intended to be a state of discipline for a future one.

I. Every species of creatures is, we see, designed for a particular way of life; to which, the nature, the capacities, temper, and qualifications, of each species, are as necessary as their external circumstances. Both come into the notion of such state, or particular way of life, and are constituent parts of it. Change a man's capacities or character, to the degree in which it is conceivable they may be changed, and he would be altogether incapable of a human course of life, and human happiness; as incapable, as if, his nature continuing unchanged, he were placed in a world, where he had no sphere of action, nor any objects to answer his appetites, passions, and affections of any sort. One thing is set over against another, as an ancient writer expresses it.[a] Our nature corresponds to our external condition. Without this correspondence, there would be no possibility of any such thing as human life and happiness: which life and happiness are, therefore, a *result* from our nature and condition jointly: meaning by human life, not living in the literal sense, but the whole complex notion commonly understood by those words. So that without determining what will be the employment and happiness, the particular life, of good men hereafter; there must be some determinate capacities, some necessary character and qualifications, without which persons cannot but be utterly incapable of it: in like manner, as there must be some, without which men would be incapable of their present state of life.

II. The constitution of human creatures, and indeed of all creatures which come under our notice, is such, as that they are capable of naturally becoming qualified for states of life, for which they were once wholly unqualified. In imagination we may indeed conceive of creatures, incapable of having any of their faculties naturally enlarged, or as being unable naturally to acquire any new qualifications. But the faculties of every

[a] [That is, the son of Sirac, who says, "All things are double, one against another; and He hath made nothing imperfect: one thing establisheth the good of another:" Ecclesiasticus xlii. 24.]

species known to us, are made for enlargement; for acquirements of experience and habits. We find ourselves, in particular, endued with capacities, not only of perceiving ideas, and of knowledge or perceiving truth, but also of storing up ideas and knowledge by memory. We are capable, not only of acting, and of having different momentary impressions made upon us; but of getting a new facility in any kind of action, and of settled alterations in our temper or character. The power of the two last is the power of habits. But neither the perception of ideas, nor knowledge of any sort, are habits; though absolutely necessary to the forming of them. However, apprehension, reason, memory, which are the capacities of acquiring knowledge, are greatly improved by exercise. Whether the word habit is applicable to all these improvements, and in particular how far the powers of memory and of habits may be powers of the same nature, I shall not inquire. But that perceptions come into our minds readily and of course, by means of their having been there before, seems a thing of the same sort, as readiness in any particular kind of action, proceeding from being accustomed to it. Aptness to recollect practical observations, of service in our conduct, is plainly habit in many cases. There are habits of perception, and habits of action. An instance of the former, is our constant and even involuntary readiness, in correcting the impressions of our sight concerning magnitudes and distances, so as to substitute judgment in the room of sensation, imperceptibly to ourselves. It seems as if all other associations of ideas not naturally connected, might be called passive habits; as properly as our readiness in understanding languages upon sight, or hearing of words. Our readiness in speaking and writing them, are instances of active habits.

For distinctness, we may consider habits, as belonging to the body, or to the mind: and the latter will be explained by the former. Under the former are comprehended all bodily activities or motions, whether graceful or unbecoming, which are owing to use: under the latter, general habits of life and conduct; such as those of obedience and submission to authority, or to any particular person; those of veracity, justice, and charity; those of attention, industry, self-government, envy, revenge. Habits of this latter kind seem produced by repeated acts, as well as the former. And as habits belonging to the body are produced by external *acts*, so habits of the mind are produced by the *exertion* of inward practical principles; *i.e.* by carrying them into act, or acting upon them; the principles of obedience, of veracity, justice, and charity. Nor can those habits be formed by any external course of action, otherwise than as it proceeds from these principles: because it is only these inward principles exerted, which are strictly acts of obedience, of veracity, of justice, and of charity.

So likewise habits of attention, industry, self-government, are in the same manner acquired by exercise; and habits of envy and revenge by indulgence, whether in outward act, or in thought and intention; *i.e.* inward act: for such intention is an act. Resolutions to do well, are also properly acts. And endeavoring to enforce upon our own minds a practical sense of virtue, or to beget in others that practical sense of it, which a man really has himself, is a virtuous act. All these, therefore, may and will contribute towards forming good habits. But going over the theory of virtue in one's thoughts, talking well, and drawing fine pictures, of it; this is so far from necessarily or certainly conducing to form a habit of it, in him who thus employs himself, that it may harden the mind in a contrary course, and render it gradually more insensible; *i.e.* form a habit of insensibility to all moral considerations. For, from our very faculty of habits, passive impressions, by being repeated, grow weaker. Thoughts, by often passing through the mind, are felt less sensibly: being accustomed to danger, begets intrepidity, *i.e.* lessens fear; to distress, lessens the passion of pity; to instances of others' mortality, lessens the sensible apprehension of our own.

From these two observations together, that practical habits are formed and strengthened by repeated acts, and that passive impressions grow weaker by being repeated upon us, it must follow, that active habits may be gradually forming and strengthening, by a course of acting upon such and such motives and excitements, while these motives and excitements themselves are, by proportionable degrees, growing less sensible; *i.e.* are continually less and less sensibly felt, even as the active habits strengthen. And experience confirms this: for active principles, at the very time that they are less lively in perception than they were, are found to be, somehow, wrought more thoroughly into the temper and character, and become more effectual in influencing our practice. The three things just mentioned may afford instances of it. Perception of danger is a natural excitement of passive fear, and active caution: and by being inured to danger, habits of the latter are gradually wrought, at the same time that the former gradually lessens. Perception of distress in others is a natural excitement, passively to pity, and actively to relieve it: but let a man set himself to attend to, inquire out, and relieve distressed persons, and he cannot but grow less and less sensibly affected with the various miseries of life, with which he must become acquainted; when yet, at the same time, benevolence, considered not as a passion, but as a practical principle of action, will strengthen: and while he passively compassionates the distressed less, he will acquire a greater aptitude actively to assist and befriend them. So also at the same time that the daily instances of men's dying around us give us daily a less sensible passive feeling or apprehension of our own mortality, such instances greatly contribute to the strengthening a practical regard to it in serious men; *i.e.* to forming a habit of acting with a constant view to it.

This seems further to show, that passive impressions made upon our minds by admonition, experience, or example, though they may have a remote efficacy, and a very great one, towards forming active habits, yet can have this efficacy no otherwise than by inducing us to such a course of action: and that it is not being *affected* so and so, but acting, which forms those habits: only it must be always remembered, that real endeavors to enforce good impressions upon ourselves are a species of virtuous action. Nor do we know how far it is possible, in the nature of things, that effects should be wrought in us at once, equivalent to habits; *i.e.* what is wrought by use and exercise. The thing insisted on is, not what may be possible, but what is in fact the appointment of nature: which is, that active habits are to be formed by exercise. Their progress may be so gradual, as to be imperceptible in its steps: it may be hard to explain the faculty, by which we are capable of habits, throughout its several parts; and to trace it up to its original, so as to distinguish it from all others in our mind: and it seems as if contrary effects were to be ascribed to it. But the thing in general, that our nature is formed to yield to use and exercise, in some such manner as this, is matter of certain experience.

Thus, by accustoming ourselves to any course of action, we get an aptness to go on, a facility, readiness, and often pleasure, in it. The inclinations which rendered us averse to it, grow weaker; the difficulties in it, not only the imaginary but the real ones, lessen; the reasons for it offer themselves of course to our thoughts upon all occasions; and the least glimpse of them is sufficient to make us go on, in a course of action, to which we have been accustomed. Practical principles appear to grow stronger, absolutely in themselves, by exercise; as well as relatively, with regard to contrary principles; which, by being accustomed to submit, do so habitually, and of course. Thus a new character, in several respects, may be formed; and many habitudes of life, not given by nature, but which nature directs us to acquire.

III. Indeed we may be assured, that we should never have had these capacities of improving by experience, acquired knowledge, and habits, had they not been necessary, and intended to be made use of. And accordingly we find them so necessary, and so much intended, that without them we should be utterly incapable of that which was the end for which we were made, considered in our temporal capacity only: the employments and satisfactions of our mature state of life.

Nature does in no wise qualify us wholly, much less at once, for this mature state of life. Even maturity of understanding, and bodily strength, not only are arrived at gradually, but are also very much owing to the continued exercise of our powers of body and mind from infancy. If we suppose a person brought into the world with both these in maturity, as far as this is conceivable, he would plainly at first be as unqualified for the human life of mature age, as an idiot. He would be in a manner distracted, with astonishment, and apprehension, and curiosity, and suspense: nor can one guess, how long it would be, before he would be familiarized to himself and the objects about him, enough even to set himself to any thing. It may be questioned too, whether the natural information of his sight and hearing would be of any manner of use to him in acting, before experience. And it seems, that men would be strangely headstrong and self-willed, and disposed to exert themselves with an impetuosity, which would render society insupportable, and the living in it impracticable, were it not for some acquired moderation and self-government, some aptitude and readiness in restraining themselves, and concealing their sense of things. Want of every thing of this kind which is learnt would render a man as incapable of society, as want of language would; or as his natural ignorance of any of the particular employments of life would render him incapable of providing himself with the common conveniences, or supplying the necessary wants of it. In these respects, and probably in many more of which we have no particular notion, mankind is left by nature, an unformed, unfinished creature; utterly deficient and unqualified, before the acquirement of knowledge, experience, and habits, for that mature state of life, which was the end of his creation, considering him as related only to this world.

But, as nature has endued us with a power of supplying those deficiencies, by acquired knowledge, experience, and habits; so likewise we are placed in a condition, in infancy, childhood, and youth, fitted for it; fitted for our acquiring those qualifications of all sorts, which we stand in need of in mature age. Hence children, from their very birth, are daily growing acquainted with the objects about them, with the scene in which they are placed, and to have a future part; and learning something or other, necessary to the performance of it. The subordinations, to which they are accustomed in domestic life, teach them self-government in common behavior abroad, and prepare them for subjection and obedience to civil authority.[b] What passes before their eyes, and daily happens to them, gives them experience, caution against treachery and deceit, together with numberless little rules of action and conduct, which we could not live without; and which are learnt so insensibly and so perfectly, as to be mistaken perhaps for instinct, though they are the effect of long experience and exercise; as much so as language, or knowledge in particular business, or the qualifications and behavior belonging to the several ranks and professions. Thus the beginning of our days is adapted to be, and is, a state of education in the theory and practice of mature life. We are much assisted in it by example, instruction, and the care of others; but a great deal is left to

[b] [Consult MILLMAN'S Hist. of Christ, vol. i.: PRIESTLEY'S Institutes of Nat. and Rev. Rel., vol. i. ch. i · and WHATELY'S Pol. Econ., sec. 5.]

ourselves to do. And of this, as part is done easily and of course; so part requires diligence and care, the voluntary foregoing many things which we desire, and setting ourselves to what we should have no inclination to, but for the necessity or expedience of it. For that labor and industry, which the station of so many absolutely requires, they would be greatly unqualified for, in maturity, as those in other stations would be for any other sorts of application; if both were not accustomed to them in their youth. And, according as persons behave themselves, in the general education which all go through, and in the particular ones adapted to particular employments, their character is formed,[c] and made to appear; they recommend themselves more or less; and are capable of, and placed in, different stations in society.

The former part of life, then, is to be considered as an important opportunity, which nature puts into our hands; and which, when lost is not to be recovered. And our being placed in a state of discipline throughout this life, for another world, is a providential disposition of things, exactly of the same kind, as our being placed in a state of discipline during childhood, for mature age. Our condition in both respects is uniform and of a piece, and comprehended under one and the same general law of nature.

If we were not able at all to discern, how or in what way the present life could be our preparation for another; this would be no objection against the credibility of its being so. We do not discern, how food and sleep contribute to the growth of the body; nor could have any thought that they would, before we

[c] [We are too apt to overlook the effect of actions on the actor; (which is often the chief effect) in improving or impairing his own powers. A razor used to cut wood or stone, is not only put to an improper use, but spoiled for the use which is proper. But this is a faint illustration. The razor may be sharpened again; but how shall we restore a blunted sensibility, an enfeebled judgment, or a vitiated appetite? Our wrong-doing inflicts worse results on ourselves than on our victims; and the evil may spread disaster over our whole future. Hence the young make a fatal blunder when they suppose that an occasional indulgence in impropriety may be compatible with general welfare, and improvement. Instead of balancing the pros and cons of a particular act, in the scale of utility or pleasure, they should mark well its effects on themselves. See the description of how an upright being may fall; in a subsequent part of this chapter.]

had experience. Nor do children at all think, on the one hand, that the sports and exercises, to which they are so much addicted, contribute to their health and growth; nor, on the other, of the necessity which there is for their being restrained in them. Nor are they capable of understanding the use of many parts of discipline, which nevertheless they must be made to go through, in order to qualify them for the business of mature age. Were we not able then to discover, in what respects the present life could form us for a future one; yet nothing would be more supposable than that it might, in some respects or other, from the general analogy of Providence. And this, for aught I see, might reasonably be said, even though we should not take in the consideration of God's moral government over the world. But,

IV. Take in this consideration, and consequently, that the character of virtue and piety is a necessary qualification for the future state, and then we may distinctly see, how, and in what respects, the present life may be a preparation for it; since we *want, and are capable of, improvement in that character, by moral and religious habits;* and *the present life is fit to be a state of discipline for such improvement:* in like manner as we have already observed, how, and in what respects, infancy, childhood, and youth, are a necessary preparation, and a natural state of discipline, for mature age.

Nothing which we at present see, would lead us to the thought of a solitary inactive state hereafter. If we judge at all from the analogy of nature, we must suppose, according to the Scripture account of it, that it will be a community. And there is no shadow of any thing unreasonable in conceiving, though there be no analogy for it, that this community will be, as the Scripture represents it, under the more immediate, or, if such an expression may be used, the more sensible government of God. Nor is our ignorance, what will be the employments of this happy community, nor our consequent ignorance, what particular scope or occasion there will be for the exercise of veracity, justice, and charity, among the members of it with regard to each other, any proof, that there will be no sphere of exercise for those virtues. Much less, if that were possible, is our ignorance any proof, that there will be no occasion for that frame of mind, or character, which is formed by the daily practice of those particular virtues here, and which is a result from it.[d] This at least must be owned in general, that, as the government established in the universe is moral, the character of virtue and piety must, in some way or other, be the *condition* of our happiness or the qualification for it.

From what is above observed, concerning our natural power of habits, it is easy to see, that we are *capable* of moral improvement by discipline. And how greatly we *want* it, need not be proved to any one who is acquainted with the great wickedness of mankind; or even with those imperfections, which the best are conscious of. But it is not perhaps distinctly attended to by every one, that the occasion which human creatures have for discipline, to improve in them this character of virtue and piety, is to be traced up higher than to excess in the passions, by indulgence and habits of vice. Mankind, and perhaps all finite creatures, from the very constitution of their nature, before habits of virtue, are deficient, and in danger of deviating from what is right; and therefore stand in need of virtuous habits, for a security against this danger. For, together with the general principle of moral understanding, we have in our inward frame various affections towards particular external objects. These affections are naturally, and of right, subject to the government of the moral principle, as to the occasions upon which they may be gratified; as to the times, degrees, and manner, in which the objects of them may be pursued. But the principle of virtue can neither excite them, nor prevent their being excited. On the contrary, they are naturally felt, when the objects of them are present to the mind, not only before all consideration whether

d ["It might seem, at first sight, that if our state hereafter presented no temptations to falsehood, injustice, &c., our habit of indulging these vices here would be no disqualification for such a state; and our forming the contrary habits no qualification. But *habits* of veracity, justice, &c. are not merely securities against temptations to the contrary, but needful for conserving the *principles* of love of truth, justice, &c. As our happiness depends upon *the ratio* between our circumstances and our dispositions, our happiness, in a state where things are ordered so as to give no scope for the practice of falsehood, injustice, &c., *must depend on our having formed a love for their opposites.*

Besides, the circumstances of the future life may be such as only to remove temptations from characters formed by such moral discipline as we undergo in this life, and not all things that could be temptations to any one."—PROF. FITZGERALD.]

they can be obtained by lawful means, but after it is found they cannot. The natural objects of affection continue so; the necessaries, conveniences, and pleasures of life, remain naturally desirable, though they cannot be obtained innocently: nay, though they cannot possibly be obtained at all. And when the objects of any affection whatever cannot be obtained without unlawful means; but may be obtained by them: such affection, though its being excited, and its continuing some time in the mind, be as innocent as it is natural and necessary, yet cannot but be conceived to have a *tendency* to incline persons to venture upon such unlawful means: and therefore must be conceived as putting them in some danger of it. Now what is the general security against this danger, against their actually deviating from right? As the danger is, so also must the security be, from within: from the practical principle of virtue.* The strengthening or improving this principle, considered as practical, or as a principle of action, will lessen the danger, or increase the security against it. And this moral principle is capable of improvement, by proper discipline and exercise: by recollecting the practical impressions which example and experience have made upon us: and, instead of following humor and mere inclination, by continually attending to the equity and right of the case, in whatever we are engaged, be it in greater or less matters; and accustoming ourselves always to act upon it, as being itself the just and natural motive of action; and as this moral course of behavior must necessarily, under the divine government, be our final interest. *Thus the principle of*

* It may be thought, that a sense of interest would as effectually restrain creatures from doing wrong. But if by a *sense of interest* is meant a speculative conviction or belief, that such and such indulgence would occasion them greater uneasiness, upon the whole, than satisfaction; it is contrary to present experience to say, that this sense of interest is sufficient to restrain them from thus indulging themselves. And if by a *sense of interest* is meant a practical regard to what is upon the whole our happiness; this is not only coincident with the principle of virtue or moral rectitude, but is a part of the idea itself. And it is evident this reasonable self-love wants to be improved, as really as any principle in our nature. For we daily see it overmatched, not only by the more boisterous passions, but by curiosity, shame, love of imitation, by any thing, even indolence: especially if the interest, the temporal interest, suppose, which is the end of such self-love, be at a distance. So greatly are profligate men mistaken, when they affirm they are wholly governed by interestedness and self-love; and so little cause is there for moralists to disclaim this principle.—See p. 131.

virtue, improved into a habit, of which improvement we are thus capable, will plainly be, in proportion to the strength of it, a security against the danger which finite creatures are in, from the very nature of propension, or particular affections. This way of putting the matter, supposes particular affections to remain in a future state; which it is scarce possible to avoid supposing. And if they do; we clearly see, that acquired habits of virtue and self-government may be necessary for the regulation of them. However, though we were not distinctly to take in this supposition, but to speak only in general; the thing really comes to the same. For habits of virtue, thus acquired by discipline, are improvement in virtue: and improvement in virtue must be advancement in happiness, if the government of the universe be moral.

From these things we may observe, (and it will further show this our natural and original need of being improved by discipline,) how it comes to pass, that creatures made upright, fall; and how those who preserve their uprightness, raise themselves by so doing, to a more secure state of virtue. To say that the former is accounted for by the nature of liberty, is to say no more, than that an event's actually happening is accounted for by a mere possibility of its happening. But it seems distinctly conceivable from the very nature of particular affections or propensions. For, suppose creatures intended for such a particular state of life, for which such propensions were necessary: suppose them endued with such propensions, together with moral understanding, as well including a practical sense of virtue as a speculative perception of it; and that all these several principles, both natural and moral, forming an inward constitution of mind, were in the most exact proportion possible; *i.e.* in a proportion the most exactly adapted to their intended state of life; such creatures would be made upright, or finitely perfect. Now particular propensions, from their very nature, must be felt, the objects of them being present; though they cannot be gratified at all, or not with the allowance of the moral principle. If they can be gratified without its allowance, or by contradicting it, then they must be conceived to have some tendency, in how low a degree soever, yet some tendency, to induce persons to such forbidden gratification. This tendency, in some one particular propension, may be increased, by the greater frequency of occasions naturally exciting it, than of occasions exciting others. The least voluntary indulgence in forbidden circumstances,[e] though but in thought, will increase this wrong tendency; and may increase it further, till, peculiar conjunctures perhaps conspiring, it becomes effect; and danger of deviating from right, ends in actual deviation from it; a danger necessarily arising from the very nature of propension, and which therefore could not have been prevented, though it might have been escaped, or got innocently through. The case would be, as if we were to suppose a straight path marked out for a person, in which a certain degree of attention would keep him steady: but if he would not attend, in this degree, any one of a thousand objects, catching his eye, might lead him out of it.

Now it is impossible to say, how much even the first full overt act of irregularity might disorder the inward constitution; unsettle the adjustments, and alter the proportions, which formed it, and in which the uprightness of its make consisted: but repetition of irregularities would produce habits. Thus the constitution would be spoiled; and creatures made upright, become corrupt and depraved in their settled character, proportionably to their repeated irregularities in occasional acts.[f] On the contrary,

[e] [Discipline is mainly promoted by a careful regard to acts of small individual moment. The subjecting of trivial acts to moral considerations, is the sure, and the only mode of self-culture. These acts are embryo habits, and we may often see clearly the moral character of a habit, when the single act seems indifferent. Thus viewed, the importance of single acts will seldom seem small. A single cigar, one glass of wine for convivial purposes, one story told with exaggerations, may change the complexion of our character, and of our whole destiny!

It is doing or refusing to do, from a law-abiding regard to consequences, that constitutes self-discipline. Papists wholly err in teaching the repression of bodily desires as in itself virtuous. Indulgence may be either an obstacle or an aid to moral progress, according to our reason for indulgence. When we can repress an appetite or passion whenever indulgence would be wrong, its mastery over us is broken; and when the passions and appetites act rightly, from force of virtuous habit, without direct volition, discipline is complete. Ascetic acts are only useful as *means*, and so long as they are *ascetic* (askesis) are proofs of imperfect obedience. Discipline is good only *as* discipline; and when complete, changes from a struggle between principle and inclination, to a spontaneous habit, and permanent mental peace.]

[f] [Chalmers objects to this hypothetical fall of man, that it wants harmony with the Scripture account. But I do not see the force of the objection. Butler *of course* does not copy the Scripture account, for he would then depart from the

these creatures might have improved and raised themselves, to a higher and more secure state of virtue, by the contrary behavior: by steadily following the moral principle, supposed to be one part of their nature: and thus *withstanding* that unavoidable danger of defection, which necessarily arose from propension, the other part of it. For, by thus preserving their integrity for some time, their danger would lessen; since propensions, by being inured to submit, would do it more easily and of course: and their security against this lessening danger would increase; since the moral principle would gain additional strength by exercise: both which things are implied in the notion of virtuous habits.

Thus vicious indulgence is not only criminal in itself, but also depraves the inward constitution and character. And virtuous self-government is not only right in itself, but also improves the inward constitution or character: and may improve it to such a degree, that though we should suppose it impossible for particular affections to be absolutely coincident with the moral principle; and consequently should allow, that such creatures as have been above supposed, would forever remain defectible, yet their danger of actually deviating from right may be almost infinitely lessened, and they fully fortified against what remains of it; if that may be called danger, against which there is an adequate, effectual security. Still, this their higher perfection may continue to consist in habits of virtue formed in a state of discipline, and this their more complete security remain to proceed from them.

Thus it is plainly conceivable, that creatures without blemish, as they came out of the hands of God, may be in danger of going wrong; and so may stand in need of the security of virtuous habits, additional to the moral principle wrought into their natures by him. That which is the ground of their danger, or their want of security, may be considered as a deficiency in themselves,

aim and nature of his book. The Bible says man fell *suddenly*, no less in his state than in his character. Butler says that we could not reason out *how much* disorder and damage would ensue from the first sin: and in saying this, avoids any incongruity with the Mosaic account, which tells us how much. What B. says of the formation of habit, by repeated transgressions, certainly cannot be gainsayed.

Adam "died," the very day he ate the forbidden fruit. The sinner "lives" the very day he believes on the only-begotten Son of God. Increase of guilt, or growth in grace are predicable in both instances. In both also there is an instant transition into a new relationship with God.]

to which virtuous habits are the natural supply. And as they are naturally capable of being raised and improved by discipline, it may be a thing fit and requisite, that they should be placed in circumstances with an eye to it: in circumstances peculiarly fitted to be to them a state of discipline for their improvement in virtue.

But how much more strongly must this hold with respect to those who have corrupted their natures, are fallen from their original rectitude, and whose passions are become excessive by repeated violations of their inward constitution! Upright creatures may want to be improved: depraved creatures want to be renewed. Education and discipline, which may be in all degrees and sorts of gentleness and of severity, are expedient for those: but must be absolutely necessary for these. For these, discipline of the severer sort too, and in the higher degrees of it, must be necessary, in order to wear out vicious habits; to recover their primitive strength of self-government, which indulgence must have weakened; to repair, as well as raise into a habit, the moral principle, in order to their arriving at a secure state of virtuous happiness.

Whoever will consider the thing, may clearly see that the present world is *peculiarly fit* to be a state of discipline for this purpose, to such as will set themselves to mend and improve. For, the various temptations with which we are surrounded; our experience of the deceits of wickedness; having been in many instances led wrong ourselves; the great viciousness of the world; the infinite disorders consequent upon it; our being made acquainted with pain and sorrow, either from our own feeling of it, or from the sight of it in others; these things, though some of them may indeed produce wrong effects upon our minds, yet when duly reflected upon, have, all of them, a direct tendency to bring us to a settled moderation and reasonableness of temper: the contrary both to thoughtless levity, and also to that unrestrained self-will, and violent bent to follow present inclination, which may be observed in undisciplined minds.

Such experience, as the present state affords, of the frailty of our nature; of the boundless extravagance of ungoverned passion; of the power which an infinite being has over us, by the various capacities of misery which he has given us; in short, that kind and degree of experience, which the present state affords us, that the constitution of nature is such as to admit the possibility, the danger, and the actual event, of creatures losing their innocence and happiness, and becoming vicious and wretched; has a tendency to give us a practical sense of things very different from a mere speculative knowledge, that we are liable to vice, and capable of misery. And who knows, whether the security of creatures in the highest and most settled state of perfection, may not in part arise, from their having had such a sense of things as this, formed, and habitually fixed within them, in some state of probation. And passing through the present world with that moral attention, which is necessary to the acting a right part in it, may leave everlasting impressions of this sort upon our minds.

To be a little more distinct: allurements to what is wrong, difficulties in the discharge of our duty, our not being able to act a uniform right part without some thought and care, and the opportunities which we have, or imagine we have, of avoiding what we dislike or obtaining what we desire, by unlawful means, when we either cannot do it at all, or at least not so easily, by lawful ones, these things, *i.e.* the snares and temptations of vice, are what render the present world peculiarly fit to be a state of discipline, to those who will preserve their integrity: because they render being upon our guard, resolution, and the denial of our passions, necessary in order to that end. The exercise of such particular recollection, intention of mind, and self-government, in the practice of virtue, has, from the make of our nature, a peculiar tendency to form habits of virtue; as implying, not only a real, but also a more continued, and a more intense exercise of the virtuous principle, or a more constant and a stronger effort of virtue exerted into act. Thus suppose a person to know himself to be in particular danger, for some time, of doing any thing wrong, which yet he fully resolves not to do; continued recollection and keeping upon his guard, in order to make good his resolution, is a *continued* exerting of that act of virtue in a *high degree,* which need have been, and perhaps would have been, only *instantaneous* and *weak,* had the temptation been so.

It is indeed ridiculous to assert, that self-denial is essential to virtue and piety:[g] but it would have been nearer the truth, though not strictly the truth itself, to have said, that it is essential to discipline and improvement. For though actions materially virtuous, which have no sort of difficulty, but are perfectly agreeable to our particular inclinations, may possibly be done only from these particular inclinations, and so may not be any exercise of the principle of virtue, *i.e.* not be virtuous actions at all; yet, on the contrary, they *may* be an exercise of that principle: and when they are, they have a tendency to form and fix the habit of virtue. But when the exercise of the virtuous principle is more continued, oftener repeated, and more intense; as it must be in circumstances of danger, temptation, and difficulty, of any kind and in any degree; this tendency is increased proportionably, and a more confirmed habit is the consequence.

This undoubtedly holds to a certain length: but how far it may hold, I know not. Neither our intellectual powers, nor our bodily strength can be improved beyond a certain degree: and both may be overwrought. Possibly there may be something analogous to this, with respect to the moral character; which is scarce worth considering. I mention it only, lest it should come into some persons' thoughts, not as an exception to the foregoing observations, which perhaps it is; but as a confutation of them, which it is not. And there may be several other exceptions. Observations of this kind cannot be supposed to hold minutely, and in every case. It is enough that they hold in general. And these plainly hold so far, as that from them may be seen distinctly, (which is all that is intended by them,) that *the present world is peculiarly fit to be a state of discipline, for our improvement in virtue and piety:* in the same sense as some sciences, by requiring and engaging the attention, not to be sure of such persons as will not, but of such as will, set themselves to them, are fit to form the mind to habits of attention.

[g] [A forced or reluctant obedience is wholly incompatible with earthly happiness; but may, in the highest degree promote our *future* happiness. It will not *long* mar our happiness, even here; because being based on principle, and established by habit, it will, in process of time, be superseded by prompt and pleasurable submission. Thus a person *habitually* virtuous, is hardly conscious of self-denial; a fact noticed by Aristotle. "He who abstains from bodily pleasures and delights, is virtuous in this very abstinence; but he who is troubled by it is undisciplined." Ethic. Nic. ii. 3.]

Indeed the present state is so far from proving, in event, a discipline of virtue to the generality of men, that on the contrary they seem to make it a discipline of vice. And the viciousness of the world is, in different ways, the great temptation which renders it a state of virtuous discipline, in the degree it is, to good men. The whole end, and the whole occasion, of mankind's being placed in such a state as the present, is not pretended to be accounted for. That which appears amidst the general corruption, is, that there are some persons, who, having within them the principle of amendment and recovery, attend to and follow the notices of virtue and religion, be they more clear or more obscure, which are afforded them; and that the present world is not only an exercise of virtue in these persons, but an exercise of it in ways and degrees, peculiarly apt to improve it: apt to improve it, in some respects, even beyond what would be, by the exercise of it, required in a perfectly virtuous society, or in a society of equally imperfect virtue with themselves. But that the present world does not actually become a state of moral discipline to many, even to the generality, *i.e.* that they do not improve or grow better in it, cannot be urged as a proof, that it was not intended for moral discipline, by any who at all observe the analogy of nature. For, of the numerous seeds of vegetables and bodies of animals, which are adapted and put in the way to improve to such a point or state of natural maturity and perfection, we do not see perhaps that one in a million actually does. Far the greatest part of them decay before they are improved to it; and appear to be absolutely destroyed. Yet no one, who does not deny all final causes, will deny, that those seeds and bodies, which do attain to that point of maturity and perfection, answer the end for which they were really designed by nature; and therefore that nature designed them for such perfection. I cannot forbear adding, though it is not to the present purpose, that the *appearance* of such an amazing *waste* in nature, with respect to these seeds and bodies, by foreign causes, is to us as unaccountable, as, what is much more terrible, the present and future ruin of so many moral agents by themselves, *i.e.* by vice.

Against this whole notion of moral discipline, it may be objected, in another way; that so far as a course of behavior, materially virtuous, proceeds from hope and fear, so far it is only a discipline and strengthening of self-love. But doing what God commands, because he commands it, is obedience, though it proceeds from hope or fear. A course of such obedience will form habits of it. And a constant regard to veracity, justice, and charity, may form distinct habits of these particular virtues; and will certainly form habits of self-government, and of denying our inclinations, whenever veracity, justice, or charity requires it. Nor is there any foundation for this great nicety, with which some affect to distinguish in this case, in order to depreciate all religion proceeding from hope or fear. For, veracity, justice, and charity, regard to God's authority, and to our own chief interest, are not only all three coincident; but each of them is, in itself, a just and natural motive or principle of action. He who begins a good life from any one of them, and perseveres in it, as he is already in some degree, so he cannot fail of becoming more and more, of that character which is correspondent to the constitution of nature as moral; and to the relation which God stands in to us as moral governor of it: nor consequently can he fail of obtaining that happiness, which this constitution and relation necessarily suppose connected with that character.

These several observations, concerning the active principle of virtue and obedience to God's commands, are applicable to passive submission or resignation to his will: which is another essential part of a right character, connected with the former, and very much in our power to form ourselves to. It may be imagined, that nothing but afflictions can give occasion for or require this virtue; that it can have no respect to, nor be any way necessary to qualify for, a state of perfect happiness: but it is not experience which can make us think thus. Prosperity itself, while any thing supposed desirable is not ours, begets extravagant and unbounded thoughts. Imagination is altogether as much a source of discontent, as any thing in our external condition. It is indeed true, that there can be no scope for *patience*, when sorrow shall be no more; but there may be need of a temper of mind, which shall have been formed by patience. For, though self-love, considered merely as an active principle leading us to pursue our chief interest, cannot but be uniformly coincident with the principle of obedience to God's commands, our interest being rightly understood; because this obedience, and the pursuit of our own chief interest, must be in every case one and the same thing: yet it may be questioned, whether self-love, considered merely as the desire of our own interest or happiness, can, from its nature, be thus absolutely and uniformly coincident with the will of God; any more than particular affections can:* coincident in such sort, as not to be liable to be excited upon occasions and in degrees, impossible to be gratified consistently with the constitution of things, or the divine appointments. So that *habits* of resignation may, upon this account, be requisite for all creatures: habits, I say; which signify what is formed by use. However, in general it is obvious that both self-love and particular affection in human creatures considered only as passive feelings, distort and rend the mind; and therefore stand in need of discipline. Now denial of those particular affections, in a course of active virtue and obedience to God's will, has a tendency to moderate them; and seems also to have a tendency to habituate the mind, to be easy and satisfied with that degree of happiness which is allotted us, *i.e.* to moderate self-love. But the proper discipline for resignation is affliction. A right behavior under that trial; recollecting ourselves so as to consider it in the view, in which religion teaches us to consider it, as from the hand of God, receiving it as what he appoints, or thinks proper to permit, in his world and under his government; this will habituate the mind to a dutiful submission. Such submission, together with the active principle of obedience, make up the temper and character in us, which answers to his sovereignty; and which absolutely belongs to the condition of our being, as dependent creatures. Nor can it be said, that this is only breaking the mind to a submission to mere power; for mere power may be accidental, and precarious, and usurped: but it is forming within ourselves the temper of resignation to His rightful authority, who is, by nature, supreme over all.

Upon the whole: such a character, and such qualifications, are necessary for a mature state of life in the present world, as nature alone does in no wise bestow; but has put it upon us, in great part, to acquire, in our progress from one stage of life to another, from childhood to mature age; put it upon us to acquire them, by giving us capacities of doing it, and by placing us, in the

* P. 145.

beginning of life, in a condition fit for it. And this is a general analogy to our condition in the present world, as in a state of moral discipline for another.

It is in vain to object against the credibility of the present life's being intended for this purpose, that all the trouble and the danger unavoidably accompanying such discipline, might have been saved us, by our being made at once the creatures and the characters, *which we were to be*. For we experience, that *what we were to be*, was to be the effect of *what we would do:* and that the general conduct of nature is, not to save us trouble or danger, but to make us capable of going through them, and to put it upon us to do so. Acquirements of our own, experience and habits, are the *natural* supply to our deficiencies, and security against our dangers: since it is as plainly natural to set ourselves to acquire the qualifications, as the external things, which we stand in need of. In particular, it is as plainly a general law of nature, that we should with regard to our temporal interest, form and cultivate practical principles within us, by attention, use, and discipline, as any thing whatever is a natural law; chiefly in the beginning of life, but also throughout the whole course of it. The alternative is left to our choice: either to improve ourselves, and better our condition; or, in default of such improvement, to remain deficient and wretched. It is therefore perfectly credible, from the analogy of nature, that the same may be our case, with respect to the happiness of a future state, and the qualifications necessary for it.

There is a third thing, which may seem implied in the present world's being a state of probation; that it is a *theatre of action*, for the manifestation of persons' characters, with respect to a future one: not, to be sure, to an all-knowing Being, but to his creation or part of it. This may, perhaps, be only a consequence of our being in a state of probation in the other senses. However, it is not impossible, that men's showing and making manifest, what is in their heart, what their real character is, may have respect to a future life, in ways and manners with which we are not acquainted: particularly it may be a means, (for the Author of nature does not appear to do any thing without means,) of their being disposed of suitably to their characters; and of its being known to the creation, by way of example, that they are thus disposed of. But not to enter upon any conjectural account of this; one may just mention, that the manifestation of persons' characters contributes very much, in various ways, to the carrying on a great part of that general course of nature, respecting mankind, which comes under our observation at present. I shall only add, that probation, in both these senses, as well as in that treated of in the foregoing chapter, is implied in moral government; since by persons' behavior under it, their characters cannot but be manifested, and if they behave well, improved.

CHAPTER VI.

THE OPINION OF NECESSITY, CONSIDERED AS INFLUENCING PRACTICE.

THROUGHOUT the foregoing treatise it appears, that the condition of mankind, considered as inhabitants of this world only, and under the government of God which we experience, is greatly analogous to our condition, as designed for another world, or as under that farther government, which religion teaches us. If therefore any assert, as a fatalist must, that the opinion of universal necessity is reconcilable with the former; there immediately arises a question in the way of analogy, whether he must not also own it to be reconcilable with the latter, *i.e.* with the system of religion itself, and the proof of it. The reader then will observe, that the question now before us is not absolute, *i.e.* whether the opinion of fate be reconcilable with religion; but hypothetical, whether, upon supposition of its being reconcilable with the constitution of nature, it be not reconcilable with religion also. Or, what pretence a fatalist, not other persons, but a fatalist, has to conclude from his opinion, that there can be no such thing as religion. And as the puzzle and obscurity, which must unavoidably arise from arguing upon so absurd a supposition as that of universal necessity, will, I fear, easily be seen; it will, I hope, as easily be excused.[a]

[a] [The student should learn to distinguish between the *kinds* of necessity. There is—1. "Logical necessity," which requires the admission of a consequent to a premise 2. "Moral necessity," which requires means in order to ends.

Since it has been all along taken for granted, as a thing proved, that there is an intelligent Author of nature, or natural Governor of the world; and since an objection may be made against the proof of this, from the opinion of universal necessity, as it may be supposed, that such necessity will itself account for the origin and preservation of all things; it is requisite, that this objection be distinctly answered; or that it be shown, that a fatality supposed consistent with what we certainly experience, does not destroy the proof of an intelligent Author and Governor of nature; before we proceed to consider, whether it destroys the proof of a moral Governor of it, or of our being in a state of religion.

When it is said by a fatalist, that the whole constitution of nature, the actions of men, every thing, and every mode and circumstance of every thing, is necessary, and could not possibly have been otherwise; it is to be observed, that this necessity does not exclude deliberation, choice, preference, and acting from certain principles, and to certain ends: because all this is matter of undoubted experience, acknowledged by all, and what every man may, every moment, be conscious of. Hence it follows, that necessity, alone and of itself, is in no sort an account of the constitution of nature, and how things came *to be* and *to continue* as they are; but only an account of this *circumstance* relating to their origin and continuance, that they could not have been otherwise, than they are and have been. The assertion, that every thing is by necessity of nature, is not an answer to the question; Whether the world came into being as it is, by an intelligent Agent forming it thus, or not: but to quite another question; Whether it came into being as it is, in that way and manner which we call *necessarily*, or in that way and manner which we call

3. "Physical necessity," which is the compulsory connection of sequences to antecedents, in the material world. 4. "Metaphysical necessity," which belongs to God only, as existing eternally and immutably. All these exist and operate, and by them we govern ourselves.

But there are various other kinds of necessity, erroneous and pernicious, which may be grouped under two heads:—1. "Atheistic," sometimes called the Democritic, which ascribes all things to the mechanical laws of matter. 2. "Theistic," which admits the existence of God, but denies to him moral character, and makes him the arbitrary and only agent in the universe, and creatures not responsible. See COLLINGS on Providence, PRICE'S Dissertations, RUTHERFORD on Providence, CHARNOCK'S Sermons, and WHATELY'S Logic.]

freely? For suppose farther, that one who was a fatalist, and one who kept to his natural sense of things, and believed himself a free agent, were disputing together, and vindicating their respective opinions; and they should happen to instance a house; they would agree that it was built by an architect. Their difference concerning necessity and freedom would occasion no difference of judgment concerning this; but only concerning another matter; whether the architect built it necessarily or freely.

Suppose they should proceed to inquire concerning the constitution of nature. In a lax way of speaking, one of them might say, it was by necessity; and the other, by freedom: but if they had any meaning to their words, as the latter must mean a free agent, so the former must at length be reduced to mean an agent, whether he would say one or more, acting by necessity: for abstract notions can do nothing. We indeed ascribe to God a necessary existence, uncaused by any agent. For we find within ourselves the idea of infinity, *i.e.* immensity and eternity, impossible, even in imagination, to be removed out of being. We seem to discern intuitively, that there must, and cannot but be, something, external to ourselves, answering this idea, or the archetype of it. Hence, (for *this abstract*, as much as any other, implies a *concrete*) we conclude, that there is, and cannot but be, an infinite and immense eternal being, existing prior to all design contributing to his existence, and exclusive of it. From the scantiness of language, a manner of speaking has been introduced; that necessity is the foundation, the reason, the account of the existence of God. But it is not alleged, nor can it be at all intended, that *every thing* exists as it does, by this kind of necessity: a necessity antecedent in nature to design: it cannot, I say, be meant that every thing exists as it does, by this kind of necessity, upon several accounts; and particularly because it is admitted, that design, in the actions of men, contributes to many alterations in nature. If any deny this, I shall not pretend to reason with them.

From these things it follows; *First,* That when a fatalist asserts, that every thing is *by necessity,* he must mean, *by an agent acting necessarily;* he *must,* I say, mean this, for I am very sensible he would not choose to mean it. *Secondly,* That the necessity, by which such an agent is supposed to act, does not exclude intelligence and design. So that, were the system of fatality admitted, it would just as much account for the formation of the world, as for the structure of a house, and no more. Necessity as much requires and supposes a necessary agent, as freedom requires and supposes a free agent, to be the former of the world. And the appearances of *design* and of *final causes* in the constitution of nature as really prove this acting agent to be an *intelligent designer*, or to act from choice; upon the scheme of necessity, supposed possible, as upon that of freedom.

It appearing thus, that the notion of necessity does not destroy the proof that there is an intelligent Author of nature and natural Governor of the world; the present question, which the analogy before mentioned suggests,* and which, I think, it will answer, is this: Whether the opinion of necessity, supposed consistent with possibility, with the constitution of the world, and the natural government which we experience exercised over it, destroys all reasonable ground of belief, that we are in a state of religion: or whether that opinion be reconcilable with religion; with the system, and the proof of it.

Suppose then a fatalist to educate any one, from his youth up, in his own principles; that the child should reason upon them, and conclude, that since he cannot possibly behave otherwise than he does, he is not a subject of blame or commendation, nor can deserve to be rewarded or punished. Imagine him to eradicate the very perceptions of blame and commendation out of his mind, by means of this system; to form his temper, and character, and behavior to it; and from it to judge of the treatment he was to expect, say, from reasonable men, upon his coming abroad into the world: as the fatalist judges from this system, what he is to expect from the Author of nature, and with regard to a future state. I cannot forbear stopping here to ask, whether any one of common sense would think fit, that a child should be put upon these speculations, and be left to apply them to practice. And a man has little pretence to reason, who is not sensible, that we are all children in speculations of this kind. However, the child would doubtless be highly delighted to find himself freed from the restraints of fear and shame, with which

* P. 157.

his play-fellows were fettered and embarrassed; and highly conceited in his superior knowledge, so far beyond his years. But conceit and vanity would be the least bad part of the influence, which these principles must have, when thus reasoned and acted upon, during the course of his education. He must either be allowed to go on and be the plague of all about him, and himself too, even to his own destruction, or else correction must be continually made use of, to supply the want of those natural perceptions of blame and commendation, which we have supposed to be removed; and to give him a practical impression, of what he had reasoned himself out of the belief of, that he was in fact an accountable child, and to be punished for doing what he was forbid. It is therefore in reality impossible, but that the correction which he must meet with, in the course of his education, must convince him, that if the scheme he was instructed in were not false, yet that he reasoned inconclusively upon it, and somehow or other misapplied it to practice and common life; as what the fatalist experiences of the conduct of Providence at present, ought in all reason to convince him, that this scheme is misapplied, when applied to the subject of religion.* But supposing the child's temper could remain still formed to the system, and his expectation of the treatment he was to have in the world, be regulated by it; so as to expect that no reasonable man would blame or punish him, for any thing which he should do, because he could not help doing it: upon this supposition it is manifest he would, upon his coming abroad into the world, be insupportable to society, and the treatment which he would receive from it would render it so to him; and he could not fail of doing something very soon, for which he would be delivered over into the hands of civil justice. And thus, in the end, he would be convinced of the obligations he was under to his wise instructor.

Suppose this scheme of fatality, in any other way, applied to practice, such practical application of it will be found equally absurd; equally fallacious in a practical sense. For instance, that if a man be destined to live such a time, he shall live to it, though he take no care of his own preservation; or if he be destined to die before that time, no care can prevent it, therefore all care about preserving one's life is to be neglected: which

* P. 158.

is the fallacy instanced in by the ancients. On the contrary, none of these practical absurdities can be drawn from reasoning, upon the supposition that we are free; but all such reasoning with regard to the common affairs of life is justified by experience. Therefore, though it were admitted that this opinion of necessity were *speculatively* true; yet, with regard to practice, it is as if it were false, so far as our experience reaches: that is, to the whole of our present life. For, the constitution of the present world, and the condition in which we are actually placed, is, as if we were free. And it may perhaps justly be concluded, that since the whole process of action, through every step of it, suspense, deliberation, inclining one way, determining, and at last doing as we determine, is as if we were free, therefore we are so [b]

The thing here insisted upon is, that under the present natural government of the world, we find we are treated and dealt with, as if we were free, prior to all consideration whether we are so or not. Were this opinion therefore of necessity admitted to be ever so true; yet such is in fact our condition and the natural course of things, that whenever we apply it to life and practice, this application of it always misleads us, and cannot but mislead us, in a most dreadful manner, with regard to our present interest. How then can people think themselves so very secure, that the same application of the same opinion may not mislead them also, in some analogous manner, with respect to a future, a more general, and more important interest? For, religion being a practical subject; and the analogy of nature showing us, that we have not faculties to apply this opinion, were it a true one, to practical subjects; whenever we do apply it to the subject of religion, and thence conclude, that we are free from its obligations, it is plain this conclusion cannot be depended upon. There will still remain just reason to think, whatever appearances are, that we deceive ourselves; in somewhat of a like manner, as when people fancy they can draw contradictory conclusions from the idea of infinity.

[b] [HUME says, "though man, in truth, is a necessary agent, having all his actions determined by fixed and immutable laws, yet, this being concealed from him, he acts with the conviction of being a free agent."

Which is the same as to say that God intended to conceal from men an important fact, involving the whole subject of right and wrong, but Mr. Hume found him out!]

From these things together, the attentive reader will see it follows, that if upon supposition of freedom the evidence of religion be conclusive, it remains so, upon supposition of necessity, because the notion of necessity is not applicable to practical subjects: *i.e.* with respect to them, is as if it were not true. Nor does this contain any reflection upon reason, but only upon what is unreasonable. For to pretend to act upon reason, in opposition to practical principles, which the Author of our nature gave us to act upon; and to pretend to apply our reason to subjects, with regard to which, our own short views, and even our experience, will show us, it cannot be depended upon; and such, at best, the subject of necessity must be; this is vanity, conceit, and unreasonableness.

But this is not all. We find within ourselves a will, and are conscious of a character. Now if this, in us, be reconcilable with fate, it is reconcilable with it in the Author of nature. Besides, natural government and final causes imply a character and a will in the Governor and Designer;* a will concerning the creatures whom he governs. The Author of nature then being certainly of some character or other, notwithstanding necessity; it is evident this necessity is as reconcilable with the particular character of benevolence, veracity, and justice, in him, which attributes are the foundation of religion, as with any other character: since we find this necessity no more hinders *men* from being benevolent, than cruel; true, than faithless; just, than unjust; or, if the fatalist pleases, what we call unjust. It is said indeed, that what, upon supposition of freedom, would be just punishment, upon supposition of necessity, becomes manifestly unjust: because it is punishment inflicted for doing that which persons could not avoid doing. As if the necessity, which is supposed to destroy the injustice of murder, for instance, would not also destroy the injustice of punishing it! However, as little to the purpose as this objection is in itself, it is very much to the purpose to observe from it, how the notions of justice and injustice remain, even while we endeavor to suppose them removed; how they

* By *will* and *character* is meant that which, in speaking of men, we should express, not only by these words, but also by the words *temper, taste, dispositions, practical principles: that whole frame of mind, from whence we act in one manner rather than another.*

force themselves upon the mind, even while we are making suppositions destructive of them: for there is not, perhaps, a man in the world, but would be ready to make this objection at first thought.

But though it is most evident, that universal necessity, if it be reconcilable with any thing, is reconcilable with that character in the Author of nature, which is the foundation of religion; "Yet, does it not plainly destroy the *proof* that he is of that character, and consequently the proof of religion?" By no means. For we find, that happiness and misery are not our *fate*, in any such sense as not to be the consequences of our behavior; but that they are the consequences of it.* We find God exercises the same kind of government over us, which a father exercises over his children, and a civil magistrate over his subjects. Now, whatever becomes of abstract questions concerning liberty and necessity, it evidently appears to us, that veracity and justice must be the natural rule and measure of exercising this authority or government, to a Being who can have no competitions, or interfering of interests, with his creatures and his subjects.

But as the doctrine of liberty, though we experience its truth, may be perplexed with difficulties, which run up into the most abstruse of all speculations; and as the opinion of necessity seems to be the very basis upon which infidelity grounds itself; it may be of some use to offer a more particular proof of the obligations of religion, which may distinctly be shown not to be destroyed by this opinion.

The proof from final causes of an intelligent Author of nature is not affected by the opinion of necessity; supposing necessity a thing possible in itself, and reconcilable with the constitution of things.† It is a matter of fact, independent on this or any other speculation, that he governs the world by the method of rewards and punishments:‡ and also that he hath given us a moral faculty, by which we distinguish between actions, and approve some as virtuous and of good desert, and disapprove others as vicious and of ill desert.§ This moral discernment implies, in the notion of it, a rule of action, and a rule of a very peculiar kind: for it carries in it authority and a right of direction; authority in such a sense, as that we cannot depart from it without being self-con-

* Chap. ii. † P. 157, &c. ‡ Chap. ii. § Dissert. II.

demned.* And that the dictates of this moral faculty, which are by nature a rule to us, are moreover the laws of God, laws in a sense including sanctions; may be thus proved. Consciousness of a rule or guide of action, in creatures who are capable of considering it as given them by their Maker, not only raises immediately a sense of duty, but also a sense of security in following it, and of danger in deviating from it. A direction of the Author of nature, given to creatures capable of looking upon it as such, is plainly a command from him: and a command from him necessarily includes in it, at least, an implicit promise in case of obedience, or threatening in case of disobedience. But then the sense or perception of good and ill desert,† which is contained in the moral discernment, renders the sanction explicit, and makes it appear, as one may say, expressed. For since his method of government is to reward and punish actions, his having annexed to some actions an inseparable sense of good desert, and to others of ill, this surely amounts to declaring, upon whom his punishments shall be inflicted, and his rewards be bestowed. He must have given us this discernment and sense of things, as a presentiment of what is to be hereafter: that is, by way of information beforehand, what we are finally to expect in this world. There is then most evident ground to think, that the government of God, upon the whole, will be found to correspond to the nature which he has given us: and that, in the upshot and issue of things, happiness and misery shall, in fact and event, be made to follow virtue and vice respectively; as he has already, in so peculiar a manner, associated the ideas of them in our minds. And hence might easily be deduced the obligations of religious worship, were it only to be considered as a means of preserving upon our minds a sense of this moral government of God, and securing our obedience to it: which yet is an extremely imperfect view of that most important duty.

No objection from necessity can lie against this general proof of religion. None against the proposition reasoned upon, that we have such a moral faculty and discernment; because this is a mere matter of fact, a thing of experience, that human kind is thus constituted: none against the conclusion; because it is immediate and wholly from this fact. For the conclusion, that

* Serm. 2, at the *Rolls*.

† Dissert. II.

God will finally reward the righteous and punish the wicked, is not here drawn, from its appearing to us fit* that *he should;* but from its appearing, that he has told us, *he will.* And this he hath certainly told us, in the promise and threatening, which it hath been observed the notion of a command implies, and the sense of good and ill desert which he has given us, more distinctly expresses. This reasoning from fact is confirmed, and in some degree even verified, by other facts; by the natural tendencies of virtue and of vice;† and by this, that God, in the natural course of his providence, punishes vicious actions as mischievous to society; and also vicious actions as such in the strictest sense.‡ So that the general proof of religion is unanswerably real, even upon the wild supposition which we are arguing upon.

It must be observed further, that natural religion has, besides this, an external evidence; which the doctrine of necessity, if it could be true, would not affect. For suppose a person, by the observations and reasoning above, or by any other, convinced of the truth of religion; that there is a God, who made the world, who is the moral governor and judge of mankind, and will upon the whole deal with every one according to his works: I say, suppose a person convinced of this by reason, but to know nothing at all of antiquity, or the present state of mankind: it would be natural for such a one to be inquisitive, what was the history of this system of doctrine; at what time, and in what manner, it came first into the world; and whether it were believed by any considerable part of it. Were he upon inquiry to

* However, I am far from intending to deny, that the will of God is determined, by what is fit, by the right and reason of the case; though one chooses to decline matters of such abstract speculation, and to speak with caution when one does speak of them. But if it be intelligible to say, that *it is fit and reasonable for every one to consult his own happiness,* then *fitness of action, or the right and reason of the case,* is an intelligible manner of speaking. And it seems as inconceivable, to suppose God to approve one course of action, or one end, preferably to another, which yet his acting at all from design implies that he does, without supposing somewhat prior in that end, to be the ground of the preference; as to suppose him to discern an abstract proposition to be true, without supposing somewhat prior in it, to be the ground of the discernment. It doth not therefore appear, that moral right is any more relative to perception, than abstract truth is; or that it is any more improper to speak of the fitness and rightness of actions and ends, as founded in the nature of things, than to speak of abstract truth, as thus founded.

† P. 118. ‡ P. 110, &c.

find, that a particular person, in a late age, first of all proposed it, as a deduction of reason, and that mankind were before wholly ignorant of it; then, though its evidence from reason would remain, there would be no additional probability of its truth, from the account of its discovery.

But instead of this being the fact, he would find, on the contrary, what could not but afford him a very strong confirmation of its truth: *First*, That somewhat of this system, with more or fewer additions and alterations, hath been professed in all ages and countries, of which we have any certain information relating to this matter. *Secondly*, That it is certain historical fact, so far as we can trace things up, that this whole system of belief, that there is one God, the creator and moral governor of the world, and that mankind is in a state of religion, was received in the first ages. And *Thirdly*, That as there is no hint or intimation in history, that this system was first reasoned out; so there is express historical or traditional evidence, as ancient as history, that it was taught first by revelation.

Now these things must be allowed to be of great weight. The first of them, general consent, shows this system to be conformable to the common sense of mankind. The second, namely, that religion was believed in the first ages of the world, especially as it does not appear that there were then any superstitious or false additions to it, cannot but be a further confirmation of its truth. For it is a proof of this alternative: either that it came into the world by revelation; or that it is natural, obvious, and forces itself upon the mind. The former of these is the conclusion of learned men. And whoever will consider, how unapt for speculation rude and uncultivated minds are, will, perhaps from hence alone, be strongly inclined to believe it the truth. And as it is shown in the second part* of this treatise, that there is nothing of such peculiar presumption against a revelation in the beginning of the world, as there is supposed to be against subsequent ones; a sceptic could not, I think, give any account, which would appear more probable even to himself, of the early pretences to revelation; than by supposing some real original one, from whence they were copied.

And the third thing above mentioned, that there is express

* Chap. ii.

historical or traditional evidence, as ancient as history, of the system of religion being taught mankind by revelation, this must be admitted as some degree of real proof, that it was so taught. For why should not the most ancient tradition be admitted as some additional proof of a fact, against which there is no presumption? This proof is mentioned here, because it has its weight to show, that religion came into the world by revelation, prior to all consideration of the proper authority of any book supposed to contain it; and even prior to all consideration, whether the revelation itself be uncorruptly handed down, or mixed and darkened with fables. Thus the historical account, which we have of the origin of religion, taking in all circumstances, is a real confirmation of its truth, no way affected by the opinion of necessity. And the *external* evidence, even of natural religion, is by no means inconsiderable.

It is carefully to be observed, and ought to be recollected after all proofs of virtue and religion, which are only general, that as speculative reason may be neglected, prejudiced, and deceived, so also may our moral understanding be impaired and perverted, and the dictates of it not impartially attended to. This indeed proves nothing against the reality of our speculative or practical faculties of perception; against their being intended by nature, to inform us in the theory of things, and instruct us how we are to behave, and what we are to expect in consequence of our behavior. Yet our liableness, in the degree we are liable, to prejudice and perversion, is a most serious admonition to us to be upon our guard, with respect to what is of such consequence, as our determinations concerning virtue and religion; and particularly not to take custom, and fashion, and slight notions of honor, or imaginations of present ease, use, and convenience to mankind, for the only moral rule.*

The foregoing observations, drawn from the nature of the thing, and the history of religion, amount, *when taken together*, to a real practical proof of it, not to be confuted: such a proof as, considering the infinite importance of the thing, I apprehend, would be admitted fully sufficient, in reason, to influence the actions of men, who act upon thought and reflection, if it were admitted that there is no proof of the contrary. But it may be said;

* Dissertation II.

"There are many probabilities, which cannot indeed be confuted, *i.e.* shown to be no probabilities, and yet may be overbalanced by greater probabilities, on the other side; much more by demonstration. And there is no occasion to object against particular arguments alleged for an opinion, when the opinion itself may be clearly shown to be false, without meddling with such arguments at all, but leaving them just as they are.* Now the method of government by rewards and punishments, and especially rewarding and punishing good and ill desert as such respectively, must go upon supposition, that we are free and not necessary agents. And it is incredible, that the Author of nature should govern us upon a supposition as true, which he knows to be false; and therefore absurd to think, he will reward or punish us for our actions hereafter; especially that he will do it under the notion, that they are of good or ill desert."

Here then the matter is brought to a point. And the answer is full, and not to be evaded,—viz.: that the whole constitution and course of things, the whole analogy of Providence, shows beyond possibility of doubt, that the conclusion from this reasoning is false; wherever the fallacy lies. The doctrine of freedom indeed clearly shows where: in supposing ourselves necessary, when in truth we are free agents. But, upon the supposition of necessity, the fallacy lies in taking for granted, that it is incredible necessary agents should be rewarded and punished. That, somehow or other, the conclusion now mentioned is false, is most certain. For it is fact, that God does govern even brute creatures by the method of rewards and punishments, in the natural course of things. Men are rewarded and punished for their actions, punished for actions mischievous to society as being so, punished for vicious actions as such; by the natural instrumentality of each other, under the present conduct of Providence. Nay, even the affection of gratitude, and the passion of resentment, and the rewards and punishments following from them, which in general are to be considered as natural, *i.e.* from the Author of nature; these rewards and punishments, being *naturally*† annexed to actions considered as implying good intention and good desert, ill intention and ill desert; these natural rewards and punishments, I say, are as much a contradiction to

* Pp. 68, 71.

† Serm. 8th, at the *Rolls*.

the conclusion above, and show its falsehood, as a more exact and complete rewarding and punishing of good and ill desert as such. So that if it be incredible, that necessary agents should be thus rewarded and punished; then, men are not necessary but free; since it is matter of fact, that they are thus rewarded and punished. If, on the contrary, which is the supposition we have been arguing upon, it be insisted that men are necessary agents; then, there is nothing incredible in the further supposition of necessary agents being thus rewarded and punished: since we ourselves are thus dealt with.

From the whole therefore it must follow, that a necessity supposed possible, and reconcilable with the constitution of things, does in no sort prove that the Author of Nature will not, nor destroy the proof that he will, finally and upon the whole, in his eternal government, render his creatures happy or miserable, by some means or other, as they behave well or ill. Or, to express this conclusion in words conformable to the title of the chapter, the analogy of nature shows us, that the opinion of necessity, considered as practical, is false. And if necessity, upon the supposition above mentioned, doth not destroy the proof of natural religion, it evidently makes no alteration in the proof of revealed.

From these things likewise we may learn, in what sense to understand that general assertion, that the opinion of necessity is essentially destructive of all religion. First, in a practical sense; that by this notion, atheistical men pretend to satisfy and encourage themselves in vice, and justify to others their disregard to all religion. And secondly, in the strictest sense; that it is a contradiction to the whole constitution of nature, and to what we may every moment experience in ourselves, and so overturns every thing. But by no means is this assertion to be understood, as if necessity, supposing it could possibly be reconciled with the constitution of things, and with what we experience, were not also reconcilable with religion: for upon this supposition, it demonstrably is so.[c]

[c] [Consult, in favor of the doctrine of necessity, atheistical writers generally; such as Fichte, Hegel, D'Holback, Comte, Crousse, Martineau, Leroux, and Holyoake — also, BELSHAM'S Essays, COLLINS on Liberty, CROMBIE on Phil. Necessity, HOBBES' Liberty and Necessity, and Leviathan, PRIESTLEY on Liberty, HARTLEY on Man, and EDWARDS on the Will.

Against the doctrine, see BEATTIE'S Works, Part 2; Replies to Hobbes by

CHAPTER VII.

THE GOVERNMENT OF GOD, CONSIDERED AS A SCHEME OR CONSTITUTION, IMPERFECTLY COMPREHENDED.

THOUGH it be acknowledged, as it cannot but be, that the analogy of nature gives a strong credibility to the general doctrine of religion, and to the several particular things contained in it, considered as so many matters of fact; and likewise that it shows this credibility not to be destroyed by any notions of necessity: still, objections may be insisted upon, against the wisdom, equity, and goodness of the divine government implied in the notion of religion, and against the method by which this government is conducted; to which objections analogy can be no direct answer. For the credibility, or the certain truth, of a matter of fact, does not immediately prove any thing concerning the wisdom or goodness of it; and analogy can do no more, immediately or directly, than show such and such things to be true or credible, considered only as matters of fact. But if, upon supposition of a moral constitution of nature and a moral government over it, analogy suggests and makes it credible, that this government must be a scheme, system, or constitution of government, as distinguished from a number of single unconnected acts of distributive justice and goodness; and likewise, that it must be a scheme, so imperfectly comprehended, and of such a sort in other respects, as to afford a direct general answer to all objections against the justice and goodness of it: then analogy is, remotely, of great service in answering those objections; both by suggesting the answer, and showing it to be a credible one.

Now this, upon inquiry, will be found to be the case. For, *First*, Upon supposition that God exercises a moral government over the world, the analogy of his natural government suggests and makes it credible, that his moral government *must* be a scheme, quite beyond our comprehension: and this affords a

BRAMHALL and LAWSON; Replies to Priestley by PALMER and BRYANT; GROVE on Liberty; CLARKE'S Sermons at the Boyle Lectures; GIBB'S Contemplations; KING'S Origin of Evil; REID on the Mind; WATTS on Liberty; HARRIS' Boyle Lectures; JACKSON'S Defence; BUTTERWORTH on Moral Government.]

general answer to all objections against the justice and goodness of it. *Secondly*, A more distinct observation of some particular things contained in God's scheme of natural government, the like things being supposed, by analogy, to be contained in his moral government, will further show, how little weight is to be laid upon these objections.

I. Upon supposition that God exercises a moral government over the world, the analogy of his natural government suggests and makes it credible, that his moral government must be a scheme, quite beyond our comprehension; and this affords a general answer to all objections against the justice and goodness of it. It is most obvious, analogy renders it highly credible, that, upon supposition of a moral government, it must be a scheme. For the world, and the whole natural government of it, appears to be so: to be a scheme, system, or constitution, whose parts correspond to each other, and to a whole, as really as any work of art, or as any particular model of a civil constitution and government. In this great scheme of the natural world, individuals have various peculiar relations to other individuals of their own species. Whole species are, we find, variously related to other species, upon this earth. Nor do we know, how much further these kinds of relations may extend. And, as there is not any action or natural event, which we are acquainted with, so single and unconnected, as not to have a respect to some other actions and events; so possibly each of them, when it has not an immediate, may yet have a remote, natural relation to other actions and events, much beyond the compass of this present world. There seems indeed nothing, from whence we can so much as make a conjecture, whether all creatures, actions, and events, throughout the whole of nature, have relations to each other But, as it is obvious, that all events have future unknown consequences; so if we trace any event, as far as we can, into what is connected with it, we shall find, that if it were not connected with something further in nature, unknown to us, something both past and present, such event could not possibly have been at all. Nor can we give the whole account of any one thing whatever; of all its causes, ends, and necessary adjuncts; those adjuncts, I mean, without which it could not have been. By this most astonishing connection, these reciprocal correspondences and mutual relations, every thing which we see in the course of nature is actually brought about. Things seemingly the most insignificant imaginable, are perpetually observed to be necessary conditions to other things of the greatest importance; so that any one thing whatever, may for aught we know to the contrary, be a necessary condition to any other.

The natural world then, and natural government of it, being such an incomprehensible scheme; so incomprehensible, that a man must, really in the literal sense, know nothing at all, who is not sensible of his ignorance in it; this immediately suggests, and strongly shows the credibility, that the moral world and government of it may be so too.[a] Indeed the natural and moral constitution and government of the world are so connected, as to make up together but one scheme: and it is highly probable, that the first is formed and carried on merely in subserviency to the latter; as the vegetable world is for the animal, and organized bodies for minds. But the thing intended here is, without inquiring how far the administration of the natural world is subordinate to that of the moral, only to observe the credibility, that one should be analogous or similar to the other: that therefore every act of divine justice and goodness may be supposed to look much beyond itself, and its immediate object; may have some reference to other parts of God's moral administration, and to a general moral plan; and that every circumstance of this his moral government may be adjusted beforehand with a view to the whole of it. For example: the determined length of time, and the degrees and ways, in which virtue is to remain in a state of warfare and discipline, and in which wickedness is permitted to have

[a] [MAIMONIDES makes use of the following similitude. "Suppose one of good understanding, whose mother had died soon after he was born to be brought up on an island, where he saw no human being but his father nor the female of any beast. This person when grown up inquires how men are produced. He is told that they are bred in the womb of one of the same species and that while in the womb we are very small and there move and are nourished. The young man inquires whether when thus in the womb we did not eat, and drink, and breathe, as we do now, and is answered, No. Then he denies it, and offers demonstration that it could not be so. For says he, if either of us cease to breathe our life is gone; and how could we have lived close shut up in a womb for months? So if we cease to eat and drink, we die, and how could the child live so for months? and thus he satisfies himself that it is *impossible* man should come into existence in such a manner."]

its progress; the times appointed for the execution of justice; the appointed instruments of it; the kinds of rewards and punishments, and the manners of their distribution; all particular instances of divine justice and goodness, and every circumstance of them, may have such respects to each other, as to make up altogether a whole, connected and related in all its parts; a scheme or system, which is as properly such, as the natural world is, and of the like kind. Supposing this to be the case, it is most evident, that we are not competent judges of this scheme, from the small parts of it which come within our view in the present life: therefore no objections against any of these parts can be insisted upon by reasonable men.[b]

This our ignorance, and the consequence here drawn from it, are universally acknowledged upon *other* occasions; and though scarce denied, yet are universally forgot, when persons come to argue against religion. And it is not perhaps easy, even for the most reasonable men, always to bear in mind the degree of our ignorance, and make due allowances for it. Upon these accounts, it may not be useless to go a little further, in order to show more distinctly, how just an answer our ignorance is, to objections against the scheme of Providence. Suppose then a person boldly to assert,[c] that the things complained of, the origin and continuance of evil, might easily have been prevented by repeated interpositions;* interpositions so guarded and circumstanced, as would

[b] [Let us imagine a person to be taken to view some great historical painting, before which hangs a thick curtain. The attendant raises the curtain a few inches. Can the spectator, from the unmeaning strip of foreground, derive any conception of the figures yet concealed? Much less is he able to criticize their proportions, or beauty, or perspective, or even the design of the artist? The small fragment of a tree, or flower, or animal, or building, may seem quite unmeaning and even ugly, though the whole would present beauty, fitness, or grandeur. Now the portion of God's dominions within our survey, is as utterly insignificant, compared to the universe, and its interminable duration, as an atom compared to a planet or a man's age to eternity.

The concluding observations of this chapter, abundantly remove every difficulty as to such ignorance being as valid against the *proofs* of religion, as it is against *objections* to it.]

[c] [No truly philosophical mind can be arrogant; because the wider the range of thought, the greater are the discoveries of our ignorance. The young student may well hesitate to decide points, on which the profoundest thinkers take opposite sides, and when conscious of inability intrust himself to the guidance of those whose lives are best.

* Pp. 177, 178.

preclude all mischief arising from them. Or, if this were impracticable, that a *scheme* of government is itself an imperfection, since more good might have been produced, without any scheme, system, or constitution at all, by continued single unrelated acts of distributive justice and goodness; because these would have occasioned no irregularities. Farther than this, it is presumed, the objections will not be carried. Yet the answer is obvious: that were these assertions true, still the observations above, concerning our ignorance in the scheme of divine government and the consequence drawn from it, would hold, in great measure; enough to vindicate religion, against all objections from the disorders of the present state. Were these assertions true, yet the government of the world might be just and good notwithstanding; for, at the most, they would infer nothing more than that it might have been better. But they are mere arbitrary assertions; no man being sufficiently acquainted with the possibilities of things, to bring any proof of them to the lowest degree of probability. For however possible what is asserted may seem, yet many instances may be alleged, in things much less out of our reach, of suppositions absolutely impossible, and reducible to the most palpable self contradictions, which, not every one would perceive to be such; nor perhaps any one, at first sight suspect.

From these things, it is easy to see distinctly, how our ignorance, as it is the common, so it is really a satisfactory answer, to all objections against the justice and goodness of Providence. If a man, contemplating any one providential dispensation, which had no relation to any others, should object, that he discerned in it a disregard to justice, or a deficiency of goodness; nothing would be less an answer to such objection, than our ignorance in other parts of providence, or in the possibilities of things, no way related to what he was contemplating. But when we know not but the part objected against may be relative to other parts unknown to us; and when we are unacquainted with what is, in the nature of the thing, practicable in the case before us; then our ignorance is a satisfactory answer; because, some unknown relation, or some unknown impossibility, may render what is objected against, just and good; nay good in the highest practicable degree.

II. How little weight is to be laid upon such objections, will further appear, by a more distinct observation of some particular things contained in the natural government of God, the like to which may be supposed, from analogy, to be contained in his moral government.

First, As in the scheme of the natural world, no ends appear to be accomplished without means: so we find that means very undesirable, often conduce to bring about ends in such a measure desirable, as greatly to overbalance the disagreeableness of the means. And in cases where such means are conducive to such ends, it is not reason, but *experience,* which shows us, that they are thus conducive. Experience also shows many means to be conducive and necessary to accomplish ends, which means, before experience, we should have thought, would have had even a contrary tendency. From these observations relating to the natural scheme of the world, the moral being supposed analogous to it, arises a great credibility, that the putting our misery in each other's power to the degree it is, and making men liable to vice to the degree we are; and in general, that those things which are objected against the moral scheme of Providence, may be, upon the whole, friendly and assistant to virtue, and productive of an overbalance of happiness: *i.e.* the things objected against may be means, by which an overbalance of good, will in the end, be found produced. And from the same observations, it appears to be no presumption against this, that we do not, if indeed we do not, see those means to have any such tendency, or that they seem to us to have a contrary one. Thus those things, which we call irregularities, may not be so at all; because they may be means of accomplishing wise and good ends more considerable. It may be added, as above, that they may also be the only means, by which these wise and good ends are capable of being accomplished.

It may be proper to add, in order to obviate an absurd and wicked conclusion from any of these observations, that though the constitution of our nature, from whence we are capable of vice and misery, may, as it undoubtedly does, contribute to the perfection and happiness of the world; and though the actual permission of evil may be beneficial to it: (*i.e.* it would have been more mischievous, not that a wicked person had himself abstained from his own wickedness, but that any one had forcibly prevented it, than that it was permitted:) yet notwithstanding, it might have been much better for the world, if this very evil had never been done. Nay it is most clearly conceivable, that the very commission of wickedness may be beneficial to the world, and yet, that it would be infinitely more beneficial for men to refrain from it. For thus, in the wise and good constitution of the natural world, there are disorders which bring their own cures; diseases, which are themselves remedies. Many a man would have died, had it not been for the gout or a fever; yet it would be thought madness to assert, that sickness is a better or more perfect state than health; though the like, with regard to the moral world, has been asserted.

Secondly, The natural government of the world is carried on by general laws. For this there may be wise and good reasons: the wisest and best, for aught we know to the contrary. And that there are such reasons, is suggested to our thoughts by the analogy of nature; by our being made to experience good ends to be accomplished, as indeed all the good which we enjoy is accomplished, by this means,—viz.: that the laws, by which the world is governed, are general. We have scarce any kind of enjoyments, but what we are, in some way or other, instrumental in procuring ourselves, by acting in a manner which we *foresee* likely to procure them: now this foresight could not be at all, were not the government of the world carried on by general laws. And though, for aught we know to the contrary, every single case may be, at length, found to have been provided for even by these: yet to prevent all irregularities, or remedy them as they arise, by the wisest and best general laws, may be impossible in the nature of things; as we see it is absolutely impossible in civil government.

But then we are ready to think, that, the constitution of nature remaining as it is, and the course of things being permitted to go on, in other respects, as it does, there might be interpositions to prevent irregularities; though they could not have been prevented, or remedied by any general laws. There would indeed be reason to wish, which, by-the-way, is very different from a right to claim, that all irregularities were prevented or remedied by present interpositions, if these interpositions would have no other effect than this. But it is plain they would have some visible and immediate *bad* effects: for instance, they would encourage idleness and negligence; and they would render doubtful the natural rule of life, which is ascertained by this very thing, that the course of the world is carried on by general laws. And further, it is certain they would have *distant* effects, and very great ones too; by means of the wonderful connections before mentioned.* So that we cannot so much as guess, what would be the whole result of the interpositions desired. It may be said, any bad result might be prevented by further interpositions, whenever there was occasion for them: but this again is talking quite at random, and in the dark.†

Upon the whole then, we see wise reasons, why the course of the world should be carried on by general laws, and good ends accomplished by this means: and for aught we know, there may be the wisest reasons for it, and the best ends accomplished by it. We have no ground to believe, that all irregularities could be remedied as they arise, or could have been precluded, by general laws. We find that interpositions would produce evil, and prevent good: and, for aught we know, they would produce greater evil than they would prevent; and prevent greater good than they would produce. And if this be the case, then the not interposing is so far from being a ground of complaint, that it is an instance of goodness. This is intelligible and sufficient: and going further, seems beyond the utmost reach of our faculties.

It may be said, that "after all, these supposed impossibilities and relations are what we are unacquainted with; and we must judge of religion, as of other things, by what we do know, and look upon the rest as nothing: or however, that the answers here given to what is objected against religion, may equally be made use of to invalidate the proof of it; since their stress lies so very much upon our ignorance." But,

First, Though total ignorance in any matter does indeed equally destroy, or rather preclude, all proof concerning it, and objections against it; yet partial ignorance does not. For we may in any degree be convinced, that a person is of such a character, and consequently will pursue such ends; though we are greatly ignorant, what is the proper way of acting, in order the most effectually to obtain those ends: and in this case, objections

* P. 173, &c. † P. 175

against his manner of acting, as seemingly not conducive to obtain them, might be answered by our ignorance; though the proof that such ends were intended, might not at all be invalidated by it. Thus, the proof of religion is a proof of the moral character of God, and consequently that his government is moral, and that every one upon the whole shall receive according to his deserts; a proof that this is the designed end of his government. But we are not competent judges, what is the proper way of acting, in order the most effectually to accomplish this end.* Therefore our ignorance is an answer to objections against the conduct of Providence, in permitting irregularities, as seeming contradictory to this end. Now, since it is so obvious, that our ignorance may be a satisfactory answer to objections against a thing, and yet not affect the proof of it; till it can be shown, it is frivolous to assert, that our ignorance invalidates the proof of religion, as it does the objections against it.

Secondly, Suppose unknown impossibilities, and unknown relations, might justly be urged to invalidate the proof of religion, as well as to answer objections against it; and that, in consequence of this, the proof of it were doubtful. Still, let the assertion be despised, or let it be ridiculed, it is undeniably true, that moral obligations would remain certain, though it were not certain what would, upon the whole, be the consequences of observing or violating them. For, these obligations arise, immediately and necessarily, from the judgment of our own mind, unless perverted, which we cannot violate without being self-condemned. And they would be certain too, from considerations of interest. For though it were doubtful, what will be the future consequences of virtue and vice; yet it is, however, credible, that they may have those consequences, which religion teaches us they will: and this credibility is a certain† obligation in point of prudence, to abstain from all wickedness, and to live in the conscientious practice of all that is good.

Thirdly, The answers above given to the objections against religion cannot be made use of to invalidate the proof of it. For, upon suspicion that God exercises a moral government over the world, analogy does most strongly lead us to conclude, that this moral government must be a scheme, or constitution, beyond

* Pp. 72, 73. † P. 68, and Part II. chap. vi.

our comprehension. A thousand particular analogies show us, that parts of such a scheme, from their relation to other parts, may conduce to accomplish ends, which we should have thought they had no tendency to accomplish : nay ends, which before experience, we should have thought such parts were contradictory to, and had a tendency to prevent. Therefore all these analogies show, that the way of arguing made use of in objecting against religion is delusive : because they show it is not at all incredible, that, could we comprehend the whole, we should find the permission of the disorders objected against to be consistent with justice and goodness; and even to be instances of them. Now this is not applicable to the proof of religion, as it is to the objections against it;* and therefore cannot invalidate that proof, as it does these objections.

Lastly, From the observation now made, it is easy to see, that the answers above given to the objections against Providence, though, in a general way of speaking, they may be said to be taken from our ignorance; yet are by no means taken merely from that, but from something which analogy shows us concerning it. For analogy shows us positively, that our ignorance in the possibilities of things, and the various relations in nature, renders us incompetent judges, and leads us to false conclusions, in cases similar to this, in which we pretend to judge and to object. So that the things above insisted upon are not mere suppositions of unknown impossibilities and relations : but they are suggested to our thoughts, and even forced upon the observation of serious men, and rendered credible too, by the analogy of nature. Therefore to take these things into the account, is to judge by experience and what we do know : and it is not judging so, to take no notice of them.

CONCLUSION

THE observations of the last chapter lead us to consider this little scene of human life, in which we are so busily engaged, as having a reference, of some sort or other, to a much larger plan of things. Whether we are, any way, related to the more dis-

* Serm. at the *Rolls*, p. 312, 2d ed.

tant parts of the boundless universe, into which we are brought, is altogether uncertain. But it is evident, that the course of things, which comes within our view, is connected with some things, past, present, and future, beyond it.* So that we are placed, as one may speak, in the middle of a scheme, not fixed but progressive, every way incomprehensible: incomprehensible, in a manner equally, with respect to what has been, what now is, and what shall be. This scheme cannot but contain in it some things as wonderful, and as much beyond our thought and conception,† as any thing in that of religion. For, will any man in his senses say, that it is less difficult to conceive, how the world came to be and to continue as it is, without, than with, an intelligent Author and Governor of it? Or, admitting an intelligent Governor of it, that there is some other rule of government more natural, and of easier conception, than that which we call moral? Indeed, without an intelligent Author and Governor of nature, no account at all can be given, how this universe, or the part of it particularly in which we are concerned, came to be, and the course of it to be carried on, as it is: nor any, of its general end and design, without a moral governor of it. That there is an intelligent Author of nature, and natural Governor of the world, is a principle gone upon in the foregoing treatise; as proved, and generally known, and confessed to be proved. And the very notion of an intelligent Author of nature, proved by particular final causes, implies a will and a character.‡

Now, as our whole nature, the nature which he has given us, leads us to conclude his will and character to be moral, just, and good: so we can scarce in imagination conceive, what it can be otherwise. However, in consequence of this his will and character, whatever it be, he formed the universe as it is, and carries on the course of it as he does, rather than in any other manner; and has assigned to us, and to all living creatures, a part and a lot in it. Irrational creatures act this their part, and enjoy and undergo the pleasures and the pains allotted them, without any reflection. But one would think it impossible, that creatures endued with reason could avoid reflecting sometimes upon all this; reflecting, if not from whence we came, yet, at least, whither we are going; and what the mysterious scheme, in the

* P. 172, &c. † See Part II. ch. ii. ‡ P. 173.

midst of which we find ourselves, will, at length, come out and produce: a scheme in which it is certain we are highly interested, and in which we may be interested even beyond conception.[d]

For many things prove it palpably absurd to conclude, that we shall cease to be, at death. Particular analogies do most sensibly show us, that there is nothing to be thought strange, in our being to exist in another state of life. And that we are now living beings, affords a strong probability that we shall *continue* so; unless there be some positive ground, and there is none from reason or analogy, to think death will destroy us. Were a persuasion of this kind ever so well grounded, there would, surely, be little reason to take pleasure in it. Indeed it can have no other ground, than some such imagination, as that of our gross bodies being ourselves; which is contrary to experience. Experience too most clearly shows us the folly of concluding, from the body and the living agent affecting each other mutually, that the dissolution of the former is the destruction of the latter. And there are remarkable instances of their *not* affecting each other, which lead us to a contrary conclusion. The supposition, then, which in all reason we are to go upon, is, that our living nature will *continue* after death. And it is infinitely unreasonable to form an institution of life, or to act, upon any other supposition.

All expectation of immortality, whether more or less certain, opens an unbounded prospect to our hopes and our fears: since we see the constitution of nature is such, as to admit of misery, as well as to be productive of happiness, and experience ourselves to partake of both in some degree; and since we cannot but know, what higher degrees of both we are capable of. And there is no presumption against believing further, that our future interest depends upon our present behavior: for we see our present interest doth; and that the happiness and misery, which are naturally annexed to our actions, very frequently do not follow, till long after the actions are done, to which they are respectively annexed. So that were speculation to leave us uncertain, whether it were likely, that the Author of nature, in giving happiness and misery to his creatures, hath regard to their actions or not yet, since we find by experience that he hath such regard, the

[d] [The remainder of this chapter is a recapitulation of the whole argument from the beginning; and should be carefully conned.]

whole sense of things which he has given us, plainly leads us, at once and without any elaborate inquiries, to think that it may, indeed must, be to good actions chiefly that he hath annexed happiness, and to bad actions misery; or that he will, upon the whole, reward those who do well, and punish those who do evil.

To confirm this from the constitution of the world, it has been observed, that some sort of moral government is necessarily implied in that natural government of God, which we experience ourselves under; that good and bad actions, at present, are naturally rewarded and punished, not only as beneficial and mischievous to society, but also as virtuous and vicious: and that there is, in the very nature of the thing, a tendency to their being rewarded and punished in a much higher degree than they are at present. And though this higher degree of distributive justice, which nature thus points out and leads towards, is prevented for a time from taking place; it is by obstacles, which the state of this world unhappily throws in its way, and which therefore are in their nature temporary. Now, as these things in the natural conduct of Providence are observable on the side of virtue; so there is nothing to be set against them on the side of vice. A moral scheme of government then is visibly established, and, in some degree, carried into execution: and this, together with the essential tendencies of virtue and vice duly considered, naturally raise in us an apprehension, that it will be carried on further towards perfection in a future state, and that every one shall there receive according to his deserts.

And if this be so, then our future and general interest, under the moral government of God, is appointed to depend upon our behavior; notwithstanding the difficulty, which this may occasion, of securing it, and the danger of losing it: just in the same manner as our temporal interest, under his natural government, is appointed to depend upon our behavior; notwithstanding the like difficulty and danger. For, from our original constitution, and that of the world which we inhabit, we are naturally trusted with ourselves; with our own conduct and our own interest. And from the same constitution of nature, especially joined with that course of things which is owing to men, we have temptations to be unfaithful in this trust; to forfeit this interest, to neglect it, and run ourselves into misery and ruin. From these temptations arise the difficulties of behaving so as to secure our temporal interest, and the hazard of behaving so as to miscarry in it. There is therefore nothing incredible in supposing there may be the like difficulty and hazard with regard to that chief and final good, which religion lays before us.

The whole account, how it came to pass that we were placed in such a condition as this, must indeed be beyond our comprehension. But it is in part accounted for by what religion teaches us, that the character of virtue and piety must be a necessary qualification for a future state of security and happiness, under the moral government of God; in like manner, as some certain qualifications or other are necessary for every particular condition of life, under his natural government: and that the present state was intended to be a school of discipline, for improving in ourselves that character. Now this intention of nature is rendered highly credible by observing; that we are plainly made for improvement of all kinds; that it is a general appointment of Providence, that we cultivate practical principles, and form within ourselves habits of action, in order to become fit for what we were wholly unfit for before; that in particular, childhood and youth is naturally appointed to be a state of discipline for mature age; and that the present world is peculiarly fitted for a state of moral discipline. And, whereas objections are urged against the whole notion of moral government and a probationary state, from the opinion of necessity; it has been shown, that God has given us the evidence, as it were, of experience, that all objections against religion, on this head, are vain and delusive. He has also, in his natural government, suggested an answer to all our short-sighted objections, against the equity and goodness of his moral government; and in general he has exemplified to us the latter by the former.

These things, which it is to be remembered, are matters of fact, ought, in all common sense, to awaken mankind; to induce them to consider in earnest their condition, and what they have to do. It is absurd, absurd to the degree of being ridiculous, if the subject were not of so serious a kind, for men to think themselves secure in a vicious life; or even in that immoral thoughtlessness, into which far the greatest part of them are fallen. The credibility of religion, arising from experience and facts here considered, is fully sufficient, in reason, to engage them to live in the general practice of all virtue and piety; under the serious apprehension, though it should be mixed with some doubt,* of a righteous administration established in nature, and a future judgment in consequence of it: especially when we consider, how very questionable it is, whether any thing at all can be gained by vice,† how unquestionably little as well as precarious, the pleasures and profits of it are at the best, and how soon they must be parted with at the longest. For, in the deliberations of reason, concerning what we are to pursue and what to avoid, as temptations to any thing from mere passion are supposed out of the case, so inducements to vice, from cool expectations of pleasure and interest so small and uncertain and short, are really so insignificant, as, in the view of reason to be almost nothing in *themselves;* and in comparison with the importance of religion they quite disappear and are lost.

Mere passion may indeed be alleged, though not as a reason, yet as an excuse, for a vicious course of life. And how sorry an excuse it is, will be manifest by observing, that we are placed in a condition in which we are unavoidably inured to govern our passions, by being necessitated to govern them: and to lay ourselves under the same kind of restraints, and as great ones too, from temporal regards, as virtue and piety, in the ordinary course of things, require. The plea of ungovernable passion then, on the side of vice, is the poorest of all things; for it is no reason, and a poor excuse. The proper *motives* to religion are the proper *proofs* of it, from our moral nature, from the presages of conscience, and our natural apprehension of God under the character of a righteous Governor and Judge: a nature, and conscience, and apprehension, given us by him; and from the confirmation of the dictates of reason, by *life and immortality brought to light by the Gospel; and the wrath of God revealed from heaven against all ungodliness and unrighteousness of men.*

* Part II. ch. vi.

† P. 108.

END OF THE FIRST PART.

PART II.

Revealed Religion.

CHAPTER I.

THE IMPORTANCE OF CHRISTIANITY.[a]

SOME persons, upon pretence of the sufficiency of the light of nature, avowedly reject all revelation, as in its very notion incredible, and what must be fictitious. And indeed it is certain, no revelation would have been given, had the light of nature been sufficient in such a sense, as to render one not wanted and useless. But no man, in seriousness and simplicity of mind, can possibly think it so, who considers the state of religion in the heathen world before revelation, and its present state in those places which have borrowed no light from it: particularly the doubtfulness of some of the greatest men, concerning things of the utmost importance, as well as the natural inattention and ignorance of mankind in general. It is impossible to say, who would have been able to have reasoned out that whole system, which we call Natural Religion, in its genuine simplicity, clear

[a] [There is a slight indication in this chapter that Butler falls into the old plan of settling the necessity of Christianity, before determining its truth. Paley discards this order of arrangement, in his very first sentence; and with good reason. The necessity of revelation is an abstraction; the proofs of it are patent facts. To hold in abeyance the credentials presented by Christianity, till we first satisfy ourselves that God could or would make any such announcements, is unphilosophical and irreverent. This chapter discusses the *importance* rather than the necessity of revelation; and so is a fitting commencement of the discussion. Every truth disclosed in revelation, over and above the truths which natural religion furnishes, proves the *necessity* of revelation, if we would know any thing of *such* truths. And it is such truths which constitute the very peculiarities of revelation, and teach the *way of salvation*, for the sinful and helpless.]

of superstition: but there is certainly no ground to affirm that the generality could. If they could, there is no sort of probability that they would. Admitting there were, they would highly want a standing admonition to remind them of it, and inculcate it upon them.

And further, were they as much disposed to attend to religion, as the better sort of men are; yet even upon this supposition, there would be various occasions for supernatural instruction and assistance, and the greatest advantages might be afforded by them.[b] So that to say revelation is a thing superfluous, what there was no need of, and what can be of no service, is, I think, to talk quite wildly and at random. Nor would it be more extravagant to affirm, that mankind is so entirely at ease in the present state, and life so completely happy, that it is a contradiction to suppose our condition capable of being, in any respect, better.

There are other persons, not to be ranked with these, who seem to be getting into a way of neglecting, and as it were, overlooking revelation, as of small importance provided natural religion be kept to. With little regard either to the evidence of the former, or to the objections against it, and even upon supposition of its truth; "the only design of it," say they, "must be, to establish a belief of the moral system of nature, and to enforce the practice of natural piety and virtue. The belief and practice of these were, perhaps, much promoted by the first publication of Christianity: but whether they are believed and practised, upon the evidence and motives of nature or of revelation, is no great matter."* This way of considering revelation, though

[b] [No one can read the writings of the great sages of antiquity without a full and sad conviction that in relation to the character of God, the sinfulness of man, the future state, and the rules of living, those prime points on which we need knowledge, they were almost profoundly ignorant. See on this point, LELAND's Adv. and Necess.: CHALMERS' Nat. Theol.: McCOSH's Div. Gov.: PASCAL's Thoughts: WARBURTON's Div. Legation.]

* Invenis multos———propterea nolle fieri Christianos, quia quasi sufficiunt sibi de bona vita sua. Bene vivere opus est, ait. Quid mihi præcepturus est Christus? Ut bene vivam? Jam bene vivo. Quid mihi necessarius est Christus; nullum homicidium, nullum furtum, nullam rapinam facio, res alienas non concupisco, nullo adulterio contaminor? Nam inveniatur in vita mea aliquid quod reprehendatur, et qui reprehenderit faciat Christianum. *Aug in Psal* xxxi. [You find many who refuse to become Christians, because they feel sufficient of themselves to lead a good life. "We ought to live well.

it is not the same with the former, yet borders nearly upon it, and very much, at length runs up into it: and requires to be particularly considered, with regard to the persons who seem to be getting into this way. The consideration of it will likewise further show the extravagance of the former opinion, and the truth of the observations in answer to it, just mentioned. And an inquiry into the importance of Christianity, cannot be an improper introduction to a treatise concerning the credibility of it.

Now, if God has given a revelation to mankind, and commanded those things which are commanded in Christianity; it is evident, at first sight, that it cannot in any wise be an indifferent matter, whether we obey or disobey those commands: unless we are certainly assured, that we know all the reasons for them, and that all those reasons are now ceased, with regard to mankind in general, or to ourselves in particular. It is absolutely impossible we can be assured of this.[c] For our ignorance of these reasons proves nothing in the case: since the whole analogy of nature shows, what is indeed in itself evident, that there may be infinite reasons for things, with which we are not acquainted.

But the importance of Christianity will more distinctly appear, by considering it more distinctly: *First*, as a republication, and external institution, of natural or essential religion, adapted to the present circumstances of mankind, and intended to promote natural piety and virtue: *Secondly*, as containing an account of a dispensation of things, not discoverable by reason, in consequence of which several distinct precepts are enjoined us. For though natural religion is the foundation and principal part of Christianity, it is not in any sense the whole of it.

I. Christianity is a republication of Natural religion. It instructs mankind in the moral system of the world: that it is the work of an infinitely perfect Being, and under his government, that virtue is his law, and that he will finally judge mankind in

says one. "What will Christ teach me? To live well? I do live well, what need then have I of Christ? I commit no murder, no theft, no robbery. I covet no man's goods, and am polluted by no adultery. Let some one find in me any thing to censure, and he who can do so, may make me a Christian."]

[c] [The true mode of distinguishing a temporary, local, or individual command from such as are of universal and perpetual obligation, is well laid down by WAYLAND, *M r. Sci.* ch. ix. sec. 2.]

righteousness, and render to all according to their works, in a future state. And, which is very material, it teaches natural religion in its genuine simplicity; free from those superstitions, with which it was totally corrupted, and under which it was in a manner lost.

Revelation is, further, an *authoritative* publication of natural religion, and so affords the evidence of testimony for the truth of it. Indeed the miracles and prophecies recorded in Scripture, were intended to prove a particular dispensation of Providence, *i.e.* the redemption of the world by the Messiah: but this does not hinder, but that they may also prove God's general providence over the world, as our moral governor and judge. And they evidently do prove it; because this character of the Author of nature, is necessarily connected with and implied in that particular revealed dispensation of things: it is likewise continually taught expressly, and insisted upon, by those persons who wrought the miracles and delivered the prophecies. So that indeed natural religion seems as much proved by the Scripture revelation, as it would have been, had the design of revelation been nothing else than to prove it.

But it may possibly be disputed, how far miracles can prove natural religion; and notable objections may be urged against this proof of it, considered as a matter of speculation: but considered as a practical thing, there can be none. For suppose a person to teach natural religion to a nation, who had lived in total ignorance or forgetfulness of it; and to declare that he was commissioned by God so to do; suppose him, in proof of his commission, to foretell things future, which no human foresight could have guessed at; to divide the sea with a word; feed great multitudes with bread from heaven; cure all manner of diseases; and raise the dead, even himself, to life; would not this give additional credibility to his teaching, a credibility beyond what that of a common man would have; and be an authoritative publication of the law of nature, *i.e.* a new proof of it? It would be a practical one, of the strongest kind, perhaps, which human creatures are capable of having given them. The Law of Moses then, and the Gospel of Christ, are authoritative publications of the religion of nature; they afford a proof of God's general providence, as moral Governor of the world, as well as of his particular dispensations of providence towards sinful creatures, revealed in the Law and the Gospel. As they are the only evidence of the latter, so they are an additional evidence of the former.

To show this further, let us suppose a man of the greatest and most improved capacity, who had never heard of revelation, convinced upon the whole, notwithstanding the disorders of the world, that it was under the direction and moral government of an infinitely perfect Being; but ready to question, whether he were not got beyond the reach of his faculties: suppose him brought, by this suspicion, into great danger of being carried away by the universal bad example of almost every one around him, who appeared to have no sense, no practical sense at least, of these things: and this, perhaps, would be as advantageous a situation with regard to religion, as nature alone ever placed any man in. What a confirmation now must it be to such a person, all at once, to find, that this moral system of things was revealed to mankind, in the name of that infinite Being, whom he had from principles of reason believed in: and that the publishers of the revelation proved their commission from him, by making it appear, that he had intrusted them with a power of suspending and changing the general laws of nature.

Nor must it by any means be omitted, for it is a thing of the utmost importance, that life and immortality are eminently brought to light by the Gospel. The great doctrines of a future state, the danger of a course of wickedness[d] and the efficacy of repentance, are not only confirmed in the Gospel, but are taught, especially the last is, with a degree of light, to which that of nature is but darkness.

Further. As Christianity served these ends and purposes, when it was first published, by the miraculous publication itself, so it was intended to serve the same purposes in future ages, by means of the settlement of a visible church:[e] of a society, dis-

[d] [Natural religion shows us the danger of sin; but not the infinite danger of eternal retribution, and the hopelessness of restoration after death. And as to the efficacy of repentance, it rather opposes that doctrine than teaches it. At least it does not teach that repentance may be accepted, so as not only to cancel guilt, but restore to the favor of God.]

[e] [" Christianity was left with Christians, to be transmitted, in like manner as the religion of nature had been left, with mankind in general. There was

tinguished from common ones, and from the rest of the world, by peculiar religious institutions; by an instituted method of instruction, and an instituted form of external religion. Miraculous powers were given to the first preachers of Christianity, in order to their introducing it into the world: a visible church was established, in order to continue it, and carry it on successively throughout all ages. Had only Moses and the prophets, Christ and his apostles, taught, and by miracles proved, religion to their contemporaries; the benefits of their instructions would have reached but a small part of mankind. Christianity must have been, in a great degree, sunk and forgot in a very few ages. To prevent this, appears to have been one reason why a visible church was instituted; to be like a city upon a hill, a standing memorial to the world of the duty which we owe our Maker: to call men continually, both by example and instruction, to attend to it, and, by the form of religion, ever before their eyes, remind them of the reality; to be the repository of the oracles of God; to hold up the light of revelation in aid to that of nature, and to propagate it, throughout all generations, to the end of the world—the light of revelation, considered here in no other view, than as designed to enforce natural religion. And in proportion as Christianity is professed and taught in the world, religion, natural or essential religion, is thus distinctly and advantageously laid before mankind, and brought again and again to their thoughts, as a matter of infinite importance.

A visible church has also a further tendency to promote natural religion, as being an instituted method of education, originally intended to be of peculiar advantage to those who conform to it. For one end of the institution was, that, by admonition and reproof, as well as instruction, by a general regular discipline, and public exercises of religion, *the body of Christ*, as the Scripture speaks, should be *edified; i.e.* trained up in piety and virtue for a higher and better state. This settlement, then, appearing thus

however this difference that by an institution of external religion with a standing ministry for instruction and discipline, it pleased God to unite Christians into *visible churches*, and all along to preserve them over a great part of the world, and thus perpetuate a general publication of the Gospel." BUTLER'S sermon before the Soc. for Prop. the Gospel. He goes on to show, in that discourse, that these churches, however corrupt any may become, are repositories for the written oracles of God, and so carry the antidote to their heresies.]

beneficial, tending in the nature of the thing to answer, and, in some degree, actually answering, those ends, it is to be remembered, that the very notion of it implies positive institutions; for the visibility of the church consists in them. Take away every thing of this kind, and you lose the very notion itself. So that if the things now mentioned are advantages, the reason and importance of positive institutions in general is most obvious; since without them these advantages could not be secured to the world. And it is mere idle wantonness, to insist upon knowing the reasons, *why* such particular ones were fixed upon rather than others.

The benefit arising from this supernatural assistance, which Christianity affords to natural religion, is what some persons are very slow in apprehending. And yet it is a thing distinct in itself, and a very plain obvious one. For will any in good earnest really say, that the bulk of mankind in the heathen world were in as advantageous a situation, with regard to natural religion, as they are now among us: that it was laid before them, and enforced upon them, in a manner as distinct, and as much tending to influence their practice?

The objections against all this, from the perversion of Christianity, and from the supposition of its having had but little good influence, however innocently they may be proposed, cannot be insisted upon as conclusive, upon any principles, but such as lead to downright Atheism; because the manifestation of the law of nature by reason, which, upon all principles of Theism, must have been from God, has been perverted and rendered ineffectual in the same manner. It may indeed, I think, truly be said, that the good effects of Christianity have not been small; nor its supposed ill effects, any effects at all of it, properly speaking. Perhaps, too, the things done have been aggravated; and if not, Christianity hath been often only a pretence, and the same evils in the main would have been done upon some other pretence. However, great and shocking as the corruptions and abuses of it have really been, they cannot be insisted upon as arguments against it, upon principles of Theism. For one cannot proceed one step in reasoning upon natural religion, any more than upon Christianity, without laying it down as a first principle, that the dispensations of Providence are not to be judged of by their per versions, but by their genuine tendencies: not by what they do actually seem to effect, but by what they would effect if mankind did their part; that part which is justly put and left upon them. It is altogether as much the language of one as of the other: *He that is unjust, let him be unjust still: and he that is holy, let him be holy still.** The light of reason does not, any more than that of revelation, force men to submit to its authority; both admonish them of what they ought to do and avoid, together with the consequences of each; and after this, leave them at full liberty to act just as they please, till the appointed time of judgment. Every moment's experience shows, that this is God's general rule of government.[f]

To return then: Christianity being a promulgation of the law of nature; being moreover an authoritative promulgation of it; with new light, and other circumstances of peculiar advantage, adapted to the wants of mankind; these things fully show its importance.

It is to be observed further, that as the nature of the case requires, so all Christians are commanded to contribute, by their profession of Christianity, to preserve it in the world, and render it such a promulgation and enforcement of religion. For it is the very scheme of the Gospel, that each Christian should, in his degree, contribute towards continuing and carrying it on: all by uniting in the public profession and external practice of Christianity; some by instructing, by having the oversight and taking care of this religious community, the church of God. Now this further shows the importance of Christianity; and, which is what I chiefly intend, its importance in a practical sense: or the high obligations we are under, to take it into our most serious consideration; and the danger there must necessarily be, not only in treating

* Rev. xxii. 11.

[f] ["It is no real objection to this, though it may seem so at first sight, to say that since Christianity is a *remedial* system, designed to obviate those very evils which have been produced by the neglect and abuse of the light of nature, it ought not to be *liable* to the same perversions. Because—1. Christianity is not designed primarily to remedy the defects of *nature*, but of an unnatural state of ruin into which men were brought by *the Fall.* And 2. It is remedial of the defects of nature in a *great degree*, by its giving additional advantages. 3. It might be impossible that it should be remedial in a greater degree than it is, without destroying man's free agency; which would be to destroy its own end, the practice of virtue."—FITZGERALD'S Notes.]

it despitefully, which I am not now speaking of, but in disregarding and neglecting it. For this is neglecting to do what is expressly enjoined us, for continuing those benefits to the world, and transmitting them down to future times. And all this holds, even though the only thing to be considered in Christianity were its subserviency to natural religion.

II. Christianity is to be considered in a further view; as containing an account of a dispensation of things, not at all discoverable by reason, in consequence of which several distinct precepts are enjoined us. Christianity is not only an external institution of natural religion, and a new promulgation of God's general providence, as righteous governor and judge of the world; but it contains also a revelation of a particular dispensation of Providence, carrying on by his Son and Spirit, for the recovery and salvation of mankind, who are represented in Scripture to be in a state of ruin. And in consequence of this revelation being made, we are commanded *to be baptized*, not only *in the name of the Father*, but also, *of the Son, and of the Holy Ghost:* and other obligations of duty, unknown before, to the Son and the Holy Ghost, are revealed. Now the importance of these duties may be judged of, by observing that they arise, not from positive command merely, but also from the offices which appear, from. Scripture, to belong to those divine persons in the Gospel dispensation; or from the relations, which we are there informed, they stand in to us. By *reason* is revealed the relation, which God the Father stands in to us. Hence arises the obligation of duty which we are under to him. In *Scripture* are revealed the relations, which the Son and Holy Spirit stand in to us. Hence arise the obligations of duty,[g] which we are under to them. The truth of the case, as one may speak, in each of these three respects being admitted: that God is the governor of the world, upon the evidence of reason; that Christ is the mediator between God and man, and the Holy Ghost our guide and sanctifier, upon the evidence of revelation: the truth of the

[g] [CHALMERS (Nat. Theol., b. v. ch. iv.) makes this very plain. He shows the *ethics* of natural religion to be one thing and its *objects* another. Natural religion discloses no Redeemer or Sanctifier; but it teaches how we should regard such a person, if there be one. It teaches love and conformity to such a being by the *relation* in which we of course stand to him. How we are to *express* that love and obedience it cannot teach.]

case, I say, in each of these respects being admitted, it is no more a question, why it should be commanded, that we be baptized in the name of the Son and of the Holy Ghost, than that we be baptized in the name of the Father. This matter seems to require to be more fully stated.*

Let it be remembered then, that religion comes under the twofold consideration of internal and external: for the latter is as real a part of religion, of true religion, as the former. Now, when religion is considered under the first notion, as an inward principle, to be exerted in such and such inward acts of the mind and heart, the essence of natural religion may be said to consist in religious regards to *God the Father Almighty:* and the essence of revealed religion, as distinguished from natural, to consist in religious regards to *the Son*, and to *the Holy Ghost.* The obligation we are under, of paying these religious regards to each of these divine persons respectively, arises from the respective relations which they each stand in to us. How these relations are made known, whether by reason or revelation, makes no alteration in the case: because the duties arise out of the relations themselves, not out of the manner in which we are informed of them. The Son and Spirit have each his proper office in that great dispensation of Providence, the redemption of the world; the one our Mediator, the other our Sanctifier. Does not then the duty of religious regards to both these divine persons, as immediately arise to the view of reason, out of the very nature of these offices and relations; as the good-will and kind intention, which we owe to our fellow-creatures, arise out of the common relations between us and them? But it will be asked, "What are the inward religious regards, appearing thus obviously due to the Son and Holy Spirit; as arising, not merely from command in Scripture, but from the very nature of the revealed relations, which they stand in to us?" I answer, the religious regards of reverence, honor, love, trust, gratitude, fear, hope.

In what external manner this inward worship is to be expressed, is a matter of pure revealed command, as perhaps the external manner, in which God the Father is to be worshipped, may be more so than we are ready to think. But the worship,

* See The Nature, Obligation, and Efficacy, of the Christian Sacraments, &c., [by WATERLAND,] and COLLIBER of Revealed Religion, as there quoted.

the internal worship itself, to the Son and Holy Ghost, is no further matter of pure revealed command, than as the relations they stand in to us are matter of pure revelation: for the relations being known, the obligations to such internal worship are obligations of reason, arising out of those relations themselves. In short, the history of the gospel as immediately shows us the reason of these obligations, as it shows us the meaning of the words, Son and Holy Ghost.

If this account of the Christian religion be just, those persons who can speak lightly of it, as of little consequence, provided natural religion be kept to, plainly forget, that Christianity, even what is peculiarly so called, as distinguished from natural religion, has yet somewhat very important, even of a moral nature. For the office of our Lord being made known, and the relation he stands in to us, the obligation of religious regards to him is plainly moral, as much as charity to mankind is; since this obligation arises, before external command, immediately out of that his office and relation itself. Those persons appear to forget, that revelation is to be considered, as informing us of somewhat new, in the state of mankind,[h] and in the government of the world: as acquainting us with some relations we stand in, which could not otherwise have been known. These relations being real (though before revelation we could be under no obligations from them, yet upon their being revealed), there is no reason to think, but that neglect of behaving suitably to them will be attended with the same kind of consequences under God's government, as neglecting to behave suitably to any other relations, made known to us by reason. Ignorance, whether unavoidable or voluntary, so far as we can possibly see, will just as much, and just as little, excuse in one case as in the other: the ignorance being supposed equally unavoidable, or equally voluntary, in both cases.

If therefore Christ be indeed the mediator between God and man, *i.e.* if Christianity be true; if he be indeed our Lord, our Savior, and our God, no one can say, what may follow, not only

[h] [If Christianity were but "a republication of natural religion," or as Tindall says, "as old as creation," why do deists oppose it? It does indeed republish natural religion, but it adds stupendous truths beside. If it gave us no new light, no new motives, it would be but a tremendous curse, making us all the more responsible, and none the more instructed or secure.]

the obstinate, but the careless disregard to him, in those high relations. Nay, no one can say, what may follow such disregard, even in the way of natural consequence.* For, as the natural consequences of vice in this life are doubtless to be considered as judicial punishments inflicted by God, so for aught we know, the judicial punishments of the future life may be, in a like way or a like sense, the natural consequence of vice:† of men's violating or disregarding the relations which God has placed them in here, and made known to them.

If mankind are corrupted and depraved in their moral character, and so are unfit for that state, which Christ is gone to prepare for his disciples; and if the assistance of God's Spirit be necessary to renew their nature, in the degree requisite to their being qualified for that state; (all which is implied in the express, though figurative declaration, *Except a man be born of the Spirit, he cannot enter into the kingdom of God:*‡) supposing this, is it possible any serious person can think it a slight matter, whether or no he makes use of the means, expressly commanded by God, for obtaining this divine assistance? Especially since the whole analogy of nature shows, that we are not to expect any benefits, without making use of the appointed means for obtaining or enjoying them. Now reason shows us nothing, of the particular immediate means of obtaining either temporal or spiritual benefits. This therefore we must learn, either from experience or revelation. And experience, the present case does not admit of.

The conclusion from all this evidently is, that Christianity being supposed either true or credible, it is unspeakable irreverence, and really the most presumptuous rashness, to treat it as a light matter. It can never justly be esteemed of little consequence, till it be positively supposed false. Nor do I know a higher and more important obligation which we are under, than that of examining most seriously into its evidence, supposing its credibility; and of embracing it, upon supposition of its truth.

The two following deductions may be proper to be added, in order to illustrate the foregoing observations, and to prevent their being mistaken.

* P. 94. † Ch. v. ‡ John iii. 5.

First, Hence we may clearly see, where lies the distinction between what is positive and what is moral in religion. Moral *precepts,* are precepts the reasons of which we see: positive *precepts,* are precepts the reasons of which we do not see.* Moral *duties* arise out of the nature of the case itself, prior to external command. Positive *duties* do not arise out of the nature of the case, but from external command; nor would they be duties at all, were it not for such command, received from Him whose creatures and subjects we are. But the manner in which the nature of the case or the fact of the relation, is made known, this doth not denominate any duty either positive or moral. That we be baptized in the name of the Father is as much a positive duty, as that we be baptized in the name of the Son, because both arise equally from revealed command: though the relation which we stand in to God the Father is made known to us by reason, and the relation we stand in to Christ, by revelation only. On the other hand, the dispensation of the Gospel being admitted, gratitude as immediately becomes due to Christ, from his being the voluntary minister of this dispensation, as it is due to God the Father, from his being the fountain of all good; though the first is made known to us by revelation only, the second by reason. Hence also we may see, and, for distinctness' sake, it may be worth mentioning, that positive institutions come under a twofold consideration. They are either institutions founded on natural religion, as baptism in the name of the Father; (though this has also a particular reference to the gospel dispensation, for it is in the name of God, as the Father of our Lord Jesus Christ:) or they are external institutions founded on revealed religion; as baptism in the name of the Son, and of the Holy Ghost.

Secondly, From the distinction between what is moral and what is positive in religion, appears the ground of that peculiar preference, which the Scripture teaches us to be due to the former.

The reason of positive institutions in general, is very obvious;

* This is the distinction between moral and positive precepts considered respectively as such. But yet, since the latter have somewhat of a moral nature, we may see the reason of them, considered in this view. Moral and positive precepts are in some respects alike, in other respects different. So far as they are alike, we discern the reasons of both; so far as they are different, we discern the reasons of the former, but not of the latter. See p. 189, &c.

though we should not see the reason, why particular ones are pitched upon rather than others. Whoever, therefore, instead of cavilling at words, will attend to the thing itself, may clearly see, that positive institutions in general, as distinguished from this or that particular one, have the nature of moral commands; since the reasons of them appear. Thus, for instance, the *external* worship of God is a moral duty, though no particular mode of it be so. Care then is to be taken, when a comparison is made between positive and moral duties, that they be compared no further than as they are different; no further than as the former are positive, or arise out of mere external command, the reasons of which we are not acquainted with; and as the latter are moral, or arise out of the apparent reason of the case, without such external command. Unless this caution be observed, we shall run into endless confusion.

Now this being premised, suppose two standing precepts enjoined by the same authority; that, in certain conjunctures, it is impossible to obey both; that the former is moral, *i.e.* a precept of which we see the reasons, and that they hold in the particular case before us; but that the latter is positive, *i.e.* a precept of which we do not see the reasons: it is indisputable that our obligations are to obey the former; because there is an apparent reason for this preference, and none against it. Further, positive institutions, all those I suppose which Christianity enjoins, are means to a moral end: and the end must be acknowledged more excellent than the means.[1] Nor is observance of these institutions any religious obedience at all, or of any value, otherwise than as it proceeds from a moral principle. This seems to be the strict logical way of stating and determining this matter; but will, perhaps, be found less applicable to practice, than may be thought at first sight.

Therefore, in a more practical, though more lax way of con-

[1] [Without offering the least objection to what is here said of the comparative value of moral and positive institutions, it should not be overlooked that sometimes, obedience to a positive rite is more indicative of an obedient spirit, than obedience to a moral rule. The latter is urged by its intrinsic propriety, over and above the command, and appeals to several of our finer impulses. The former rests singly on our reverence for the will of God. There are many who would repel a temptation to steal, or to lie, who yet are insensible to the duty of baptism or the Lord's supper.]

sideration, and taking the words, *moral law* and *positive institutions*, in the popular sense, I add, that the whole moral law is as much matter of revealed command, as positive institutions are: for the Scripture enjoins every moral virtue. In this respect then they are both upon a level. But the moral law is, moreover, written upon our hearts; interwoven into our very nature. And this is a plain intimation of the Author of it, which is to be preferred, when they interfere.

But there is not altogether so much necessity for the determination of this question, as some persons seem to think. Nor are we left to reason alone to determine it. For, *First*, Though mankind have, in all ages, been greatly prone to place their religion in peculiar positive rites, by way of equivalent for obedience to moral precepts; yet, without making any comparison at all between them, and consequently without determining which is to have the preference, the nature of the thing abundantly shows all notions of that kind to be utterly subversive of true religion, as they are, moreover, contrary to the whole general tenor of Scripture; and likewise to the most express particular declarations of it, that nothing can render us accepted of God, without moral virtue.

Secondly, Upon the occasion of mentioning together positive and moral duties, the Scripture always puts the stress of religion upon the latter, and never upon the former. This, though no sort of allowance to neglect the former, when they do not interfere with the latter, is yet a plain intimation, that when they do, the latter are to be preferred. And as mankind are for placing the stress of their religion anywhere, rather than upon virtue; lest both the reason of the thing, and the general spirit of Christianity, appearing in the intimation now mentioned, should be ineffectual against this prevalent folly, our Lord himself, from whose command alone the obligation of positive institutions arises, has taken occasion to make the comparison between them and moral precepts; when the Pharisees censured him, for *eating with publicans and sinners;* and also when they censured his disciples, for *plucking the ears of corn on the Sabbath day.* Upon this comparison, he has determined expressly, and in form, which shall have the preference when they interfere. And by delivering his authoritative determination in a proverbial manner of expression, he has made it general: *I will have mercy, and not sacrifice.** The propriety of the word *proverbial,* is not the thing insisted upon: though I think the manner of speaking is to be called so. But that the manner of speaking very remarkably renders the determination general, is surely indisputable. For, had it been said only, that God preferred mercy to the rigid observance of the Sabbath, even then, by parity of reason, most justly might we have argued, that he preferred mercy likewise, to the observance of other ritual institutions; and in general, moral duties, to positive ones. And thus the determination would have been general; though its being so were inferred and not expressed. But as the passage really stands in the Gospel, it is much stronger. For the sense and t' very literal words of our Lord's answer, are as applicable to any other instance of a comparison, between positive and moral duties, as to that upon which they were spoken. And if, in case of competition, mercy is to be preferred to positive institutions, it will scarce be thought, that justice is to give place to them. It is remarkable too, that, as the words are a quotation from the Old Testament, they are introduced, on both the forementioned occasions, with a declaration, that the Pharisees did not understand the meaning of them. This, I say, is very remarkable. For, since it is scarce possible, for the most ignorant person, not to understand the literal sense of the passage in the prophet;† and since understanding the literal sense would not have prevented their *condemning the guiltless,*‡ it can hardly be doubted, that the thing which our Lord really intended in that declaration was, that the Pharisees had not learned from it, as they might, wherein the *general* spirit of religion consists: that it consists in moral piety and virtue, as distinguished from ritual observances. However, it is certain we may learn this from his divine application of the passage, in the Gospel.

But, as it is one of the peculiar weaknesses of human nature, when, upon a comparison of two things, one is found to be of greater importance than the other, to consider this other as of scarce any importance at all: it is highly necessary that we remind ourselves, how great presumption it is, to make light of any institutions of divine appointment; that our obligations to obey

* Matt. ix. 13, and xii. 7. † Hosea vi. 6. ‡ See Matt. xii. 7.

all God's commands whatever are absolute and indispensable; and that commands merely positive, admitted to be from him, lay us under a moral obligation to obey them: an obligation moral in the strictest and most proper sense.

To these things I cannot forbear adding, that the account now given of Christianity most strongly shows and enforces upon us the obligation of searching the Scriptures, in order to see, what the scheme of revelation really is; instead of determining beforehand, from reason, what the scheme of it must be.* Indeed if in revelation there be found any passages, the seeming meaning of which is contrary to natural religion; we may most certainly conclude, such seeming meaning not to be the real one.[J] But it is not any degree of presumption against an interpretation of Scripture, that such interpretation contains a doctrine, which the light of nature cannot discover;† or a precept, which the law of nature does not oblige to.

CHAPTER II.

SUPPOSED PRESUMPTION AGAINST A REVELATION CONSIDERED AS MIRACULOUS.

HAVING shown the importance of the Christian revelation, and the obligations which we are under seriously to attend to it, upon supposition of its truth, or its credibility, the next thing in

* See ch. iii.

J [Dr. ANGUS judiciously remarks on this sentence, "This sentiment, as understood by Butler, is just, but very liable to abuse. Clearly, the Bible must be so interpreted as to agree with *all* known truth, whether of natural religion or natural science. At the same time, to correct the theology of the Bible by the theology of nature, as finite and guilty men understand it, may involve the rejection of Bible theology entirely; and of the very light and teaching it was intended to supply. The converse of Butler's statement is equally true, and even more important. If in natural theology there be found any facts, the seeming lesson of which is contrary to revealed religion, such seeming lesson is not the real one." Practically, it will be found that seeming meanings of Scripture, really erroneous, are corrected by other parts of Scripture itself. I understand Butler as only affirming that we must interpret Scripture according to immutable principles, and *known truth.* The infidel rejects it for not conforming to his *assumed hypothesis.*]

† P. 203.

order, is to consider the supposed presumptions against revelation in general; which shall be the subject of this chapter: and the objections against the Christian in particular, which shall be the subject of some following ones.* For it seems the most natural method, to remove the prejudices against Christianity, before we proceed to the consideration of the positive evidence for it, and the objections against that evidence.†

It is, I think, commonly supposed, that there is some peculiar presumption, from the analogy of nature, against the Christian scheme of things, at least against miracles; so as that stronger evidence is necessary to prove the truth and reality of them, than would be sufficient to convince us of other events, or matters of fact. Indeed the consideration of this supposed presumption cannot but be thought very insignificant, by many persons. Yet, as it belongs to the subject of this treatise; so it may tend to open the mind, and remove some prejudices, however needless the consideration of it be, upon its own account.

I. I find no appearance of a presumption, from the analogy of nature, against the *general scheme* of Christianity, that God created and invisibly governs the world by Jesus Christ; and by him also will hereafter judge it in righteousness, *i.e.* render to every one according to his works; and that good men are under the secret influence of his Spirit. Whether these things are, or are not, to be called miraculous, is perhaps only a question about words; or however, is of no moment in the case. If the analogy of nature raises any presumption against this general scheme of Christianity, it must be, either because it is not discoverable by reason or experience; or else, because it is unlike that course of nature, which is. But analogy raises no presumption against the truth of this scheme, upon either of these accounts.

First, There is no presumption, from analogy, against the truth of it, upon account of its not being discoverable by reason or experience. Suppose one who never heard of revelation, of the most improved understanding, and acquainted with our whole system of natural philosophy and natural religion; such a one could not but be sensible, that it was but a very small part of the natural and moral system of the universe, which he was acquainted with. He could not but be sensible, that there must be innumerable

* Chaps. iii., iv., v., vi.

† Chap. vii.

things, in the dispensations of Providence past, in the invisible government over the world at present carrying on, and in what is to come; of which he was wholly ignorant,* and which could not be discovered without revelation. Whether the scheme of nature be, in the strictest sense, infinite or not; it is evidently vast, even beyond all possible imagination. And doubtless that part of it, which is open to our view, is but as a point in comparison of the whole plan of Providence, reaching throughout eternity past and future; in comparison of what is even now going on, in the remote parts of the boundless universe, nay, in comparison of the whole scheme of this world. And therefore, that things lie beyond the natural reach of our faculties, is no sort of presumption against the truth and reality of them; because it is certain, there are innumerable things, in the constitution and government of the universe, which are thus beyond the natural reach of our faculties.

Secondly, Analogy raises no presumption against any of the things contained in this general doctrine of Scripture now mentioned, upon account of their being unlike the known course of nature. For there is no presumption at all from analogy, that the *whole* course of things, or divine government naturally unknown to us, and *every thing* in it, is like to any thing in that which is known; and therefore no peculiar presumption against any thing in the former, upon account of its being unlike to any thing in the latter. And in the constitution and natural government of the world, as well as in the moral government of it, we see things, in a great degree, unlike one another: and therefore ought not to wonder at such unlikeness between things visible and invisible. However, the scheme of Christianity is by no means entirely unlike the scheme of nature; as will appear in the following part of this treatise.

The notion of a miracle, considered as a proof of a divine mission, has been stated with great exactness by divines; and is, I think, sufficiently understood by every one. There are also invisible miracles,[a] the Incarnation of Christ, for instance, which,

* P. 172.

[a] [Papists urge that the actual conversion of the bread and wine in the Eucharist is an invisible miracle. But an invisible miracle is such because wrought under circumstances which *exclude* examination: while transubstan-

being secret, cannot be alleged as a proof of such a mission; but require themselves to be proved by visible miracles. Revelation itself too is miraculous; and miracles are the proof of it; and the supposed presumption against these shall presently be considered. All which I have been observing here is, that, whether we choose to call every thing in the dispensations of Providence, not discoverable without revelation, nor like the known course of things, miraculous; and whether the general Christian dispensation now mentioned is to be called so, or not; the foregoing observations seem certainly to show, that there is no presumption against it from the analogy of nature.

II. There is no presumption, from analogy, against some operations, which we should now call miraculous; particularly none against a revelation at the beginning of the world: nothing of such presumption against it, as is supposed to be implied or expressed in the word, *miraculous.*[b] A miracle, in its very notion, is relative to a course of nature; and implies something different from it, considered as being so. Now, either there was no course of nature at the time which we are speaking of; or if there were, we are not acquainted what the course of nature is, upon the first peopling of worlds. Therefore the question, whether mankind had a revelation made to them at *that* time, is to be considered, not as a question concerning a miracle, but as a common question of fact. And we have the like reason, be it more or less, to admit the report of tradition, concerning this question, and concerning common matters of fact of the same antiquity; for instance, what part of the earth was first peopled.

Or thus: When mankind was first placed in this state, there was a power exerted, totally different from the present course of nature. Now, whether this power, thus wholly different from the present course of nature, (for we cannot properly apply to it the word *miraculous;*) whether this power *stopped* immediately after it had made man, or went on, and exerted itself further in giving him a revelation, is a question of the same kind, as whether an

tiation *invites* and *facilitates* examination. It is wrought publicly, and constantly, and yet cannot be discovered to be a miracle. Indeed it supposes the working of a second miracle, to make the first invisible.]

[b] [Paley shows conclusively that a denial of miracles leads not only to a denial of revelation, but a denial of the existence of God, all of whose extraordinary acts are necessarily miraculous.]

ordinary power exerted itself in such a particular *degree* and manner, or not.

Or suppose the power exerted in the formation of the world be considered as miraculous, or rather, be called by that name; the case will not be different: since it must be acknowledged, that such a power was exerted. For supposing it acknowledged, that our Savior spent some years in a course of working miracles:[c] there is no more presumption, worth mentioning, against his having exerted this miraculous power, in a certain degree greater, than in a certain degree less; in one or two more instances, than in one or two fewer; in this, than in another manner.

It is evident then, that there can be no peculiar presumption, from the analogy of nature, against supposing a revelation, when man was first placed upon earth.[d]

Add, that there does not appear the least intimation in history or tradition, that religion was first reasoned out: but the whole of history and tradition makes for the other side, that it came into the world by revelation. Indeed the state of religion, in the first ages of which we have any account, seems to suppose and imply, that this was the original of it among mankind.[e] And these reflections together, without taking in the peculiar authority of Scripture, amount to real and a very material degree of evidence, that there was a revelation at the beginning of the world.

[c] [WHATELY, in his *Logic*, b. iii., has shown the folly of the Deistical attempts to explain our Savior's miracles as mere natural events. Having labored to show this of some *one* of the miracles, they then do so as to *another*, and thence infer that *all* were accidental conjunctures of natural circumstances. He says, they might as well argue "that because it is not improbable one may throw sixes once in a hundred throws, therefore it is no more improbable that one may throw sixes a hundred times running."

FITZGERALD says, "the improbability of a whole series of strange natural events, taking place unaccountably, one after another, amounts to a far greater improbability than is involved in the admission of miracles."]

[d] [That man, at first, must have had supernatural *instructions*, or in other words some revelations, is shown by Archbishop WHATELY in his "Origin of Civilization." Rev. SAMUEL STANHOPE SMITH expresses his conviction, both from reason and history, that man in his savage state could not even have preserved life without instruction from his Creator.]

[e] [The maintenance by the Jews, of a system of pure Theism, through so many and so rude ages, without being superior, or even equal to their neighbors, in science and civilization, can only be accounted for on the presumption of a revelation.]

Now this, as it is a confirmation of natural religion, and therefore mentioned in the former part of this treatise;* so likewise it has a tendency to remove any prejudices against a subsequent revelation.

III. But still it may be objected, that there is some peculiar presumption, from analogy, against miracles; particularly against revelation, after the settlement and during the continuance of a course of nature.

Now with regard to this supposed presumption, it is to be observed in general, that before we can have ground for raising what can, with any propriety, be called an *argument* from analogy, for or against revelation considered as something miraculous, we must be acquainted with a similar or parallel case. But the history of some other world, seemingly in like circumstances with our own, is no more than a parallel case: and therefore nothing short of this can be so. Yet, could we come at a presumptive proof, for or against a revelation, from being informed, whether such world had one, or not; such a proof, being drawn from one single instance only, must be infinitely precarious. More particularly:

First. There is a very strong presumption against common speculative truths, and against the most ordinary facts, before the proof[r] of them; which yet is overcome by almost any proof.

* P. 166, &c.

r [MILLS (Logic, chap. 24, § 5,) points out what he deems a mistake of "some of the writers against Hume on Miracles," in confounding the improbability of an event, before its occurrence, with the improbability afterwards; that is, considering them equal in degree. He fully proves that the great Laplace fell into this error, and the student should consult the passage.

Prof. FITZGERALD holds Butler to have fallen into the mistake adverted to by Mills; and quotes the latter author in a way which seems to make him say that such is his opinion also. I do not so understand Mills, nor do I see that Butler has confounded these meanings; but the very contrary. He expressly affirms, and most truly, that the strongest presumption may lie against "the most ordinary facts *before the proof* which yet is overcome by almost any proof." Butler's position here, may be thus illustrated. Suppose a hundred numbers to be put in a box, and it is proposed to draw out the number 42. Now there are 99 chances to 1 against drawing that, or any other *given* number. But suppose a child tells you he put the hundred numbers into a box, and drew out one, and it proved to be 42; you at once believe, for that was as likely to come as any other.

The proof of Christianity from prophecy becomes amazingly strong, thus viewed. There are many predictions, for instance that Christ should be born

There is a presumption of millions to one, against the story of Cæsar, or of any other man. For suppose a number of common facts so and so circumstanced, of which we had no kind of proof, should happen to come into one's thoughts; every one would, without any possible doubt, conclude them to be false. And the like may be said of a single common fact. Hence it appears, that the question of importance, as to the matter before us, is, concerning the *degree* of the peculiar presumption supposed against miracles; not whether there be any peculiar presumption at all against them. For, if there be the presumption of millions to one, against the most common facts; what can a small presumption, additional to this, amount to, though it be peculiar? It cannot be estimated, and is as nothing. The only material question is, whether there be any such presumptions against miracles, as to render them in any sort incredible.

Secondly, If we leave out the consideration of religion, we are in such total darkness, upon what causes, occasions, reasons, or circumstances, the present course of nature depends; that there does not appear any improbability for or against supposing, that five or six thousand years may have given scope[8] for causes, occasions, reasons, or circumstances, from whence miraculous interpositions may have arisen. And from this, joined with the foregoing observation, it will follow, that there must be a presumption, beyond all comparison greater, against the *particular* common facts just now instanced in, than against miracles *in general;* before any evidence of either.

Thirdly, Take in the consideration of religion, or the moral system of the world, and then we see distinct particular reasons for miracles: to afford mankind instruction additional to that of nature, and to attest the truth of it. This gives a real credibility to the supposition, that it might be part of the original plan of things, that there should be miraculous interpositions.

at a certain time, and place, and under certain very particular circumstances. The probabilities against such a *conjuncture* of events are almost infinite; yet they happened exactly as foretold.]

8 [For instance, a mass of ice or snow, may imperceptibly accumulate for an age, and then suddenly fall and overwhelm a village. Or a planet, or comet, may have been gradually nearing our earth for a million of years, without producing, *as yet*, any effect on our orbit; but in process of time, its proximity may work great changes in our condition.]

Lastly, Miracles must not be compared to common natural events, or to events which, though uncommon, are similar to what we daily experience: but to the extraordinary phenomena of nature. And then the comparison will be between the presumption against miracles, and the presumption against such uncommon appearances, suppose, as comets, and against there being any such powers in nature as magnetism and electricity, so contrary to the properties of other bodies not endued with these powers. And before any one can determine, whether there be any peculiar presumption against miracles, more than against other extraordinary things; he must consider, what, upon first hearing, would be the presumption against the last mentioned appearances and powers, to a person acquainted only with the daily, monthly, and annual course of nature respecting this earth, and with those common powers of matter which we every day see.

Upon all this I conclude; that there certainly is no such presumption against miracles, as to render them in any wise incredible: that, on the contrary, our being able to discern reasons for them, gives a positive credibility to the history of them, in cases where those reasons hold: and that it is by no means certain, that there is any *peculiar* presumption at all, from analogy, even in the lowest degree, against miracles, as distinguished from other extraordinary phenomena: though it is not worth while to perplex the reader with inquiries into the abstract nature of evidence, in order to determine a question, which, without such inquiries, we see* is of no importance.

CHAPTER III.

OUR INCAPACITY OF JUDGING, WHAT WERE TO BE EXPECTED IN A REVELATION; AND THE CREDIBILITY, FROM ANALOGY, THAT IT MUST CONTAIN THINGS LIABLE TO OBJECTIONS.

BESIDES the objections against the *evidence* for Christianity, many are alleged against the *scheme* of it; against the whole manner in which it is put and left with the world; as well as against several particular relations in Scripture: objections drawn

* P. 208.

from the deficiencies of revelation: from things in it appearing to men *foolishness*;* from its containing matters of offence, which have led, and it must have been foreseen would lead, into strange enthusiasm and superstition, and be made to serve the purposes of tyranny and wickedness; from its not being universal; and, which is a thing of the same kind, from its evidence not being so convincing and satisfactory as it might have been: for this last is sometimes turned into a positive argument against its truth.†

It would be tedious, indeed impossible, to enumerate the several particulars comprehended under the objections here referred to; they being so various, according to the different fancies of men. There are persons who think it a strong objection against the authority of Scripture, that it is not composed by rules of art, agreed upon by critics, for polite and correct writing. And the scorn is inexpressible, with which some of the prophetic parts of Scripture are treated: partly through the rashness of interpreters; but very much also, on account of the hieroglyphical and figurative language, in which they are left us.

Some of the principal things of this sort shall be particularly considered in the following chapters. But my design at present is to observe in general, with respect to this whole way of arguing, that, upon supposition of a revelation, it is highly credible beforehand, that we should be incompetent judges of it to a great degree: and that it would contain many things appearing to us liable to great objections; in case we judge of it otherwise, than by the analogy of nature. Therefore, though objections against the *evidence* of Christianity are most seriously to be considered, yet objections against Christianity itself are, in a great measure, frivolous: almost all objections against it, excepting those which are alleged against the particular proofs of its coming from God. I express myself with caution, lest I should be mistaken to vilify reason; which is indeed the only faculty we have wherewith to judge concerning any thing, even revelation itself: or be misunderstood to assert, that a supposed revelation cannot be proved false, from internal characters. For, it may contain clear immoralities or contradictions; and either of these would prove it false. Nor will I take upon me to affirm, that nothing else can possibly

* 1 Cor. i. 28.

† See Chap. vi.

render any supposed revelation incredible. Yet still the observation above, is, I think, true beyond doubt; that objections against Christianity, as distinguished from objections against its evidence, are frivolous. To make out this, is the general design of the present chapter.

With regard to the whole of it, I cannot but particularly wish, that the *proofs* might be attended to; rather than the assertions cavilled at, upon account of any unacceptable *consequences*, real or supposed, which may be drawn from them. For, after all, that which is true, must be admitted, though it should show us the shortness of our faculties: and that we are in no wise judges of many things, of which we are apt to think ourselves very competent ones. Nor will this be any objection with reasonable men; at least upon second thought it will not be any objection with such, against the justness of the following observations.

As God governs the world and instructs his creatures, according to certain laws or rules, in the known course of nature; known by reason together with experience: so the Scripture informs us of a scheme of divine Providence, additional to this. It relates, that God has, by revelation, instructed men in things concerning his government, which they could not otherwise have known; and reminded them of things, which they might otherwise know; and attested the truth of the whole by miracles. Now if the natural and the revealed dispensation of things are both from God, if they coincide with each other, and together make up one scheme of Providence; our being incompetent judges of one, must render it credible, that we may be incompetent judges also of the other. Upon experience, the acknowledged constitution and course of nature is found to be greatly different from what, before experience, would have been expected; and such as, men fancy, there lie great objections against. This renders it beforehand highly credible, that they may find the revealed dispensation likewise, if they judge of it as they do of the constitution of nature, very different from expectations formed beforehand; and liable, in appearance, to great objections: objections against the scheme itself, and against the degrees and manners of the miraculous interpositions by which it was attested and carried on. Thus, suppose a prince to govern his dominions in the wisest manner possible, by common known laws; and that upon some exigencies he should suspend these laws; and govern, in several instances, in a different manner. If one of his subjects were not a competent judge beforehand, by what common rules the government should or would be carried on; it could not be expected, that the same person would be a competent judge, in what exigencies, or in what manner, or to what degree, those laws commonly observed would be suspended or deviated from. If he were not a judge of the wisdom of the ordinary administration, there is no reason to think he would be a judge of the wisdom of the extraordinary. If he thought he had objections against the former; doubtless, it is highly supposable, he might think also, that he had objections against the latter. And thus, as we fall into infinite follies and mistakes, whenever we pretend, otherwise than from experience and analogy, to judge of the constitution and course of nature; it is evidently supposable beforehand, that we should fall into as great, in pretending to judge in like manner concerning revelation. Nor is there any more ground to expect that this latter should appear to us clear of objections, than that the former should.

These observations, relating to the whole of Christianity, are applicable to inspiration in particular. As we are in no sort judges beforehand, by what laws or rules, in what degree, or by what means, it were to have been expected, that God would naturally instruct us; so upon supposition of his affording us light and instruction by revelation, additional to what he has afforded us by reason and experience, we are in no sort judges, by what methods, and in what proportion, it were to be expected that this supernatural light and instruction would be afforded us. We know not beforehand, what degree or kind of natural information it were to be expected God would afford men, each by his own reason and experience: nor how far he would enable and effectually dispose them to communicate it, whatever it should be, to each other; nor whether the evidence of it would be certain, highly probable, or doubtful; nor whether it would be given with equal clearness and conviction to all. Nor could we guess, upon any good ground I mean, whether natural knowledge, or even the faculty itself, by which we are capable of attaining it, reason, would be given us at once, or gradually.

In like manner, we are wholly ignorant, what degree of new

knowledge, it were to be expected, God would give mankind by revelation, upon supposition of his affording one: or how far, or in what way, he would interpose miraculously, to qualify them, to whom he should originally make the revelation, for communicating the knowledge given by it; and to secure their doing it to the age in which they should live; and to secure its being transmitted to posterity. We are equally ignorant, whether the evidence of it would be certain or highly probable, or doubtful:* or whether all who should have any degree of instruction from it, and any degree of evidence of its truth, would have the same: or whether the scheme would be revealed at once, or unfolded gradually.[a] Nay we are not in any sort able to judge, whether it were to have been expected, that the revelation should have been committed to writing; or left to be handed down, and consequently corrupted, by verbal tradition, and at length sunk under it, if mankind so pleased, and during such time as they are permitted, in the degree they evidently are, to act as they will.

But it may be said, "that a revelation in some of the above-mentioned circumstances, one, for instance, which was not committed to writing, and thus secured against danger of corruption, would not have answered its purpose." I ask, what purpose? It would not have answered all the purposes, which it has now answered, and in the same degree: but it would have answered others, or the same in different degrees. And which of these were the purposes of God, and best fell in with his general government, we could not at all have determined beforehand.

Now since we have no principles of reason, upon which to judge beforehand, how it were to be expected that revelation should have been left, or what was most suitable to the divine plan of government, in any of the forementioned respects; it must be quite frivolous to object afterwards as to any of them, against its being left in one way, rather than another: for this would be to object against things, upon account of their being different from expectations, which has been shown to be without reason.

Thus we see, that the only question concerning the truth of Christianity is, whether it be a real revelation; not whether it be attended with every circumstance which we should have

* See Chap. vi.

[a] [See note, page 218.]

looked for: and concerning the authority of Scripture, whether it be what it claims to be; not whether it be a book of such sort, and so promulged, as weak men are apt to fancy a book containing a divine revelation should be. Therefore, neither obscurity, nor seeming inaccuracy of style, nor various readings, nor early disputes about the authors of particular parts, nor any other things of the like kind, though they had been much more considerable in degree than they are, could overthrow the authority of the Scripture: unless the prophets, apostles, or our Lord, had promised, that the book containing the divine revelation should be exempt from those things. Nor indeed can any objections overthrow such a kind of revelation as the Christian claims to be, (since there are no objections against the morality of it,*) but such as can show, that there is no proof of miracles wrought originally in attestation of it; no appearance of any thing miraculous in its obtaining in the world; nor any of prophecy, that is, of events foretold, which human sagacity could not foresee. If it can be shown, that the proof alleged for all these is absolutely none at all, then is revelation overturned. But were it allowed, that the proof of any one or all of them is lower than is allowed; yet, whilst *any* proof of them remains, revelation will stand upon much the same foot it does at present, as to all the purposes of life and practice, and ought to have the like influence upon our behavior.

From the foregoing observations too, it will follow, and those who will thoroughly examine into revelation will find it worth remarking, that there are several ways of arguing, which though just with regard to other writings, are not applicable to Scripture: at least not to its prophetic parts. We cannot argue, for instance, that such and such cannot be the sense or intent of a passage of Scripture, for, if it had, it would have been expressed more plainly, or represented under a more apt figure or hieroglyphic. Yet we may justly argue thus, with respect to common books. And the reason of this difference is very evident. In Scripture we are not competent judges, as we are in common books, how plainly it were to have been expected, that the sense should have been expressed, or under how apt an image figured. The only question is, what appearance there is, that this *is* the sense;

* P. 220.

and scarce at all, how much more determinately or accurately it might have been expressed or figured.[b]

"But is it not self-evident, that internal improbabilities of all kinds weaken external probable proof?" Doubtless. But to what practical purpose can this be alleged here, when it has been proved before,* that real internal improbabilities, which rise even to moral certainty, are overcome by the most ordinary testimony; and when it now has been made to appear, that we scarce know what are improbabilities, as to the matter we are here considering: as it will further appear from what follows.

From the observations made above it is manifest, that we are not in any sort competent judges, what supernatural instruction were to have been expected; and it is self-evident, that the objections of an incompetent judgment must be frivolous. Yet it may be proper to go one step further, and observe, that if men will be regardless of these things, and pretend to judge of the Scripture by preconceived expectations; the analogy of nature shows beforehand, not only that it is highly credible they may, but also probable that they will, imagine they have strong objections against it, however really unexceptionable. For so, prior to experience, they would think they had, against the circumstances, and degrees, and the whole manner of that instruction, which is afforded by the ordinary course of nature. Were the instruction which God affords to brute creatures by instincts and mere propensions, and to mankind by these together with reason, matter of probable proof, and not of certain observation; it would be rejected as incredible, in many instances of it, only upon account of the means by which this instruction is given, the seeming disproportions, the limitations, necessary conditions, and circumstances of it. For instance: would it not have been thought highly improbable, that men should have been so much more

[b] [It is not to be understood that Butler would not have the ordinary rules of interpretation applied to the Holy Scriptures. Because the interpretation, "if not gathered *out* of the words, must be brought *into* them." We cannot interpret them as if we knew beforehand, what the Holy Ghost meant to say; as SPINOZA proposes to do, in his Philosophia Scripturæ Interpretes. The student will do well to consult BENSON'S Hulsean Lectures on Scripture Difficulties: KING'S Morsels of Criticism: STORR, Exertationes Exeget.: MICHAELIS, Introd. ad. Nov. Test.: and FEATLEY'S Key.]

* Pp. 207 208.

capable of discovering, even to certainty, the general laws of matter, and the magnitudes, paths, and revolutions, of heavenly bodies; than the occasions and cures of distempers, and many other things in which human life seems so much more nearly concerned, than in astronomy? How capricious and irregular a way of information would it be said, is that of *invention*, by means of which nature instructs us in matters of science, and in many things, upon which the affairs of the world greatly depend: that a man should, by this faculty, be made acquainted with a thing in an instant, (when perhaps he is thinking of something else,) which he has in vain been searching after, it may be, for years.

So likewise the imperfections attending the only method, by which nature enables and directs us to communicate our thoughts to each other, are innumerable. Language is, in its very nature, inadequate, ambiguous, liable to infinite abuse, even from negligence; and so liable to it from design, that every man can deceive and betray by it. And, to mention but one instance more; that brutes, without reason, should act, in many respects, with a sagacity and foresight vastly greater than what men have in those respects, would be thought impossible. Yet it is certain they do act with such superior foresight: whether it be their own, indeed, is another question. From these things, it is highly credible beforehand, that upon supposition that God should afford men some additional instruction by revelation, it would be with circumstances, in manners, degrees, and respects, against the credibility of which we should be apt to fancy we had great objections. Nor are the objections against the Scripture, nor against Christianity in general, at all more or greater, than the analogy of nature would beforehand—not perhaps give ground to *expect;* (for the analogy may not be sufficient, in some cases, to ground an expectation upon;) but no more nor greater, than analogy would show it, beforehand, to be supposable and *credible*, that there might seem to lie against revelation.

By applying these general observations to a particular objection, it will be more distinctly seen, how they are applicable to others of the like kind; and indeed to almost all objections against Christianity, as distinguished from objections against its evidence. It appears from Scripture, that, as it was not unusual in the apostolic age, for persons, upon their conversion to Christianity, to be endued with miraculous gifts; so, some of those persons exercised these gifts in a strangely irregular and disorderly manner;[c] and this is made an objection against their being really miraculous. Now the foregoing observations quite remove this objection, how considerable soever it may appear at first sight. For, consider a person endued with any of these gifts, for instance that of tongues: it is to be supposed, that he had the same power over this miraculous gift, as he would have had over it, had it been the effect of habit, of study and use, as it ordinarily is; or the same power over it, as he had over any other natural endowment. Consequently, he would use it in the same manner as he did any other; either regularly, and upon proper occasions only, or irregularly, and upon improper ones: according to his sense of decency, and his character of prudence.[d] Where then is the objection? Why, if this miraculous power was indeed given to the world to propagate Christianity, and attest the truth of it, we might, it seems, have expected, that other sort of persons should have been chosen to be invested with it; or that these should, at the same time, have been endued with prudence; or that they should have been continually restrained and directed in the exercise of it: *i.e.* that God should have miraculously interposed, if at all, in a different manner, or higher degree. But, from the observations made above, it is undeniably evident, that we are not judges in what degrees and manners it were to have been expected he should miraculously interpose; upon supposition of his doing it in some degree and manner. Nor, in the natural course of Providence, are superior gifts of memory, eloquence, knowledge, and other talents of great influence, conferred only on persons of prudence and decency, or such as are disposed to make the properest use

[c] [See 1 Cor. xii. 1–10: xiii. 1: and xiv. 1–19.]

[d] ["The power of healing, or working miracles, is, during the whole course of its operation, one continued arrest or diversion of the general laws of matter and motion. It was therefore fit that this power should be given occasionally. But the *speaking with tongues*, when once the gift was conferred, became thenceforth a natural power; just as the free use of members of the body, after being restored, by miracle, to the exercise of their natural functions. In healing, the apostles are to be considered as the workers of a miracle; in speaking strange tongues, as persons on whom a miracle is performed."—WARBURTON, Doct. of Grace, b. i. ch. iii.]

of them. Nor is the instruction and admonition naturally afforded us for the conduct of life, particularly in our education, commonly given in a manner the most suited to recommend it; but often with circumstances apt to prejudice us against such instruction.

One might go on to add, there is a great resemblance between the light of nature and of revelation, in several other respects. Practical Christianity, or that faith and behavior which renders a man a Christian, is a plain and obvious thing: like the common rules of conduct, with respect to ordinary temporal affairs. The more distinct and particular knowledge of those things, the study of which the apostle calls *going on unto perfection*,* and of the prophetic parts of revelation, like many parts of natural and even civil knowledge, may require very exact thought, and careful consideration. The hinderances too, of natural, and of supernatural light and knowledge, have been of the same kind. And as it is owned the whole scheme of Scripture is not yet understood; so, if it ever comes to be understood, before the *restitution of all things*,† and without miraculous interpositions, it must be in the same way as natural knowledge is come at: by the continuance and progress of learning and of liberty;[e] and by particular persons attending to, comparing, and pursuing, intimations scattered up and down it, which are overlooked and disregarded by the generality of the world. For this is the way in which all improvements are made; by thoughtful men's tracing on obscure hints, dropped us by nature as it were, accidentally, or which seem to come into our minds by chance. Nor is it at all incredible, that a book which has been so long in the possession of mankind, should contain many truths as yet undiscovered. For, all the same phenomena, and the same faculties of investigation,

* Heb. vi. 1. † Acts iii. 21.

[e] [The doctrine of "development" has of late been popular in some quarters. Butler here shows the only *safe* notion we may entertain on that subject. "Exact thought, and careful consideration" may show us how to confute specious heresies, expound embarrassing passages, dissipate painful doubts, and remove many prejudices or misapprehensions. But revelation is complete as it stands.

We may hope for progress in theology as in other sciences; not in the development of new facts or faith, as Papists and Socinians pretend, but in the increase of sound wisdom, aided by a more perfect interpretation of God's word.]

from which such great discoveries in natural knowledge have been made in the present and last age, were equally in the possession of mankind, several thousand years before. And possibly it might be intended, that events, as they come to pass, should open and ascertain the meaning of several parts of Scripture.

It may be objected, that this analogy fails in a material respect: for that natural knowledge is of little or no consequence. But I have been speaking of the general instruction which nature does or does not afford us. And besides, some parts of natural knowledge, in the more common restrained sense of the words, are of the greatest consequence to the ease and convenience of life. But suppose the analogy did, as it does not, fail in this respect; yet it might be abundantly supplied, from the whole constitution and course of nature: which shows, that God does not dispense his gifts according to *our* notions of the advantage and consequence they would be of to us. And this in general, with his method of dispensing knowledge in particular, would together make out an analogy full to the point before us.

But it may be objected still further and more generally; "The Scripture represents the world as in a state of ruin, and Christianity as an expedient to recover it, to help in these respects where nature fails: in particular, to supply the deficiencies of natural light. Is it credible then, that so many ages should have been let pass, before a matter of such a sort, of so great and so general importance, was made known to mankind; and then that it should be made known to so small a part of them? Is it conceivable, that this supply should be so very deficient, should have the like obscurity and doubtfulness, be liable to the like perversions, in short, lie open to all the like objections, as the light of nature itself?*

Without determining how far this, in fact, is so, I answer; it is by no means incredible, that it might be so, if the light of nature and of revelation be from the same hand. Men are naturally liable to diseases: for which God, in his good providence, has provided natural remedies.† But remedies existing in nature have been unknown to mankind for many ages; are known but to few now; probably many valuable ones are not known yet. Great has been and is the obscurity and difficulty,

* Chap. vi.

† Chap. v.

in the nature and application of them. Circumstances *seem* often to make them very improper, where they are absolutely necessary. It is after long labor and study, and many unsuccessful endeavors, that they are brought to be as useful as they are; after high contempt and absolute rejection of the most useful we have; and after disputes and doubts, which have seemed to be endless. The best remedies too, when unskilfully, much more when dishonestly applied, may produce new diseases; and with the rightest application the success of them is often doubtful. In many cases they are not effectual: where they are, it is often very slowly: and the application of them, and the necessary regimen accompanying it, is not uncommonly so disagreeable, that some will not submit to them; and satisfy themselves with the excuse, that if they would, it is not certain whether it would be successful. And many persons, who labor under diseases, for which there are known natural remedies, are not so happy as to be always, if ever, in the way of them. In a word, the remedies which nature has provided for diseases are neither certain, perfect, nor universal. And indeed the same principles of arguing, which would lead us to conclude, that they must be so, would lead us likewise to conclude, that there could be no occasion for them; *i.e.* that there could be no diseases at all. And therefore our experience that there are diseases, shows that it is credible beforehand, upon supposition nature has provided remedies for them, that these remedies may be, as by experience we find they are, neither certain, nor perfect, nor universal; because it shows, that the principles upon which we should expect the contrary are fallacious.

And now, what is the just consequence from all these things? Not that reason is no judge of what is offered to us as being of divine revelation. For this would be to infer that we are unable to judge of any thing, because we are unable to judge of all things. Reason can, and it ought to judge, not only of the meaning, but also of the morality and the evidence of revelation.

First, It is the province of reason to judge of the morality of the Scripture; *i.e.* not whether it contains things different from what we should have expected from a wise, just, and good Being; (for objections from hence have been now obviated:) but whether it contains things plainly contradictory to wisdom, justice, or goodness; to what the light of nature teaches us of God. And I know nothing of this sort objected against Scripture, excepting such objections as are formed upon suppositions, which would equally conclude, that the constitution of nature is contradictory to wisdom, justice, or goodness; which most certainly it is not. There are, indeed, some particular precepts in Scripture, given to particular persons, requiring actions, which would be immoral and vicious, were it not for such precepts. But it is easy to see, that all these are of such a kind, as that the precept changes the whole nature of the case and of the action; and both constitutes and shows that not to be unjust or immoral, which, prior to the precept, must have appeared and really been so: which may well be, since none of these precepts are contrary to immutable morality. If it were commanded, to cultivate the *principles*, and act from the spirit of treachery, ingratitude, cruelty; the command would not alter the nature of the case or of the action, in any of these instances. But it is quite otherwise in precepts, which require only the doing an *external action:* for instance, taking away the property, or life of any. For men have no right, either to life or property, but what arises solely from the grant of God. When this grant is revoked, they cease to have any right at all in either: and when this revocation is made known, as surely it is possible it may be, it must cease to be unjust to deprive them of either. And though a course of external acts, which without command would be immoral, must make an immoral habit; yet a few detached commands have no such natural tendency. I thought proper to say thus much of the few Scripture precepts, which require, not vicious actions, but actions which would have been vicious, but for such precepts; because they are sometimes weakly urged as immoral, and great weight is laid upon objections drawn from them.

To me there seems no difficulty at all in these precepts, but what arises from their being offences: *i.e.* from their being liable to be perverted, as indeed they are, by wicked designing men, to serve the most horrid purposes; and perhaps to mislead the weak and enthusiastic. And objections from this head are not objections against revelation; but against the whole notion of religion, as a trial: and against the general constitution of nature.

Secondly, Reason is able to judge, and must, of the evidence of revelation, and of the objections urged against that evidence: which shall be the subject of a following chapter.*

The consequence of the foregoing observations is, that the question upon which the truth of Christianity depends, is scarcely at all what objections there are against its scheme, since there are none against the morality of it, but *what objections there are against its evidence;* or, *what proof there remains of it, after due allowances are made for the objections against that proof:* because it has been shown, that the *objections against Christianity, as distinguished from objections against its evidence, are frivolous.* For surely very little weight, if any at all, is to be laid upon a way of arguing and objecting, which, when applied to the general constitution of nature, experience shows not to be conclusive: and such, I think, is the whole way of objecting treated of throughout this chapter. It is resolvable into principles, and goes upon suppositions, which mislead us to think, that the Author of nature would not act, as we experience he does; or would act, in such and such cases, as we experience he does not in like cases. But the unreasonableness of this way of objecting will appear yet more evidently from hence, that the chief things thus objected against are justified, as shall be further shown,† by distinct, particular, and full analogies, in the constitution and course of nature.

It is to be remembered, that, as frivolous as objections of the foregoing sort against revelation are, yet, when a supposed revelation is more consistent with itself, and has a more general and uniform tendency to promote virtue, than, all circumstances considered, could have been expected from enthusiasm and political views, this is a presumptive proof of its not proceeding from them, and so of its truth: because we are competent judges, what might have been expected from enthusiasm and political views.[f]

* Chap. vii.

† Chap. iv. latter part, and v. vi.

[f] [This pregnant paragraph should receive very full attention. We know much of men, little of God. What men are likely to do, or say, in certain circumstances, is often very clear; and generally may be guessed at. But what God would do or say in new contingencies, who shall attempt to prescribe or predict? We are poorly qualified to assert that such and such declarations could not have come from infinite wisdom; but we are quite competent to affirm that such and such things could not have come from human contrivance or enthusiasm.]

CHAPTER IV.

CHRISTIANITY, CONSIDERED AS A SCHEME OR CONSTITUTION, IMPERFECTLY COMPREHENDED.

As hath been now shown,* the analogy of nature renders it highly credible beforehand, that, supposing a revelation to be made, it must contain many things very different from what we should have expected, and such as appear open to great objections: and that this observation, in good measure, takes off the force of those objections, or rather precludes them. It may be alleged, that this is a very partial answer to such objections, or a very unsatisfactory way of obviating them: because it does not show at all, that the things objected against can be wise, just, and good; much less, that it is credible they are so. It will therefore be proper to show this distinctly; by applying to these objections against the wisdom, justice, and goodness of Christianity, the answer above† given to the like objections against the constitution of nature: before we consider the particular analogies in the latter, to the particular things objected against in the former. Now that which affords a sufficient answer to objections against the wisdom, justice, and goodness of the constitution of nature, is its being a constitution, a system, or scheme, imperfectly comprehended;[a] a scheme in which means are made use of to accomplish ends; and which is carried on by general laws. For from these things it has been proved, not only to be possible, but also to be credible, that those things which are objected against may be consistent with wisdom, justice, and goodness; nay, may be instances of them: and even

* In the foregoing chapter.

† Part I. ch. vii., to which this all along refers.

[a] ["It is the last step of reason to know there is an infinity of things which surpass it."—PASCAL. "The wall of adamant which bounds human inquiry, has scarcely ever been discovered by any adventurer, till he was aroused by the shock that drove him back."—Sir JAS. MACKINTOSH. "Of the dark parts of revelation there are two sorts: one which may be cleared up by the studious; the other which will always reside within the shadow of God's throne where it would be impiety to intrude."—WARBURTON. "A Christianity without mystery is as unphilosophical as it is unscriptural."—ANGUS.]

that the constitution and government of nature may be perfect in the highest possible degree. If Christianity then be a scheme, and of the like kind; it is evident, the like objections against it must admit of the like answer. And,

I. Christianity is a scheme, quite beyond our comprehension.

The moral government of God is exercised, by gradually conducting things so in the course of his providence, that every one, at length and upon the whole, shall receive according to his deserts; and neither fraud nor violence, but truth and right, shall finally prevail. Christianity is a particular scheme under this general plan of Providence, and a part of it, conducive to its completion, with regard to mankind: consisting itself also of various parts, and a mysterious economy, which has been carrying on from the time the world came into its present wretched state, and is still carrying on, for its recovery, by a divine person, the Messiah; who is to *gather together in one the children of God, that are scattered abroad,** and establish *an everlasting kingdom, wherein dwelleth righteousness.*† In order to it; after various manifestations of things, relating to this great and general scheme of Providence, through a succession of many ages: (For *the Spirit of Christ which was in the prophets, testified beforehand his sufferings, and the glory that should follow: unto whom it was revealed, that not unto themselves, but unto us they did minister the things which are now reported unto us by them that have preached the Gospel; which things the angels desire to look into:*‡)—after various dispensations looking forward and preparatory to, this final salvation: *in the fulness of time,* when infinite wisdom thought fit; He, *being in the form of God,—made himself of no reputation, and took upon him the form of a servant, and was made in the likeness of men: and being found in fashion as a man, he humbled himself, and became obedient to death, even the death of the cross. Wherefore God also hath highly exalted him, and given him a name, which is above every name: that at the name of Jesus every knee should bow, of things in heaven, and things in the earth, and things under the earth: and that every tongue should confess, that Jesus Christ is Lord, to the glory of God the Father.*§ Parts likewise of this economy are the miraculous mission of the Holy Ghost. and his

* John xi. 52. † 2 Peter iii. 13. ‡ 1 Peter i. 11, 12. § Phil. ii. [6-11.]

ordinary assistances given to good men:[b] the invisible government, which Christ at present exercises over his church: that which he himself refers to in these words: *In my Father's house are many mansions—I go to prepare a place for you:** and his future return to *judge the world in righteousness,* and completely re-establish the kingdom of God. *For the Father judgeth no man; but hath committed all judgment unto the Son: that all men should honor the Son, even as they honor the Father.*† *All power is given unto him in heaven and in earth.*‡ *And he must reign, till he hath put all enemies under his feet. Then cometh the end, when he shall have delivered up the kingdom to God, even the Father; when he shall have put down all rule, and all authority and power. And when all things shall be subdued unto him, then shall the Son also himself be subject unto him that put all things under him, that God may be all in all.*§ Surely little need be said to show, that this system, or scheme of things, is but imperfectly comprehended by us. The Scripture expressly asserts it to be so. And indeed one cannot read a passage relating to this *great mystery of godliness,*|| but what immediately runs up into something which shows us our ignorance in it; as every thing in nature shows us our ignorance in the constitution of nature. And whoever will seriously consider that part of the Christian scheme, which is revealed in Scripture, will find so much more unrevealed, as will convince him, that, to all the purposes of judging and objecting, we know as little of it, as of the constitution of nature. Our ignorance, therefore, is as much an answer to our objections against the perfection of one, as against the perfection of the other.¶

II. It is obvious too, that in the Christian dispensation, as much as in the natural scheme of things, means are made use of to accomplish ends.

The observation of this furnishes us with the same answer, to objections against the perfection of Christianity, as to objections of the like kind, against the constitution of nature. It shows

[b] [The influences of the Holy Spirit are not only "given to good men," but are sent upon many who live unmindful of eternity, quickening their consciences, enlightening their understandings and arresting their passions, and thus it is they are converted unto the truth in Christ.]

* John xiv. 2. † John v. 22, 23. ‡ Matt. xxviii. 18.

§ 1 Cor. xv. 28. || 1 Tim. iii. 16. ¶ P. 174, &c.

the credibility, that the things objected against, how *foolish** soever they appear to men, may be the very best means of accomplishing the very best ends. And their appearing *foolishness* is no presumption against this, in a scheme so greatly beyond our comprehension.†

III. The credibility, that the Christian dispensation may have been, all along, carried on by general laws,‡ no less than the course of nature, may require to be more distinctly made out.

Consider then, upon *what ground* it is we say, that the whole common course of nature is carried on according to general foreordained laws. We know indeed several of the general laws of matter; and a great part of the natural behavior of living agents is reducible to general laws. But we know in a manner nothing, by what laws, storms, tempests, earthquakes, famine, pestilence, become the instruments of destruction to mankind. And the laws by which persons born into the world at such a time and place are of such capacities, geniuses, tempers; the laws by which thoughts come into our mind, in a multitude of cases; and by which innumerable things happen, of the greatest influence upon the affairs and state of the world. These laws are so wholly unknown to us, that we call the events which come to pass by them, accidental; though all reasonable men know certainly, that there cannot, in reality, be any such thing as chance; and conclude that the things which have this appearance are the result of general laws, and may be reduced to them. It is but an exceeding little way, and in but a very few respects, that we can trace up the natural course of things before us, to general laws. It is only from analogy, that we conclude the whole of it to be capable of being reduced to them: only from our seeing that part is so. It is from our finding, that the course of nature, in some respects and so far, goes on by general laws, that we conclude this of the rest.

If that be a just ground for such a conclusion, it is a just ground also, if not to conclude, yet to apprehend, to render it supposable and credible, which is sufficient for answering objections, that God's miraculous interpositions may have been, all along in like manner, by *general* laws of wisdom. Thus, that miraculous powers should be exerted, at such times, upon such

* 1 Cor. i. [18–25.] † Pp. 178, 179. ‡ Pp. 180, 181.

occasions, in such degrees and manners, and with regard to such persons, rather than others; that the affairs of the world, being permitted to go on in their natural course so far, should, just at such a point, have a new direction given them by miraculous interpositions; that these interpositions should be exactly in such degrees and respects only; all this may have been by general laws. These laws are indeed unknown to us: but no more unknown than the laws from whence it is, that some die as soon as they are born, and others live to extreme old age; that one man is so superior to another in understanding; with innumerable more things, which, as was before observed, we cannot reduce to any laws or rules, though it is taken for granted, they are as much reducible to general ones, as gravitation. If the revealed dispensations of Providence, and miraculous interpositions, be by general laws, as well as God's ordinary government in the course of nature, made known by reason and experience; there is no more reason to expect that every exigence, as it arises, should be provided for by these general laws or miraculous interpositions, than that every exigence in nature should be, by the general laws of nature. Yet there might be wise and good reasons, why miraculous interpositions should be by general laws; and why these laws should not be broken in upon, or deviated from, by other miracles.

Upon the whole then, the appearance of deficiencies and irregularities in nature is owing to its being a scheme but in part made known, and of such a certain particular kind in other respects. We see no more reason why the frame and course of nature should be such a scheme, than why Christianity should. And that the former is such a scheme, renders it credible, that the latter, upon supposition of its truth, may be so too. And as it is manifest, that Christianity is a scheme revealed but in part, and a scheme in which means are made use of to accomplish ends, like to that of nature: so the credibility, that it may have been all along carried on by general laws, no less than the course of nature, has been distinctly proved. From all this it is beforehand credible that there might, I think probable that there would, be the like appearance of deficiencies and irregularities in Christianity, as in nature: *i.e.* that Christianity would be liable to the like objections, as the frame of nature. And these objections are answered by these observations concerning Christianity; as the like objections against the frame of nature are answered by the like observations concerning the frame of nature.

The objections against Christianity, considered as a matter of fact,* having, in general, been obviated in the preceding chapter; and the same, considered as made against the wisdom and goodness of it, having been obviated in this: the next thing, according to the method proposed, is to show, that the principal objections, in particular, against Christianity, may be answered, by particular and full analogies in nature. And as one of them is made against the whole scheme of it together, as just now described, I choose to consider it here, rather than in a distinct chapter by itself.

The thing objected against this scheme of the gospel is, "that it seems to suppose God was reduced to the necessity of a long series of intricate means, in order to accomplish his ends, the recovery and salvation of the world: in like sort as men, for want of understanding or power, not being able to come at their ends directly, are forced to go roundabout ways, and make use of many perplexed contrivances to arrive at them." Now every thing which we see shows the folly of this, considered as an objection against the truth of Christianity. For, according to our manner of conception, God makes use of variety of means, what we often think tedious ones, in the natural course of providence, for the accomplishment of all his ends. Indeed it is certain there is somewhat in this matter quite beyond our comprehension: but the mystery is as great in nature as in Christianity. We know what we ourselves aim at, as final ends: and what courses we take, merely as means conducing to those ends. But we are greatly ignorant how far things are considered by the Author of nature, under the single notion of means and ends; so as that it may be said, this is merely an end, and that merely a means, in his regard. And whether there be not some peculiar absurdity in our very manner of conception, concerning this matter, something contradictory arising from our extremely imperfect views of things, it is impossible to say.

* P. 172, &c.

However, this much is manifest, that the whole natural world and government of it, is a scheme or system; not a fixed, but a progressive one: a scheme in which the operation of various means takes up a great length of time, before the ends they tend to can be attained. The change of seasons, the ripening of fruits, the very history of a flower, are instances of this: and so is human life. Thus vegetable bodies, and those of animals, though possibly formed at once, yet grow up by degrees to a mature state. And thus rational agents, who animate these latter bodies, are naturally directed to form each his own manners and character, by the gradual gaining of knowledge and experience, and by a long course of action. Our existence is not only successive, as it must be of necessity; but one state of our life and being is appointed by God, to be a preparation for another; and that to be the means of attaining to another succeeding one: infancy to childhood; childhood to youth; youth to mature age. Men are impatient, and for precipitating things: but the Author of nature appears deliberate throughout his operations; accomplishing his natural ends by slow successive steps.[c] And there is a plan of things beforehand laid out, which, from the nature of it, requires various systems of means, as well as length of time, in order to the carrying on its several parts into execution.

Thus, in the daily course of natural providence, God operates in the very same manner, as in the dispensation of Christianity; making one thing subservient to another; this, to something further; and so on, through a progressive series of means, which extend, both backward and forward, beyond our utmost view. Of this manner of operation, every thing we see in the course of nature is as much an instance, as any part of the Christian dispensation.

[c] ["Providence hurries not himself to display to-day the consequence of the principle he yesterday announced. He will draw it out in the lapse of ages. Even according to our reasoning logic is none the less sure, because it is slow." —GUIZOT on Civilization, Lect. I.

How impressively is this sentiment sustained by modern geology, and astronomy!]

CHAPTER V.

THE PARTICULAR SYSTEM OF CHRISTIANITY; THE APPOINTMENT OF A MEDIATOR, AND THE REDEMPTION OF THE WORLD BY HIM.

THERE is not, I think, any thing relating to Christianity, which has been more objected against, than the mediation of Christ, in some or other of its parts. Yet upon thorough consideration, there seems nothing less justly liable to it.[a] For,

I. The whole analogy of nature removes all imagined presumption against the general notion of *a Mediator between God and man.** For we find all living creatures are brought into the world, and their life in infancy is preserved, by the instrumentality of others: and every satisfaction of it, some way or other, is bestowed by the like means. So that the visible government, which God exercises over the world, is by the instrumentality and mediation of others. How far his invisible government be or be not so, it is impossible to determine at all by reason. The supposition, that part of it is so, appears, to say the least, altogether as credible, as the contrary. There is then no sort of objection, from the light of nature, against the general notion of a mediator between God and man, considered as a doctrine of Christianity, or as an appointment in this dispensation: since we find by experience, that God does appoint mediators, to be the instruments of good and evil to us: the instruments of his justice and his mercy. And the objection here referred to is urged, not against mediation in that high, eminent, and peculiar sense, in

[a] ["Philosophers make shameful and dangerous mistakes, when they judge of the Divine economy. He cannot, they tell us, act thus, it would be contrary to his wisdom, or his justice, &c. But while they make these peremptory assertions they show themselves to be unacquainted with the fundamental rules of their own science, and with the origin of all late improvements. True philosophy would begin the other way, with observing the constitution of the world, how God has made us, and in what circumstances he has placed us, and *then* from what he has done, form a sure judgment what he would do. Thus might they learn 'the invisible things of God from those which are clearly seen' the things which are not accomplished from those which are."—POWELL'S *Use and Abuse of Philosophy.*]

* 1 Tim. ii. 5.

which Christ is our mediator; but absolutely against the whole notion itself of a mediator at all.

II. As we must suppose, that the world is under the proper moral government of God, or in a state of religion, before we can enter into consideration of the revealed doctrine, concerning the redemption of it by Christ: so that supposition is here to be distinctly noticed. Now the divine moral government which religion teaches us, implies that the consequence of vice shall be misery, in some future state, by the righteous judgment of God. That such consequent punishment shall take effect by his appointment, is necessarily implied. But, as it is not in any sort to be supposed, that we are made acquainted with all the ends or reasons, for which it is fit that future punishments should be inflicted, or why God has appointed such and such consequent misery to follow vice; and as we are altogether in the dark, how or in what manner it shall follow, by what immediate occasions, or by the instrumentality of what means; so there is no absurdity in supposing it may follow in a way analogous to that in which many miseries follow such and such courses of action at present; poverty, sickness, infamy, untimely death by diseases, death from the hands of civil justice. There is no absurdity in supposing future punishment may follow wickedness *of course*, as we speak, or in the way of natural consequence from God's original constitution of the world; from the nature he has given us, and from the condition in which he places us; or in a like manner, as a person rashly trifling upon a precipice, in the way of natural consequence, falls down; in the way of natural consequence of this, breaks his limbs, and in the way of natural consequence, without help, perishes.

Some good men may perhaps be offended with hearing it spoken of as a supposable thing that future punishments of wickedness may be in the way of natural consequence: as if this were taking the execution of justice out of the hands of God, and giving it to nature. But they should remember, that when things come to pass according to the course of nature, this does not hinder them from being his doing, who is the God of nature: and that the Scripture ascribes those punishments to divine justice, which are known to be natural; and which must be called so, when distinguished from such as are miraculous. After all, this supposition, or rather this way of speaking, is here made use of only by way of illustration of the subject before us. For since it must be admitted, that the future punishment of wickedness is not a matter of arbitrary appointment, but of reason, equity, and justice; it comes for aught I see, to the same thing, whether it is supposed to be inflicted in a way analogous to that in which the temporal punishments of vice and folly are inflicted, or in any other way. And though there were a difference, it is allowable, in the present case, to make this supposition, plainly not an incredible one, that future punishment may follow wickedness in the way of natural consequence, or according to some general laws of government already established in the universe.

III. Upon this supposition, or even without it, we may observe somewhat, much to the present purpose, in the constitution of nature or appointments of Providence: the provision which is made, that all the bad natural consequences of men's actions should not always actually follow; or that such bad consequences, as, according to the settled course of things, would inevitably have followed if not prevented, should, in certain degrees, be prevented. We are apt presumptuously to imagine, that the world might have been so constituted, as that there would not have been any such thing as misery or evil. On the contrary we find the Author of nature permits it: but then he has provided reliefs, and in many cases perfect remedies for it, after some pains and difficulties; reliefs and remedies even for that evil, which is the fruit of our own misconduct; and which, in the course of nature, would have continued, and ended in our destruction, but for such remedies. And this is an instance both of severity and of indulgence, in the constitution of nature. Thus all the bad consequences, now mentioned, of a man's trifling upon a precipice, might be prevented. And though all were not, yet some of them might, by proper interposition, if not rejected:[b] by another's coming to the rash man's relief, with his own laying hold on that relief, in such sort as the case required. Persons may do a great

[b] [The interposition of a man of known probity and worth often saves the thoughtless or the guilty from punishment. Mediation is seen in a thousand forms in the arrangements of social life; and the common sense of all mankind approves of it. The release of the offending, by the intercession of the good, and all the benefits of advice, caution, example, instruction, persuasion, and authority, are instances of mediation.]

deal themselves towards preventing the bad consequences of their follies: and more may be done by themselves, together with the assistance of others their fellow-creatures; which assistance nature requires and prompts us to. This is the general constitution of the world.

Now suppose it had been so constituted, that after such actions were done, as were foreseen naturally to draw after them misery to the doer, it should have been no more in human power to have prevented that naturally consequent misery, in any instance, than it is in all: no one can say, whether such a more severe constitution of things might not yet have been really good. But, on the contrary, provision being made by nature, that we may and do, to so great degree, prevent the bad natural effects of our follies; this may be called mercy or compassion in the original constitution of the world: compassion, as distinguished from goodness in general. And, the whole known constitution and course of things affording us instances of such compassion, it would be according to the analogy of nature, to hope, that however ruinous the natural consequences of vice might be, from the general laws of God's government over the universe; yet provision might be made, possibly might have been originally made, for preventing those ruinous consequences from inevitably following: at least from following universally, and in all cases.

Many, I am sensible, will wonder at finding this made a question, or spoken of as in any degree doubtful. The generality of mankind are so far from having that awful sense of things, which the present state of vice and misery and darkness seems to make but reasonable, that they have scarce any apprehension or thought at all about this matter, any way: and some serious persons may have spoken unadvisedly concerning it. But let us observe, what we experience to be, and what, from the very constitution of nature cannot but be, the consequences of irregular and disorderly behavior: even of such rashness, wilfulness, neglects, as we scarce call vicious. Now it is natural to apprehend, that the bad consequences of irregularity will be greater, in proportion as the irregularity is so. And there is no comparison between these irregularities, and the greater instances of vice, or a dissolute profligate disregard to all religion; if there be any thing at all in religion. For consider what it is for creatures, moral agents, presumptuously to introduce that confusion and misery into the kingdom of God, which mankind have in fact introduced: to blaspheme the Sovereign Lord of all; to contemn his authority; to be injurious, to the degree they are, to their fellow-creatures, the creatures of God. Add that the effects of vice in the present world are often extreme misery, irretrievable ruin, and even death: and upon putting all this together, it will appear, that as no one can say, in what degree fatal the unprevented consequences of vice may be, according to the general rule of divine government; so it is by no means intuitively certain, how far these consequences could possibly, in the nature of the thing, be prevented, consistently with the eternal rule of right, or with what is, in fact, the moral constitution of nature. However, there would be large ground to hope, that the universal government was not so severely strict, but that there was room for pardon, or for having those penal consequences prevented. Yet,

IV. There seems no probability, that any thing we could do would alone and of itself prevent them: prevent their following, or being inflicted. But one would think at least, it were impossible that the contrary should be thought certain. For we are not acquainted with the whole of the case. We are not informed of all the reasons, which render it fit that future punishments should be inflicted: and therefore cannot know, whether any thing we could do would make such an alteration, as to render it fit that they should be remitted. We do not know what the whole natural or appointed consequences of vice are; nor in what way they would follow, if not prevented: and therefore can in no sort say, whether we could do any thing which would be sufficient to prevent them. Our ignorance being thus manifest, let us recollect the analogy of nature or Providence. For, though this may be but a slight ground to raise a positive opinion upon, in this matter; yet it is sufficient to answer a mere arbitrary assertion, without any kind of evidence, urged by way of objection against a doctrine, the proof of which is not reason, but revelation. Consider then: people ruin their fortunes by extravagance; they bring diseases upon themselves by excess; they incur the penalties of civil laws; and surely civil government is natural; will sorrow for these follies past, and behaving well for the future, alone and of itself prevent the natural consequences of them?

On the contrary, men's natural abilities of helping themselves are often impaired; or if not, yet they are forced to be beholden to the assistance of others, upon several accounts, and in different ways; assistance which they would have had no occasion for, had it not been for their misconduct; but which, in the disadvantageous condition they have reduced themselves to, is absolutely necessary to their recovery, and retrieving their affairs. Since this is our case, considering ourselves merely as inhabitants of this world, and as having a temporal interest here, under the natural government of God, which however has a great deal moral in it; why is it not supposable that this may be our case also, in our more important capacity, as under his perfect moral government, and having a more general and future interest depending?[c] If we have misbehaved in this higher capacity, and rendered ourselves obnoxious to the future punishment, which God has annexed to vice: it is plainly credible, that behaving well for the time to come may be—not useless, God forbid—but wholly insufficient, alone and of itself, to prevent that punishment: or to put us in the condition which we should have been in, had we preserved our innocence.

Though we ought to reason with all reverence, whenever we reason concerning the divine conduct: yet it may be added, that it is clearly contrary to all our notions of government, as well as to what is, in fact, the general constitution of nature, to suppose, that doing well for the future should, in all cases, prevent all the judicial bad consequences of having done evil, or all the punishment annexed to disobedience. We have manifestly nothing from whence to determine, in what degree, and in what cases, reformation would prevent this punishment, even supposing that it would in some. And though the efficacy of repentance itself

[c] [MR. NEWMAN notices a distinction between the facts of revelation, and its principles; and considers the argument from analogy more concerned with its principles than with its facts. "The revealed facts are special and singular, from the nature of the case, but the revealed principles are common to all the works of God; and if the Author of nature be the author of grace, it may be expected that the principles displayed in them will be the same, and form a connecting link between them. In this identity of *principle*, lies the analogy of natural and revealed religion, in Butler's sense of the word. The Incarnation is a fact, and cannot be paralleled by any thing in nature: the doctrine of mediation is a principle, and is abundantly exemplified in nature."—*Essay on Developments.*]

alone, to prevent what mankind had rendered themselves obnoxious to, and recover what they had forfeited, is now insisted upon, in opposition to Christianity; yet, by the general prevalence of propitiatory sacrifices over the heathen world, this notion of repentance alone being sufficient to expiate guilt, appears to be contrary to the general sense of mankind.[d]

Upon the whole then; had the laws, the general laws of God's government been permitted to operate, without any interposition in our behalf, the future punishment, for aught we know to the contrary, or have any reason to think, must inevitably have followed, notwithstanding any thing we could have done to prevent it.

V. In this darkness, or this light of nature, call it which you please, revelation comes in; and confirms every doubting fear, which could enter into the heart of man, concerning the future unprevented consequence of wickedness. It supposes the world to be in a state of ruin (a supposition which seems the very ground of the Christian dispensation, and which, if not provable by reason, yet is in no wise contrary to it;) and teaches us too, that the rules of divine government are such, as not to admit of pardon immediately and directly upon repentance, or by the sole efficacy of it. But teaches at the same time, what nature might justly have hoped, that the moral government of the universe was not so rigid, but that there was room for an interposition, to avert the fatal consequences of vice; which therefore, by this means, does admit of pardon. Revelation teaches us, that the unknown laws of God's more general government, no less than the particular laws by which we experience he governs us at present, are compassionate,* as well as good in the more general notion of goodness: and that he hath mercifully provided, that there should be an interposition to prevent the destruction of human kind; whatever that destruction unprevented would have been. *God so loved the world, that he gave his only begotten Son, that whosoever believeth,* not, to be sure, in a speculative, but in a practical sense, *that whosoever believeth in him, should*

[d] [The student will find the inadequacy of repentance to cancel guilt, beautifully exhibited by WAYLAND, Mor. Science: MAGEE, Atonement: HOWE. Living Temple.]

* P 232, &c.

*not perish:** gave his Son in the same way of goodness to the world, as he affords particular persons the friendly assistance of their fellow-creatures, when, without it, their temporal ruin would be the certain consequence of their follies: in the same way of goodness, I say, though in a transcendent and infinitely higher degree. And the Son of God *loved us, and gave himself for us*, with a love, which he himself compares to that of human friendship: though, in this case, all comparisons must fall infinitely short of the thing intended to be illustrated by them. He interposed in such a manner as was necessary and effectual to prevent that execution of justice upon sinners, which God had appointed should otherwise have been executed upon them; or in such a manner, as to prevent that punishment from actually following, which, according to the general laws of divine government, must have followed the sins of the world, had it not been for such interposition.†

If any thing here said should appear, upon first thought, inconsistent with divine goodness; a second, I am persuaded, will entirely remove that appearance. For were we to suppose the constitution of things to be such, as that the whole creation must

* John iii. 16.

† It cannot, I suppose, be imagined, even by the most cursory reader, that it is, in any sort, affirmed or implied in any thing said in this chapter, that none can have the benefit of the general redemption, but such as have the advantage of being made acquainted with it in the present life. But it may be needful to mention, that several questions, which have been brought into the subject before us, and determined, are not in the least entered into here. questions which have been, I fear, rashly determined, and perhaps with equal rashness contrary ways. For instance, whether God could have saved the world by other means than the death of Christ, consistently with the general laws of his government. And had not Christ come into the world, what would have been the future condition of the better sort of men; those just persons over the face of the earth, for whom Manasses in his prayer[e] asserts, repentance was not appointed. The meaning of the first of these questions is greatly ambiguous: and neither of them can properly be answered, without going upon that infinitely absurd supposition, that we know the whole of the case. And perhaps the very inquiry, *What would have followed, if God had not done as he has*, may have in it some very great impropriety: and ought not to be carried on any further than is necessary to help our partial and inadequate conceptions of things.

[e] [The "prayer of Manasses" is one of the apocryphal books of the Old Testament, which next precedes "Maccabees."]

have perished, had it not been for something, which God had appointed should be, in order to prevent that ruin: even this supposition would not be inconsistent, in any degree, with the most absolutely perfect goodness. Still it may be thought, that this whole manner of treating the subject before us supposes mankind to be naturally in a very strange state. And truly so it does. But it is not Christianity which has put us into this state. Whoever will consider the manifold miseries, and the extreme wickedness of the world; that the best have great wrongnesses within themselves, which they complain of, and endeavor to amend; but that the generality grow more profligate and corrupt with age; that even moralists thought the present state to be a state of punishment: and, that the earth our habitation has the appearances of being a ruin: whoever, I say, will consider all these, and some other obvious things, will think he has little reason to object against the Scripture account, that mankind is in a state of degradation; against this being *the fact:* how difficult soever he may think it to account for, or even to form a distinct conception of the occasions and circumstances of it. But that the crime of our first parents was the occasion of our being placed in a more disadvantageous condition, is a thing throughout and particularly analogous to what we see in the daily course of natural providence; as the recovery of the world by the interposition of Christ has been shown to be so in general.

VI. The particular manner in which Christ interposed in the redemption of the world, or his office as *Mediator*, in the largest sense, *between God and man*, is thus represented to us in the Scripture. *He is the light of the world;** the revealer of the will of God in the most eminent sense. He is a propitiatory sacrifice;† *the Lamb of God:*‡ and, as he voluntarily offered himself up, he is styled our High Priest.§ And, which seems of peculiar weight, he is described beforehand in the Old Testament, under the same characters of a priest, and an expiatory victim.‖ And whereas it is objected, that all this is merely by

* John i., and viii. 12.

† Rom. iii. 25, v. 11: 1 Cor. v. 7: Eph. v. 2: 1 John ii. 2: Matt. xxvi 28.

‡ John i. 29, 36, and throughout the book of Revelation.

§ Throughout the epistle to the Hebrews.

‖ Isa. liii. Dan. ix. 24: Ps. cx 4.

way of allusion to the sacrifices of the Mosaic law, the Apostle on the contrary affirms, that the *law was a shadow of good things to come, and not the very image of the things:** and that *the priests that offer gifts according to the law—serve unto the example and shadow of heavenly things, as Moses was admonished of God, when he was about to make the tabernacle. For see, saith he, that thou make all things according to the pattern showed to thee in the mount:*† *i.e.* the Levitical priesthood was a shadow of the priesthood of Christ; in like manner as the tabernacle made by Moses was according to that showed him in the mount. The priesthood of Christ, and the tabernacle in the mount, were the originals; of the former of which the Levitical priesthood was a type; and of the latter the tabernacle made by Moses was a copy. The doctrine of this epistle then plainly is, that the legal sacrifices were allusions to the great and final atonement to be made by the blood of Christ; and not that this was an allusion to those. Nor can any thing be more express and determinate than the following passage. *It is not possible that the blood of bulls and of goats should take away sin. Wherefore when he cometh into the world, he saith, Sacrifice and offering, i.e.* of bulls and of goats, *thou wouldest not, but a body hast thou prepared me. Lo! I come to do thy will, O God. By which will we are sanctified, through the offering of the body of Jesus Christ once for all.*‡ And to add one passage more of the like kind: *Christ was once offered to bear the sins of many: and unto them that look for him shall he appear the second time, without sin; i.e.* without bearing sin, as he did at his first coming, by being an offering for it; without having our *iniquities* again *laid upon him,* without being any more a sin-offering: —*unto them that look for him shall he appear the second time, without sin, unto salvation.*§ Nor do the inspired writers at all confine themselves to this manner of speaking concerning the satisfaction of Christ; but declare an efficacy in what he did and suffered for us, additional to and beyond mere instruction, example, and government, in great variety of expression: *That Jesus should die for that nation,* the Jews: *and not for that nation only, but that also,* plainly by the efficacy of his death,

* Heb. x. 1. † Heb. viii. 4, 5.
‡ Heb. x. 4, 5, 7, 9, 10. § Heb. ix. 28.

*he should gather together in one the children of God that were scattered abroad:** that *he suffered for sins, the just for the unjust:*† that *he gave his life, himself, a ransom:*‡ that *we are bought, bought with a price:*§ that *he redeemed us with his blood: redeemed us from the curse of the law, being made a curse for us:*‖ that he is our *advocate, intercessor,* and *propitiation:*¶ that *he was made perfect,* or consummate, *through sufferings; and being* thus *made perfect, he became the author of salvation:*** that *God was in Christ reconciling the world to himself; by the death of his Son, by the cross; not imputing their trespasses unto them:*†† and lastly, that *through death he destroyed him that had the power of death.*‡‡ Christ having thus *humbled himself, and become obedient to death, even the death of the cross; God also hath highly exalted him, and given him a name, which is above every name: hath given all things into his hands: hath committed all judgment unto him; that all men should honor the Son, even as they honor the Father.*§§ For, *worthy is the Lamb that was slain, to receive power, and riches, and wisdom, and strength, and honor, and glory, and blessing. And every creature which is in heaven, and on the earth, heard I, saying, Blessing, and honor, and glory, and power, be unto him that sitteth upon the throne, and unto the Lamb forever and ever.*‖‖

These passages of Scripture seem to comprehend and express the chief parts of Christ's office, as Mediator between God and man, so far, I mean, as the nature of this his office is revealed; and it is usually treated of by divines under three heads.

First, He was, by way of eminence, the Prophet: *that Prophet that should come into the world,*¶¶ to declare the divine will. He published anew the law of nature, which men had corrupted; and the very knowledge of which, to some degree, was lost among them. He taught mankind, taught us authoritatively, to *live soberly, righteously, and godly in this present world,* in expectation of the future judgment of God. He confirmed

* John xi. 51, 52. † 1 Pet. iii. 18.
‡ Matt. xx. 28: Mark x. 45: 1 Tim. ii. 6.
§ 2 Pet. ii. 1: Rev. xiv. 4: 1 Cor. vi. 20.
‖ 1 Pet. i. 19: Rev. v. 9: Gal. iii. 13. ¶ Heb. vii. 25: 1 John ii. 1, 2.
** Heb. ii. 10.: v. 9. †† 2 Cor. v. 19: Rom. v. 10: Eph. ii. 16.
‡‡ Heb. ii. 14. See also a remarkable passage in the book of Job, xxxiii. 24.
§§ Phil. ii. 8, 9: John iii. 35, and v. 22, 23. ‖‖ Rev. v. 12, 13. ¶¶ John vi. 14.

the truth of this moral system of nature, and gave us additional evidence of it; the evidence of testimony.* He distinctly revealed the manner, in which God would be worshipped, the efficacy of repentance, and the rewards and punishments of a future life. Thus he was a prophet in a sense in which no other ever was. To which is to be added, that he set us a perfect *example, that we should follow his steps.*

Secondly, He has a *kingdom which is not of this world.* He founded a Church, to be to mankind a standing memorial of religion, and invitation to it; which he promised to be with always even to the end. He exercises an invisible government over it, himself, and by his Spirit: over that part of it which is militant here on earth, a government of discipline, *for the perfecting of the saints, for the edifying his body: till we all come in the unity of the faith, and of the knowledge of the Son of God, unto a perfect man, unto the measure of the stature of the fulness of Christ.*† Of this Church, all persons scattered over the world, who live in obedience to his laws, are members. For these he is *gone to prepare a place,* and *will come again to receive them unto himself, that where he is, there they may be also; and reign with him forever and ever:*‡ and likewise *to take vengeance on them that know not God, and obey not his Gospel.*§

Against these parts of Christ's office I find no objections, but what are fully obviated in the beginning of this chapter.

Lastly, Christ offered himself a propitiatory sacrifice, and made atonement for the sins of the world; which is mentioned last, in regard to what is objected against it. Sacrifices of expiation were commanded the Jews, and obtained among most other nations, from tradition, whose original probably was revelation. And they were continually repeated, both occasionally, and at the returns of stated times: and made up great part of the external religion of mankind. *But now once in the end of the world Christ appeared to put away sin by the sacrifice of himself.*‖ This sacrifice was, in the highest degree and with the most extensive influence, of that efficacy for obtaining pardon of sin, which the heathens may be supposed to have thought their sacri

* P. 188, &c. † Eph. iv. 12, 13. ‡ John xiv. 2, 3: Rev. iii. 21, and xi. 15
§ 2 Thess. i. 8. ‖ Heb. ix. 26.

fices to have been, and which the Jewish sacrifices really were in some degree, and with regard to some persons.[f]

How and in what particular *way* it had this efficacy, there are not wanting persons who have endeavored to explain: but I do not find that the Scripture has explained it. We seem to be very much in the dark concerning the manner in which the ancients understood atonement to be made, *i.e.* pardon to be obtained by sacrifices. And if the Scripture has, as surely it has, left this matter of the satisfaction of Christ mysterious, left somewhat in it unrevealed, all conjectures about it must be, if not evidently absurd, yet at least uncertain. Nor has any one reason to complain for want of further information, unless he can show his claim to it.

Some have endeavored to explain the efficacy of what Christ has done and suffered for us, beyond what the Scripture has authorized: others, probably because they could not explain it, have been for taking it away, and confining his office as Redeemer of the world, to his instruction, example, and government of the church. Whereas the doctrine of the Gospel appears to be, not only that he taught the efficacy of repentance, but rendered it of the efficacy of which it is, by what he did and suffered for us: that he obtained for us the benefit of having our repentance accepted unto eternal life: not only that he revealed to sinners, that they were in a capacity of salvation, and how they might obtain it; but moreover that he put them into this capacity of salvation, by what he did and suffered for them; put us into a capacity of escaping future punishment, and obtaining future happiness. And it is our wisdom thankfully to accept the benefit, by performing the conditions, upon which it is offered, on our part, without disputing how it was procured on his. For,

VII. Since we neither know by what means punishment in a future state would have followed wickedness in this: nor in what manner it would have been inflicted, had it not been prevented; nor all the reasons why its infliction would have been needful, nor the particular nature of that state of happiness, which Christ is gone to prepare for his disciples: and since we are ignorant

[f] [Consult MAGEE, on Atonement: STAPFERI Institutiones: TURRETIN, De Satisfactione: CHALMERS, Discourses: OWEN, Satis. of Christ.]

how far any thing which we could do, would, alone and of itself, have been effectual to prevent that punishment to which we were obnoxious, and recover that happiness which we had forfeited; it is most evident we are not judges, antecedently to revelation, whether a mediator was or was not necessary, to obtain those ends: to prevent that future punishment, and bring mankind to the final happiness of their nature. For the very same reasons, upon supposition of the necessity of a mediator, we are no more judges, antecedently to revelation, of the whole nature of his office, or of the several parts of which it consists; or of what was fit and requisite to be assigned him, in order to accomplish the ends of divine Providence in the appointment. Hence it follows, that to object against the expediency or usefulness of particular things, revealed to have been done or suffered by him, because we do not see how they were conducive to those ends, is highly absurd. Yet nothing is more common to be met with, than this absurdity. If it be acknowledged beforehand, that we are not judges in the case, it is evident that no objection can, with any shadow of reason, be urged against any particular part of Christ's mediatorial office revealed in Scripture, till it can be shown positively not to be requisite or conducive to the ends proposed to be accomplished; or that it is in itself unreasonable.

There is one objection made against the satisfaction of Christ, which looks to be of this positive kind: that the doctrine of his being appointed to suffer for the sins of the world, represents God as being indifferent whether he punished the innocent or the guilty. Now from the foregoing observations we may see the extreme slightness of all such objections; and (though it is most certain all who make them *do not see* the consequence) that they conclude altogether as much against God's whole original constitution of nature, and the whole daily course of divine Providence in the government of the world, (*i.e.* against the whole scheme of Theism and the whole notion of religion,) as against Christianity. For the world is a constitution or system, whose parts have a mutual reference to each other: and there is a scheme of things gradually carrying on, called the course of nature, to the carrying on of which God has appointed us, in various ways, to contribute. And when, in the daily course of natural providence, it is appointed that innocent people should suffer for the faults of the guilty, this is liable to the very same objection, as the instance we are now considering. The infinitely greater importance of that appointment of Christianity, which is objected against, does not hinder but it may be, as it plainly is, an appointment of the very same *kind*, with what the world affords us daily examples of. Nay, if there were any force at all in the objection, it would be stronger, in one respect, against natural providence, than against Christianity: because under the former we are in many cases commanded, and even necessitated whether we will or no, to suffer for the faults of others; whereas the sufferings of Christ were voluntary.

The world's being under the righteous government of God does indeed imply, that finally, and upon the whole, every one shall receive according to his personal deserts: and the general doctrine of the whole Scripture is, that this shall be the completion of the divine government. But during the progress, and, for aught we know, even in order to the completion of this moral scheme, vicarious punishments may be fit, and absolutely necessary. Men by their follies run themselves into extreme distress; into difficulties which would be absolutely fatal to them, were it not for the interposition and assistance of others. God commands by the law of nature, that we afford them this assistance, in many cases where we cannot do it without very great pains, and labor, and sufferings to ourselves. We see in what variety of ways one person's sufferings contribute to the relief of another: and how, or by what particular means, this comes to pass, or follows, from the constitution and laws of nature, which came under our notice: and, being familiarized to it, men are not shocked with it. So that the reason of their insisting upon objections of the foregoing kind against the satisfaction of Christ is, either that they do not consider God's settled and uniform appointments as his appointments at all; or else they forget that vicarious punishment is a providential appointment of every day's experience. And then, from their being unacquainted with the more general laws of nature or divine government over the world, and not seeing how the sufferings of Christ could contribute to the redemption of it, unless by arbitrary and tyrannical will, they conclude his sufferings could not contribute to it any other way. And yet, what has been often alleged in justification of this doctrine, even from the apparent natural tendency of this method of our redemption; its tendency to vindicate the authority of God's laws, and deter his creatures from sin; this has never yet been answered, and is I think plainly unanswerable: though I am far from thinking it an account of the whole of the case. But, without taking this into consideration, it abundantly appears, from the observations above made, that this objection is not an objection against Christianity, but against the whole general constitution of nature. And if it were to be considered as an objection against Christianity, or considering it as it is, an objection against the constitution of nature; it amounts to no more in conclusion than this, that a divine appointment cannot be necessary or expedient, because the objector does not discern it to be so: though he must own that the nature of the case is such, as renders him incapable of judging, whether it be so or not; or of seeing it to be necessary, though it were so!

It is indeed a matter of great patience to reasonable men, to find people arguing in this manner: objecting against the credibility of such particular things revealed in Scripture, that they do not see the necessity or expediency of them. For though it is highly right, and the most pious exercise of our understanding, to inquire with due reverence into the ends and reasons of God's dispensations: yet when those reasons are concealed, to argue from our ignorance, that such dispensations cannot be from God, is infinitely absurd. The presumption of this kind of objections seems almost lost in the folly of them. And the folly of them is yet greater, when they are urged, as usually they are, against things in Christianity analogous or like to those natural dispensations of Providence, which are matter of experience. Let reason be kept to: and if any part of the Scripture account of the redemption of the world by Christ can be shown to be really contrary to it, let the Scripture, in the name of God, be given up. But let not such poor creatures as we are, go on objecting against an infinite scheme, that we do not see the necessity or usefulness of all its parts, and call this reasoning; and, which still further heightens the absurdity in the present case, parts which we are not actively concerned in. For it may be worth mentioning,

Lastly, That not only the reason of the thing, but the whole analogy of nature, should teach us, not to expect to have the like information concerning the divine conduct, as concerning our own duty. God instructs us by experience, (for it is not reason, but experience which instructs us,) what good or bad consequences will follow from our acting in such and such manners: and by this he directs us how we are to behave ourselves. But, though we are sufficiently instructed for the common purposes of life: yet it is but an almost infinitely small part of natural providence, which we are at all let into. The case is the same with regard to revelation. The doctrine of a mediator between God and man, against which it is objected, that the expediency of some things in it is not understood, relates only to what was done on God's part in the appointment, and on the Mediator's in the execution of it. For what is *required of us*, in consequence of this gracious dispensation, is another subject, in which none can complain for want of information. The constitution of the world, and God's natural government over it, is all mystery, as much as the Christian dispensation. Yet under the first he has given men all things pertaining to life; and under the other all things pertaining unto godliness. And it may be added, that there is nothing hard to be accounted for in any of the common precepts of Christianity: though if there were, surely a divine command is abundantly sufficient to lay us under the strongest obligations to obedience. But the fact is, that the reasons of all the Christian precepts are evident. Positive institutions are manifestly necessary to keep up and propagate religion among mankind. And our duty to Christ, the internal and external worship of him; this part of the religion of the Gospel manifestly arises out of what he has done and suffered, his authority and dominion, and the relation which he is revealed to stand in to us.*

* P. 194, &c.

CHAPTER VI.

THE WANT OF UNIVERSALITY IN REVELATION; AND THE SUPPOSED DEFICIENCY IN THE PROOF OF IT

It has been thought by some persons, that if the evidence of revelation appears doubtful, this itself turns into a positive argument against it: because it cannot be supposed, that, if it were true, it would be left to subsist upon doubtful evidence. And the objection against revelation from its not being universal is often insisted upon as of great weight.

The weakness of these opinions may be shown, by observing the suppositions on which they are founded: which are really such as these; that it cannot be thought God would have bestowed any favor at all upon us, unless in the degree which we think he might, and which, we imagine, would be most to our particular advantage; and also that it cannot be thought he would bestow a favor upon any, unless he bestowed the same upon all; suppositions, which we find contradicted, not by a few instances in God's natural government of the world, but by the general analogy of nature together.

Persons who speak of the evidence of religion as doubtful, and of this supposed doubtfulness as a positive argument against it, should be put upon considering, what that evidence is, which they act upon with regard to their temporal interests. It is not only extremely difficult, but in many cases absolutely impossible, to balance pleasure and pain, satisfaction and uneasiness, so as to be able to say on which side is the overplus. There are the like difficulties and impossibilities in making the due allowances for a change of temper and taste, for satiety, disgusts, ill health: any of which render men incapable of enjoying, after they have obtained what they most eagerly desired. Numberless too are the accidents, besides that one of untimely death, which may even probably disappoint the best-concerted schemes: and strong objections are often seen to lie against them, not to be removed or answered, but which seem overbalanced by reasons on the other side; so as that the certain difficulties and dangers of the pursuit are, by every one, thought justly disregarded, upon account of the appearing greater advantages in case of success, though there be but little probability of it. Lastly, every one observes our liableness, if we be not upon our guard, to be deceived by the falsehood of men, and the false appearances of things: and this danger must be greatly increased, if there be a strong bias within, suppose from indulged passion, to favor the deceit. Hence arises that great uncertainty and doubtfulness of proof, *wherein* our temporal interest really consists; what are the most probable *means* of attaining it; and whether those means will eventually be *successful*. And numberless instances there are, in the daily course of life, in which all men think it reasonable to engage in pursuits, though the probability is greatly against succeeding; and to make such provision for themselves, as it is supposable they may have occasion for, though the plain acknowledged probability is, that they never shall.

Those who think the objection against revelation, from its light not being universal, to be of weight,[a] should observe, that the Author of nature, in numberless instances, bestows that upon some, which he does not upon others, who seem equally to stand in need of it. Indeed he appears to bestow all his gifts with the most promiscuous variety among creatures of the same species: health and strength, capacities of prudence and of knowledge, means of improvement, riches, and all external advantages. As there are not any two men found, of exactly like shape and features; so it is probable there are not any two, of an exactly like constitution, temper, and situation, with regard to the goods and evils of life. Yet, notwithstanding these uncertainties and varieties, God does exercise a natural government over the world; and there is such a thing as a prudent and imprudent institution of life, with regard to our health and our affairs, under that his natural government.

As neither the Jewish nor Christian revelation have been universal; and as they have been afforded to a greater or less part

[a] [This objection is ably urged by TINDALL. The answer of our author is complete. We should remember, that twice in the history of mankind, revelation *has been* universal. The first pair, and the occupants of the ark, comprised the whole population. But how soon was light rejected! Christianity is universal, in nature and intention; is to become so in fact; and according to a very probable construction of prophecy, will continue to be universal, for three hundred and sixty thousand years.]

of the world, at different times; so likewise at different times, both revelations have had different degrees of evidence. The Jews who lived during the succession of prophets, that is, from Moses till after the Captivity, had higher evidence of the truth of their religion, than those had, who lived in the interval between the last-mentioned period, and the coming of Christ. And the first Christians had higher evidence of the miracles wrought in attestation of Christianity, than what we have now. They had also a strong presumptive proof of the truth of it, perhaps of much greater force, in way of argument, than many think, of which we have very little remaining; I mean the presumptive proof of its truth, from the influence which it had upon the lives of the generality of its professors. And we, or future ages, may possibly have a proof of it, which they could not have, from the conformity between the prophetic history, and the state of the world[b] and of Christianity.

And further: if we were to suppose the evidence, which some have of religion, to amount to little more than seeing that it *may* be true; but that they remain in great doubts and uncertainties about both its evidence and its nature, and great perplexities concerning the rule of life: others to have a *full conviction* of the truth of religion, with a distinct knowledge of their duty; and others severally to have all the intermediate degrees of religious light and evidence, which lie between these two—if we put the case, that for the present, it was intended that revelation should be no more than a small light, in the midst of a world greatly overspread, notwithstanding it, with ignorance and darkness: that certain glimmerings of this light should extend, and be directed, to remote distances, in such a manner as that those who really partook of it should not discern whence it originally came: that some in a nearer situation to it should have its light obscured, and, in different ways and degrees, intercepted: and that others should be placed within its clearer influence, and be much more enlivened, cheered, and directed by it; but yet that even to these

[b] [May not this be a principal object of the Apocalypse? As the book of Daniel furnished a constant and powerful support to the faith of the Jew, by the constant development of prophecy, so the Apocalypse, rightly studied must powerfully, and through all time, support the faith of the Christian by the continual unfolding and verification of its predictions.]

it should be no more than *a light shining in a dark place:* all this would be perfectly uniform, and of a piece with the conduct of Providence, in the distribution of its other blessings. If the fact of the case really were, that some have received no light at all from the Scripture; as many ages and countries in the heathen world: that others, though they have, by means of it, had essential or natural religion enforced upon their consciences, yet have never had the genuine Scripture revelation, with its real evidence, proposed to their consideration; and the ancient Persians and modern Mahometans may possibly be instances of people in a situation somewhat like to this; that others, though they have had the Scripture laid before them as of divine revelation, yet have had it with the system and evidence of Christianity so interpolated, the system so corrupted, the evidence so blended with false miracles, as to leave the mind in the utmost doubtfulness and uncertainty about the whole; which may be the state of some thoughtful men, in most of those nations who call themselves Christian: and lastly, that others have had Christianity offered to them in its genuine simplicity, and with its proper evidence, as persons in countries and churches of civil and of Christian liberty; but that even these persons are left in great ignorance in many respects, and have by no means light afforded them enough to satisfy their curiosity, but only to regulate their life, to teach them their duty, and encourage them in the careful discharge of it. I say, if we were to suppose this somewhat of a general true account of the degrees of moral and religious light and evidence, which were intended to be afforded mankind, and of what has actually been and is their situation, in their moral and religious capacity; there would be nothing in all this ignorance, doubtfulness, and uncertainty, in all these varieties, and supposed disadvantages of some in comparison of others, respecting religion, but may be paralleled by manifest analogies in the natural dispensations of Providence at present, considering ourselves merely in our temporal capacity.

Nor is there any thing shocking in all this, or which would seem to bear hard upon the moral administration in nature, if we would really keep in mind, that every one shall be dealt equitably with: instead of forgetting this, or explaining it away, after it is acknowledged in words. All shadow of injustice, and indeed all harsh appearances, in this various economy of Providence, would be lost, if we would keep in mind, that every merciful allowance shall be made, and no more be required of any one, than what might have been equitably expected of him, from the circumstances in which he was placed; and not what might have been expected, had he been placed in other circumstances: *i.e.* in Scripture language, that every man shall be *accepted according to what he had, not according to what he had not.** This however does not by any means imply, that all persons' condition here is equally advantageous with respect to futurity. And Providence's designing to place some in greater darkness with respect to religious knowledge, is no more a reason why they should not endeavor to get out of that darkness, and others to bring them out of it, than why ignorant and slow people in matters of other knowledge should not endeavor to learn, or should not be instructed.

It is not unreasonable to suppose, that the same wise and good principle, whatever it was, which disposed the Author of nature to make different kinds and orders of creatures, disposed him also to place creatures of like kinds in different situations. And that the same principle which disposed him to make creatures of different moral capacities, disposed him also to place creatures of like moral capacities in different religious situations; and even the same creatures, in different periods of their being. The account or reason of this is also most probably the account why the constitution of things is such, as that creatures of moral natures or capacities, for a considerable part of that duration in which they are living agents, are not at all subjects of morality and religion; but grow up to be so, and grow up to be so more and more, gradually from childhood to mature age.

What, in particular, is the account or reason of these things, we must be greatly in the dark, were it only that we know so very little even of our own case. Our present state may possibly be the consequence of something past, of which we are wholly ignorant: as it has a reference to somewhat to come, of which we know scarce any more than is necessary for practice. A system or constitution, in its notion, implies variety; and so complicated a one as this world, very great variety. So that

* 2 Cor. viii. 12.

were revelation universal, yet, from men's different capacities of understanding, from the different lengths of their lives, their different educations and other external circumstances, and from their difference of temper and bodily constitution, their religious situations would be widely different, and the disadvantage of some in comparison of others, perhaps, altogether as much as at present. The true account, whatever it be, why mankind, or such a part of mankind, are placed in this condition of ignorance, must be supposed also the true account of our further ignorance, in not knowing the reasons why, or whence it is, that they are placed in this condition.

The following practical reflections may deserve the serious consideration of those persons, who think the circumstances of mankind or their own, in the forementioned respects, a ground of complaint.

First, The evidence of religion not appearing obvious, may constitute one particular part of some men's trial in the religious sense: as it gives scope, for a virtuous exercise, or vicious neglect of their understanding, in examining or not examining into that evidence. There seems no possible reason to be given, why we may not be in a state of moral probation, with regard to the exercise of our understanding upon the subject of religion, as we are with regard to our behavior in common affairs. The former is as much a thing within our power and choice as the latter. And I suppose it is to be laid down for certain, that the same character, the same inward principle, which, after a man is convinced of the truth of religion, renders him obedient to the precepts of it, would, were he not thus convinced, set him about an examination of it, upon its system and evidence being offered to his thoughts: and that in the latter state his examination would be with an impartiality, seriousness, and solicitude, proportionable to what his obedience is in the former. And as inattention, negligence, want of all serious concern, about a matter of such a nature and such importance, when offered to men's consideration, is, before a distinct conviction of its truth, as real depravity and dissoluteness, as neglect of religious practice after such conviction: so active solicitude about it, and fair impartial consideration of its evidence before such conviction, is as really an exercise of a morally right temper; as is religious practice after. Thus, that religion is not intuitively true, but a matter of deduction and inference; that a conviction of its truth is not forced upon every one, but left to be, by some, collected with heedful attention to premises; this as much constitutes religious probation, as much affords sphere, scope, opportunity, for right and wrong behavior, as any thing whatever does. And their manner of treating this subject, when laid before them, shows what is in their heart, and is an exertion of it.

Secondly, It appears to be a thing as evident, though it is not so much attended to, that if, upon consideration of religion, the evidence of it should seem to any persons doubtful, in the highest supposable degree; even this doubtful evidence will, however, put them into a *general state of probation* in the moral and religious sense. For, suppose a man to be really in doubt, whether such a person had not done him the greatest favor; or, whether his whole temporal interest did not depend upon that person; no one, who had any sense of gratitude and of prudence, could possibly consider himself in the same situation, with regard to such person, as if he had no such doubt. In truth, it is as just to say, that certainty and doubt are the same, as to say the situations now mentioned would leave a man as entirely at liberty in point of gratitude or prudence, as he would be, were he certain he had received no favor from such person; or that he no way depended upon him. Thus, though the evidence of religion which is afforded to some men should be little more than they are given to see, the system of Christianity, or religion in general, to be supposable and credible; this ought in all reason to beget a serious practical apprehension, that it *may* be true. And even this will afford matter of exercise for religious suspense and deliberation, for moral resolution and self-government; because the apprehension that religion may be true does as really lay men under obligations, as a full conviction that it is true. It gives occasion and motives to consider further the important subject; to preserve attentively upon their minds a general implicit sense that they may be under divine moral government, an awful solicitude about religion, whether natural or revealed. Such apprehension ought to turn men's eyes to every degree of new light which may be had, from whatever side it comes; and induce them to refrain, in the mean time, from all immoralities, and live in the conscientious practice of every common virtue. Especially are they bound to keep at the greatest distance from all dissolute profaneness, for this the very nature of the case forbids; and to treat with highest reverence a matter, upon which their own whole interest and being, and the fate of nature, depend. This behavior, and an active endeavor to maintain within themselves this temper, is the business, the duty, and the wisdom of those persons, who complain of the doubtfulness of religion: is what they are under the most proper obligations to. And such behavior is an exertion of, and has a tendency to improve in them, that character, which the practice of all the several duties of religion, from a full conviction of its truth, is an exertion of, and has a tendency to improve in others: others, I say, to whom God has afforded such conviction. Nay, considering the infinite importance of religion, revealed as well as natural, I think it may be said in general, that whoever will weigh the matter thoroughly may see, there is not near so much difference, as is commonly imagined, between what ought in reason to be the rule of life, to those persons who are fully convinced of its truth, and to those who have only a serious doubting apprehension, that it may be true. Their hopes, and fears, and obligations, will be in various degrees: but, as the subject-matter of their hopes and fears is the same, so the subject-matter of their obligations, what they are bound to do and to refrain from, is not so very unlike.

It is to be observed further, that, from a character of understanding, or a situation of influence in the world, some persons have it in their power to do infinitely more harm or good, by setting an example of profaneness and avowed disregard to all religion, or, on the contrary, of a serious, though perhaps doubting, apprehension of its truth, and of a reverent regard to it under this doubtfulness; than they can do, by acting well or ill in all the *common intercourses* among mankind. Consequently they are most highly accountable for a behavior, which, they may easily foresee, is of such importance, and in which there is most plainly a right and a wrong; even admitting the evidence of religion to be as doubtful as is pretended.

The ground of these observations, and that which renders them just and true, is, that doubting necessarily implies *some* degree of evidence for that, of which we doubt. For no person would be in doubt concerning the truth of a number of facts so and so circumstanced, which should accidentally come into his thoughts, and of which he had no evidence at all. And though in the case of an even chance, and where consequently we were in doubt, we should in common language say, that we had no evidence at all for either side; yet that situation of things, which renders it an even chance and no more, that such an event will happen, renders this case equivalent to all others, where there is such evidence on both sides of a question,* as leaves the mind in doubt concerning the truth. Indeed in all these cases, there is no more evidence on one side than on the other; but there is (what is equivalent to) much more for either, than for the truth of a number of facts, which come into one's thoughts at random. Thus, in all these cases, doubt as much presupposes evidence, in lower degrees, as belief presupposes higher, and certainty higher still. Any one, who will a little attend to the nature of evidence, will easily carry this observation on, and see, that between no evidence at all, and that degree of it which affords ground of doubt, there are as many intermediate degrees, as there are, between that degree which is the ground of doubt, and demonstration. And though we have not faculties to distinguish these degrees of evidence with any sort of exactness; yet, in proportion as they are discerned, they ought to influence our practice. It is as real an imperfection in the moral character, not to be influenced in practice by a lower degree of evidence when discerned, as it is in the understanding, not to discern it. And as, in all subjects which men consider, they discern the lower as well as higher degrees of evidence, proportionably to their capacity of understanding; so, in practical subjects, they are influenced in practice, by the lower as well as higher degrees of it, proportionably to their fairness and honesty. And as, in proportion to defects in the understanding, men are unapt to see lower degrees of evidence, are in danger of overlooking evidence when it is not glaring, and are easily imposed upon in such cases; so, in proportion to the corruption of the heart, they seem capable of satisfying themselves with having no regard in practice to evidence acknowledged to be real, if it be not overbearing. From these things it must follow, that doubting concerning religion implies

* Introduction.

such a degree of evidence for it, as, joined with the consideration of its importance, unquestionably lays men under the obligations before mentioned, to have a dutiful regard to it in all their behavior.

Thirdly, The difficulties in which the evidence of religion is involved, which some complain of, is no more a just ground of complaint, than the external circumstances of temptation, which others are placed in; or than difficulties in the practice of it, after a full conviction of its truth. Temptations render our state a more improving state of discipline,* than it would be otherwise: as they give occasion for a more attentive exercise of the virtuous principle, which confirms and strengthens it more, than an easier or less attentive exercise of it could. Speculative difficulties are, in this respect, of the very same nature with these external temptations. For the evidence of religion not appearing obvious, is to some persons a temptation to reject it, without any consideration at all; and therefore requires such an attentive exercise of the virtuous principle, seriously to consider that evidence, as there would be no occasion for, but for such temptation. And the supposed doubtfulness of its evidence, after it has been in some sort considered, affords opportunity to an unfair mind of explaining away, and deceitfully hiding from itself, that evidence which it might see; and also for men's encouraging themselves in vice, from hopes of impunity, though they do clearly see thus much at least, that these hopes are uncertain. In like manner the common temptation to many instances of folly, which end in temporal infamy and ruin, is the ground for hope of not being detected, and of escaping with impunity; *i.e.* the doubtfulness of the proof beforehand, that such foolish behavior will thus end in infamy and ruin. On the contrary, supposed doubtfulness in the evidence of religion calls for a more careful and attentive exercise of the virtuous principle, in fairly yielding themselves up to the proper influence of any real evidence, though doubtful; and in practising conscientiously all virtue, though under some uncertainty, whether the government in the universe may not possibly be such, as that vice may escape with impunity. And in general, temptation, meaning by this word the lesser allurements to wrong and difficulties in the discharge of our duty, as

* Part I. chap. v.

well as the greater ones; temptation, I say, as such and of every kind and degree, as it calls forth some virtuous efforts, additional to what would otherwise have been wanting, cannot but be an additional discipline and improvement of virtue, as well as probation of it in the other senses of that word.* So that the very same account is to be given, why the evidence of religion should be left in such a manner, as to require, in some, an attentive, solicitous, perhaps painful exercise of their understanding about it; as why others should be placed in such circumstances, as that the practice of its common duties, after a full conviction of the truth of it, should require attention, solicitude, and pains: or, why appearing doubtfulness should be permitted to afford matter of temptation to some; as why external difficulties and allurements should be permitted to afford matter of temptation to others. The same account also is to be given, why some should be exercised with temptations of both these kinds; as why others should be exercised with the latter in such very high degrees, as some have been, particularly as the primitive Christians were.

Nor does there appear any absurdity in supposing, that the speculative difficulties, in which the evidence of religion is involved, may make even the principal part of some persons' trial. For as the chief temptations of the generality of the world are the ordinary motives to injustice, or unrestrained pleasure, or to live in the neglect of religion, from that frame of mind which renders many persons almost without feeling as to any thing distant, or which is not the object of their senses; so there are other persons without this shallowness of temper, persons of a deeper sense as to what is invisible and future; who not only see, but have a general practical feeling, that what is to come will be present, and that things are not less real for their not being the objects of sense; and who, from their natural constitution of body and of temper, and from their external condition, may have small temptations to behave ill, small difficulty in behaving well, in the common course of life. Now when these latter persons have a distinct full conviction of the truth of religion, without any possible doubts or difficulties, the practice of it is to them unavoidable, unless they do a constant violence to their own minds; and religion is scarce any more a discipline to them, than

* Part I. chap. iv. and pp. 156, 157.

it is to creatures in a state of perfection. Yet these persons may possibly stand in need of moral discipline and exercise, in a higher degree than they would have by such an easy practice of religion. Or it may be requisite, for reasons unknown to us, that they should give some further manifestation* what is their moral character, to the creation of God, than such a practice of it would be. Thus in the great variety of religious situations in which men are placed, what constitutes, what chiefly and peculiarly constitutes, the probation, in all senses, of some persons, may be the difficulties in which the evidence of religion is involved: and their principal and distinguished trial may be, how they will behave under and with respect to these difficulties. Circumstances in men's situation in their temporal capacity, analogous in good measure to this respecting religion, are to be observed. We find some persons are placed in such a situation in the world, as that their chief difficulty with regard to conduct, is not the doing what is prudent when it is known; for this, in numberless cases, is as easy as the contrary: but to some the principal exercise is, recollection and being upon their guard against deceits, the deceits suppose of those about them; against false appearances of reason and prudence. To persons in some situations, the principal exercise with respect to conduct is, attention in order to inform themselves what is proper, what is really the reasonable and prudent part to act.

[*Fourthly.*] As I have hitherto gone upon supposition, that men's dissatisfaction with the evidence of religion is not owing to their neglects or prejudices; it must be added, on the other hand, in all common reason, and as what the truth of the case plainly requires should be added, that such dissatisfaction possibly may be owing to those, possibly may be men's own fault. For,

If there are any persons, who never set themselves heartily and in earnest to be informed in religion: if there are any, who secretly wish it may not prove true; and are less attentive to evidence than to difficulties, and more to objections than to what is said in answer to them: these persons will scarce be thought in a likely way of seeing the evidence of religion, though it were most certainly true, and capable of being ever so fully proved

* Pp. 156, 157.

If any accustom themselves to consider this subject in the way of mirth and sport: if they attend to forms and representations, and inadequate manners of expression, instead of the real things intended by them: (for signs often can be no more than inadequately expressive of the things signified:) or if they substitute human errors in the room of divine truth; why may not all, or any of these things, hinder some men from seeing that evidence, which really is seen by others; as a like turn of mind, with respect to matters of common speculation and practice, does, we find by experience, hinder them from attaining that knowledge and right understanding, in matters of common speculation and practice, which more fair and attentive minds attain to? And the effect will be the same, whether their neglect of seriously considering the evidence of religion, and their indirect behavior with regard to it, proceed from mere carelessness, or from the grosser vices; or whether it be owing to this, that forms and figurative manners of expression, as well as errors, administer occasions of ridicule, when the things intended, and the truth itself, would not. Men may indulge a ludicrous turn so far as to lose all sense of conduct and prudence in worldly affairs, and even, as it seems, to impair their faculty of reason. And in general, levity, carelessness, passion, and prejudice *do* hinder us from being rightly informed, with respect to common things: and they *may*, in like manner, and perhaps, in some further providential manner, with respect to moral and religious subjects: may hinder evidence from being laid before us, and from being seen when it is. The Scripture* does declare, that every one *shall not understand*. And it makes no difference, by what providential conduct this comes to pass: whether the evidence of Christianity was, originally and with design, put and left so, as that those who are desirous of evading moral obligations should not see it; and

* Dan. xii. 10. See also Isa. xxix. 13, 14: Matt. vi. 23, and xi. 25, and xiii. 11, 12: John iii. 19, and v. 44: 1 Cor. ii. 14, and 2 Cor. iv. 4: 2 Tim. iii. 13: and that affectionate as well as authoritative admonition, so very many times inculcated, *He that hath ears to hear, let him hear.* Grotius saw so strongly the thing intended in these and other passages of Scripture of the like sense, as to say, that the proof given us of Christianity was less than it might have been, for this very purpose: *Ut ita sermo Evangelii tanquam lapis esset Lydius ad quem ingenia sanabilia explorarentur.* De Ver. R. C. lib. ii. [So that the Gospel should be a touchstone, to test the honesty of men's dispositions.]

that honest-minded persons should: or, whether it comes to pass by any other means.

Further: [*Fifthly.*] The general proof of natural religion and of Christianity does, I think, lie level to common men: even those, the greatest part of whose time, from childhood to old age, is taken up with providing for themselves and their families the common conveniences, perhaps necessaries, of life: those I mean, of this rank, who ever think at all of asking after proof, or attending to it. Common men, were they as much in earnest about religion, as about their temporal affairs, are capable of being convinced upon real evidence, that there is a God who governs the world: and they feel themselves to be of a moral nature, and accountable creatures. And as Christianity entirely falls in with this their natural sense of things, so they are capable, not only of being persuaded, but of being made to see, that there is evidence of miracles wrought in attestation of it, and many appearing completions of prophecy.

This proof, though real and conclusive, is liable to objections, and may be run up into difficulties; which however persons who are capable not only of talking of, but of really seeing, are capable also of seeing through: *i.e.* not of clearing up and answering them, so as to satisfy their curiosity, for of such knowledge we are not capable with respect to any one thing in nature; but capable of seeing that the proof is not lost in these difficulties, or destroyed by these objections. But then a thorough examination into religion with regard to these objections, which cannot be the business of every man, is a matter of pretty large compass, and, from the nature of it, requires some knowledge, as well as time and attention; to see, how the evidence comes out, upon balancing one thing with another, and what, upon the whole, is the amount of it. If persons who pick up these objections from others, and take for granted they are of weight, upon the word of those from whom they received them, or, by often retailing of them, come to see or fancy they see them to be of weight; will not prepare themselves for such an examination, with a competent degree of knowledge; or will not give that time and attention to the subject, which, from the nature of it, is necessary for attaining such information: in this case, they must remain in doubtfulness, ignorance, or error: in the same way as they must, with regard to common sciences, and matters of common life, if they neglect the necessary means of being informed in them.

Perhaps it will still be objected, that if a prince or common master were to send directions to a servant, he would take care, that they should always bear the certain marks, who they came from, and that their sense should be always plain: so as that there should be no possible doubt if he could help it, concerning the authority or meaning of them. The proper answer to all this kind of objections is, that, wherever the fallacy lies, it is even certain we cannot argue thus with respect to Him who is the Governor of the world: and that he does not afford us such information, with respect to our temporal affairs and interests, experience abundantly shows.

However, there is a full answer to this objection, from the very nature of religion. The reason why a prince would give his directions in this plain manner is, that he absolutely desires an external action done, without concerning himself with the motive or principle upon which it is done: *i.e.* he regards only the external event, or the thing's being done; and not at all, properly speaking, the doing of it, or the action. Whereas the whole of morality and religion consisting merely in action itself, there is no sort of parallel between the cases. But if the prince be supposed to regard only the action; *i.e.* only to desire to exercise, or in any sense prove, the understanding or loyalty of a servant; he would not always give his orders in such a plain manner. It may be proper to add, that the will of God, respecting morality and religion, may be considered either as absolute, or as only conditional. If it be absolute, it can only be thus, that we should act virtuously in such given circumstances; not that we should be brought to act so, by this changing of our circumstances. And if God's will be thus absolute, then it is in our power, in the highest and strictest sense, to do or to contradict his will; which is a most weighty consideration. Or his will may be considered only as conditional, that if we act so and so, we shall be rewarded; if otherwise, punished: of which conditional will of the Author of nature, the whole constitution of it affords most certain instances.

Upon the whole: that we are in a state of religion necessarily implies, that we are in a state of probation : and the credibility of our being at all in such a state being admitted, there seems no peculiar difficulty in supposing our probation to be, just as it is, in those respects which are above objected against. There seems no pretence, from *the reason of the thing*, to say, that the trial cannot equitably be any thing, but whether persons will act suitably to certain information, or such as admits no room for doubt; so as that there can be no danger of miscarriage, but either from their not attending to what they certainly know, or from overbearing passion hurrying them on to act contrary to it. For, since ignorance and doubt, afford scope for probation in all senses, as really as intuitive conviction or certainty; and since the two former are to be put to the same account as difficulties in practice; men's moral probation may also be, whether they will take due care to inform themselves by impartial consideration, and afterwards whether they will act as the case requires, upon the evidence which they have, however doubtful. And this, we find by *experience*, is frequently our probation,* in our temporal capacity. For, the information which we want with regard to our worldly interests is by no means always given us of course, without any care of our own. And we are greatly liable to self-deceit from inward secret prejudices, and also to the deceits of others. So that to be able to judge what is the prudent part, often requires much and difficult consideration. Then after we have judged the very best we can, the evidence upon which we must act, if we will live and act at all, is perpetually doubtful to a very high degree. And the constitution and course of the world in fact is such, as that want of impartial consideration what we have to do, and venturing upon extravagant courses because it is doubtful what will be the consequence, are often naturally, *i.e.* providentially, altogether as fatal, as misconduct occasioned by heedless inattention to what we certainly know, or disregarding it from overbearing passion.

Several of the observations here made may well seem strange, perhaps unintelligible, to many good men. But if the persons for whose sake they are made think so, (persons who object as above, and throw off all regard to religion under pretence of want of evidence;) I desire them to consider again, whether their think-

* Pp. 100, 257, &c.

ng so be owing to any thing unintelligible in these observations, or to their own not having such a sense of religion and serious solicitude about it, as even their state of scepticism does in all reason require? It ought to be forced upon the reflection of these persons, that our nature and condition necessarily require us, in the daily course of life, to act upon evidence much lower than what is commonly called probable: to guard, not only against what we fully believe will, but also against what we think it supposable may, happen; and to engage in pursuits when the probability is greatly against success, if it even be credible, that possibly we may succeed in them.

CHAPTER VII.

THE PARTICULAR EVIDENCE FOR CHRISTIANITY.

The presumptions against revelation, and objections against the general scheme of Christianity, and particular things relating to it, being removed, there remains to be considered, what positive evidence we have for the truth of it; chiefly in order to see, what the analogy of nature suggests with regard to that evidence, and the objections against it: or to see what is, and is allowed to be, the plain natural rule of judgment and of action, in our temporal concerns, in cases where we have the same kind of evidence, and the same kind of objections against it, that we have in the case before us.

In the evidence of Christianity there seem to be several things of great weight, not reducible to the head, either of miracles, or the completion of prophecy, in the common acceptation of the words. But these two are its direct and fundamental proofs: and those other things, however considerable they are, yet ought never to be urged apart from its direct proofs, but always to be joined with them. Thus the evidence of Christianity will be a long series of things, reaching, as it seems, from the beginning of the world to the present time, of great variety and compass, taking in both the direct and also the collateral, proofs, and making up, all of them together, one argument. The conviction arising from this kind of proof may be compared to what they call *the effect*, in architecture or other works of art; a result from a great number of things, so and so disposed, and taken into one view. I shall therefore, *first*, make some observations relating to miracles, and the appearing completions of prophecy; and consider what analogy suggests, in answer to the objections brought against this evidence. And, *secondly*, I shall endeavor to give some account of the general argument now mentioned, consisting both of the direct and collateral evidence, considered as making up one argument: this being the kind of proof, upon which we determine most questions of difficulty, concerning common facts, alleged to have happened, or seeming likely to happen; especially questions relating to conduct.

First, I shall make some observations upon the direct proof of Christianity from miracles and prophecy, and upon the objections alleged against it.[a]

I. Now the following observations relating to the *historical evidence of miracles* wrought in attestation of Christianity appear to be of great weight.

1. The Old Testament affords us the same historical evidence of the miracles of Moses and of the prophets, as of the common civil history of Moses and the kings of Israel; or, as of the affairs of the Jewish nation. And the *Gospels* and *the Acts* afford us the same historical evidence of the miracles of Christ and the apostles, as of the common matters related in them. This indeed could not have been affirmed by any reasonable man, if the authors of these books, like many other historians, had appeared to aim at an entertaining manner of writing, and hence interspersed miracles in their works, at proper distances and upon proper occasions. These might have animated a dull relation, amused the reader, and engaged his attention. And the same account would naturally have been given of them, as of the speeches and descriptions given by such authors: the same account, in a manner, as is to be given, why the poets make use of wonders and prodigies. But the facts, both miraculous and natural, in Scripture, are related in plain unadorned narratives,

[a] [See WITSII Meletemeta, Diss. IV.: PFAFII Disput: CAMPBELL on Miracles: DOUGLASS' Criterion: FARMER's Dissertations: PALEY's Evid.: TAYLOR's Apol. of Ben Mordecai: TUCKER's Light of Nat.: WATSON's Tracts, vol. iv.: JORTIN's Sermons: Bp. FLEETWOOD's Essays: BOYLE Lectures: LARDNER's Credibility.]

and both of them appear, in all respects, to stand upon the same foot of historical evidence.[b]

Further: some parts of Scripture, containing an account of miracles fully sufficient to prove the truth of Christianity, are quoted as genuine, from the age in which they are said to be written, down to the present: and no other parts of them, material in the present question, are omitted to be quoted in such manner, as to afford any sort of proof of their not being genuine. And, as common history, when called in question in any instance, may often be greatly confirmed by contemporary or subsequent events more known and acknowledged; and as the common Scripture history, like many others, is thus confirmed; so likewise is the miraculous history of it, not only in particular instances, but in general. For, the establishment of the Jewish and Christian religions, which were events contemporary with the miracles related to be wrought in attestation of both, or subsequent to them, these events are just what we should have *expected*, upon supposition such miracles were really wrought to attest the truth of those religions. These miracles are a satisfactory account of those events: of which no other satisfactory account can be given; nor any account at all, but what is merely imaginary and invented

It is to be added, that the most obvious, the most easy and direct account of this history, how it came to be written, and to be received in the world as a true history, is that it really is so; nor can any other account of it be easy and direct. Now, though an account, not at all obvious, but very far-fetched and indirect, may be and often is, the true account of a matter, yet it cannot be admitted on the authority of its being asserted. Mere guess, supposition, and possibility, when opposed to historical evidence, prove nothing, but that historical evidence is not demonstrative.

The just consequence from all this, I think is, that the Scripture history in general is to be admitted as an authentic genuine history, till something positive be alleged sufficient to invalidate

[b] ["The miracles of the Jewish historian, are intimately connected with all the civil affairs, and make a necessary and inseparable part. The whole history is founded in them; it consists of little else; and if it were not a history of them, it would be a history of nothing."—BOLINGBROKE, Posthumous Works, vol. iii. p. 279.]

it. No man will deny the consequence to be, that it cannot be rejected, or thrown by as of no authority, till it can be proved to be of none; even though the evidence now mentioned for its authority were doubtful. This evidence may be confronted by historical evidence on the other side, if there be any: or general incredibility in the things related, or inconsistence in the general turn of the history, would prove it to be of no authority. But since, upon the face of the matter, upon a first and general view, the *appearance* is, that it is an authentic history, it cannot be determined to be fictitious, without some proof that it is so. The following observations in support of these, and coincident with them, will greatly confirm the historical evidence for the truth of Christianity.

2. The Epistles of Paul, from the nature of epistolary writing, and moreover from several of them being written, not to particular persons but to churches, carry in them evidences of their being genuine, beyond what can be in a mere historical narrative, left to the world at large. This evidence,[c] joined with that which they have in common with the rest of the New Testament, seems not to leave so much as any particular pretence for denying their genuineness, considered as an ordinary matter of fact, or of criticism: I say *particular* pretence, for *denying* it; because any single fact, of such a kind and such antiquity, may have *general doubts* raised concerning it, from the very nature of human affairs and human testimony. There is also to be mentioned a distinct and particular evidence of the genuineness of the epistle chiefly referred to here, the first to the Corinthians; from the manner in which it is quoted by Clemens Romanus, in an epistle of his own to that church.* Now these epistles afford

[c] [An admirable work on this recondite mode of proving the truth of the New Testament narrative, is PALEY'S Horæ Paulinæ. The same department of evidence is ably handled by BIRK, in his Horæ Evangelicæ, and Horæ Apostolicæ: GRAVES on the Pentateuch: and BLUNT in his "Undesigned Coincidences both of the Old and New Testament." GROTIUS, De Veritate, has some excellent passages on the same subject.]

* [Clem. Rom. Ep. 1. c. 47.] CLEMENT, who is here quoted, lived in the first century, and is mentioned Phil. iv. 3. His epistle to the Corinthians, written in Greek, contains the passage here referred to, which may be thus translated: "Take the letter of the blessed Paul the Apostle. What did he write to you, in the first beginning of the Gospel? Truly he sent you a divinely inspired letter about himself, and Cephas, and Apollos."

a proof of Christianity, detached from all others, which is, I think, a thing of weight; and also a proof of a nature and kind peculiar to itself. For,

In them the author declares, that he received the Gospel in general, and the institution of the Communion in particular, not from the rest of the apostles, or jointly together with them, but alone, from Christ himself; whom he declares likewise, conformably to the history in the Acts, that he saw after his ascension.* So that the testimony of Paul is to be considered, as detached from that of the rest of the apostles.

He declares further, that he was endued with a power of working miracles, as what was publicly known to those very people, speaks of frequent and great variety of miraculous gifts as then subsisting in those very churches, to which he was writing; which he was reproving for several irregularities, and where he had personal opposers. He mentions these gifts incidentally, in the most easy manner, and without effort; by way of reproof to those who had them, for their indecent use of them; and by way of depreciating them, in comparison of moral virtues. In short he speaks to these churches, of these miraculous powers, in the manner any one would speak to another of a thing, which was as familiar, and as much known in common to them both, as any thing in the world.† And this, as hath been observed by several persons, is surely a very considerable thing.

3. It is an acknowledged historical fact, that Christianity offered itself to the world, and demanded to be received, upon the allegation, (*i.e.* as unbelievers would speak, upon the pretence,) of miracles, publicly wrought to attest the truth of it, in such an age; and that it was actually received by great numbers in that very age, and upon the professed belief of the reality of these miracles. And Christianity, including the dispensation of the Old Testament, seems distinguished by this from all other religions. I mean, that this does not *appear* to be the case with regard to any other; for surely it will not be supposed to lie upon any person, to prove by positive historical evidence, that it was not. It does in no sort appear that Mahometanism was first

* Gal. i.: 1 Cor. xi. 23, &c.: 1 Cor. xv. 8.

† Rom. xv. 19: 1 Cor. xii. 8, 9, 10–28, &c., and xiii. 1, 2, 8, and the whole 14th chapter: 2 Cor. xii. 12, 13: Gal. iii. 2, 5.

received in the world upon the foot of supposed miracles,* *i.e.* public ones:[d] for, as revelation is itself miraculous, all pretence to it must necessarily imply some pretence of miracles. And it is a known fact, that it was immediately, at the very first, propagated by other means. And as particular institutions, whether in Paganism or Popery, said to be confirmed by miracles *after* those institutions had obtained, are not to the purpose: so, were there what might be called historical proof, that any of them were introduced by a supposed divine command, believed to be attested by miracles; these would not be in any wise parallel. For single things of this sort are easy to be accounted for, after parties are formed, and have power in their hands; and the leaders of them are in veneration with the multitude; and political interests are blended with religious claims, and religious distinctions. But *before* any thing of this kind, for a few persons, and those of the lowest rank, all at once, to bring over such great numbers to a new religion, and get it to be received upon the particular evidence of miracles; this is quite another thing.

I think it will be allowed by any fair adversary, that the fact now mentioned, taking in all the circumstances, is peculiar to the Christian religion. However, the fact itself is allowed, that Christianity obtained, *i.e.* was professed to be received in the world, upon the belief of miracles, immediately in the age in which it is said those miracles were wrought: or that this is what its first converts would have alleged, as the reason for their embracing it. It is not to be supposed that such numbers of men, in the most distant parts of the world, should forsake the religion of their country, in which they had been educated; separate themselves from their friends, particularly in their festival shows and solemnities, to which the common people are so greatly addicted, and which were of a nature to engage them much more, than any thing of that sort among us: and embrace

* See the Koran, chap. xiii. and chap. xvii.

[d] [MAHOMET expressly declares that he worked no *public* miracles in confirmation of his mission, "because the former nations have charged them with imposture." He claims, however, to have had private miraculous assurances of his mission, and most preposterous they were.

WHATELY, in his Christian Evidences, has handled this aspect of miracles with great ability. See also PALEY'S Evidences, sec. 3: and GIBBON'S Decline and Fall, chap. 1.]

a religion, which could not but expose them to many inconveniences, and indeed must have been a giving up the world in a great degree, even from the very first, and before the empire engaged in form against them: it cannot be supposed, that such numbers should make so great, and to say the least, so inconvenient a change in their whole institution of life, unless they were really convinced of the truth of those miracles, upon the knowledge or belief of which they professed to make it. And it will, I suppose, readily be acknowledged, that the generality of the first converts to Christianity must have believed them: that as by becoming Christians they declared to the world, they were satisfied of the truth of those miracles; so this declaration was to be credited. And this their testimony is the same kind of evidence for those miracles, as if they had put it in writing, and these writings had come down to us. And it is real evidence, because it is of facts, which they had capacity and full opportunity to inform themselves of.

It is also distinct from the direct or express historical evidence, though it is of the same kind: and would be allowed to be distinct in all cases. For were a fact expressly related by one or more ancient historians, and disputed in after ages; that this fact is acknowledged to have been *believed* by great numbers of the age in which the historian says it was done, would be allowed an additional proof of such fact, quite distinct from the express testimony of the historian. The credulity of mankind is acknowledged: and the suspicions of mankind ought to be acknowledged too; and their backwardness even to believe, and greater still to practise, what makes against their interest. And it must particularly be remembered, that education, and prejudice, and authority, were against Christianity, in the age I am speaking of. So that the immediate conversion of such numbers is a real presumption of somewhat more than human in this matter.[e] I

[e] [ALEXANDER, in his Evidences, and several other writers have placed this argument in a very convincing light. ARNOBIUS, one of the earliest Christian writers, asks, "Shall we say that the men of those times were inconsiderate, deceitful, stupid, and brutish enough to feign having seen what they never saw? and that when they might have lived in peace and comfort, they chose gratuitous hatred and obloquy?"

The *rejection* of Christianity by so many in the first age was the result of the continued action of personal and hereditary prejudice and depravity say presumption, for it is not alleged as a proof alone and by itself. Nor need any one of the things mentioned in this chapter be considered as a proof by itself: and yet all of them together may be one of the strongest.*

Upon the whole: as there is large historical evidence, both direct and circumstantial, of miracles wrought in attestation of Christianity, collected by those who have writ upon the subject; it lies upon unbelievers to show why this evidence is not to be credited. This way of speaking is, I think, just; and what persons who write in defence of religion naturally fall into. Yet, in a matter of such unspeakable importance, the proper question is, not whom it lies upon, according to the rules of argument, to maintain or confute objections: but whether there really are any, against this evidence, sufficient, in reason, to destroy the credit of it. However, unbelievers seem to take upon them the part of showing that there are.

They allege, that numberless enthusiastic people, in different ages and countries, expose themselves to the same difficulties which the primitive Christians did; and are ready to give up their lives for the most idle follies imaginable. It is not very clear, to what purpose this objection is brought. For surely, every one, in every case, must distinguish between opinions and facts. And though testimony is no proof of enthusiastic opinions, or of any *opinion* at all; yet it is allowed, in all other cases, to be a proof of *facts*. A person's laying down his life in attestation of facts or of opinions, is the strongest proof of his believing them. And if the apostles and their contemporaries did believe the facts, in attestation of which they exposed themselves to sufferings and death; this their belief, or rather knowledge, must be a proof of those facts: for they were such as came under the observation of their senses. And though it is not of equal weight, yet it is of weight, that the martyrs of the next age, notwithstanding they were not eye-witnesses of those facts,

capable of resisting any supposable evidence. The *reception* of Christianity by multitudes, under the same evidences, and to their immediate personal damage, shows strongly that there was enough evidence to produce those effects. Thus the rejection by some does not countervail the acceptance by others.]

* P. 294, &c.

as were the apostles and their contemporaries, had, however. full opportunity to inform themselves whether they were true or not. and gave equal proof of their believing them to be true.

But enthusiasm, it is said, greatly weakens the evidence of testimony even for facts, in matters relating to religion: some seem to think it totally and absolutely destroys the evidence of testimony upon this subject. The powers of enthusiasm, and of diseases too, which operate in a like manner, are indeed very wonderful, in particular instances. But if great numbers of men, not appearing in any peculiar degree weak, nor under any peculiar suspicion of negligence, affirm that they saw and heard such things plainly, with their eyes and their ears, and are admitted to be in earnest; such testimony is evidence of the strongest kind we can have, for any matter of fact. Possibly it may be overcome, strong as it is, by incredibility in the things thus attested, or by contrary testimony. And in an instance where one thought it was so overcome, it might be just to consider, how far such evidence could be accounted for by enthusiasm; for it seems as if no other imaginable account were to be given of it. But till such incredibility be shown, or contrary testimony produced, it cannot surely be expected, that so far-fetched, so indirect and wonderful an account of such testimony, as that of enthusiasm must be; an account so strange, that the generality of mankind can scarce be made to understand what is meant by it; it cannot, I say, be expected that such an account will be admitted of such evidence; when there is this direct, easy, and obvious account of it, that people really saw and heard a thing not incredible, which they affirm, sincerely and with full assurance, they did see and hear.

Granting then that enthusiasm is not (strictly speaking) an absurd, but a possible account of such testimony, it is manifest, that the very mention of it goes upon the previous supposition, that the things so attested are incredible: and therefore need not be considered, till they are shown to be so. Much less need it be considered, after the contrary has been proved. And I think it has been proved, to full satisfaction, that there is no incredibility in a revelation, in general; or in such a one as the Christian, in particular. However, as religion is supposed peculiarly liable to enthusiam, it may just be observed, that prejudices almost without number, and without name, such as romance, affection, humor, a desire to engage attention, or to surprise, party spirit, custom, little competitions, unaccountable likings and dislikings; these influence men strongly in common matters. And as these prejudices are often scarce known or reflected upon by the persons themselves who are influenced by them, they are to be considered as influences of a like kind to enthusiasm. Yet human testimony, in common matters, is naturally and justly believed, notwithstanding.

It is intimated further, in a more refined way of observation, that though it should be proved, that the apostles and first Christians could not, in some respects, be deceived themselves, and in other respects, cannot be thought to have intended to impose upon the world, yet it will not follow that their general testimony is to be believed, though truly handed down to us: because they might still in part, *i.e.* in other respects, be deceived themselves, and in part also designedly impose upon others; which, it is added, is a thing very credible, from that mixture of real enthusiasm, and real knavery, to be met with in the same characters.[f]

I must confess, I think the matter of fact contained in this observation upon mankind is not to be denied; and that something very much akin to it is often supposed in Scripture as a very common case, and most severely reproved. But it were to have been expected, that persons capable of applying this observation as applied in the objection, might also frequently have met with the like mixed character, in instances where religion was quite out of the case. The thing plainly is, that mankind are naturally endued with reason, or a capacity of distinguishing between truth and falsehood; and as naturally they are endued with veracity, or a regard to truth in what they say: but from many occasions they are liable to be prejudiced and biassed and deceived themselves, and capable of intending to deceive others, in every degree: insomuch that, as we are all liable to be deceived by prejudice, so likewise it seems to be not an uncommon thing, for persons who, from their regard to truth, would not invent a lie entirely without any foundation at all, to propagate it with heightening circumstances, after it is once invented and

[f] [Compare BUTLER's Sermons; on Balaam, and on Self-deceit.]

set a-going. And others, though they would not *propagate* a lie, yet, which is a lower degree of falsehood, will let it pass without contradiction. But notwithstanding all this, *human testimony* remains still a natural ground of assent; and this assent a natural principle of action.

It is objected further, that however it has happened, the *fact* is, that mankind have, in different ages, been strangely deluded with pretences to miracles and wonders. But it is by no means to be admitted, that they have been oftener, or are at all more liable to be deceived by these than by other pretences.

It is added, that there is a very considerable degree of historical evidence for miracles, which are, on all hands, acknowledged to be fabulous. But suppose there were even *the like* historical evidence for these, to what there is for those alleged in proof of Christianity, which yet is in no wise allowed, but suppose this; the consequence would not be, that the evidence of the latter is not to be admitted. Nor is there a man in the world, who in common cases, would conclude thus. For what would such a conclusion really amount to but this, that evidence, confuted by contrary evidence, or any way overbalanced, destroys the credibility of other evidence, neither confuted nor overbalanced? To argue that because there is, if there were, like evidence from testimony, for miracles acknowledged false, as for those in attestation of Christianity, therefore the evidence in the latter case is not to be credited; this is the same as to argue, that if two men of equally good reputation had given evidence in different cases no way connected, and one of them had been convicted of perjury, this confuted the testimony of the other!

Upon the whole then, the general observation, that human creatures are so liable to be deceived, from enthusiasm in religion, and principles equivalent to enthusiasm in common matters, and in both from negligence; and that they are so capable of dishonestly endeavoring to deceive others; this does indeed weaken the evidence of testimony in all cases, but does not destroy it in any. And these things will appear, to different men, to weaken the evidence of testimony, in different degrees: in degrees proportionable to the observations they have made, or the notions they have any way taken up, concerning the weakness and negligence and dishonesty of mankind; or concerning the powers of enthusiasm, and prejudices equivalent to it. But it seems to me, that people do not know what they say, who affirm these things to destroy the evidence from testimony which we have, of the truth of Christianity. Nothing can destroy the evidence of testimony in any case, but a proof or probability, that persons are not competent judges of the facts to which they give testimony; or that they are actually under some indirect influence in giving it, in such particular case. Till this be made out, the *natural* laws of human actions require, that testimony be admitted. It can never be sufficient to overthrow direct historical evidence, indolently to say, that there are so many principles, from whence men are liable to be deceived themselves, and disposed to deceive others, especially in matters of religion, that one knows not what to believe. And it is surprising persons can help reflecting, that this very manner of speaking supposes they are not satisfied that there is nothing in the evidence, of which they speak thus; or that they can avoid observing, if they do make this reflection, that it is on such a subject, a very material one.*

Over against all these objections is to be set the *importance* of Christianity, as what must have engaged the attention of its first converts, so as to have rendered them less liable to be deceived from carelessness, than they would in common matters; and likewise the strong *obligations to veracity*, which their religion laid them under: so that the first and most obvious presumption is, that they could not be deceived themselves nor deceive others. And this presumption, in this degree, is peculiar to the testimony we have been considering.

In argument, assertions are nothing in themselves, and have an air of positiveness which sometimes is not very easy: yet they are necessary, and necessary to be repeated; in order to connect a discourse, and distinctly to lay before the view of the reader, what is proposed to be proved, and what is left as proved. Now the conclusion from the foregoing observations is, I think, beyond all doubt, this: that unbelievers must be forced to admit the external evidence for Christianity, *i.e.* the proof of miracles wrought to attest it, to be of real weight and very considerable; though they cannot allow it to be sufficient, to convince them of the

* See the foregoing chapter.

reality of those miracles. And as they must, in all reason, admit this; so it seems to me, that upon consideration they would, in fact, admit it; those of them, I mean, who know any thing at all of the matter; in like manner as persons, in many cases, own they see strong evidence from testimony, for the truth of things, which yet they cannot be convinced are true: cases, suppose, where there is contrary testimony; or things which they think, whether with or without reason, to be incredible. But there is no testimony contrary to that which we have been considering: and it has been fully proved, that there is no incredibility in Christianity in general, or in any part of it.

II. As to the evidence for Christianity from prophecy, I shall only make some few general observations, which are suggested by the analogy of nature; *i.e.* by the acknowledged natural rules of judging in common matters, concerning evidence of a like kind to this from prophecy.

1. The obscurity or unintelligibleness of one part of a prophecy does not, in any degree, invalidate the proof of foresight, arising from the appearing completion of those other parts, which are understood. For the case is evidently the same, as if those parts which are not understood were lost, or not written at all, or written in an unknown tongue. Whether this observation be commonly attended to or not, it is so evident, that one can scarce bring oneself to set down an instance in common matters, to exemplify it. However, suppose a writing, partly in cipher, and partly in plain words at length; and that in the part one understood, there appeared mention of several known facts; it would never come into any man's thoughts to imagine, that if he understood the whole, perhaps he might find, that those facts were not in reality known by the writer. Indeed, both in this example and in the thing intended to be exemplified by it, our not understanding the whole (the whole, suppose, of a sentence or a paragraph) might sometimes occasion a doubt, whether one understood the literal meaning of such a part: but this comes under another consideration.

For the same reason, though a man should be incapable, for want of learning, or opportunities of inquiry, or from not having turned his studies this way, even so much as to judge whether particular prophecies have been throughout completely fulfilled;

yet he may see, in general, that they have been fulfilled to such a degree, as, upon very good ground, to be convinced of foresight more than human in such prophecies, and of such events being intended by them. For the same reason also, though, by means of the deficiencies in civil history, and the different accounts of historians, the most learned should not be able to make out to satisfaction, that such parts of the prophetic history have been minutely and throughout fulfilled; yet a very strong *proof of foresight* may arise, from that general completion of them, which is made out. As much perhaps, as the giver of prophecy intended should ever be afforded by such parts of prophecy.

2. A long series of prophecy being applicable to such and such events, is itself a proof that it was intended of them: as the rules by which we naturally judge and determine, in common cases parallel to this, will show.[g] This observation I make in answer to the common objection against the application of the prophecies, that, considering each of them distinctly by itself, it does not at all appear, that they were intended of those particular events to which they are applied by Christians; and therefore it is to be supposed, that if they meant any thing, they were intended of other events unknown to us, and not of these at all.

Now there are two kinds of writing, which bear a great resemblance to prophecy, with respect to the matter before us: the mythological, and the satirical, where the satire is to a certain degree concealed. And a man might be assured, that he understood what an author intended by a fable or parable related without any application or moral, merely from seeing it to be easily capable of such application, and that such a moral might naturally be deduced from it. And he might be fully assured, that such persons and events were intended in a satirical writing, merely from its being applicable to them. And, agreeable to the last observation, he might be in a good measure satisfied of it,

[g] ["Whenever a general scheme is known to be pursued by a writer, that scheme becomes the true key in the hands of his reader, for unlocking the meaning of particular parts, which would otherwise not be seen clearly to refer to such scheme. The inspired writers had one common and predominant scheme in view, which was to *bear testimony to Jesus*. Whatever passages occur in their writings, which bear an apt and easy resemblance to the history of Jesus, may, or rather must in all reasonable construction, be applied to him."—HURD on the Proph., p. 117.]

though he were not enough informed in affairs, or in the story of such persons to understand half the satire. For, his satisfaction that he understood the meaning, the intended meaning, of these writings, would be greater or less in proportion as he saw the general turn of them to be capable of such application; and in proportion to the number of particular things capable of it. And thus, if a long series of prophecy is applicable to the present state of the church, and to the political situations of the kingdoms of the world, some thousand years after these prophecies were delivered; and a long series of prophecy delivered before the coming of Christ is applicable to him; these things are in themselves a proof, that the prophetic history was intended of him, and of those events: in proportion as the general turn of it is capable of such application, and to the number and variety of particular prophecies capable of it. And though, in all just way of consideration, the obvious completion of prophecies is to be allowed to be thus explanatory of, and to determine, their meaning; yet it is to be remembered further, that the ancient Jews applied the prophecies to a Messiah before his coming,[h] in much the same manner as Christians do now: and that the primitive Christians interpreted the prophecies respecting the state of the church and of the world in the last ages, in the sense which the event seems to confirm and verify. From these things it may be made appear:

3. That the showing even to a high probability, if that could be, that the prophets thought of some other events, in such and such predictions, and not those which Christians allege to be completions of those predictions; or that such and such prophecies are capable of being applied to other events than those, to which Christians apply them—that this would not confute or destroy the force of the argument from prophecy, even with regard to those very instances. For, observe how this matter really is. If one knew such a person to be the sole author of such a book, and was certainly assured, or satisfied to any degree, that one knew the whole of what he intended in it; one should be assured or satisfied to such degree, that one knew the whole

[h] [Consult on this point, GULICK, Theologia Prophetica: VITRINGA, Observationes: HENGSTENBURG, Christologia: HORSLEY'S Tracts and Sermons: KING'S Morsels of Criticism: WAUGH'S Dissertations: LYALL'S Propœdia Prophetica.]

meaning of that book: for the meaning of a book is nothing but the meaning of the author. But if one knew a person to have *compiled* a book out of memoirs, which he received from another, of vastly superior knowledge in the subject of it, especially if it were a book full of great intricacies and difficulties; it would in no wise follow, that one knew the whole meaning of the book, from knowing the whole meaning of the compiler: for the original author of them, might have, and there would be no presumption, in many cases, against supposing him to have, some further meaning than the compiler saw. To say then that the Scriptures, and the things contained in them, can have no other or further meaning than those persons had, who first recited or wrote them, is evidently saying, that those persons were the original, proper, and sole authors of those books, *i.e.* that they are not inspired: which is absurd, while the authority of these books is under examination; *i.e.* till you have determined they are of no divine authority at all. Till this be determined, it must in all reason be supposed, not indeed that they have, (for this is taking for granted that they are inspired;) but that they may have, some further meaning than what the compilers saw or understood. And, upon this supposition, it is supposable also, that this further meaning may be fulfilled.

Events corresponding to prophecies, interpreted in a different meaning from that, in which the prophets are supposed to have understood them; affords in a manner, the same proof, that this different sense was originally intended, as it would have afforded, if the prophets had not understood their predictions in the sense it is supposed they did: because there is no presumption of *their* sense of them being the whole sense of them. And it has been already shown, that the apparent completions of prophecy must be allowed to be explanatory of its meaning. So that the question is, whether a series of prophecy has been fulfilled, in a natural or proper, *i.e.* in any real sense of the words of it. For such completion is equally a proof of foresight more than human, whether the prophets are, or are not, supposed to have understood it in a different sense. I say, supposed: for, though I think it clear, that the prophets did not understand the full meaning of their predictions, it is another question, how far they thought they did; and in what sense they understood them

Hence may be seen, to how little purpose those persons busy themselves, who endeavor to prove, that the prophetic history is applicable to events of the age in which it was written, or of ages before it. To have proved this, before there was any appearance of a further completion of it, might have answered some purpose; for it might have prevented the expectation of any such further completion. Thus could Porphyry have shown, that some principal parts of the book of Daniel, for instance the seventh verse of the seventh chapter, which the Christians interpreted of the latter ages, was applicable to events, which happened before or about the age of Antiochus Epiphanes; this might have prevented them from expecting any further completion of it. And, unless there was then, as I think there must have been, external evidence concerning that book, more than is come down to us; such a discovery might have been a stumbling-block in the way of Christianity itself: considering the authority which our Savior has given to the book of Daniel, and how much the general scheme of Christianity presupposes the truth of it. But even this discovery, had there been any such,* would be of very little weight with reasonable men now; if this passage, thus applicable to events before the age of Porphyry, appears to be applicable also to events, which succeeded the dissolution of the Roman empire. I mention this, not at all as intending to insinuate, that the division of this empire into ten parts, for it plainly was divided into about that number, were, alone and by itself, of any moment in verifying the prophetic history: but only as an example of the thing I am speaking of. Thus upon the whole, the matter of inquiry evidently must be, as above put, Whether the prophecies are applicable to Christ, and to the present state of the world, and of the church; applicable in such a degree, as to imply foresight: not whether they are *capable* of any other appli-

* It appears that Porphyry did nothing worth mentioning in this way. For Jerome on the place says: *Duas posteriores bestias—in uno Macedonum regno ponit.* And as to the ten kings; *Decem reges enumerat, qui fuerunt sævissimi: ipsosque reges non unius ponit regni, verbi gratia, Macedoniæ, Syriæ, Asiæ, et Ægypti; sed de diversis regnis unum efficit regum ordinem.* ["The two latter beasts he places in one of the Macedonian kingdoms." "He reckons up ten kings who had been excessively cruel and these not kings of one country, as Macedonia, for instance, or Syria, or Asia, or Egypt; but makes up his set of kings out of different kingdoms."] In this way of interpretation, any thing may be made of any thing.

cation. Though I know no pretence for saying the general turn of them is capable of any other.

These observations are, I think, just, and the evidence referred to in them real: though there may be people who will not accept of such imperfect information from Scripture. Some too have not integrity and regard enough to truth, to attend to evidence, which keeps the mind in doubt, perhaps perplexity, and which is much of a different sort from what they expected. It plainly requires a degree of modesty and fairness, beyond what every one has, for a man to say, not to the world but to himself, that there is a real appearance of great weight in this matter, though he is not able thoroughly to satisfy himself about it; but that it shall have its influence upon him, in proportion to its apparent reality and weight. It is much more easy, and more falls in with the negligence, presumption, and wilfulness of the generality, to determine at once, with a decisive air, There is nothing in it. The prejudices arising from that absolute contempt and scorn, with which this evidence is treated in the world, I do not mention. For what can be said to persons, who are weak enough in their understandings to think this any presumption against it; or, if they do not, are yet weak enough in their temper to be influenced by such prejudices, upon such a subject?

Secondly, I shall endeavor to give some account of the general argument for the truth of Christianity, consisting both of the direct and circumstantial evidence considered as making up one argument. To state and examine this argument fully, would be a work much beyond the compass of this whole treatise; nor is so much as a proper abridgment of it to be expected here. Yet the present subject requires to have some brief account of it given. For it is the kind of evidence, upon which most questions of difficulty, in common practice, are determined: evidence arising from various coincidences, which support and confirm each other, and in this manner prove, with more or less certainty, the point under consideration. I choose to do it also: First, because it seems to be of the greatest importance, and not duly attended to by every one, that the proof of revelation is not some direct and express things only, but a great variety of circumstantial things also; and that though each of these direct and circumstantial things is indeed to be considered separately, yet they are afterwards to be joined together; for that the proper force of the evidence consists in the result of those several things, considered in their respects to each other, and united into one view. In the next place, because it seems to me, that the matters of fact here set down, which are acknowledged by unbelievers, must be acknowledged by them also to contain together a degree of evidence of great weight, if they could be brought to lay these several things before themselves distinctly, and then with attention consider them together; instead of that cursory thought of them, to which we are familiarized. For being familiarized to the cursory thought of things as really hinders the weight of them from being seen, as from having its due influence upon practice.

The thing asserted, and the truth of which is to be inquired into, is this: That over and above our reason and affections, which God has given us for the information of our judgment and the conduct of our lives, he has also, by external revelation, given us an account of himself and his moral government over the world, implying a future state of rewards and punishments; *i.e.* hath revealed the system of natural religion: (for natural religion may be externally* revealed by God, as the ignorant may be taught it by their fellow-creatures)—that God, I say, has given us the evidence of revelation, as well as the evidence of reason, to ascertain this moral system; together with an account of a particular dispensation of Providence, which reason could no way have discovered, and a particular institution of religion founded on it, for the recovery of mankind out of their present wretched condition, and raising them to the perfection and final happiness of their nature.

This revelation, whether real or supposed, may be considered as wholly historical. For prophecy is nothing but the history of events before they come to pass; doctrines also are matters of fact; and precepts come under the same notion. The general design of Scripture, which contains in it this revelation, thus considered as historical, may be said to be, to give us an account of the world in this one single view, as God's world: by which it appears essentially distinguished from all other books, so far as I have found, except such as are copied from it. It begins with an account of God's creation of the world, in order to ascertain,

* P. 189, &c.

and distinguish from all others, who is the object of our worship, by what he has done: in order to ascertain, who he is, concerning whose providence, commands, promises, and threatenings, this sacred book, all along, treats; [viz.] the Maker and Proprietor of the world, he whose creatures we are, the God of nature: in order likewise to distinguish him from the idols of the nations, which are either imaginary beings, *i.e.* no beings at all; or else part of that creation, the historical relation of which is here given. And John, not improbably with an eye to this Mosaic account of the creation, begins his Gospel with an account of our Savior's pre-existence, and that *all things were made by him; and without him was not any thing made that was made:** agreeably to the doctrine of Paul, that *God created all things by Jesus Christ.*† This being premised, the Scripture, taken together, seems to profess to contain a kind of an abridgment of the history of the world, in the view just now mentioned: that is, a general account of the condition of religion and its professors, during the continuance of that apostasy from God, and state of wickedness, which it everywhere supposes the world to lie in. And this account of the state of religion carries with it some brief account of the political state of things, as religion is affected by it. Revelation indeed considers the common affairs of this world, and what is going on in it, as a mere scene of distraction; and cannot be supposed to concern itself with foretelling at what time Rome, or Babylon, or Greece, or any particular place, should be the most conspicuous seat of that tyranny and dissoluteness, which all places equally aspire to be; cannot, I say, be supposed to give any account of this wild scene for its own sake. But it seems to contain some very general account of the chief governments of the world, as the general state of religion has been, is, or shall be, affected by them, from the first transgression, and during the whole interval of the world's continuing in its present state, to a certain future period, spoken of both in the Old and New Testament, very distinctly, and in great variety of expression: *The times of the restitution of all things:*‡ when *the mystery of God shall be finished, as he hath declared to his servants the prophets:*§ when *the God of heaven shall set up a kingdom, which shall never be destroyed: and the kingdom shall not be left to other*

* John i. 3. † Eph. iii. 9. ‡ Acts iii. 21. § Rev. x. 7.

people,* as it is represented to be during this apostasy, but *judgment shall be given to the saints*,† and *they shall reign*:‡ *and the kingdom and dominion, and the greatness of the kingdom under the whole heaven, shall be given to the people of the saints of the Most High.*§

Upon this general view of the Scripture, I would remark, how great a length of time the whole relation takes up, near six thousand years of which are past; and how great a variety of things it treats of; the natural and moral system or history of the world, including the time when it was formed, all contained in the very first book, and evidently written in a rude and unlearned age; and in subsequent books, the various common and prophetic history, and the particular dispensation of Christianity. Now all this together gives the largest scope for criticism; and for the confutation of what is capable of being confuted, either from reason, or from common history, or from any inconsistence in its several parts. And it deserves, I think, to be mentioned, that whereas some imagine the supposed doubtfulness of the evidence for revelation implies a positive argument that it is not true; it appears, on the contrary, to imply a positive argument that it is true. For, could any common relation of such antiquity, extent, and variety (for in these things the stress of what I am now observing lies) be proposed to the examination of the world: that it could not, in an age of knowledge and liberty, be confuted, or shown to have nothing in it, to the satisfaction of reasonable men; would be thought a strong presumptive proof of its truth. Indeed it must be a *proof* of it, just in proportion to the probability, that if it were false, it might be shown to be so: which, I think, is scarce pretended to be shown, but upon principles and in ways of arguing, which have been clearly obviated.|| Nor does it at all appear, that any set of men, who believe natural religion, are of the opinion, that Christianity has been thus confuted. But to proceed:

Together with the moral system of the world, the Old Testament contains a chronological account of the beginning of it, and from thence, an unbroken genealogy of mankind for many ages before common history begins; and carried on as much

* Dan. ii. 44. † Dan. vii. 22. ‡ Rev. xi. 17, 18; xx. 6.
§ Dan. vii. 27. || Chap. ii. iii. &c.

farther as to make up a continued thread of history, of the length of between three and four thousand years. It contains an account of God's making a covenant with a particular nation, that they should be his people, and he would be their God, in a peculiar sense; of his often interposing miraculously in their affairs; giving them the promise, and long after, the possession, of a particular country; assuring them of the greatest national prosperity in it, if they would worship him, in opposition to the idols which the rest of the world worshipped, and obey his commands; and threatening them with unexampled punishments if they disobeyed him, and fell into the general idolatry: insomuch that this one nation should continue to be the observation and the wonder of all the world. It declares particularly, that *God would scatter them among all people, from one end of the earth unto the other;* but that *when they should return unto the Lord their God, he would have compassion upon them, and gather them from all the nations, whither he had scattered them:* that *Israel should be saved in the Lord, with an everlasting salvation; and not be ashamed or confounded world without end.** And as some of these promises are conditional, others are as absolute as any thing can be expressed: that the time should come, when *the people should be all righteous, and inherit the land forever:* that *though God would make a full end of all nations whither he had scattered them, yet would he not make a full end of them:* that *he would bring again the captivity of his people Israel, and plant them upon their land, and they should be no more pulled up out of their land:* that *the seed of Israel should not cease from being a nation forever.*† It foretells, that God would raise them up a particular person, in whom all his promises should finally be fulfilled; the Messiah, who should be, in a high and eminent sense, their anointed Prince and Savior. This was foretold in such a manner, as raised a general expectation of such a person in the nation, as appears from the New Testament, and is an acknowledged fact; an expectation of his coming at such a particular time, before any one appeared claiming to be that person, and when there was no ground for such an expectation, but from the prophecies: which expectation, therefore, must in all

* Deut. xxviii. 64; xxx. 2, 3: Isa. xlv. 17.

† Isa. lx. 21: Jer. xxx. 11; xlvi. 28: Amos ix. 14, 15: Jer. xxxi. 36

reason be presumed to be explanatory of those prophecics, if there were any doubt about their meaning. It seems moreover to foretell, that this person should be rejected by the nation to whom he had been so long promised, though he was so much desired by them.* And it expressly foretells, that he should be the Savior of the Gentiles; and that the completion of the scheme contained in this book, and then begun, and in its progress, should be something so great, that in comparison with it, the restoration of the Jews alone would be but of small account. *It is a light thing that thou shouldest be my servant to raise up the tribes of Jacob, and to restore the preserved of Israel: I will also give thee for a light to the Gentiles, that thou mayest be for salvation unto the end of the earth.* And, *In the last days, the mountain of the Lord's house shall be established in the top of the mountains, and shall be exalted above the hills; and all nations shall flow into it—for out of Zion shall go forth the law, and the word of the Lord from Jerusalem. And he shall judge among the nations—and the Lord alone shall be exalted in that day, and the idols he shall utterly abolish.*†

The Scripture further contains an account, that at the time the Messiah was expected, a person rose up in this nation, claiming to be that Messiah, to be the person to whom all the prophecies referred, and in whom they should center: that he spent some years in a continued course of miraculous works; and endued his immediate disciples and followers with a power of doing the same, as a proof of the truth of that religion, which he commissioned them to publish: that invested with this authority and power, they made numerous converts in the remotest countries, and settled and established his religion in the world; to the end of which the Scripture professes to give a prophetic account of the state of this religion among mankind.[1]

Let us now suppose a person utterly ignorant of history, to have

* Isa. viii. 14, 15; xlix. 5; chap. liii.: Mal. i. 10, 11, and chap. iii.

† Isa. xlix. 6, chap. ii., chap. xi., chap. lvi. 7: Mal. i. 11. To which must be added, the other prophecies of the like kind, several in the New Testament, and very many in the Old; which describe what shall be the completion of the revealed plan of Providence.

[See DAVIDSON'S Disc. on Proph.: BLANEY on Daniel's LXX. Weeks: HURD'S Introd. to the Study of Proph.: JORTIN'S Ser. at Boyle Lect.: FULLER'S Gosp its own Witness, part ii.: WAUGH'S Diss.: APTHORPE'S Discourses.]

all this related to him out of the Scripture. Or suppose such an one, having the Scripture put into his hands, to remark these things in it, not knowing but that the whole, even its civil history, as well as the other parts of it, might be, from beginning to end, an entire invention; and to ask, What truth was in it, and whether the revelation here related was real, or a fiction? And, instead of a direct answer, suppose him, all at once, to be told the following confessed facts; and then to unite them into one view.

Let him first be told, in how great a degree the profession and establishment of natural religion, the belief that there is one God to be worshipped, that virtue is his law, and that mankind shall be rewarded and punished hereafter, as they obey and disobey it here; in how very great a degree, I say, the profession and establishment of this moral system in the world is owing to the revelation, whether real or supposed, contained in this book: the establishment of this moral system, even in those countries which do not acknowledge the proper authority of the Scripture.* Let him be told also, what number of nations do acknowledge its proper authority. Let him then take in the consideration, of what importance religion is to mankind. And upon these things he might, I think, truly observe, that this supposed revelation's obtaining and being received in the world, with all the circumstances and effects of it, considered together as one event, is the most conspicuous and important event in the history of mankind: that a book of this nature, and thus promulged and recommended to our consideration, demands, as if by a voice from heaven, to have its claims most seriously examined; and that, before such examination, to treat it with any kind of scoffing and ridicule, is an offence against natural piety. It is to be remembered, that how much soever the establishment of natural religion in the world is owing to the Scripture revelation, this does not destroy the proof of religion from reason, any more than the proof of Euclid's Elements is destroyed, by a man's knowing or thinking, that he should never have seen the truth of the several propositions contained in it, nor had those propositions come into his thoughts, but for that mathematician.

Let such a person as we are speaking of be, in the next place,

* P. 250.

informed of the acknowledged antiquity of the first parts of this book; and that its chronology, its account of the time when the earth, and the several parts of it, were first peopled with human creatures, is no way contradicted, but is really confirmed, by the natural and civil history of the world, collected from common historians, from the state of the earth, and from the late invention of arts and sciences.

And as the Scripture contains an unbroken thread of common and civil history, from the creation to the captivity, for between three and four thousand years; let the person we are speaking of be told, in the next place, that this general history, as it is not contradicted, but confirmed by profane history[k] as much as there would be reason to expect, upon supposition of its truth; so there is nothing in the whole history *itself*, to give any reasonable ground of suspicion of its not being, in the general, a faithful and literally true genealogy of men, and series of things. I speak here only of the common Scripture history, or of the course of ordinary events related in it, as distinguished from miracles, and from the prophetic history. In all the Scripture narrations of this kind, following events arise out of foregoing ones, as in all other histories. There appears nothing related as done in any age, not conformable to the manners of that age: nothing in the account of a succeeding age, which one would say could not be true, or was improbable, from the account of things in the preceding one. There is nothing in the characters, which would raise a thought of their being feigned; but all the internal marks imaginable of their being real. It is to be added also, that mere genealogies, bare narratives of the number of

[k] [Hundreds of instances might be adduced, in which profane historians corroborate the statements of the Scriptures. The following are merely specimens: DIODORUS SICULUS, STRABO, TACITUS, PLINY, and SOLINUS, speak of the destruction of Sodom and Gomorrah. The lives of David and Solomon are given in the remains of the PHŒNICIAN ANNALS, in DAMASCENUS, and EUPOLEMUS. MENANDER describes the carrying away of the Ten Tribes by Salmanasor. SUETONIUS, TACITUS, PLINY the younger, and NUMENIUS, speak of Jesus Christ. His miracles are owned by CELSUS, PORPHYRY, JULIAN, and Jewish writers opposed to Christianity. SUETONIUS, TACITUS, PLINY, JULIAN, and others describe his being put to death; and TACITUS says that many were put to death for adhering to his religion. PHLEGON mentions the miracles of Peter; and Paul is enumerated among eminent authors, in a fragment of LONGINUS.]

years, which persons called by such and such names lived, do not carry the face of fiction; perhaps do carry some presumption of veracity: and all unadorned narratives, which have nothing to surprise, may be thought to carry somewhat of the like presumption too. And the domestic and the political history is plainly credible. There may be incidents in Scripture, which, taken alone in the naked way they are told, may appear strange; especially to persons of other manners, temper, education: but there are also incidents of undoubted truth, in many or most persons' lives, which, in the same circumstances, would appear to the full as strange.[1] There may be mistakes of transcribers, there may be other real or seeming mistakes, not easy to be particularly accounted for: but there are certainly no more things of this kind in the Scripture, than what were to have been expected in books of such antiquity; and nothing, in any wise, sufficient to discredit the general narrative.

Now, that a history, claiming to commence from the creation, and extending in one continued series, through so great a length of time, and variety of events, should have such appearances of reality and truth in its whole contexture, is surely a very remarkable circumstance in its favor. And as all this is applicable to the common history of the New Testament, so there is a further credibility, and a very high one, given to it by profane authors: many of these writing of the same times, and confirming the truth of customs and events, which are incidentally as well as more purposely mentioned in it. And this credibility of the common Scripture-history, gives some credibility to its miraculous history:

[1] [This thought is elaborated with skill by WHATELY in his "*Historic Doubts.*" He takes up all the popular infidel objections as to the life of Christ, and applies them with undiminished or even increased force against the evidences that such a man as Buonaparte ever existed.

JOHNSON in a lively sally once said—"It is easy to be on the negative side. I deny that Canada is taken. The French are a much more numerous people than we; and it is not likely they would allow us to take it.' 'But the Government have announced the fact.' 'Very true. But the ministry have put us to an enormous expense by the war in America, and it is their interest to persuade us that we have got something for our money.' 'But the fact is confirmed by thousands who were at the taking of it.' 'Aye, but these men have an interest in deceiving us: they don't want you should think the French have beat them. Now suppose you go over and find it so, that would only satisfy yourself; for when you come back we will not believe you. We will say you have been bribed.'"—BOSWELL.]

especially as this is interwoven with the common, so as that they imply each other, and both together make up one relation.

Let it then be more particularly observed to this person, that it is an acknowledged matter of fact, which is indeed implied in the foregoing observation, that there was such a nation as the Jews, of the greatest antiquity, whose government and general polity was founded on the law, here related to be given them by Moses as from heaven: that natural religion, with rites additional yet no way contrary to it, was their established religion, which cannot be said of the Gentile world: and that their very being as a nation, depended upon their acknowledgment of one God, the God of the universe. For, suppose in their captivity in Babylon, they had gone over to the religion of their conquerors, there would have remained no bond of union, to keep them a distinct people. And while they were under their own kings, in their own country, a total apostasy from God would have been the dissolution of their whole government. They in such a sense nationally acknowledged and worshipped the Maker of heaven and earth, when the rest of the world were sunk in idolatry, as rendered them, in fact, the peculiar people of God. This remarkable establishment and preservation of natural religion among them, seems to add peculiar credibility to the historical evidence for the miracles of Moses and the prophets. Because these miracles are a full satisfactory account of this event, which plainly needs to be accounted for, and cannot be otherwise.

Let this person, supposed wholly ignorant of history, be acquainted further, that one claiming to be the Messiah, of Jewish extraction, rose up at the time when this nation, from the prophecies above mentioned, expected the Messiah: that he was rejected, as it seemed to have been foretold he should, by the body of the people, under the direction of their rulers: that in the course of a very few years, he was believed on and acknowledged as the promised Messiah, by great numbers among the Gentiles, agreeably to the prophecies of Scripture, yet not upon the evidence of prophecy, but of miracles,* of which miracles we have also strong historical evidence; (by which I mean here no more than must be acknowledged by unbelievers; for let pious frauds and follies be admitted to weaken, it is absurd to say they

* P. 267, &c.

destroy our evidence of miracles wrought in proof of Christianity:)* that this religion approving itself to the reason of mankind, and carrying its own evidence with it, so far as reason is a judge of its system, and being no way contrary to reason in those parts of it which require to be believed upon the mere authority of its Author; that this religion, I say, gradually spread and supported itself for some hundred years, not only without any assistance from temporal power, but under constant discouragements, and often the bitterest persecutions from it; and then became the religion of the world: that in the mean time the Jewish nation and government were destroyed in a very remarkable manner, and the people carried away captive and dispersed through the most distant countries; in which state of dispersion they have remained fifteen hundred years: and that they remain a numerous people, united among themselves, and distinguished from the rest of the world, as they were in the days of Moses, by the profession of his law; and everywhere looked upon in a manner, which one scarce knows how distinctly to express, but in the words of the prophetic account of it, given so many ages before it came to pass: *Thou shalt become an astonishment, a proverb, and a byword, among all nations whither the Lord shall lead thee.*†

The appearance of a standing miracle, in the Jews remaining a distinct people in their dispersion, and the confirmation which this event appears to give to the truth of revelation, may be thought to be answered, by their religion's forbidding them intermarriages with those of other nations, and prescribing them many peculiarities in their food, by which they are debarred from incorporating with the people in whose countries they live. This is not, I think, a satisfactory account of that which it pretends to account for. But what does it pretend to account for? The correspondence between this event and the prophecies; or the coincidence of both, with a long dispensation of Providence, of a peculiar nature, towards that people? No. It is only the event itself, which is offered to be thus accounted for: which single event, taken alone, abstracted from all such correspondence and coincidence, perhaps would not have appeared miraculous: but that correspondence and coincidence may be so, though the event

* P. 270, &c.

† Deut. xxviii. 37

itself be supposed not. Thus the concurrence of our Saviour's being born at Bethlehem, with a long foregoing series of prophecy and other coincidences, is doubtless miraculous; the series of prophecy, and other coincidences, and the event, being admitted: though the event itself appears to have been brought about in a natural way; of which, however, no one can be certain.

As several of these events seem, in some degree expressly, to have verified the prophetic history already, so likewise they may be considered further, as having a peculiar aspect towards the full completion of it; as affording some presumption that the whole of it shall, one time or other, be fulfilled. Thus, that the Jews have been so wonderfully preserved in their long and wide dispersion; which is indeed the direct fulfilling of some prophecies, but is now mentioned only as looking forward to somewhat yet to come: that natural religion came forth from Judea, and spread, in the degree it has done over the world, before lost in idolatry; which, together with some other things, have distinguished that very place, in like manner as the people of it are distinguished: that this great change of religion over the earth was brought about under the profession and acknowledgment, that Jesus was the promised Messiah: things of this kind naturally turn the thoughts of serious men towards the full completion of the prophetic history, concerning the final restoration of that people; concerning the establishment of the everlasting kingdom among them, the kingdom of the Messiah; and the future state of the world, under this sacred government. Such circumstances and events, compared with these prophecies, though no completions of them, yet would not, I think, be spoken of as nothing in the argument, by a person upon his first being informed of them. They fall in with the prophetic history of things still future, give it some additional credibility, and have the appearance of being somewhat in order to the full completion of it.

Indeed it requires a good degree of knowledge, and great calmness and consideration, to be able to judge thoroughly of the evidence for the truth of Christianity, from that part of the prophetic history which relates to the situation of the kingdoms of the world, and to the state of the church, from the establishment of Christianity to the present time. But it appears from a general view of it, to be very material. And those persons who have thoroughly examined it, and some of them were men of the coolest tempers, greatest capacities, and least liable to imputations of prejudice, insist upon it as determinately conclusive.

[CONCLUSION.] Suppose now a person quite ignorant of history, first to recollect the passages above mentioned out of Scripture, without knowing but that the whole was a late fiction, then to be informed of the correspondent facts now mentioned, and to unite them all into one view: that the profession and establishment of natural religion in the world is greatly owing, in different ways, to this book, and the supposed revelation which it contains; that it is acknowledged to be of the earliest antiquity; that its chronology and common history are entirely credible; that this ancient nation, the Jews, of whom it chiefly treats, appear to have been, in fact, the people of God, in a distinguished sense; that, as there was a national expectation among them, raised from the prophecies, of a Messiah to appear at such a time, so one at this time appeared claiming to be that Messiah; that he was rejected by this nation, but received by the Gentiles, not upon the evidence of prophecy, but of miracles; that the religion he taught supported itself under the greatest difficulties, gained ground, and at length became the religion of the world; that in the mean time the Jewish polity was utterly destroyed, and the nation dispersed over the face of the earth; that notwithstanding this, they have remained a distinct numerous people for so many centuries, even to this day; which not only appears to be the express completion of several prophecies concerning them, but also renders it, as one may speak, a visible and easy possibility that the promises made to them as a nation, may yet be fulfilled.

To these acknowledged truths, let the person we have been supposing add, as I think he ought, whether every one will allow it or no, the obvious appearances which there are, of the state of the world, in other respects besides what relates to the Jews, and of the Christian church, having so long answered, and still answering to the prophetic history. Suppose, I say, these facts set over against the things before mentioned out of the Scripture, and seriously compared with them; the joint view of both together must, I think, appear of very great weight to a considerate reasonable person: of much greater indeed, upon having them first laid before him, than is easy for us, who are so familiarized to them, to conceive, without some particular attention for that purpose.

All these things, and the several particulars contained under them, require to be distinctly and most thoroughly examined into; that the weight of each may be judged of, upon such examination, and such conclusion drawn, as results from their *united force.* But this has not been attempted here. I have gone no further than to show, that the general imperfect view of them now given, the confessed historical evidence for miracles, and the many obvious appearing completions of prophecy, together with the collateral things* here mentioned, and there are several others of the like sort; that all this together, which, being fact, must be acknowledged by unbelievers, amounts to real evidence of somewhat more than human in this matter: evidence much more important, than careless men, who have been accustomed only to transient and partial views of it, can imagine; and indeed abundantly sufficient to act upon. And these things, I apprehend, must be acknowledged by unbelievers. For though they may say, that the historical evidence of miracles wrought in attestation of Christianity, is not sufficient to convince them, that such miracles were really wrought: they cannot deny, that there is such historical evidence, it being a known matter of fact that there is. They may say, the conformity between the prophecies and events is by accident: but there are many instances in which such conformity itself cannot be denied. They may say, with regard to such kind of collateral things as those above mentioned, that any odd accidental events, without meaning, will have a meaning found in them by fanciful people: and that such as are fanciful in any one certain way, will make out a thousand coincidences, which seem to favor their peculiar follies. Men, I say, may talk thus: but no one who is serious, can possibly think these things to be nothing, if he considers the importance of collateral things, and even of lesser circumstances, in the evidence of probability, as distinguished in nature, from the evidence of demonstration. In many cases indeed it seems to require the truest judgment, to determine with exactness the weight of cir-

* All the particular things mentioned in this chapter, not reducible to the head of certain miracles, or determinate completions of prophecy. See p. 263.

cumstantial evidence: but it is very often altogether as convincing, as that which is the most express and direct.

This general view of the evidence for Christianity, considered as making one argument, may also serve to recommend to serious persons, to set down every thing which they think may be of any real weight at all in proof of it, and particularly the many seeming completions of prophecy: and they will find, that, judging by the natural rules, by which we judge of probable evidence in common matters, they amount to a much higher degree of proof, upon such a *joint review*, than could be supposed upon considering them separately, at different times; how strong soever the proof might before appear to them, upon such separate views of it. For probable proofs, by being added, not only *increase* the evidence, but *multiply* it.[m] Nor should I dissuade any one from setting down, what he thought made for the contrary side. But then it is to be remembered, not in order to influence his judgment, but his practice, that a mistake on one side may be, in its consequences, much more dangerous, than a mistake on the other. And what course is most safe, and what most dangerous, will be thought a very material consideration, when we deliberate, not concerning events, but concerning conduct in our temporal affairs. To be influenced by this consideration in our judgment, to believe or disbelieve upon it, is indeed as much prejudice, as any thing whatever. And, like other prejudices, it operates contrary ways, in different men; for some are

[m] [Butler states this argument with more than his usual brevity, and its force is not seen without reflection. "If contrivance or accident could have given to Christianity *any* of its apparent testimonies, its miracles, its prophecies, its morals, its propagation, or [the character of] its founder, there could be no room to believe, or even imagine, that *all* these appearances of great credibility, could be *united together*, by any such means. If successful craft could have contrived its public miracles, or the pretence of them, it requires another reach of craft, to adopt its prophecies to the same object. Further, it required not only a different, but a totally opposite art to conceive and promulgate its admirable morals. Again, its propagation, in defiance of the powers and terrors of the world, implied still other qualities of action. Lastly, the model of the life of its founder, is a work of such originality and wisdom, as could be the offspring only of consummate powers of invention, or rather never could have been *devised*, but must have come from real life. The hypothesis sinks under its incredibility. Each of these suppositions of contrivance, being arbitrary and unsupported, the climax of them is an extravagance."—DAVISON, on Prophecy.]

inclined to believe what they hope, and others what they fear. And it is manifest unreasonableness to apply to men's passions in order to gain their assent. But in deliberations concerning conduct, there is nothing which reason more requires to be taken into the account, than the importance of it. For, suppose it doubtful, what would be the consequence of acting in this, or in the contrary manner: still, that taking one side could be attended with little or no bad consequence, and taking the other might be attended with the greatest, must appear, to unprejudiced reason, of the highest moment towards determining how we are to act. The truth of our religion, like the truth of common matters, is to be judged of by all the evidence taken together. And unless the whole series of things which may be alleged in this argument, and every particular thing in it, can reasonably be supposed to have been by accident (for here the stress of the argument for Christianity lies); then is the truth of it proved: in like manner, as if in any common case, numerous events acknowledged, were to be alleged in proof of any other event disputed; the truth of the disputed event would be proved, not only if any one of the acknowledged ones did of itself clearly imply it, but, though no one of them singly did so, if the whole of the acknowledged events taken together could not in reason be supposed to have happened, unless the disputed one were true.

It is obvious, how much advantage the nature of this evidence gives to those persons who attack Christianity, especially in conversation. For it is easy to show, in a short and lively manner, that such and such things are liable to objection, that this and another thing is of little weight in itself; but impossible to show, in like manner, the united force of the whole argument in one view.

Lastly, as it has been made appear, that there is no presumption against a revelation as miraculous; that the general scheme of Christianity, and the principal parts of it, are conformable to the experienced constitution of things, and the whole perfectly credible: so the account now given of the positive evidence for it, shows, that this evidence is such, as, from the nature of it, cannot be destroyed, though it should be lessened.

CHAPTER VIII.

OBJECTIONS AGAINST ARGUING FROM THE ANALOGY OF NATURE, TO RELIGION.

If every one would consider, with such attention as they are bound, even in point of morality, to consider, what they judge and give characters of; the occasion of this chapter would be, in some good measure at least, superseded. But since this is not to be expected; for some we find do not concern themselves to understand even what they write against: since this treatise, in common with most others, lies open to objections, which may appear very material to thoughtful men at first sight; and, besides that, seems peculiarly liable to the objections of such as can judge without thinking, and of such as can censure without judging; it may not be amiss to set down the chief of these objections which occur to me, and consider them to their hands. They are such as these:

"That it is a poor thing to solve difficulties in revelation, by saying, that there are the same in natural religion; when what is wanting is to clear both of them of these their common, as well as other their respective, difficulties; that it is a strange way indeed of convincing men of the obligations of religion, to show them, that they have as little reason for their worldly pursuits: and a strange way of vindicating the justice and goodness of the Author of nature, and of removing the objections against both, to which the system of religion lies open, to show, that the like objections lie against natural providence; a way of answering objections against religion, without so much as pretending to make out, that the system of it, or the particular things in it objected against, are reasonable—especially, perhaps some may be inattentive enough to add, must this be thought strange, when it is confessed that analogy is no answer to such objections: that when this sort of reasoning is carried to the utmost length it can be imagined capable of, it will yet leave the mind in a very unsatisfied state; and that it must be unaccountable ignorance of mankind, to imagine they will be prevailed with to forego their present interests and pleasures, from regard to religion, upon doubtful evidence."

Now, as plausible as this way of talking may appear, that appearance will be found in a great measure owing to half views, which show but part of an object, yet show that indistinctly, and to undeterminate language. By these means weak men are often deceived by others, and ludicrous men, by themselves. And even those, who are serious and considerate, cannot always readily disentangle, and at once clearly see through the perplexities, in which subjects themselves are involved; and which are heightened by the deficiencies and the abuse of words. To this latter sort of persons, the following reply to each part of this objection severally, may be of some assistance; as it may also tend a little to stop and silence others.

First, The thing wanted, *i.e.* what men require, is to have *all* difficulties cleared. And this is, or at least for any thing we know to the contrary, it may be, the same as requiring to comprehend the divine nature, and the whole plan of Providence from everlasting to everlasting! But it hath always been allowed to argue from what is acknowledged, to what is disputed. And it is in no other sense a poor thing, to argue from natural religion to revealed, in the manner found fault with, than it is to argue in numberless other ways of probable deduction and inference, in matters of conduct, which we are continually reduced to the necessity of doing. Indeed the epithet *poor* may be applied, I fear as properly, to great part or the whole of human life, as it is to the things mentioned in the objection. Is it not a poor thing, for a physician to have so little knowledge in the cure of diseases, as even the most eminent have? To act upon conjecture and guess, where the life of man is concerned? Undoubtedly it is: but not in comparison of having no skill at all in that useful art, and being obliged to act wholly in the dark.

Further: since it is as unreasonable, as it is common, to urge objections against revelation, which are of equal weight against natural religion; and those who do this, if they are not confused themselves, deal unfairly with others, in making it seem that they are arguing only against revelation, or particular doctrines of it, when in reality they are arguing against moral providence; it is a thing of consequence to show, that such objections are as much levelled against natural religion, as against revealed. Objections, which are equally applicable to both, are properly speaking answered, by its being shown that they are so, provided the former be admitted to be true. And without taking in the consideration how distinctly this is admitted, it is plainly very material to observe, that as the things objected against in natural religion are of the same kind with what is certain matter of experience in the course of providence, and in the information which God affords us concerning our temporal interest under his government; so the objections against the system of Christianity, and the evidence of it, are of the very same kind with those which are made against the system and evidence of natural religion. However, the reader upon review may see, that most of the analogies insisted upon, even in the latter part of this treatise, do not necessarily require to have more taken for granted than is in the former; [viz.] that there is an Author of nature, or natural Governor of the world: and Christianity is vindicated, not from its analogy to natural religion, but chiefly from its analogy to the experienced constitution of nature.

Secondly, Religion is a practical thing, and consists in such a determinate course of life, as what, there is reason to think, is commanded by the Author of nature, and will, upon the whole, be our happiness under his government. If men can be convinced, that they have the like reason to believe this, as to believe that taking care of their temporal affairs will be to their advantage; such conviction cannot but be an argument to them for the practice of religion. And if there be really any reason for believing one of these, and endeavoring to preserve life, and secure ourselves the necessaries and conveniences of it; then there is reason also for believing the other, and endeavoring to secure the interest it proposes to us. And if the interest, which religion proposes to us, be infinitely greater than our whole temporal interest; then there must be proportionably greater reason for endeavoring to secure one, than the other; since, by the supposition, the probability of our securing one is equal to the probability of our securing the other. This seems plainly unanswerable; and has a tendency to influence fair minds, who consider what our condition really is, or upon what evidence we are naturally appointed to act; and who are disposed to acquiesce in the terms upon which we live, and attend to and follow that practical instruction, whatever it be, which is afforded us.

But the chief and proper force of the argument referred to in the objection, lies in another place. The proof of religion, it is said, is involved in such inextricable difficulties, as to render it doubtful; and that it cannot be supposed that if it were true, it would be left upon doubtful evidence. Here then, over and above the force of each particular difficulty or objection, these difficulties and objections taken together are turned into a positive argument against the truth of religion; which argument would stand thus. If religion were true, it would not be left doubtful, and open to objections to the degree in which it is: therefore that it is thus left, not only renders the evidence of it weak, and lessens its force, in proportion to the weight of such objections, but also shows it to be false, or is a general presumption of its being so. Now the observation, that from the natural constitution and course of things, we must in our temporal concerns, almost continually, and even in matters of great consequence, act upon evidence of a like kind and degree to the evidence of religion, is an answer to this argument. Because it shows, that it is according to the conduct and character of the Author of nature to appoint we should act upon evidence like to that, which this argument presumes he cannot be supposed to appoint we should act upon: it is an instance, a general one, made up of numerous particular ones, of somewhat in his dealing with us, similar to what is said to be incredible. As the force of this answer lies merely in the parallel, which there is between the evidence for religion and for our temporal conduct; the answer is equally just and conclusive, whether the parallel be made out, by showing the evidence of the former to be higher, or the evidence of the latter to be lower.

Thirdly, The design of this treatise is not to vindicate the character of God, but to show the obligations of men: it is not to justify his providence, but to show what belongs to us to do. These are two subjects, and ought not to be confounded. Though they may at length run up into each other, yet observations may immediately tend to make out the latter, which do not appear, by any immediate connection, to the purpose of the former; which is less our concern, than many seem to think. For, first,

It is not necessary we should justify the dispensations of Providence against objections, any farther than to show, that the things objected against may, for aught we know, be consistent with justice and goodness. Suppose then, that there are things in the system of this world, and plan of Providence relating to it, which taken alone would be unjust: yet it has been shown unanswerably, that if we could take in the reference, which these things may have to other things, present past and to come; to the whole scheme, which the things objected against are parts of; these very things might, for aught we know, be found to be, not only consistent with justice, but instances of it. Indeed it has been shown, by the analogy of what we see, not only possible that this may be the case, but credible that it is. And thus objections, drawn from such things, are answered, and Providence is vindicated, as far as religion makes its vindication necessary.

Hence it appears, Secondly, that objections against the Divine justice and goodness are not endeavored to be *removed*, by showing that the like objections, allowed to be really conclusive, lie against natural providence: but those objections being supposed and shown not to be *conclusive*, the things objected against, considered as matters of fact, are farther shown to be credible, from their conformity to the constitution of nature; for instance, that God will reward and punish men for their actions hereafter, from the observation, that he does reward and punish them for their actions here. And this, I apprehend, is of weight.

Thirdly, it would be of weight, even though those objections were not answered. For, there being the proof of religion above set down; and religion implying several facts; for instance again, the fact last mentioned, that God will reward and punish men for their actions hereafter; the observation, that his present method of government is by rewards and punishments, shows that future fact not to be incredible: whatever objections men may think they have against it, as unjust or unmerciful, according to their notions of justice and mercy; or as improbable from their belief of necessity. I say, *as improbable:* for it is evident no objection against it, *as unjust*, can be urged from necessity; since this notion as much destroys injustice, as it does justice.

Fourthly, Though objections against the reasonableness of the system of religion cannot indeed be answered without entering into consideration of its reasonableness; yet objections against the credibility or truth of it may. Because the system of it is reducible into what is properly matter of fact: and the truth, the probable truth of facts, may be shown without consideration of their reasonableness. Nor is it necessary, though, in some cases and respects, it is highly useful and proper, yet it is not necessary, to give a proof of the reasonableness of every precept enjoined us, and of every particular dispensation of Providence, which comes into the system of religion. Indeed the more thoroughly a person of a right disposition is convinced of the perfection of the Divine nature and conduct, the farther he will advance towards that perfection of religion, which John* speaks of.[a] But the general obligations of religion are fully made out, by proving the reasonableness of the practice of it. And that the practice of religion *is* reasonable, may be shown, though no more could be proved, than that the system of it *may be* so, for aught we know to the contrary: and even without entering into the distinct consideration of this.

Fifthly, It is easy to see, that though the analogy of nature is not an immediate answer to objections against the wisdom, the justice, or goodness, of any doctrine or precept of religion; yet it may be, as it is, an immediate and direct answer to what is really intended by such objections; which is, to show that the things objected against are incredible.

Fourthly, It is most readily acknowledged, that the foregoing treatise is by no means satisfactory; very far indeed from it: but so would any natural institution of life appear, if reduced into a system, together with its evidence. Leaving religion out of the case, men are divided in their opinions, whether our pleasures overbalance our pains: and whether it be, or be not, eligible to live in this world.[b] And were all such controversies settled, which perhaps, in speculation, would be found involved in great

* 1 John iv. 18.—["There is no fear in love," &c.]

[a] [Obedience from dread, if it continue to be the only motive, precludes advance toward perfection; for "He that feareth is not made perfect in love." But obedience from a discernment of the reasonableness and beneficence of religion, and of the perfections of its Author, increases love till it "casteth out fear."]

[b] [See a discussion of this subject, in BAYLE's Historical and Biographical Dictionary: art. XENOPHANES: notes D, E, F, G.]

difficulties; and were it determined upon the evidence of reason, as nature has determined it to our hands, that life is to be preserved: still, the rules which God has been pleased to afford us, for escaping the miseries of it, and obtaining its satisfactions, the rules, for instance, of preserving health, and recovering it when lost, are not only fallible and precarious, but very far from being exact. Nor are we informed by nature, as to future contingencies and accidents, so as to render it at all certain, what is the best method of managing our affairs. What will be the success of our temporal pursuits, in the common sense of the word success, is highly doubtful. And what will be the success of them in the proper sense of the word; *i.e.* what happiness or enjoyment we shall obtain by them, is doubtful in a much higher degree. Indeed the unsatisfactory nature of the evidence, with which we are obliged to take up, in the daily course of life, is scarce to be expressed. Yet men do not throw away life, or disregard the interests of it, upon account of this doubtfulness. The evidence of religion then being admitted real, those who object against it, as not satisfactory, *i.e.* as not being what they wish it, plainly forget the very condition of our being: for satisfaction, in this sense, does not belong to such a creature as man.

And, what is more material, they forget also the very nature of religion. For, religion presupposes, in all those who will embrace it, a certain degree of integrity and honesty; which it was intended to try whether men have or not, and to exercise in such as have it, in order to its improvement. Religion presupposes this as much, and in the same sense, as speaking to a man presupposes he understands the language in which you speak; or as warning a man of any danger presupposes that he hath such a regard to himself, as that he will endeavor to avoid it. Therefore the question is not at all, Whether the evidence of religion be satisfactory; but Whether it be, in reason, sufficient to prove and discipline that virtue, which it presupposes. Now the evidence of it is fully sufficient for all those purposes of *probation*; how far soever it is from being satisfactory, as to the purposes of *curiosity*, or any other: and indeed it answers the purposes of the former in several respects, which it would not do, if it were as overpowering as is required. Besides, whether the motives or the evidence for any course of action be satisfactory, meaning here, by that word, what satisfies a man that such a course of action will in event be for his good; this need never be, and I think, strictly speaking, never is, the practical question in common matters. The practical question in all cases is, Whether the evidence for a course of action be such as, taking in all circumstances, makes the faculty within us, which is the guide and judge of conduct,* determine that course of action to be prudent. Indeed, satisfaction that it will be for our interest or happiness, abundantly determines an action to be prudent: but evidence almost infinitely lower than this, determines actions to be so too; even in the conduct of every day.

Fifthly, As to the objection concerning the influence which this argument, or any part of it, may, or may not be expected to have upon men; I observe, as above, that religion being intended for a trial[c] and exercise of the morality of every person's character, who is a subject of it; and there being, as I have shown, such evidence for it, as is sufficient, in reason, to influence men to embrace it: to object, that it is not to be imagined mankind will be influenced by such evidence, is nothing to the purpose of the foregoing treatise. For the purpose of it is not to inquire, what sort of creatures mankind are; but what the light and knowledge, which is afforded them, requires they should be: to show how, in reason, they ought to behave; not how, in fact, they will behave. This depends upon themselves, and is their own concern; the personal concern of each man in particular. How little regard the generality have to it, experience indeed does too fully show. But religion, considered as a probation, has had its end upon all persons, to whom it has been proposed with evidence sufficient in reason to influence their practice: for by this means they have been put into a state of probation; let

* See Dissertation II.

[c] [It is remarked by DEAN FITZGERALD, that "It is not inconceivable that the Almighty should apply such a test of men's candor and fidelity, as should require them first to act upon a thing as true, before they were so fully satisfied of its truth as to leave no doubt remaining. Such a course of action might be the appointed, and for all we know, the only possible way of overcoming habits of thought and feeling, repugnant to the belief demanded, so that a fixed religious faith might be the reward, as it were, of a sincere course of prudent behavior."]

them behave as they will in it. Thus, not only revelation, but reason also, teaches us, that by the evidence of religion being laid before men, the designs of Providence are carrying on, not only with regard to those who will be influenced by it, but likewise with regard to those who will not. Lastly, the objection here referred to, allows the thing insisted upon in this treatise to be of *some* weight; and if so, it may be hoped it will have some influence. And if there be a probability that it will have any at all, there is the same reason in kind, though not in degree, to lay it before men, as there would be, if it were likely to have a greater influence.

Further, I desire it may be considered, with respect to the whole of the foregoing objections, that in this treatise I have argued upon the principles of others,* not my own: and have omitted what I think true, and of the utmost importance, because by others thought unintelligible, or not true. Thus I have argued upon the principles of the fatalists, which I do not believe: and have omitted a thing of the utmost importance which I do believe,—[viz.] the moral fitness and unfitness of actions, prior to all will whatever; which as certainly determine the divine *conduct*, as speculative truth and falsehood necessarily determine the divine *judgment*. Indeed the principle of liberty, and that of moral fitness, so force themselves upon the mind, that moralists, ancient as well as modern, have formed their language upon it. And probably it may appear in mine, though I have endeavored to avoid it; and, in order to avoid it, have sometimes been obliged to express myself in a manner, which will appear strange to such as do not observe the reason for it. But the general argument here pursued, does not at all suppose, or proceed upon these principles.

Now, these two abstract principles of liberty and moral fitness being omitted, religion can be considered in no other view, than merely as a question of fact: and in this view it is here considered. It is obvious, that Christianity, and the proof of it, are both historical. Even natural religion is, properly, a matter

* By *arguing upon the principles of others,* the reader will observe is meant, not proving any thing *from* those principles, but *notwithstanding* them. Thus religion is proved, not *from* the opinion of necessity; which is absurd: but, *notwithstanding* or *even though* that opinion were admitted to be true.

of fact. For, that there is a righteous Governor of the world, is so: and this proposition contains the general system of natural religion. But then, several abstract truths, and in particular those two principles, are usually taken into consideration in the proof of it: whereas it is here treated of only as a matter of fact. To explain this; That the three angles of a triangle are equal to two right ones, is an abstract truth; but that they appear so to our mind, is only a matter of fact. This last must have been admitted, if any thing was, by those ancient sceptics, who would not admit the former: but pretended to doubt, whether there were any such thing as truth, or whether we could certainly depend upon our faculties of understanding for the knowledge of it in any case.

The assertion that there is, in the nature of things, an original standard of right and wrong in actions, independent upon all will, but which unalterably determines the will of God, to exercise that moral government over the world, which religion teaches, (*i.e.* finally and upon the whole to reward and punish men respectively as they act right or wrong;) contains an abstract truth, as well as matter of fact. But suppose that in the present state, every man without exception, was rewarded and punished, in exact proportion as he followed or transgressed that sense of right and wrong, which God has implanted in his nature: this would not be at all an abstract truth, but only a matter of fact. And though this fact were acknowledged by every one, yet the same difficulties might be raised as now are, concerning the abstract questions of liberty and moral fitness. And we should have a proof, even the certain one of experience, that the government of the world was perfectly moral, without taking in the consideration of those questions: and this proof would remain, in what way soever they were determined.

Thus, God having given mankind a moral faculty, the object of which is actions, and which naturally approves some actions as right, and of good desert, and condemns others as wrong, and of ill desert; that he will, finally and upon the whole, reward the former and punish the latter, is not an assertion of an abstract truth, but of what is as mere a fact, as his doing so at present would be. This future fact I have not, indeed, proved with the force with which it might be proved, from the principles of liberty and moral fitness; but without them have given a really conclusive practical proof of it, which is greatly strengthened by the general analogy of nature; a proof easily cavilled at, easily shown not to be demonstrative, (and it is not offered as such;) but impossible, I think, to be evaded, or answered. Thus the obligations of religion are made out, exclusive of the questions concerning liberty and moral fitness; which have been perplexed with difficulties and abstruse reasonings, as every thing may.

Hence therefore may be observed distinctly, what is the force of this treatise. It will be, to such as are convinced of religion upon the proof arising out of the two last mentioned principles, an *additional* proof and confirmation of it: to such as do not admit those principles, an *original* proof of it,* and a confirmation of that proof. Those who believe, will here find the scheme of Christianity cleared of objections, and the evidence of it in a peculiar manner strengthened. Those who do not believe will at least be shown the absurdity of all attempts to prove Christianity false, the plain undoubted credibility of it; and, I hope, a good deal more.

Thus, though some perhaps may seriously think, that analogy, as here urged, has too great stress laid upon it; and ridicule, unanswerable ridicule, may be applied, to show the argument from it in a disadvantageous light; yet there can be no question, but that it is a real one. For religion, both natural and revealed, implying in it numerous facts; analogy, being a *confirmation* of all facts to which it can be applied, and the *only proof* of most, cannot but be admitted by every one to be a material thing, and truly of weight on the side of religion, both natural and revealed. And it ought to be particularly regarded by such as profess to follow nature, and to be less satisfied with abstract reasonings.

CONCLUSION.

WHATEVER account may be given of the strange inattention and disregard, in some ages and countries, to a matter of such importance as religion; it would, before experience, be incredible, that there should be the like disregard in those, who have had

* P. 141, &c.

the moral system of the world laid before them, as it is by Christianity, and often inculcated upon them: because this moral system carries in it a good degree of evidence for its truth, upon its being barely proposed to our thoughts. There is no need of abstruse reasonings and distinctions, to convince an unprejudiced understanding, that there is a God who made and governs the world, and will judge it in righteousness; though they may be necessary to answer abstruse difficulties, when once such are raised: when the very meaning of those words, which express most intelligibly the general doctrine of religion, is pretended to be uncertain; and the clear truth of the thing itself is obscured by the intricacies of speculation. To an unprejudiced mind, ten thousand thousand instances of design cannot but prove a designer. And it is intuitively manifest, that *creatures* ought to live under a dutiful sense of their Maker; and that justice and charity must be his laws, to creatures whom he has made social, and placed in society.

The truth of revealed religion, peculiarly so called, is not indeed self-evident, but requires external proof, in order to its being received. Yet inattention, among us, to revealed religion, will be found to imply the same dissolute immoral temper of mind, as inattention to natural religion: because, when both are laid before us, in the manner they are in Christian countries of liberty, our obligations to inquire into both, and to embrace both upon supposition of their truth, are obligations of the same nature. Revelation claims to be the voice of God: and our obligation to attend to his voice is surely moral, in all cases. And as it is insisted, that its evidence is conclusive, upon thorough consideration of it; so it offers itself with obvious appearances of having something more than human in it, and therefore in all reason requires to have its claims most seriously examined into.

It is to be added, that though light and knowledge, in what manner soever afforded, is equally from God; yet a miraculous revelation has a peculiar tendency, from the first principles of our nature, to awaken mankind, and inspire them with reverence and awe. And this is a peculiar obligation, to attend to what claims to be so, with such appearances of truth. It is therefore most certain, that our obligations to inquire seriously into the evidence of Christianity, and, upon supposition of its truth, to embrace it, are of the utmost importance, and moral in the highest and most proper sense. Let us then suppose, that the evidence of religion in general, and of Christianity, has been seriously inquired into, by all reasonable men among us. Yet we find many professedly to reject both, upon speculative principles of infidelity. All of them do not content themselves with a bare neglect of religion, and enjoying their imaginary freedom from its restraints. Some go much beyond this. They deride God's moral government over the world. They renounce his protection, and defy his justice. They ridicule and vilify Christianity, and blaspheme the author of it; and take all occasions to manifest scorn and contempt of revelation. This amounts to an active setting themselves against religion; to what may be considered as a positive principle of irreligion, which they cultivate within themselves; and, whether they intend this effect or not, render habitual, as a good man does the contrary principle. Others, who are not chargeable with all this profligateness, yet are in avowed opposition to religion, as if discovered to be groundless

Now admitting, which is the supposition we go upon, that these persons act upon what they think principles of reason, (and otherwise they are not to be argued with,) it is really inconceivable, that they should imagine they clearly see the whole evidence of it, considered in itself, to be nothing at all: nor do they pretend this. They are far indeed from having a just notion of its evidence: but they would not say its evidence was nothing, if they thought the system of it, with all its circumstances, were credible, like other matters of science or history. Their manner of treating it must proceed, either from such kind of objections against all religion, as have been answered or obviated in the former part of this treatise; or else from objections, and difficulties, supposed more peculiar to Christianity. Thus, they entertain prejudices against the whole notion of a revelation, and miraculous interpositions. They find things in Scripture, whether in incidental passages, or in the general scheme of it, which appear to them unreasonable. They take for granted, that if Christianity were true, the light of it must have been more general, and the evidence of it more satisfactory, or rather overpowering: that it must and would have been, in some way, otherwise put and left, than it is. Now this is not imagining they see the evidence itself to be nothing, or inconsiderable; but quite another thing. It is being fortified *against* the evidence, in some degree acknowledged, by thinking they see the system of Christianity, or something which appears to them necessarily connected with it, to be incredible or false; fortified against that evidence, which might otherwise make great impression upon them. Or, lastly, if any of these persons are, upon the whole, in doubt concerning the truth of Christianity; their behavior seems owing to their taking for granted, through strange inattention, that such doubting is, in a manner, the same thing as being certain against it.

To these persons, and to this state of opinion concerning religion, the foregoing treatise is adapted. For, all the general objections against the moral system of nature having been obviated, it is shown, that there is not any peculiar presumption at all against Christianity, considered either as not discoverable by reason, or as unlike to what is so discovered; nor any, worth mentioning, against it as miraculous, if any at all; none, certainly, which can render it in the least incredible. It is shown, that, upon supposition of a divine revelation, the analogy of nature renders it beforehand highly credible, I think probable, that many things in it must appear liable to great objections; and that we must be incompetent judges of it, to a great degree. This observation is, I think, unquestionably true, and of the very utmost importance. But it is urged, as I hope it will be understood, with great caution not to vilify the faculty of reason, which is *the candle of the Lord within us*;* though it can afford no light, where it does not shine; nor judge, where it has no principles to judge upon. The objections here spoken of, being first answered in the view of objections against Christianity as a matter of fact, are in the next place considered as urged more immediately against the wisdom, justice, and goodness of the Christian dispensation. And it is fully made out, that they admit of exactly the like answer, in every respect, to what the like objections against the constitution of nature admit of: that, as partial views give the appearance of wrong to things, which, upon further consideration and knowledge of their relations to other things, are found just and good; so it is perfectly credible,

* Prov. xx. 27.

that the things objected against the wisdom and goodness of the Christian dispensation, may be rendered instances of wisdom and goodness, by their reference to other things beyond our view. Because Christianity is a scheme as much above our comprehension, as that of nature; and like that, a scheme in which means are made use of to accomplish ends, and which, as is most credible, may be carried on by general laws. And it ought to be attended to, that this is not an answer taken merely or chiefly from our ignorance: but from something positive, which our observation shows us. For, to like objections, the like answer is experienced to be just, in numberless parallel cases.

The objections against the Christian dispensation, and the method by which it is carried on, having been thus obviated, in general, and together; the chief of them are considered distinctly, and the particular things objected to are shown credible, by their perfect analogy, each apart, to the constitution of nature. Thus, if man be fallen from his primitive state, and to be restored, and infinite wisdom and power engages in accomplishing our recovery: it were to have been expected, it is said, that this should have been effected at once; and not by such a long series of means, and such a various economy of persons and things; one dispensation preparatory to another, this to a further one, and so on through an indefinite number of ages, before the end of the scheme proposed can be completely accomplished; a scheme conducted by infinite wisdom, and executed by almighty power. But now, on the contrary, our finding that every thing in the constitution and course of nature is thus carried on, shows such expectations concerning revelation to be highly unreasonable; and is a satisfactory answer to them, when urged as objections against the credibility, that the great scheme of Providence in the redemption of the world may be of this kind, and to be accomplished in this manner.

As to the particular method of our redemption, the appointment of a Mediator between God and man: this has been shown to be most obviously analogous to the general conduct of nature, *i.e.* the God of nature, in appointing others to be the instruments of his mercy, as we experience in the daily course of Providence. The condition of this world, which the doctrine of our redemption by Christ presupposes, so much falls in with natural appearances, that heathen moralists inferred it from those appearances: inferred that human nature was fallen from its original rectitude, and in consequence of this, degraded from its primitive happiness. However this opinion came into the world, these appearances kept up the tradition, and confirmed the belief of it. And as it was the general opinion under the light of nature, that repentance and reformation, alone and by itself, was not sufficient to do away sin, and procure a full remission of the penalties annexed to it; and as the reason of the thing does not at all lead to any such conclusion; so every day's experience shows us, that reformation is not, in any sort, sufficient to prevent the present disadvantages and miseries, which, in the natural course of things, God has annexed to folly and extravagance.

Yet there may be ground to think, that the punishments, which, by the general laws of divine government, are annexed to vice, may be prevented: that provision may have been, even originally, made, that they should be prevented by some means or other, though they could not by reformation alone. For we have daily instances of *such mercy*, in the general conduct of nature: compassion provided for misery,* medicines for diseases, friends against enemies. There is provision made, in the original constitution of the world, that much of the natural bad consequences of our follies, which persons themselves alone cannot prevent, may be prevented by the assistance of others; assistance which nature enables, and disposes, and appoints them to afford. By a method of goodness analogous to this, when the world lay in wickedness, and consequently in ruin, *God so loved the world, that he gave his only-begotten Son* to save it: and *he being made perfect by suffering, became the author of eternal salvation to all them that obey him.*† Indeed neither reason nor analogy would lead us to think, in particular, that the interposition of Christ, in the manner in which he did interpose, would be of that efficacy for recovery of the world, which the Scripture teaches us it was. But neither would reason nor analogy lead us to think, that other particular means would be of the efficacy, which experience shows they are, in numberless instances. Therefore, as the case before us does not admit of experience; so, that neither reason nor

* Serm. at the *Rolls*, p. 106.

† John iii. 16: Heb. v. 9.

analogy can show how, or in what particular way, the interposition of Christ, as revealed in Scripture, is of that efficacy, which it is there represented to be; this is no kind nor degree of presumption against its being really of that efficacy.

Further: the objections against Christianity, from the light of it not being universal, nor its evidence so strong as might possibly be given, have been answered by the general analogy of nature. That God has made such variety of creatures, is indeed an answer to the former: but that he dispenses his gifts in such variety, both of degrees and kinds, among creatures of the same species, and even to the same individuals at different times; is a more obvious and full answer to it. And it is so far from being the method of Providence in other cases, to afford us such overbearing evidence, as some require in proof of Christianity; that on the contrary, the evidence upon which we are naturally appointed to act in common matters, throughout a very great part of life, is doubtful in a high degree. And admitting the fact, that God has afforded to some no more than doubtful evidence of religion; the same account may be given of it, as of difficulties and temptations with regard to practice. But as it is not impossible,* surely, that this alleged doubtfulness may be men's own fault; it deserves their most serious consideration, whether it be not so. However, it is certain, that doubting implies a *degree* of evidence for that of which we doubt: and that this degree of evidence as really lays us under obligations as demonstrative evidence.

The whole of religion then is throughout credible: nor is there, I think, any thing, relating to the revealed dispensation of things, more different from the experienced constitution and course of nature, than some parts of the constitution of nature are from other parts of it. If so, the only question which remains is, What positive evidence can be alleged for the truth of Christianity? This too in general has been considered, and the objections against it estimated. Deduct, therefore, what is to be deducted from that evidence, upon account of any weight which may be thought to remain in these objections, after what the analogy of nature has suggested in answer to them: and then consider, what are the practical consequences from all this

* P. 258, &c.

upon the most sceptical principles one can argue upon (for I am writing to persons who entertain these principles): and upon such consideration it will be obvious, that immorality, as little excuse as it admits of in itself, is greatly aggravated, in persons who have been made acquainted with Chriatianity, whether they believe it or not: because the moral system of nature, or natural religiòn, which Christianity lays before us, approves itself, almost intuitively, to a reasonable mind, upon seeing it proposed.

In the next place, with regard to Christianity, it will be observed that there is a middle between a full satisfaction of the truth of it, and a satisfaction of the contrary. The middle state of mind between these two consists in a serious apprehension, that it may be true, joined with doubt whether it is so. And this, upon the best judgment I am able to make, is as far towards speculative infidelity, as any sceptic can at all be supp sed to go, who has had true Christianity, with the proper evidences of it, laid before him, and has in any tolerable measure considered them. For I would not be mistaken to comprehend all who have ever heard of it; because it seems evident, that in many countries called Christian, neither Christianity nor its evidence, is fairly laid before men. And in places where both are, there appear to be some who have very little attended to either, and who reject Christianity with a scorn proportionate to their inattention; and yet are by no means without understanding in other matters. Now it has been shown, that a serious apprehension that Christianity may be true, lays persons under the strictest obligations of a serious regard to it, throughout the whole of their life; a regard not the same exactly, but in many respects nearly the same with what a full conviction of its truth would lay them under.

Lastly, it will appear, that blasphemy and profaneness, with regard to Christianity, are absolutely without excuse. There is no temptation to it, but from the wantonness of vanity or mirth; and these, considering the infinite importance of the subject, are no such temptations as to afford any excuse for it. If this be a just account of things, and yet men can go on to vilify or disregard Christianity, which is to talk and act as if they had a demonstration of its falsehood, there is no reason to think they would alter their behavior to any purpose, though there were a demonstration of its truth.

DISSERTATIONS.

OF PERSONAL IDENTITY.

OF THE NATURE OF VIRTUE.

Advertisement.

In the first copy of these papers, I had inserted the two following dissertations into the chapters, on *a Future Life*, and on the *Moral Government of God;* with which they are closely connected. But as these do not directly fall under the *title* of the foregoing treatise, and would have kept the subject of it too long out of sight, it seems more proper to place them by themselves.

DISSERTATION I.

Personal Identity.

WHETHER we are to live in a future state, as it is the most important question which can possibly be asked, so it is the most intelligible one which can be expressed in language. Yet strange perplexities have been raised about the meaning of that identity or sameness of person, which is implied in the notion of our living now and hereafter, or in any two successive moments. And the solution of these difficulties hath been stranger than the difficulties themselves. For, personal identity has been explained so by some, as to render the inquiry concerning a future life of no consequence at all to us the persons who are making it. And though few men can be misled by such subtleties; yet it may be proper to consider them a little.

When it is asked *wherein* personal identity consists, the answer should be the same, as if it were asked wherein consists similitude, or equality; that all attempts to define would but perplex it. Yet there is no difficulty at all in ascertaining *the idea*. For as, upon two triangles being compared or viewed together, there arises to the mind the idea of similitude; or upon twice two and four, the idea of equality: so likewise, upon comparing the consciousness of one's self, or one's own existence, in any two moments, there as immediately arises to the mind the idea of personal identity. And as the two former comparisons not only give us the ideas of similitude and equality; but also show us that two triangles are alike, and twice two and four are equal: so the latter comparison not only gives us the idea of personal identity, but also shows us the identity of ourselves in those two moments; the present, suppose, and that immediately past; or the present, and that a month, a year, or twenty years past. In other words, by reflecting upon that which is myself now, and that which was myself twenty years ago, I discern they are not two, but one and the same self.

But though consciousness of what is past does thus ascertain our personal identity to ourselves, yet to say, that it *makes* personal identity, or is necessary to our being the same persons, is to say, that a person has not existed a single moment, nor done one action, but what he can remember; indeed none but what he reflects upon. And one should really think it self-evident, that consciousness of personal identity presupposes, and therefore cannot constitute, personal identity; any more than knowledge, in any other case, can constitute truth, which it presupposes.

This wonderful mistake may possibly have arisen from hence; that to be endued with consciousness is inseparable from the idea of a person, or intelligent being. For, this might be expressed inaccurately thus, that consciousness makes personality: and from hence it might be concluded to make personal identity But though present consciousness of what we at present do and feel is necessary to our being the persons we *now are;* yet present consciousness of past actions or feelings is not necessary to our being the same persons who performed those actions, or *once had* those feelings.

The inquiry, what makes vegetables the same, in the common acceptation of the word, does not appear to have any relation to this of personal identity: because, the word *same*, when applied to them and to a person, is not only applied to different subjects, but it is also used in different senses. For when a man swears to the same tree, as having stood fifty years in the same place, he means only the same as to all the purposes of property, and uses of common life; and not that the tree has been all that time the same, in the strict philosophical sense of the word. For he does not know, whether any one particle of the present tree be the same with any one particle of the tree which stood in the same place fifty years ago. And if they have not one common particle of matter, they cannot be the same tree in the proper philosophic sense of the word *same:* it being evidently a contradiction in terms, to say they are, when no part of their substance, and no one of their properties is the same: no part of their substance, by the supposition; no one of their properties, because it is allowed, that the same property cannot be transferred from one substance to another. Therefore when we say the identity or sameness of a plant consists in a continuation of the same life, communicated under the same organization, to a number of particles of matter, whether the same or not; the word *same*, when applied to life and to organization, cannot possibly be understood to signify, what it signifies in this very sentence, when applied to matter. In a loose and popular sense then, the life and the organization and the plant are justly said to be the same, notwithstanding the perpetual change of the parts. But in strict and philosophical language, no man, no being, no mode of being, no any thing, can be the same with that, with which it has indeed nothing the same. Now sameness is used in this latter sense, when applied to persons. The identity of these, therefore, cannot subsist with diversity of substance.

The thing here considered, and as I think, demonstratively determined, is proposed by Mr. Locke in these words, *Whether it*, i.e. the same self or person, *be the same identical substance?* And he has suggested what is a much better answer to the question, than that which he gives it in form. For he defines person, *a thinking intelligent being*, &c., and personal identity, *the sameness of a rational being.** The question then is, whether the same rational being is the same substance: which needs no answer, because being and substance, in this place, stand for the same idea. The ground of the doubt, whether the same person be the same substance, is said to be this; that the consciousness of our own existence, in youth and in old age, or in any two joint successive moments, is not the *same individual action*,† i.e. not the same consciousness, but different successive consciousnesses. Now it is strange that this should have occasioned such perplexities. For it is surely conceivable, that a person may have a capacity of knowing some object or other to be the same now, which it was when he contemplated it formerly: yet in this case, where, by the supposition, the object is perceived to be the same, the perception of it in any two moments cannot be one and the same perception. And thus, though the successive consciousnesses, which we have of our own existence, are not the same, yet are they consciousnesses of one and the same thing or object;

* Locke's Works, vol. i. p. 146.

† Locke, pp. 146, 147.

of the same person, self, or living agent. The person, of whose existence the consciousness is felt now, and was felt an hour or a year ago, is discerned to be, not two persons, but one and the same person; and therefore is one and the same.

Mr. Locke's observations upon this subject appear hasty: and he seems to profess himself dissatisfied with suppositions, which he has made relating to it.* But some of those hasty observations have been carried to a strange length by others; whose notion, when traced and examined to the bottom, amounts, I think, to this:† "That personality is not a permanent, but a transient thing: that it lives and dies, begins and ends continually: that no one can any more remain one and the same person two moments together, than two successive moments can be one and the same moment: that our substance is indeed continually changing; but whether this be so or not, is, it seems, nothing to the purpose; since it is not substance, but consciousness alone, which constitutes personality: which consciousness, being successive, cannot be the same in any two moments, nor consequently the personality constituted by it." Hence it must follow, that it is a fallacy upon ourselves, to charge our present selves with any thing we did, or to imagine our present selves interested in any thing which befell us yesterday; or that our present self will be interested in what will befall us to-morrow: since our present self is not, in reality, the same with the self of yesterday, but another like self or person coming in its room, and mistaken for it; to which another self will succeed to-morrow. This, I say, must follow. For if the self or person of to-day, and that of to-morrow, are not the same, but only like persons; the person of to-day is really no more interested in what will befall the person of to-morrow, than in what will befall any other person.

It may be thought, perhaps, that this is not a just representation of the opinion we are speaking of: because those who maintain it allow, that a person is the same as far back as his remembrance reaches. Indeed they use the words, *identity*, and *same person*. Nor will language permit these words to be laid aside; since if they were, there must be I know not what ridiculous

* Locke, p. 152.

† See an answer to Dr. Clarke's Third Defence of his Letter to Mr. Dodwell, 2d edit. p. 44, 56, &c.

periphrasis substituted in the room of them. But they cannot, *consistently with themselves*, mean, that the person is really the same. For it is self-evident, that the personality cannot be really the same, if, as they expressly assert, that in which it consists is not the same. And as, consistently with themselves, they cannot, so, I think it appears, they do not *mean*, that the person is *really* the same, but only that he is so in a fictitious sense: in such a sense only as they assert, for this they do assert, that any number of persons whatever may be the same person. The bare unfolding this notion, and laying it thus naked and open, seems the best confutation of it. However, since great stress is said to be put upon it, I add the following things.

First, This notion is absolutely contradictory to that certain conviction, which necessarily and every moment rises within us, when we turn our thoughts upon ourselves, when we reflect upon what is past, and look forward upon what is to come. All imagination of a daily change of that living agent which each man calls himself, for another, or of any such change throughout our whole present life, is entirely borne down by our natural sense of things. Nor is it possible for a person in his wits to alter his conduct, with regard to his health or affairs, from a suspicion, that, though he should live to-morrow, he should not, however, be the same person he is to-day. Yet, if it be reasonable to act, with respect to a future life, upon the notion that personality is transient, it is reasonable to act upon it, with respect to the present. Here then is a notion equally applicable to religion and to temporal concerns. Every one sees and feels the inexpressible absurdity of it in the latter case; therefore, if any can take up with it in the former, this cannot proceed from the reason of the thing, but must be owing to inward unfairness, and secret corruption of heart.

Secondly, It is not an idea, or abstract notion, or quality, but a *being* only, which is capable of life and action, of happiness and misery. Now all beings confessedly continue the same, during the whole time of their existence. Consider then a living being now existing, and which has existed for any time alive. This living being must have done and suffered and enjoyed, what it has done and suffered and enjoyed formerly, (this living being, I say, and not another) as really as it does and suffers and enjoys, what it does and suffers and enjoys this instant. All these successive actions, enjoyments, and sufferings, are actions, enjoyments, and sufferings, of the same living being. And they are so, prior to all consideration of its remembering or forgetting: since remembering or forgetting can make no alteration in the truth of past matter of fact. And suppose this being endued with limited powers of knowledge and memory, there is no more difficulty in conceiving it to have a power of knowing itself to be the same living being which it was some time ago, of remembering some of its actions, sufferings, and enjoyments, and forgetting others, than in conceiving it to know or remember or forget any thing else.

Thirdly, Every person is *conscious*, that he is now the same person or self he was as far back as his remembrance reaches: since when any one reflects upon a past action of his own, he is just as certain of the person who did that action, namely, himself who now reflects upon it, as he is certain that the action was done at all. Nay, very often a person's assurance of an action having been done, of which he is absolutely assured, arises wholly from the consciousness that he himself did it. This he, person, or self, must either be a substance, or the property of some substance. If he, a person, be a substance; then consciousness that he is the same person is consciousness that he is the same substance. If the person, or he, be the property of a substance, still consciousness that he is the same property is as certain a proof that his substance remains the same, as consciousness that he remains the same substance would be; since the same property cannot be transferred from one substance to another.

But though we are thus certain, that we are the same agents, living beings, or substances, now, which we were as far back as our remembrance reaches; yet it is asked, whether we may not possibly be deceived in it? And this question may be asked at the end of any demonstration whatever: because it is a question concerning the truth of perception by memory. He who can doubt, whether perception by memory can in this case be depended upon, may doubt also, whether perception by deduction and reasoning, which also include memory, or indeed whether intuitive perception can. Here then we can go no further. For it is ridiculous to attempt to prove the truth of those perceptions, whose truth we can no otherwise prove, than by other perceptions of exactly the same kind with them, and which there is just the same ground to suspect; or to attempt to prove the truth of our faculties, which can no otherwise be proved, than by the use or means of those very suspected faculties themselves.[a]

[a] ["One is continually reminded throughout this dissertation, of what is called *The common-sense school* of Scotch metaphysicians. Nor can there be any doubt that REID, in particular, was largely indebted to Butler, of whose writings he was a diligent student, for forming that sober and manly character of understanding which is, I think, his great merit."—FITZGERALD.]

DISSERTATION II.

The Nature of Virtue.

THAT which renders beings capable of moral government, is their having a moral nature, and moral faculties of perception and of action. Brute creatures are impressed and actuated by various instincts and propensions: so also are we. But additional to this, we have a capacity of reflecting upon actions and characters, and making them an object to our thought: and on doing this, we naturally and unavoidably approve some actions, under the peculiar view of their being virtuous and of good desert; and disapprove others, as vicious and of ill desert. That we have this moral approving and disapproving* faculty, is certain from our experiencing it in ourselves, and recognising it in each other. It appears from our exercising it unavoidably, in the approbation and disapprobation even of feigned characters; from the words right and wrong, odious and amiable, base and worthy, with many others of like signification in all languages applied to actions and characters: from the many written systems of morals which suppose it, since it cannot be imagined, that all these authors, throughout all these treatises, had absolutely no meaning at all to their words, or a meaning merely chimerical: from

* This way of speaking is taken from Epictetus,† and is made use of as seeming the most full, and least liable to cavil. And the moral faculty may be understood to have these two epithets, *δοκιμαστὶκὴ* and *ἀποδοκιμαστικὴ* [applauding and condemning] upon a double account; because, upon a survey of actions, whether before or after they are done, it determines them to be good or evil; and also because it determines itself to be the guide of action and of life, in contradistinction from all other faculties, or natural principles of action; in the very same manner as speculative reason *directly* and naturally judges of speculative truth and falsehood: and at the same time is attended with a consciousness upon *reflection*, that the natural right to judge of them belongs to it

† Arr. Epict. lib. i. cap. i.

our natural sense of gratitude, which implies a distinction between merely being the instrument of good, and intending it: from the distinction every one makes between injury and mere harm, which, Hobbes says, is peculiar to mankind; and between injury and just punishment, a distinction plainly natural, prior to the consideration of human laws.

It is manifest that great part of common language, and of common behavior over the world, is formed upon supposition of such a moral faculty; whether called conscience, moral reason, moral sense, or divine reason; whether considered as a sentiment of the understanding, or as a perception of the heart; or, which seems the truth, as including both. Nor is it at all doubtful in the general, what course of action this faculty, or practical discerning power within us, approves and what it disapproves. For, as much as it has been disputed wherein virtue consists, or whatever ground for doubt there may be about particulars; yet, in general, there is in reality a universally acknowledged standard of it. It is that, which all ages and all countries have made profession of in public: it is that, which every man you meet puts on the show of: it is that, which the primary and fundamental laws of all civil constitutions over the face of the earth make it their business and endeavor to enforce the practice of upon mankind: namely, justice, veracity, and regard to common good. It being manifest then, in general, that we have such a faculty or discernment as this, it may be of use to remark some things more distinctly concerning it.

First, It ought to be observed, that the object of this faculty is actions,* comprehending under that name active or practical principles: those principles from which men would act, if occasions and circumstances gave them power; and which, when fixed and habitual in any person, we call his character. It does not appear, that brutes have the least reflex sense of actions, as distinguished from events: or that will and design, which constitute the very nature of actions as such, are at all an object to their perception. But to ours they are: and they are the object, and the only one, of the approving and disapproving faculty.

* *Οὐδὲ ἡ ἀρετὴ καὶ κακία—ἐν πείσει, ἀλλὰ ἐνεργείᾳ*, [Virtue and vice are not in feeling, but in action,] M. Anton. lib. ix. 16. Virtutis laus omnis in actione consistit. [The whole praise of virtue, depends on action.] Cic. Off. lib. i. cap. 6.

Acting, conduct, behavior, abstracted from all regard to what is in fact and event the consequence of it, is itself the natural object of the moral discernment; as speculative truth and falsehood is of speculative reason. Intention of such and such consequences, is indeed, always included; for it is part of the action itself: but though the intended good or bad consequences do not follow, we have exactly the same sense of the *action*, as if they did. In like manner we think well or ill of characters, abstracted from all consideration of the good or the evil, which persons of such characters have it actually in their power to do. We never, in the moral way, applaud or blame either ourselves or others, for what we enjoy or what we suffer, or for having impressions made upon us, which we consider as altogether out of our power: but only for what we do or would have done, had it been in our power: or for what we leave undone, which we might have done, or would have left undone, though we could have done.

Secondly, Our sense or discernment of actions as morally good or evil, implies in it a sense or discernment of them as of good or ill desert. It may be difficult to explain this perception, so as to answer all the questions which may be asked concerning it: but every one speaks of such and such actions as deserving punishment; and it is not, I suppose, pretended, that they have absolutely no meaning at all to the expression. Now the meaning plainly is not, that we conceive it for the good of society, that the doer of such actions should be made to suffer. For if, unhappily, it were resolved, that a man, who by some innocent action, was infected with the plague, should be left to perish, lest, by other people's coming near him, the infection should spread; no one would say he *deserved* this treatment. Innocence and ill desert are inconsistent ideas. Ill desert always supposes guilt: and if one be no part of the other, yet they are evidently and naturally connected in our mind. The sight of a man in misery raises our compassion towards him; and if this misery be inflicted on him by another, our indignation against the author of it. But when we are informed, that the sufferer is a villain, and is punished only for his treachery or cruelty; our compassion exceedingly lessens, and in many instances our indignation wholly subsides. Now what produces this effect is the conception of that in the sufferer, which we call ill desert. Upon considering then, or viewing together, our notion of vice and that of misery, there results a third, that of ill desert. And thus there is in human creatures an association of the two ideas, natural and moral evil, wickedness and punishment. If this association were merely artificial or accidental, it were nothing: but being most unquestionably natural, it greatly concerns us to attend to it, instead of endeavoring to explain it away.

It may be observed further, concerning our perception of good and of ill desert, that the former is very weak with respect to common instances of virtue. One reason of which may be, that it does not appear to a spectator, how far such instances of virtue proceed from a virtuous principle, or in what degree this principle is prevalent: since a very weak regard to virtue may be sufficient to make men act well in many common instances. On the other hand, our perception of ill desert in vicious actions lessens, in proportion to the temptations men are thought to have had to such vices. For, vice in human creatures consisting chiefly in the absence or want of the virtuous principle; though a man be overcome, suppose by tortures, it does not from thence appear to what degree the virtuous principle was wanting. All that appears is, that he had it not in such a degree, as to prevail over the temptation; but possibly he had it in a degree, which would have rendered him proof against common temptations.

Thirdly, Our perception of vice and ill desert arises from, and is the result of, a comparison of actions with the nature and capacities of the agent. For the mere neglect of doing what we ought to do, would, in many cases, be determined by all men to be in the highest degree vicious. This determination must arise from such comparison, and be the result of it; because such neglect would not be vicious in creatures of other natures and capacities, as brutes. It is the same also with respect to positive vices, or such as consist in doing what we ought not. For every one has a different sense of harm done by an idiot, madman, or child, and by one of mature and common understanding: though the action of both, including the intention, which is part of the action, be the same: as it may be, since idiots and madmen, as well as children, are capable not only of doing mischief but also of intending it. Now this difference must arise from somewhat discerned in the nature or capacities of one, which renders the action vicious; and the want of which, in the other, renders the same action innocent or less vicious: and this plainly supposes a comparison, whether reflected upon or not, between the action and capacities of the agent, previous to our determining an action to be vicious. Hence arises a proper application of the epithets, incongruous, unsuitable, disproportionate, unfit, to actions which our moral faculty determines to be vicious.

Fourthly, It deserves to be considered, whether men are more at liberty, in point of morals, to make themselves miserable without reason, than to make other people so: or dissolutely to neglect their own greater good, for the sake of a present lesser gratification, than they are to neglect the good of others, whom nature has committed to their care. It would seem, that a due concern about our own interest or happiness, and a reasonable endeavor to secure and promote it, (which is, I think, very much the meaning of the word prudence, in our language;) it would seem, that this is virtue, and the contrary behavior faulty and blamable; since, in the calmest way of reflection, we approve of the first, and condemn the other conduct, both in ourselves and others. This approbation and disapprobation are altogether different from mere desire of our own, or of their happiness, and from sorrow upon missing it. For the object or occasion of this last kind of perception is satisfaction or uneasiness: whereas the object of the first is active behavior. In one case, what our thoughts fix upon is our condition: in the other, our conduct.

It is true indeed, that nature has not given us so sensible a disapprobation of imprudence and folly, either in *ourselves* or *others*, as of falsehood, injustice, and cruelty: I suppose, because that constant habitual sense of private interest and good, which we always carry about with us, renders such sensible disapprobation less necessary, less wanting, to keep us from imprudently neglecting our own happiness, and foolishly injuring ourselves, than it is necessary and wanting to keep us from injuring others, to whose good we cannot have so strong and constant a regard: and also because imprudence and folly, appearing to bring its own punishment more immediately and constantly than injurious behavior, it less needs the additional punishment, which would be inflicted upon it by others, had they the same sensible indignation against it, as against injustice, and fraud, and cruelty. Besides, unhappiness being in itself the natural object of compassion, the unhappiness which people bring upon themselves, though it be wilfully, excites in us some pity for them; and this of course lessens our displeasure against them. Still it is matter of experience, that we are formed so as to reflect very severely upon the greater instances of imprudent neglect and foolish rashness, both in ourselves and others. In instances of this kind, men often say of themselves with remorse, and of others with some indignation, that they deserved to suffer such calamities, because they brought them upon themselves, and would not take warning. Particularly when persons come to poverty and distress by a long course of extravagance, and after frequent admonitions, though without falsehood or injustice; we plainly, do not regard such people as alike objects of compassion with those, who are brought into the same condition by unavoidable accidents. From these things it appears, that prudence is a species of virtue, and folly of vice: meaning by *folly*, something quite different from mere incapacity; a thoughtless want of that regard and attention to our own happiness, which we had capacity for. And this the word properly includes; and, as it seems, in its usual acceptation: for we scarcely apply it to brute creatures.

However, if any person be disposed to dispute the matter, I shall very willingly give him up the words virtue and vice, as not applicable to prudence and folly: but must insist, that the faculty within us, which is the judge of actions, approves of prudent actions, and disapproves imprudent ones: I say prudent and imprudent *actions* as such, and considered distinctly from the happiness or misery which they occasion. And by the way, this observation may help to determine what justness there is in the objection against religion, that it teaches us to be interested and selfish.

Fifthly, Without inquiring how far, and in what sense, virtue is resolvable into benevolence, and vice into the want of it; it may be proper to observe, that benevolence, and the want of it, singly considered, are in no sort the *whole* of virtue and vice. For if this were the case, in the review of one's own character, or that of others, our moral understanding and moral sense would be indifferent to every thing, but the degrees in which benevo-

28*

lence prevailed, and the degrees in which it was wanting. That is, we should neither approve of benevolence to some persons rather than to others, nor disapprove injustice and falsehood upon any other account, than merely as an overbalance of happiness was foreseen likely to be produced by the first, and of misery by the second. On the contrary, suppose two men competitors for any thing whatever, which would be of equal advantage to each of them; though nothing indeed would be more impertinent, than for a stranger to busy himself to get one of them preferred to the other; yet such endeavor would be virtue, in behalf of a friend or benefactor, abstracted from all consideration of distant consequences: as that examples of gratitude, and the cultivation of friendship, would be of general good to the world. Again, suppose one man should, by fraud or violence, take from another the fruit of his labor, with intent to give it to a third, who he thought would have as much pleasure from it as would balance the pleasure which the first possessor would have had in the enjoyment, and his vexation in the loss of it; suppose also that no bad consequences would follow: yet such an action would surely be vicious. Nay further, were treachery, violence, and injustice, no otherwise vicious, than as foreseen likely to produce an overbalance of misery to society; then, if in any case a man could procure to himself as great advantage by an act of injustice, as the whole foreseen inconvenience, likely to be brought upon others by it, would amount to; such a piece of injustice would not be faulty or vicious at all: because it would be no more than, in any other case, for a man to prefer his own satisfaction to another's, in equal degrees.

The fact, then, appears to be, that we are *constituted* so as to condemn falsehood, unprovoked violence, injustice, and to approve of benevolence to some preferably to others, abstracted from all consideration, which conduct is likeliest to produce an overbalance of happiness or misery. Therefore, were the Author of nature to propose nothing to himself as an end but the production of happiness, were his moral character merely that of benevolence; yet ours is not so. Upon that supposition indeed, the only reason of his giving us the above mentioned approbation of benevolence to some persons rather than others, and disapprobation of falsehood, unprovoked violence, and injustice, must be, that he foresaw this constitution of our nature would produce more happiness, than forming us with a temper of mere general benevolence. But still, since this is our constitution, falsehood, violence, injustice, must be vice in us; and benevolence to some, preferably to others, virtue; abstracted from all consideration of the overbalance of evil or good, which they may appear likely to produce.

Now if human creatures are endued with such a moral nature as we have been explaining, or with a moral faculty, the natural object of which is actions: moral government must consist in rendering them happy and unhappy, in rewarding and punishing them, as they follow, neglect, or depart from, the moral rule of action interwoven in their nature, or suggested and enforced by this moral faculty;* in rewarding and punishing them upon account of their so doing.

I am not sensible that I have, in this fifth observation, contradicted what any author designed to assert. But some of great and distinguished merit, have, I think, expressed themselves in a manner, which may occasion some danger, to careless readers, of imagining the whole of virtue to consist in singly aiming, according to the best of their judgment, at promoting the happiness of mankind in the present state; and the whole of vice, in doing what they foresee, or might foresee, is likely to produce an overbalance of unhappiness in it: than which mistakes, none can be conceived more terrible. For it is certain, that some of the most shocking instances of injustice, adultery, murder, perjury, and even of persecution, may, in many supposable cases, not have the appearance of being likely to produce an overbalance of misery in the present state; perhaps sometimes may have the contrary appearance.

This reflection might easily be carried on, but I forbear. The happiness of the world is the concern of Him who is the lord and the proprietor of it: nor do we know what we are about, when we endeavor to promote the good of mankind in any ways, but those which he has directed; that is indeed in all ways not contrary to veracity and justice. I speak thus upon supposition of persons really endeavoring, in some sort, to do good without regard to these. But the truth seems to be, that such supposed

* P. 145.

endeavors proceed, almost always, from ambition, the spirit of party, or some indirect principle, concealed perhaps in great measure from persons themselves. And though it is our business and our duty to endeavor, within the bounds of veracity and justice, to contribute to the ease, convenience, and even cheerfulness and diversion of our fellow-creatures: yet, from our short views, it is greatly uncertain, whether this endeavor will, in particular instances, produce an overbalance of happiness upon the whole; since so many and distant things must come into the account. And that which makes it our duty is, that there is some appearance that it will, and no positive appearance sufficient to balance this, on the contrary side; and also, that such benevolent endeavor is a cultivation of that most excellent of all virtuous principles, the active principle of benevolence.

However, though veracity, as well as justice, is to be our rule of life; it must be added, otherwise a snare will be laid in the way of some plain men, that the use of common forms of speech, generally understood, cannot be falsehood; and in general, that there can be no designed falsehood, without designing to deceive. It must likewise be observed, that in numberless cases, a man may be under the strictest obligations to what he foresees will deceive, without his intending it. For it is impossible not to foresee, that the words and actions of men, in different ranks and employments, and of different educations, will perpetually be mistaken by each other. And it cannot but be so, while they will judge with the utmost carelessness, as they daily do, of what they are not, perhaps, enough informed to be competent judges of, even though they considered it with great attention.

INDEX TO PART I.

REFERENCES TO THE EDITOR'S NOTES ARE IN BRACKETS.

PAGE

Abstract reasonings may mislead. 162
  fitness of things....... *note* 166
Actions
  distinguished from their qualities.................. 111
  manifest character......... 156
  rewarded and punished...... 98
  this world a theater of...... 156
  what sort exercise virtue..... 152
Active and passive impressions.. 140
Advantages of virtue.......... 113
  may never recur.......... 161
Affections, excited by objects.... 145
  need control.............. 166
  part of our constitution...... 147
Affliction, a discipline......... 150
  chiefly of our own making.... 160
Agent, the living, not compounded 81
Alienation of parts of our body.. 84
All things made double........ 137
Allurements, use of........... 151
Analogy
  answers objections as to a present state of trial........ 135
  as to modes of existence..... 78
  carrying the force of positive argument............ [105
  deals only with facts....... 171
  indicates future punishment.. 101
  may amount to proof....... 168
  objections which it cannot answer................ 171
  the only proof of some things. 79
Antiquity of religion.......... 167

PAGE

Atheists not argued with, in this treatise............. 181

Beginnings of a righteous government seen on earth..... 107
Bible, teaches the existence of general laws.......... [99
Bodies
  not necessary to us......... 82
  not ourselves............. 83
  only instruments........ 85, 86
  their solid elements........ 88
Bodily and mental habits...... 134
Brain, does not think......... [89
Brahminical notion of death..... 92
Brutes,
  are they immortal?........ [88
  may have greater strength than man................. 119
  under man's control........ 119

Capacities,
  state of in infancy......... 88
  not destroyed by death...... 89
  not dependent on the body... 79
Causes and ends incomprehensible 172
Changes compatible with identity.............. 78, 83
Character
  manifested by probation..... 156
  not given but acquired...... 155
  what it means......... *note* 163
Conscience,
  how it acts............. 164

PAGE
Conscience
implies government........ 115
a rule............ 164
authority.......... 164
future retribution.... 165
may be impaired.......... 168
perverted................ 168
Consciousness an indiscerptible entity.............. 82
presupposes identity........ [77
Consequences
may sometimes be avoided... 102
may be foreseen........... 98
show a moral government.... 98
Course of nature constant...... 97
Creatures finitely perfect....... 147
may fall................ 148
have each a way of life..... 137

Danger of wrong doing, how increased............. 132
Death
and birth similar.......... 91
enlarges our sphere........ 92
has no power over matter.... [91
is not a suspension of our powers............... 91
is not our destruction....... 80
what it is.............. 80
Decay of vegetables, inference from.............. 92
Definitions of identity......... 77
Delivering up of the Lord Jesus Christ.............. [111
Destruction of seeds.......... 153
Different states of human existence. 89
Difficulties belong to all subjects. [96
exercise the virtuous principle. 152
Disadvantages of virtue temporary............... 126
Discipline, its true nature and use................ [148
Disease not destructive to the soul. 90
sometimes remedial........ 177
Disorder produced by sin....... 148
Distress excites passive pity and active relief......... 140

PAGE
Distributive justice a natural rule. 110
Divine government a scheme. CHAP. VII.
Domestic government......... 114
Dreams, what they prove....... 86

Earthly satisfactions attainable.. 183
Effects of actions on the actor... [143
Ends often produced by unlikely means.............. 180
Enjoyments in our own power to a great degree........ 95
Error, how spread............. [96
Evidence of natural religion..... 166
Evil, may possibly be useful.... 177
its possible origin......... 147
not a necessary part of probation.................. [128
Exceptions to the happiness of virtue.............. 108
Experience indispensable...... 141

Faculties, human, not perfect at first................ 141
Fall of man.............. 133, [148
Fallacy in fatalism........... 169
Fallen creatures require discipline. 150
Fatalism,—see *Necessity*.
Fear a proper motive to obedience.............. 154
Folly, destructive, as well as crime.............. 132
Formal notion of government.... 99
Foundation of moral improvement............... [108
Future advantages, how proportioned.............. 93
Future existence probable... CHAP. I.
of brutes...... [79
Future interest dependent on conduct............... 95
Future life,
a solemn subject.......... 95
not an inactive condition.... 144
reconcilable with atheism.... 94
this life preparatory to it. CHAP. V.
Future punishment credible..... 103
Future retribution, how proved. 125

PAGE

Future state
different from the present. . . . 78
brings us into new scenes. . . . 93
may have temptations. . . . . . [145
social. 144
will not require such virtues as does the present life. . 154

General laws
govern the world. . . . . . . 177, [99
produce punishment. 103
wisdom of them. 178
General method of God's government. 97
General system of religion. 124
Gradual improvement, a wise arrangement. 141, 142
GOD
an intelligent governor. 106
determined by what is fit. . . . [166
governs by human instruments. 111
governs justly. . . . . [108
has a will and a character. . . . 163
his aims incomprehensible. . . 97
his attributes inferred from our own. . . . . [115
his general government. 97
his government just and good. 176
his indirect commands. 165
moral government of. . . CHAP. III.
natural " . . . . . " II.
necessarily existent. 159
not indifferent to human actions. 125
not simply benevolent. 106
rewards and punishes. 169
the only necessary being. 159
Good actions, how punished. 111
Good habits necessary even to the virtuous. 149
Good men befriended as such. . . 112
cannot now all unite. 121
Good not forced upon us. . . . . . [134
Government,
civil, an ordinance of God. . . 111
considered as a scheme. CHAP. VII.
of God. . . . . CHAP. II.

PAGE

Government,
not perfected in this world. . . 107
the formal notion of it. 98
the perfection of. 106

Habits,
how formed, &c. 139
necessary to us hereafter. . . . [145
of resignation. 155
often ruinous. 101
of virtue an improvement in virtue. 147
passive. 138
shape the character. 141
Happiness
not always the *immediate* reward of virtue. 108
not given promiscuously. 138
requisites for. 137
the result of virtue. 118
Helplessness of man. . . . . [138
Higher degrees of retribution probable. 127
Hinderances to virtue. 121
History of religion. 169
Honest men befriend the honest. . 112
Hope and fear appeal to self-love. 153
are just principles of action. . 154
Human life preparatory. 144
Hume's wonderful discovery. . . . [162
Human powers may be overtasked. 152

Identity
does not depend on the sameness of the body. 83
of living agents. 77, 78
not explicable. . . . . [77
Ignorance
acknowledged on all subjects but religion. 174
answers objections. 175
the argument from. 180
total, destroys proof. 178
Illustration of the modification of an action by its intention. . . . . [111

PAGE

Imagination a source of discontent. 154
  produces much error. 81
Immortality of brutes. 88
Improvement
  by discipline. 144
  by habit. 147
  of our faculties gradual. 141
  wisdom of this. 142
Incomprehensibility of God's plans 97
Inconsiderateness destructive. . . 102
Inferiority of brute force. 119
Infidelity unjustifiable. 105
Insignificance of our knowledge. . [174
Interest coincident with virtue. . . 154
  not a sufficient restraint. . *note* 146
Interpositions to prevent irregularities. 177
  would produce evil. 178
Intentional good rewarded. 114
Irregularities perhaps unavoidable. 177
  seeming may not be such. . . . 176
Inward peace attends virtue. . . . 112

Kingdom, idea of a perfect. 123
Knowledge of man insignificant. [174

Liberty does not account for the fall. 147
  implied in our present condition 162
Life a probation. 128
  one part of it preparatory to another. . . . . [142
  what is it intended for. 137
Living agent not subject to death. 79
Living powers. . . . . see *Death.*
Locke on human identity. . . . . . . [77

Maimonides, his similitude. . . . . [173
Man
  an inferior part of creation. . . 133
  a system of parts. . . . . [98
  by nature social. . . . . [93
  capable of improvement. 145
  connected with present, past, and future. 181
  dealt with as if free. 162

AGE

Man
  has a moral nature. 115
  his fall not accounted for by his free agency. 147
  his helplessness. . . . . [138
  knows nothing fully. 173
  may become qualified for new states. 137
  not a competent judge of God's schemes. 174
  requires moral culture. 145
Mania often produced by moral causes. . . . . [85
Materialism, its philosophical absurdity. . . . . [81
Matter and mind not the same. . . [83
  affect each other. 85
Means
  learned by experience. 176
  man not a competent judge of the fitness of them. 178
  not always agreeable. 176
Men often miss possible temporal good. 129
Men's temporal interests greatly depend on themselves. . 131
Might of unarmed virtue. . . . . . [121
Mind
  influenced by the passions. . . 131
  is the man. . . . . [87
  its effects on the body. . . . . . . [85
  may survive the body. . . . . . . [89
  the only real percipient. 85
  uses the body as an instrument. . . . . [87
Miracles, properly speaking, not unnatural. 94
Miseries as contingent as conduct. 135
  generally are avoidable. 100
Mixture of suffering and enjoyment in this world. . . . [128
Moral and natural government of God similar to each other. 184
Moral attributes of God may be inferred from our own. . [115
Moral discipline. . . . . CHAP. V.

PAGE

Moral government of God. . CHAP. III.
Moral improvement, basis of. . . . [108
Moral world, its apparent irregularities. 176
Mystery of God, finished. . . . *note* 102

Natural, the true meaning of the word. 94
Natural government of God. CHAP. II.
Natural religion,
  its evidences not affected by the doctrine of necessity. . . 166
  proof of. 166
  teaches the doctrine of punishment. 102
Necessary agents may be punished 169
Necessary bulk of one's self. 84
Necessary existence of God. 159
Necessary tendencies of virtue. . . 118
Negligence and folly disastrous. . 132
Necessity
  consigns us to a fallacy. 169
  contradicts the constitution of nature. 170
  destroys no proof of religion. . 170
  different kinds of. . . . . [157
  does not exclude design. 160
  doctrine of. . . . . CHAP. VI.
  not an agent. 159
  not applicable to practice. . . . 163
  not in conflict with religion. . . 160
  our condition indicates freedom 162
  reconcilable with religion. . . . 168
  the doctrine absurd. 157
  what it means. 158
  writers for and against. . . . . [170
New scenes in the next world. . . 93

Obedience, reluctant, useful. . . . . [152
Objections
  against a proof and against a thing to be proved. 179
  against the scheme of Providence. 174
  analogy of plants. 92
  Christianity not universal. . . . 169
  course of nature. 97

PAGE

Objections,
  destruction of seeds. 153
  difference between temporal and eternal things. . . . . [135
  discipline might have been avoided. 156
  God simply benevolent. 106
  good and evil may be mixed in the next world. 124
  gratification of appetites natural and proper. 98
  ignorance, the argument from invalidates the proof of religion. 178
  immortality of brutes. 87
  incredible that necessary agents should be punished. . . . 169
  irregularities of the moral world 176
  necessity destroys the proof of religion. 165
  our powers may be overtasked 152
  probabilities may be overbalanced by probabilities. 169
  punishments are only natural events. 99
  rectitude arising from hope and fear, sordid. 153
  rewards and punishments. . . . 95
  sin need not have entered the world. 177
  society punishes good actions. 111
  special interpositions might prevent evil. 177, 178
  to the doctrine of necessity. . . . . CHAP. VI.
  to the doctrine of future punishments. 100–103
  virtue sometimes punished. . . 111
  virtues of the present life not wanted hereafter. 154
  world disciplines some to vice. 153
Obligation certain, when proofs are not. 179
Occasional disadvantages of virtue 117
Occasional indulgences in wrongdoing awfully dangerous [143

PAGE

One period of life preparatory to another. . . . . [142
Opportunities once lost irrecoverable. 143
Organs of sense mere instruments 89
Our moral nature proves a moral government. 115

Pain, no contrivance for it in man. [110
Partial ignorance does not destroy proof. 178
Passions
carry away the judgment. . . . 131
make our condition one of trial. 130
may account for the fall of man 147
may be excited where gratification is impossible or unlawful. 146
may remain in a future state. . 147
should be subject to the moral principle. 145
the bare excitement of, not criminal. 145
but dangerous. 146
Passive habits. 138
Passive impressions weakened by repetition. 139
Passive submission essential. . . . 155
Peace of the virtuous. 112
Perception, instruments of. 85
possible without instruments. . 86
Perfection of moral government 106,107
of an earthly kingdom. 123
Persecution unnatural. 111
Philosophy never arrogant. . . . . [174
what it cannot teach. . . . . . . [87
Pleasure
not a sufficient reason for action 98
and pain mostly depend on ourselves. 95
the distribution indicates moral government. 105
Powers
may be improved by exercise. . 138
may be overtasked. 152
may exist and not be exercised. 80

PAGE

Powers
no reason for supposing that death will destroy them. 81
Practical proof, what. 168
Present existence unaccounted for by atheism. 94
Presumptions that death will destroy us. 81
that it will suspend our existence. 91
Presumptuousness unjustifiable. . 105
Private vices not public benefits. [111
Probabilities in favor of religion may be overbalanced by probabilities against it. . 169
Probation. . . . . CHAP. IV.
applies to the present life as well as the future. 130
does not necessarily imply suffering. . . . . [128
implies allurements. 129
is more than moral government. 128
requires severe discipline. . . . 150
Proofs of natural religion. 166
of religion not affected by the doctrine of necessity. . . . 160
Propensions necessarily create temptations. 146
are excited by their appropriate objects. 147
Proper gratification of the appetites. 98
Prosperity of a virtuous community. 123
may beget discontent. 154
Providence, objections to God's 140, 174
Public spirit a fruit of virtue. . . . 120
Punishment
an alarming subject. 105
especially considered. 100
greater hereafter than now. . . 127
in a future state credible. 103, 125
is God's voice of instruction. . [108
is sometimes capital. 102
not unjust. 163
often long delayed. 101

PAGE

Punishment
often overtakes suddenly.... 101
of virtuous actions........ 111
religious and natural similar.. 100
results from folly as well as crime.............. 132
the result of general laws.... 103

Quotations.
Aristotle................ [152
Chalmers........ [131, 138, 148
Cicero............... [82, 86
Clarke.................. [97
Fitzgerald............... [145
Robert Hall............. [118
Hume.................. [162
Maimonides............. [173
Mandeville.............. [111
Plato................ [87, 113
Son of Sirac............ [137
Strabo.................. [92

Rashness, consequences of. 96
Reason
an incompetent judge of means 178
gives power over brute force.. 119
needs experience.......... 141
not dependent on bodily powers 89
requires a fair opportunity 119–121
Recapitulation of the whole argument. 180
Rectitude, is self-interest a proper motive to it? 153
References to other authors.
Bates.................. [128
Baxter.................. [88
Bayle................... [88
Beattie................. [170
Belsham................ [170
Berkeley................ [111
Bonnett................. [89
Bramhall................ [171
Brown.................. [111
Bryant................. [171
Butterworth............. [107
Calcott................. [128
Capp................... [109

PAGE

References to other authors.
Chalmers.......... [77, 79, 148
Charnock............... [158
Cheyne................. [88
Clarke......... 82, [81, 97, 171
Colliber................. [88
Collings............. [158, 170
Compte................. [170
Crombie................ [170
Crouse................. [170
Davies................. [109
D'Holbach.............. [170
Descartes............... [88
Ditton.................. [88
Doddridge.............. [109
Dodwell................. [81
Dwight................. [109
Edwards............. [88, 170
Fabricius............... [128
Fichtè................. [170
Gibbs.................. [171
Grove.................. [171
Haller.................. [89
Harris.................. [171
Hartley................ [170
Hègel.................. [170
Henly.................. [128
Hobbes................ [170
Holtzfusius............. [128
Holyoake............... [170
Horseley............... [109
Hume................... [88
Hunt.................. [109
Jackson................ [171
Kennicott.............. [128
King.............. [98, 171
Law.................... [98
Lawson................ [171
Le Clerc............... [128
Leland................ [109
Leroux................ [170
Liefchild.............. [109
Locke.................. [88
Manton................ [128
Martineau.............. [170
Martinius.............. [119
Milman................ [142

PAGE

References to other authors.
Morgagni. . . . . [89
Morton. . . . . [109
Musæus. . . . . [128
Palmer. . . . . [171
Pearson. . . . . [128
Polignac. . . . . [88
Porteus. . . . . [109
Price. . . . . [158
Priestley. . . . . [142, 170
Reid. . . . . [170
Rutherford. . . . . [109, 158
Search. . . . . [88
Seed. . . . . [109
Selden. . . . . [128
Shaftesbury. 108
Sherlock. . . . . [109
Shuckford. . . . . [128
Son of Sirac. . . . . [137
South. . . . . [109, 128
Stapfer. . . . . [128
Strabo. 92
Toplady. . . . . [128
Topping. . . . . [109
Twisse. . . . . [109
Wagstaff. . . . . [88
Warburton. . . . . [111
Watts. . . . . [77, 88, 171
Whately. . . . . [142, 158
Willis. . . . . [88
Wisheart. . . . . [109
Witsius. . . . . [128
Wittichius. . . . . [109
Reflection not dependent on sensation. 91
Reformation is attended with discomfort. 108
may not prevent penalties. . . . 102
Relation between us and our bodies 85
Relations of things, limitless. . . . 173
Religion
a question of fact. 165
historical evidence of. 168
professed in all ages. 167
its proofs not affected by the doctrine of necessity. . . 170
nor by our ignorance. 178

PAGE

Reluctant obedience profitable. . [152
Remedies often very disagreeable 176
Repentance may be too late. 104
Requisites to the superiority of reason. 119
of virtue. 120, 121
Resentment of injuries. 114
Resignation
a temper consonant with God's sovereignty. 155
essential to virtue. 154
the fruit of affliction. 155
the habit necessary hereafter. . 155
Retributions are divine teachings [108
Revelation,
antiquity of. 167
not improbable. 167
not universal. . . . . *note* 107
Rewards and punishments, how distributed. 126

Satisfactions of virtue. 108
Scheme of God incomprehensible. 172
Self-denial, its relations to present happiness. 134
not essential to piety. 152
Self-discipline, what. . . . . [148
Self-love
a just principle of action. . . . 154
appealed to. 153
how moderated and disciplined 155
not a sufficient restraint. . *note* 146
reasonable and safe. 130
Sensation not necessary to reflection. 91
Senses not percipients. 85
Severe discipline necessary. 150
Similitude of a historical painting [174
Simplicity of the living agent. . . 83
Sin, why not kept out of the world 177
Skepticism does not justify irreligion. 105
Social, our nature essentially such [93
Society
must punish vice. 110
natural and necessary. . . . . . [93
sometimes punishes the good 111

PAGE

Soul
a simple substance.......... 82
not destroyed with the body.. 79
not naturally immortal...... [81
Souls of brutes.............. 88
Special interpositions of Providence........... 177, 178
Stages of existence........... 78
State of probation........ CHAP. IV.
State of discipline and improvement........... CHAP. V.
Submissive temper necessary.... 155
Subordinations exceedingly beneficial............... 142
Subserviencies in nature....... 173
Sufferings may be avoided...... 95
not necessary to the cultivation of virtue........ [128

Temporal and religious probation similar............. 132
Temptations
increased by bad examples... 132
and by former errors...... 132
intended for our improvement. 136
involve probation.......... 129
may improve or injure us.... 153
security against their evils... 146
sources of, to upright beings.. 147
the necessary result of propensions............... 146
Tendencies of virtue.......... 118
hindered................ 121
essential, not accidental..... 126
Terms "nature" and "course of nature"............. [97
Theorizing no aid to virtue..... 139
Thoughtlessness often fatal..... 101
Transmigration of souls....... [87
Trials
manifest character......... 156
may exist in a future state... 147
produced by our propensions. 131
qualify for a better state..... 144
unreasonable ones are not inflicted............. 133
why we are subjected to them. 136

PAGE

Ultimate design of man........ [98
Understanding may be perverted. 168
Uneasiness produced by former sins............... 109
Union of good beings.......... 122
Unjustifiableness of religious indifference........... 105
Upright creatures may fall...... 147
need good habits.......... 149
Universe and its government immense.............. 123

Vice
actually punished by society 110,111
must produce uneasiness..... 112
never rewarded as such..... 116
not only criminal but depraving 149
often increased by trials..... 153
punished as such.......... 114
Vicious men lose their influence. [121
Virtue
a bond of union........... 122
as such, rewarded on earth... 111
"brings its own reward".... [118
has occasional disadvantages. [117
hinderances accidental...... 121
how and why rewarded..... 111
improved by trials......... 151
its benefits to a community... 123
natural, not vice.......... 116
not always rewarded in this life 108
on the whole happier than vice 113
secures peace............. 112
tendencies essential........ 126
tends to give power.... 118, [121
Virtuous beings need virtuous habits.............. 149
Virtuous habits a security...... 147
how formed.............. 139
improve virtue............ 147
necessary in a future state... [145
Voice of nature is for virtue..... 117

Waste of seeds.............. 153
Wickedness may produce some benefits............. 177
voluntary................ 136

PAGE

Will and character
  of God, how determined. . *note* 166
  what they mean. . . . . . . *note* 163
Wonderful discovery of Hume. . [162
World
  a system of subordinations. . . 173
  a theater for the manifestation
    of character. 156

PAGE

World, (*continued.*)
  disciplines some to vice. 153
  fitted for man's discipline. . . . 150
  governed by fixed laws. 110

Youth
  a determining period. 101
  if lost, not to be recovered. . . 143
  its beneficial subordinations. . 141

INDEX TO PART II.

REFERENCES TO THE EDITOR'S NOTES ARE IN BRACKETS

PAGE

A common absurdity. 243
Abstract truth distinguished from facts. . . . . 305, [186
Absurdity of some objections to Christianity. 245
Abuse of our natural endowments 217
Accidental, what events are so called. 226
Accountability gradually increases 251
Actions,
  definition of, in morals. 261
  distinguished from things done 261
  their bad consequences sometimes escaped. 232
  virtue and vice consist in them 261
Advantage, as proper a consideration in religion as in temporal affairs. 298
  variously bestowed. 249, 312
Analogy
  a confirmation of all facts to which it can be applied. . 306
  affords no argument against the scheme of Christianity. . 203
    nor against miracles. . . 203
  answers presumptions against miracles. 207
  does not prove the wisdom of God. 301
  does not teach that the *whole* of God's government is like that on earth. 204
  easily cavilled at, but unanswerable. 306

PAGE

Analogy, (*continued.*)
  between natural information and that derived from inspiration. 212
  between the remedies of nature and those of grace. 219
  between the gospel and human discoveries. 219
  between the light of nature and of revelation. 218
  between the use of natural gifts, and miraculous. . . 217
  between the government of God and that of a human master. 261
  its small influence on men. . . 303
  how used in this treatise. . . . 306
  may show our duty, but not the design of the requirement 246
  objections to this mode of arguing. . . . . CHAP. VIII.
  shows that there may be infinite reasons for things, with which we are not acquainted. 188
  the only ground for some of our knowledge. 306
Antidote to heresies. . . . . [191
Apocalypse, its principal object. . [249
Appearances of men and things deceptive. 248
Arguments proper as to human writings, are not so as to Scripture. 214

PAGE

Atonement,
how held by the ancients.... 241
makes the innocent suffer for the guilty........... 243
Author of nature taken for granted 298
Authoritativeness of revelation.. 189

Baptism
a test of obedience........ [199
commanded and important... 194
why the form of words...... 194
Bible, how to be interpreted. [202, 215
Brutes, their great sagacity..... 216
Boundary of human inquiry.... [223

Candor necessary in judging of Christianity.......... 302
Chance, really no such thing... 226
Characters drawn in Scripture evidently unfeigned ... 287
Christ
a mediator........... CHAP. V.
a prophet............... 240
a priest and king.......... 241
his history, as given in Scripture............... 285
his pre-existence taught..... 282
his satisfaction 239
his sufferings voluntary..... 243
manner of his interposition... 238
not merely a teacher and example.............. 242
offered himself a propitiatory sacrifice............. 241
Christianity
a fearful curse, if it give no more light than natural religion............ [196
a question of fact.......... 301
a remedial system......... [193
an authoritative republication of the religion of nature............ 188, 189
a particular scheme under a general plan...... 194, 224
a scheme imperfectly comprehended......... CHAP. IV.

PAGE

Christianity, (*continued.*)
a scheme revealed but in part. 226
brings life and immortality to light............... 190
could not possibly be a contrivance.......... [222, 294
demands attention, if barely probable............ 253
has evidences besides miracles and prophecy........ 263
in what degree remedial.... [193
is a real revelation......... 213
is conformable to the constitution of things........ 295
its benefits require the use of means.............. 197
its establishment and prevalence, the most conspicuous and important event in history........... 286
its evidences......... CHAP. VII.
its good effects not small.... 192
its precepts plain and obvious. 218
its proof historical 304
its proofs liable to objection.. 260
men bound to examine its evidence.............. 197
miracles and prophecy its direct and fundamental proofs. 263
must have mysteries....... [223
no objection to the morality of it........... 214, 220, 222
not merely a republication of natural religion....... [196
not primarily designed to remedy the defects of nature............... [193
not the discovery of reason... 188
objections to its evidence.... 210
objections to its nature 210
offered to some in a corrupt state............... 250
prescribes new duties....... 194
preserves natural religion in the world........... 191
propagated against all obstructions.............. [294

PAGE

Christianity, (*continued*.)
rashness of treating it lightly. 194, 196, 197
requires means to accomplish ends. 225
reveals a particular dispensation of Providence. 194
reveals important facts. 196
some of its dark parts may be cleared up, others cannot. . . . . [223
teaches more than natural religion. 194
the evils ascribed to it, are not its evils. 192
the one great question concerning it. 213, 214
the only religion professedly confirmed by miracles. . 268
to be transmitted by Christians. . . . . [190
universal, in nature and intention. . . . . [248
what alone could disprove it. . 295
why not remedial to a greater degree. 193
why not sooner promulgated. . 219
Christians
bound to spread Christianity. 190
primitive, their testimony. . . . 267
Church
men bound to support it. 193
preserves a knowledge of religion. 191
visible, its design. 190, 191
Circumstantial evidences of Christianity. 263, 281
often as convincing as direct testimony. 294
Clemens Romanus, testimony of. 266
his letter to the Corinthians. . [266
Climax of infidel extravagance. . [294
Coincidence of natural and revealed religion. . . . 211, 218
Coincidences of Scripture. 266
Comparison, how it may mislead us. 201

PAGE

Compassion distinct from goodness 233
visible in the constitution of the world. 233
Consequences of infidelity; more dangerous than those of faith. 294
of sin, often averted. 233
Conversational objections to revelation. 295
Conversion, how produced. . . . . . [225
Course of nature
different from what we might have supposed, previous to experience. 211
none at the beginning. 205
our total darkness as to its causes. 208
Creation
Mosaic account of, referred to by John. 282
a different exertion of power from government. 205
why Scripture describes it. . . 281
Creatures of like moral qualities placed in different religious situations. 251
Credulity of mankind acknowledged. 269
Cumulative proof of Christianity. [207

Daniel
his book had more evidence of authenticity than has come to us. 279
his predictions a support of Jewish faith. . . . . [249
quoted by Christ. 279
Dark parts of revelation. . . . . . . [223
Degrees of evidence have degrees of weight. 255
require nice examination. . . . 258
Deistical explanation of Christ's miracles. . . . . [206
Deists, why do they oppose Christianity. . . . . [196
Depravity of man obvious. 238
doctrine of. . . . . [218

PAGE

Desert of good and ill, the notion of. 305
Development, of truth. 218
modern, doctrine of. . . . . [218
Differences of religious advantages may have like reasons as those for different temporal advantages. 251
would remain if revelation were universal. 252
Difficulties
absurdity of requiring them to be all removed. 297
as to the evidence of religion, analogous to those attending the practice of it 256
cannot be solved by analogy. . 296
speculative, may be the chief trials of some. 257
the discernment which can see them, might suffice to see through them. 260
Direct and circumstantial evidence must be taken together. 280
Diseases of body and mind, analogous as to their remedies. 220
Disobedience, without possible excuse. 253
Dispensations, preparatory one to another. 310
Disregard of religion a great profligacy. 233
Distinction between moral and positive obligation. 198, [198
between acts and principles. . [235
between temporary, individual, and universal commands [188
Doubt
affords scope for probation. . . 262
exercises our virtuous principles. 256
implies some evidence. 252, 254, 283
involves some obligation. 263
puts us upon probation. 253
Doubtful evidence should have *some* influence. 255

PAGE

Duties arising from revealed relations. 195
moral and positive. 194

Earth, its appearances confirm Scripture. 238
Effect of Adam's transgression. . . 238
of combined probabilities. 294, [294
Efficacy of repentance. . . . . [190
not taught by the light of nature. 190
End, God's not known. 246
Enthusiasm
is not peculiar to religion. . . . 272
impairs no testimony for Christianity. 271
may often weaken testimony. . 271
sometimes mixed with knavery 272
the absence of all sign of it in Christianity, a presumptive proof in its favor. . . 222
will not account for the spread of Christianity. 270
Enthusiasts make as great sacrifices as Christians. . . . 270
Epistles of Paul, proof from. 266
Eternal retribution not taught by natural religion. . . . . . . [190
Ethics of natural religion distinguished from its objects [194
Events expound Scripture. 219
Evidence
of Christianity impregnable. . 295
collateral and direct to be viewed together. 294
from miracles and prophecy. . 267
imperfect, should yet influence practice in proportion to its degree. 255
of circumstances may be most direct. 294
of religion, open to all. 260
of religion, the same in kind as that which controls us in temporal things. 258
much lower than satisfactory often determines us. . . . 303

PAGE

Evidence, (*continued.*)
not only increased but multiplied by a combination of probabilities. . . . 294, [294
reason the proper judge of. . . 221
requires careful sifting. 256
candor in judging. . . 302, [303
safety always in admitting it. 294
why liable to objection. 257
Evil, remedies provided for it. 219, 232
Exaggeration practised by many who will not lie. 272
External manner of heart worship 195
Experience
affords no presumption against Christianity. 203
corroborates Christian doctrines. 245
teaches the effects of actions. . 246
Extravagance of some objections. 187, 188

Facts
analogy the only proof of some. 306
distinguished from abstract truths. 305
of revelation distinguished from its principles. . . . . [235
Fall of man, assumed as a fact. . . 236
confirmed by appearances. . . . 236
Falsehood, its degrees and inducements. 272
False miracles have deceived many 273
have some historic evidence. . 273
Fatalists, their principles argued upon. 304
Fear cast out by love. . . . . [301
Fitness, moral. 304, 305
Flippant objections to Christianity 295
Folly, a real vice. 280
Foresight of brutes. 216
Future punishments,
all the reasons for them not known. 234
not arbitrarily appointed. . . . 232
natural sequences. 231, 232

PAGE

Future punishments,
rendered credible by temporal punishments. 300

Genealogy of mankind given in Scripture. 283
General laws
a wise arrangement. 227
do not render miracles incredible. 227
control the Christian dispensation. 226
few events can be traced up to them. 226
miracles may be their results. 226, 227
the ground of believing there are such. 226
things called accidental governed by them. 226
Geology, its impressive lessons. . [229
GOD
a master giving laws. 261
all his reasons for giving a command must be certainly known, and known to have passed away, before we can safely disregard it. 188
duties towards him as the Father. 194, 195
governs by mediation. 230
his government shows compassion. 233
progressive. 229
his means and ends we cannot distinguish. 228
his providence, objections to it idle. 300, 301
his reasons not assigned. 246
his will, as absolute or conditional. 261
how he would act in contingencies, unknown. . . . . [222
how to be worshipped, a pure matter of revelation. . . . 195
instructs us by experience. 211, 246

PAGE

GOD, (*continued.*)
little known. . . . . [222
not indifferent as to who suffer. 243
reveals our duties, not his plans. 246
the real author of the prophecies. 276
Good and evil unequally distributed. 248
Government of God sometimes, apparently, tardy in its results. 224, 225
Gradual growth of causes. . . . . [208

Happiness not always secured by well-laid schemes. 247
Hazard of neglecting Christianity. 262
Heathen world, condition of. 186, 250
Hieroglyphic and figurative language of Scripture. 210
Hinderances to natural and spiritual knowledge similar. . 218
History
of miracles. 264
of the Jews confirmed by their condition. 289, 290
of the origin of religion. 206
furnishes no parallel to revelation. 207
prophecy is history anticipated 281
Scripture, has not been invalidated. 283
Holy Spirit, its operations on the heart. . . . . [225
Human contrivance unequal to some things. . . . . [222
Human life, in what sense it may be called poor. 297
Human testimony, reliable notwithstanding the prevalence of falsehood. 273

Identity of principle between natural and revealed religion. . . . . [235
Ignorance
of heathen writers. . . . . [187

PAGE

Ignorance
of other worlds, forbids objections to Christianity on the ground of miracles. 207
of the laws of miracles, not greater than of natural laws. 256
of the reason of our present condition. 251
much of it our own fault. . . . 259
Imagination may fancy unreal coincidences. 293
Immorality not authorized in Scripture. 221, 222
Impassable limit to human knowledge. . . . . [223
Imperceptible accumulation of forces. . . . . [208
Imperfect knowledge, better than acting in the dark. 297
Imperfection of language. 216
Importance of revelation. . . CHAP. I.
an abstraction. . . . . [186
precludes the idea that the first witnesses were careless. . 274
Improbability before and after an event. . . . . [207
of the Deistical theory greater than that of miracles. . . [206
Inadequacy of repentance. . . . . . [236
Inattention to religion, real depravity. 252, 307
prevents convincement. 258
Incarnation an invisible miracle. 204
cannot be paralleled. . . . . . . [235
Influence of the Holy Ghost. . . . [225
of the analogical argument. . 303
Innocent sometimes suffer for the guilty. 243
Inspiration, the proper kind and extent of it not discoverable by reason. 212
not to be interpreted like other writings. 211
Inspired writers, key to their meaning. . . . . [276
their one great scheme. . . . [276

PAGE

Inspired writers, (*continued.*)
show a foresight more than human. 278, 279
Instruction from God to savages. [206
Intercession by the good for the bad. . . . . [232
Interest, temporal, not always apparent. 302
Interpositions of men for each other. . . . . [232
Internal improbabilities weaken external proof. 215
Interpretation of Scripture. . . . . [215
Irregularity, really no such thing. 226
whence the appearance of. . . . 227
Irregularities of men, consequences proportioned to magnitude. 233
Irreligion an aggravated sin. . . . 233
especially in persons in high standing. 254
not justifiable on any pretence. 256, 312
Invention an irregular way of information. 216
Invisible miracles. . . . . [204
things of God, how learned. . [230

Jews
God's dealing with them 290
their continuance, a standing miracle. 290
their history confirmed by facts 291
their system of Theism. . . . . [206
Jewish miracles, a part of civil history. . . . . [265
John, his allusion to Christ, in the beginning of his gospel. 282
his doctrine agrees with that of Paul. 282

Kingdom of Christ on earth. 241
Knowledge
profound, not necessary to piety. 218
scientific and religious, have the same difficulties. . . . 218

PAGE

Knowledge of Scripture, improved in the same way as knowledge of the sciences. . . 218
unequally distributed. 249

Language necessarily ambiguous. 216
of the prophecies, often figurative. 210
Laplace, error of. . . . . [207
Levity destructive to religious influence. 259
Liberty
belief of our, unavoidable. . . . 304
of the will, not discussed. *note* 304
necessary to the progress of knowledge. 218
the principle so natural that language is formed on it. 304
Life
future, brought to light by the gospel. 190
may be taken away by command. 221
not thrown away because success is uncertain. 302
whether desirable or not. 301
Light of nature
displayed in the Scriptures. . . 188
does not teach our future condition. 190
favors the doctrine of a Mediator. 230
has left the greatest heathen in doubt. 186
Ludicrous turn, danger of. 259

Mahometanism not received on the footing of miracles. [268
Mahometans and ancient Persians, how situated as to revelation. 250
Man
accepted according to what he hath. 251
his circumstances no ground of complaint. 252

PAGE

Man, (*continued.*)
his obligation to study the Scriptures. 202, 262
must be renewed. 197
Manasses, prayer of. . . . . [237
Manner of worship a matter of pure revelation. 195
Martyrs
could not have been impostors 272
had full knowledge of facts 269, 271
the full force of their testimony 269
their obligations to veracity. . 274
were not enthusiasts. 271
Means as related to ends. 225
Mediation seen everywhere. 230
exemplified in social life. . . . [232
Mediator,
appointment of. . . . . CHAP. V.
the notion of, natural. 230
the Scripture doctrine of. 238–240
whether one was necessary. . . 243
why most objected to. 243
Medium between full satisfaction of a truth and full satisfaction to the contrary. . 313
Memory, eloquence, &c. imprudently used. 217
Men apt to be deluded by pretences. 273
their conduct may be guessed at. . . . . [222
Mercy seen in the constitution of the world. 233
Messiah came at the expected time 285
his mission. 224
Minuteness of predictions touching Christ. 207
Miracles
admitted evidence for such as are false does not impair the evidence of Christian. 273
contrary to the course of nature? 206
denying them leads to Atheism. . . . . [205
disorderly use of. 217

PAGE

Miracles, (*continued.*)
distinct reasons for them. . . . 208
large historical evidence for their truth. 270
manner in which related 264
no argument of analogy against them. 205–207
none parallel to those of Scripture. 207
not mere embellishments. . . . 264
not to be compared to common events. 209
nowise incredible. 209
occasions for them likely to arise in the course of ages. 208
of the Old Testament, inseparable from history. . . . . [265
operate by general laws. 226
Pagan and Popish, were wrought *after* those systems had obtained. 268
peculiar to the Jewish and Christian religions. 268
received as genuine from the first. 268, 269
regulated by general laws. . . . 227
satisfactorily account for the existence of Christianity 265
should be compared to uncommon events. 209
the credentials of Christianity 267
the evidence of their truth at first 249
the question of their truth only one of *degree* in point of evidence. 208
the only satisfactory account of some events. 265
the real nature of presumptions against them. 208
the term a relative one. 205
their direct proof of Christianity. 264
their evidence the same as that for common facts. 264
their force as proofs. 189

PAGE

Miracles, (*continued.*)
visible and invisible. . . . 204, [204
what evidence arises from their having been accepted as true by the first Christians. 268
writers upon. . . . . [264, 268
Miraculous power
creation not properly an act of 205
misused by some. 217, 267
pretences of, have deluded some. 273
why bestowed. 190
Misconduct creates need of assistance. 235
Mistake of some of Hume's opponents. 207
Mistakes of philosophers dangerous. . . . . [230
of transcribers, &c. 228
Modern geology, lesson from. . . . [229
Moral action, the nature of. 261
an action becomes such by command. . . . . [221
Moral duties. See *Positive.*
Moral faculty, its object. 305
Moral government. See *Government.*
Moral precepts. See *Positive.*
Moral system revealed to mankind. 190
Morality of Scripture, reason a judge of. 220
Mysteries to be expected in revelation. 223, 224
as many in nature as in Scripture. 246
Mystery of godliness. 225
Mythological writings resemble prophecy. 276

Narratives of Scripture unadorned 228
Natural consequences of vice are judicial punishments. . . 197
and spiritual things analogous in importance. 219
endowments often abused. . . . 217

PAGE

Natural light compared to revelation. 218
Natural religion
and revealed, coincide. 211
as much perverted as Christianity. 192
could not have been reasoned out. 192
discloses no Redeemer. . . . . . [194
its ethics and objects distinguished. . . . . [194
its light wholly insufficient. . . 187
might be authenticated by miracles. 190
moral system of. 187
taught and confirmed by Christianity. 188, 286, 292
what it does not teach. . . [190, 194
Nature carried on by uniform laws. 226
implies the agency of God. . . 231
its light insufficient. 186
Nature and obligation of sacraments. . . . . *note* 195
Necessity of revelation. . . . . [186
Negligence prevents the recognition of truth. 258
wholly inexcusable. 197

Obedience from dread. . . . . [301
or disobedience, an important matter. 188
to a positive rite, especially indicative of piety. 199
Objections
to certain precepts of Scripture, as immoral. 221
to prophecy, from its obscurity 275
to revelation, are of equal weight against natural religion. 97
to the analogical argument, as such. . . . . CHAP. VIII.
to the distribution of good and evil. 248–250
to the doctrine of mediation. . . . . CHAP. V.

PAGE

Objections, (*continued.*)
to the evidence for miracles. . . . . CHAP. II.
to the unequal distribution of religious knowledge. . . . 249

Objections to Christianity
as a matter of fact. 301
as a remedial system. . . . [193, 219
as a roundabout, perplexed contrivance. 228
as deficient in point of truth. . 247
as a scheme. 209
as mysterious. . . . . [223
as to its wisdom and goodness . . . . CHAP. IV.
as unimportant. . . . . CHAP. I.
atonement makes the innocent suffer for the guilty. 227, 243
contains things unlike the course of nature. 204
does not remove difficulties . . [223
has been perverted. 192
has been productive of evils. . 192
has internal improbabilities 225–227
disclosed to the world so recently. 219
disorderly use of miraculous gifts. 227
has small influence. 192, 303
if true would not be left doubtful. 299
is not satisfactory. 260, 261
its doctrine of mediation. CHAP. V.
its external proof weakened by internal improbabilities. 215
its lack of evidence. . . . CHAP. VI.
its late introduction. 219
may be advanced flippantly, but cannot be so answered. 295
natural things too unimportant to furnish analogies in its favor. 219
not just and good. . . . . . CHAP. IV.
not necessary. 147
not universal. . . . . . CHAP. VI. 248

PAGE

Objections to Christianity, (*continued.*)
slowly developed. 219
some of its precepts immoral. . 221
sufficiency of natural religion. 187
vicarious sufferings. 245

Obligation arises from the bare supposableness of Christianity. 253, 262

Obligations to God arising out of relationship. 196

Obscurity in part of a prophecy, does not impair the evidence of foresight. 275

Offenders often shielded by friends [232

Offices of Christ as a mediator 238–240

Opinions must be distinguished from facts. 270

Ordinary rules of interpretation. . [215

Pagan and Popish miracles easily accounted for. 268

Parables show what the author intended. 276

Partial views give an appearance of wrong. 309

Passion hinders correct judgment 259

Paul, his separate testimony. . . . 266
how he received the gospel. . . 267
summary of his testimony. . . 267

Perfection of religion, what? CHAP. VIII.

Persons for whom this treatise is written. 309

Philosophy, its true mode of proceeding. . . . . [230

Piety superior to ritual observances. 201

Pleasures and pains, which overbalance?. 301

Political events, how mentioned in Scripture. 282

Popish doctrine of a miracle at the Eucharist. . . . . . . [204

Popular conversational objections 295

Porphyry's mode of interpretation frivolous. . . . . *note* 279
objections to the book of Daniel 279

PAGE

Positive evidence of Christianity.........CHAP. VII.

Positive institutions
- belong to the notion of a church............. 192
- lay us under the strictest obligation.............. 202
- means to moral ends....... 199
- men disposed to depend on them............... 200
- necessary to keep up and propagate religion....... 246
- not to be made light of...... 201
- not to supersede moral obedience.............. 200
- the reason of them often obvious............... 198
- two modes of viewing them... 198

Positive precepts compared with moral...........198, 201
- create moral obligations..... 221

Power of healing............[217

Practice should be influenced by probability.......... 254

Predictions of Christ very numerous and minute... 207, 208

Prejudice a hinderance to knowledge.............. 258
- a mark of weakness........ 280
- as hostile to truth as enthusiasm.............. 272
- operates contrary ways...... 294

Preservation of the Jews as a distinct race............ 291

Presumptions
- against miracles........... 205
- against revelation as miraculous............CHAP. II.
- none against the *general scheme* of Christianity.. 203
- none peculiar to miracles.... 207
- strong, overcome by weak proof...........207, [207

Priesthood of Christ.......... 238
- Jewish, typical of Christ..... 239

Principles argued upon in this treatise............. 304

PAGE

Progressions in our existence.... 229

Progress in theology probable...[218

Probable proofs, by being added, not only increase evidence, but multiply it... 294

Probability should influence practice................ 254

Profane history corroborates Scripture statements... 287

Proofs of Christianity
- a touchstone of honesty.....[259
- level to common men....... 260
- some important ones omitted in this treatise, and why. 304
- why not more plain........ 261

Prophecy
- a joint review of prophecies furnishes a far stronger proof than examination in detail............ 294
- a series of, being applicable to certain events, is proof that it was intended of them............... 276
- compared to compiled memoirs.............. 278
- created the expectation of a Messiah............. 284
- confirmed by appearances.... 292
- evidence from............ 275
- expressed in figurative language.............. 275
- how understood by ancient Jews.............. 277
- in relation to the Jews...... 284
- is history anticipated....... 281
- its obscurity............. 275
- its proofs amazingly strong..[207
- may not *always* have been understood by the writer.. 278
- proves foresight........ 276, 279
- sometimes obscured by interpreters............. 210
- summary of, concerning Christ 284
- use of, to future ages....... 249
- writers upon.......... 277, 285

Prophet, Christ a............ 240

PAGE

Prophets
- not the *authors* of what they wrote. 278
- their sense of their predictions not necessarily the whole sense. 278
- whether they had in view the events which Christians consider fulfilments. . . . 277

Proverbial, use of the word. 201

Providence, never hasty. . . . . . . [229
- objections to it useless. . . 300, 301
- the course of, progressive. . . . 229

Province of reason. 220

Prudence, its best plans often frustrated. 247
- often requires us to act with uncertain prospect of success. 247, 248

Punishment
- follows wickedness, *of course*. . 231
- instances of vicarious. 244
- not always avoided by reformation. 235
- not promiscuously inflicted. . . 243
- provision made for escaping it. 232, 311
- we cannot of ourselves escape it. 234
- we cannot know why such and such are inflicted. 231

Quotations.
- Angus. . . . . [202, 223
- Augustine. . . . . *note* 187
- Arnobius. . . . . [269
- Clemens Romanus. . . . . [266
- Davidson. . . . . [294
- Fitzgerald. . . . . [303
- Grotius. . . . . [259
- Guizot. . . . . [229
- Hurd. . . . . [276
- Dr. Johnson. . . . . [288
- Mahomet. . . . . [268
- Powell. . . . . [230
- Warburton. . . . . [217, 223
- Whately. . . . . [206

PAGE

Rashness of interpreters. 210
- of treating religion lightly. . . 197

Reason
- could not have invented Christianity. 206
- could not ascertain the power of penitence. 194
- discovers our relation to God the Father. 194
- but not our relation to the Son and Holy Ghost. . . 194, 196
- its limits very narrow. . . . . . [223
- its proper province. 220
- must have right principles. . . 220
- needs the aid of experience in judging of the consequences of actions. 246
- not sufficient to construct a system of natural religion free from superstition. 186
- our only faculty for judging even revelation. 210
- requires the importance of a question to be taken into account. 295
- teaches nothing of the certain means of either temporal or spiritual good. 197
- very incompetent to judge what a revelation ought to be. 210–212

Reasoning by analogy to any extent, leaves the mind unsatisfied. 296

Redemption
- agreeable to our natural notions. 235
- analogous to natural remedies. 232
- conjectures about it must be uncertain. 242
- mode of, not discoverable by reason. 243
- men not competent judges of its plan. 245
- on whom are its benefits. . *note* 237
- Scripture account of 239, 240

PAGE

Redemption, (*continued.*)
we should be thankful for it, without disputing how it was procured. 242

References to other authors.
Alexander. . . . . [269
Apthorpe. . . . . [285
Bayle. . . . . [301
Benson. . . . . [215
Birk. . . . . [266
Blaney. . . . . [285
Blunt. . . . . [266
Bolingbroke. . . . . [265
Boswell. . . . . [288
Boyle. . . . . [264
Butler. . . . . [190, 272
Campbell. . . . . [264
Celsus. . . . . [287
Chalmers. . . . . [187, 194, 242
Colliber. 195
Damascenus. . . . . [287
Davidson. . . . . [285
Diodorus Siculus. . . . . [287
Eupolemus. . . . . [287
Featley. . . . . [215
Fitzgerald. . . . . [193, 206, 207
Fleetwood. . . . . [264
Fuller. . . . . [285
Gibbon. . . . . [268
Graves . . . . [266
Grotius. . . . . [266
Gulick. . . . . [277
Hengstenburg. . . . . [277
Horseley. . . . . [277
Howe. . . . . [236
Hurd. . . . . [285
Jortin. . . . . [264, 285
Julian. . . . . [257
King. . . . . [215, 277
Lardner. . . . . [264
Leland. . . . . [187
Longinus. . . . . [287
Lyall. . . . . [277
McCosh. . . . . [187
Mackintosh. . . . . [223
Magee. . . . . [236, 242
Manasses. . . . . [237

PAGE

References, (*continued.*)
Menander. . . . . [287
Michaelis. . . . . [215
Mills. . . . . [207
Newman. . . . . [235
Numenius. . . . . [287
Owen. . . . . [24?
Paley. . . . . [205, 266, 268
Pascal. . . . . [187, 223
Pfaffius. . . . . [264
Phlegon. . . . . [287
Phœnician Annals. . . . . [287
Pliny. . . . . [287
Porphyry. . . . . 279, [287
Samuel Stanhope Smith. . . . . [206
Solinus. . . . . [287
Spinoza. . . . . [215
Stapfer. . . . . [242
Storr. . . . . [215
Strabo. . . . . [287
Suetonius. . . . . [287
Tacitus. . . . . [287
Taylor. . . . . [264
Tindall. . . . . [196, 248
Tucker. . . . . [264
Turretin. . . . . [242
Vitringa. . . . . [276
Warburton. . . . . [187
Waterland. . . . . [195
Watson. . . . . [264
Waugh. . . . . [277, 285
Wayland. . . . . [188, 236
Whately. . . . . [206, 268, 288
Witsius. . . . . [264

Reformation does not always preclude punishment. 235
Regard due to the Son and Holy Spirit. 195
Regard to God as Creator, the essence of natural religion. 195
Rejection of Christ by many, at first, the argument from it. . . [269
foretold. 285
Relations, being learned, duties are perceived. 194

PAGE

Relations of man to Deity. 194
to the Son and Holy Ghost. . . 195
Religion
a practical thing. 298
a question of fact. 301, 304
affords particular reasons for miracles. 208
confirmed by the establishment of a church. 191
considered as external and internal. 195
doubt of its evidence does not release from moral obligation. 254
has its end on all persons to whom proposed. . . 303, [303
if true, why susceptible of any possible doubt?. 299
its acceptance safe. 295
its general spirit intimated 200, 201
its great importance. 254
its introduction into the world 206
its reasonableness fully shown, if it can only be proved that it *may* be reasonable. 301
its very nature overlooked by those who insist that it should have overwhelming evidence. 302
may be true, though doubtful. 299
must be judged by its evidences *taken together*. . . 294
not a thing reasoned out. 206
not equally taught to all men. 206
objections to it removed by analogy. 300
presupposes candor in those who examine it 256, 302, [303
reason may judge of its morality. 220
reasonable, for aught which can be shown to the contrary. 301
the perception of. 302
the view of it taken in this treatise. 299

PAGE

Religion, (*continued.*)
the evidence for it may be lessened, but cannot be destroyed. 295
why its evidences are allowed to admit of doubt. 249, 253, 299
Relief for evils provided. 232
Remedial nature of Christianity. [193
Remedies
provided in nature. 219, 232
may be unskilfully used. 220
show the compassion of God. 233
and also his strictness. 234
Repentance
cannot cancel guilt. . . . . 236, [236
general sense of mankind on the subject. 236
its efficacy not taught by natural religion . . . . [190
its efficacy taught in the Scriptures. 190
not sufficient to preclude disaster 234, 235
Revelation
a particular part of a great plan 224
accounts for the Theism of the Jews. . . . . [206
at the beginning of the world, would not be miraculous 205
cannot be neglected with impunity. 260–262
considered as miraculous. CHAP. II.
considered historically. 281
difference between its facts and its principles. . . . . [235
discovers new relations, and so new duties. 194
distinguished from natural religion. 195
does not compel assent. 253
has twice been universal. . . . [248
how it could be overturned. . . 214
its disclosures, of course, could not have been anticipated. 211, 212

PAGE

Revelation, (*continued.*)
its measure of evidence puts us on probation....... 253
its facts necessarily singular. [235
no more different from the course of nature than some parts of the course of nature are different from other parts....... 312
necessary............ CHAP. I.
republishes and confirms natural religion....... 188, 189
nothing incredible in it...... 271
teaches that God's laws are compassionate........ 236
the use of unwritten revelation............... 213
what is to be expected in revelation........... 210, 212
Reverence for the will of God... [199
Ridicule of Scripture
an offence against natural piety............... 286
easier than examination..... 259
the great weakness of being influenced by it....... 280
Roman Empire mentioned...... 279
Rules for health very fallible and inexact............. 302
of Biblical interpretation.... [215

Sacrifices
commanded.............. 241
expiatory................ 239
how the ancients regarded them............... 242
learned by the heathen from tradition............ 241
really efficacious.......... 242
the prevalence of.......... 236
Sacrifice of Christ
an objection to it.......... 243
how efficacious, not taught.... 242
proper and real........ 239–241
puts us into a capacity for salvation............ 242
voluntary............... 244

PAGE

Safety an important consideration in judging........... 294
Satirical writings, how understood........... 276, 277
Scheme of nature, vast........ 204
progressive............... 229
Scheme of providence, if understood, would justify facts which are objected to... 300
Schemes, the best may be disconcerted.............. 247
Science confirms Scripture history 287
Scorn of prophetic diction...... 210
Scripture
announces a general restoration of things........ 282
antiquity of.............. 287
characters evidently not feigned 287
confirmed by profane authors. 288
confirmed by the state of the earth............... 287
considered historically...... 281
contains an abridged history of the world......... 282
exposed to criticism........ 283
expounded by itself........ [202
gives a history of this world as God's world.......... 281
gives an account of civil governments only as they affected religion....... 282
has internal evidence of truth 287
history genuine........... 265
how distinguished from other books........... 281–283
how to be interpreted...... [202
if false could be shown to be so............... 283
includes a history of thousands of years........ 283
includes the chronology of nearly four thousand years............... 284
its authority the great question, not its contents... 214
its chronicles confirmed by history............. 287

PAGE

Scripture, (*continued.*)
its evidences comprise a series of things of great variety and reaching to the beginning of time....... 263
its evidences not intended to be overpowering....... 253
its great proofs are miracles and prophecy......... 264
its relation to miracles only to be accounted for on the supposition of their truth.............. 265
its strangeness not surprising. 288
its style objected to........ 210
its truth must be judged of by the evidence *taken together*.............. 295
may contain things not yet discovered........... 218
miracles, their first reception.. 265
naturalness of its statements.. 287
not composed by rules of art.. 210
nothing improbable related in any part............ 287
not to be judged by preconceived expectation..... 215
not to be judged exactly as other books.......... 214
ordinary rules of interpretation............... [215
our duty to search it.... 202, 262
precepts, some give offence... 210
reveals our relation to the Son and Holy Spirit....... 194
the possibility of its truth demands investigation.... 258
truths not discoverable by reason.............. 203
variety of topics introduced.. 283
written in a rude age....... 283
why it describes creation.... 282
Searching the Scriptures a great duty............... 202
Self-deceit, our liability to it.... 262
Serious apprehension may comport with doubt...... 313

PAGE

Shameful mistakes of philosophers [230
Similarity of objections to religion and nature....... 298
Sincerity of belief proved by dying for it.......... 270
Skepticism no justification of irreligion............... 253
Sorrow cannot of itself restore abused benefits........ 234
Speaking with tongues........ [217
Speculative difficulties similar to external temptations.... 256
the chief trial of some... 257, 259
Spread of Christianity unaccountable if it were an imposture............. 290
Standing ministry, what for.... [191
Strangeness of some Scripture events.............. 288
Stupidity of the martyrs, if insincere............. [269
Subserviences, the world a system of................. 229
Success, temporal, always uncertain................ 302
Suffering, ignorance does not prevent it either in temporal or spiritual things... 196
Sufferings of Christ vindicate God's law........... 244
of the early Christians...... 269
Sufficiency of light of nature pretended............. 186
Summary of Jewish history..... 284
of the historical evidence of Scripture............ 292
Supernatural instructions necessary from the first..... [206

Temporal interests not always discerned........ 247, 248
managed by prudent persons on the very principles proposed by religion as to spiritual interests 298, 299
Temporal interests often decided by considerations which

PAGE

fall short of demonstration. 299
Temporary commands, distinguished from perpetual. [188
Temptation
a wholesome discipline 256
earthly and spiritual similar. . 256
calls forth virtuous effort. 257
Testimony
can be destroyed only by counter-testimony, or by the incompetency of the witness 274
for miracles not mentioned in Scripture, does not impair the testimony for those there recorded. . . . 273
of Paul, separate and independent. 266
of profane authors to the truth of Scripture history. . . . [287
of the first Christians. . . . 269, 271
must be judged candidly. . . . [259
none counter to Christianity. . 275
slight, overcomes strong presumptions. 308
unconfuted, must be admitted. 273
value of, lessened by enthusiasm. 271
Theism of the Jews accounted for. . . . . [206
Theology of the Bible, not to be corrected. . . . . [202
Things which it is unreasonable to dispute. 307
Thoughtlessness of men. 233
Tradition teaches that there was a revelation at the beginning. 205
of the fall of man. 311
Transubstantiation. . . . . [205
Trial by speculative difficulties, analogous to other trials. 256
True philosophy inductive. . . . . . [230
Truth
of Christianity proved, unless the whole of its history and influence can be accounted for by accident. . 295
Truth, how developed. . . . . [218
the, of an event may be fully proved, though no *one* of sundry proofs may be complete. 295
whether there is any such thing, denied by skeptics 305
Twofold effect of the analogical argument. 308

Unbelievers, acknowledgment of. . 289
cannot deny a conformity between prophecy and events. 293
Understanding, its right use. 245
Undesigned coincidences in Bible history. . . . . [266
Undeterminate language deceives many. 297
Unequal distribution of religious knowledge. 249
Unfair dealing of objectors. 297
Unreasonableness of applying to passion for guidance. . . . 295
Unsatisfactory evidence, men often obliged to act upon it. 302

Variety in the distribution of God's gifts. 249, 312
Vastness of the scheme of nature. 204
Veracity of the first Christians. . . 274
Vicarious punishments witnessed every day. 244
deter from sin. 245
Vice
appointed to be punished. . . . 231
blinds men to just evidence. . . 255
its effects in the present world 234
its natural consequences are God's judicial inflictions. 197
its real enormity. 234
not palliated by any supposed lack of evidence for religion. 255

PAGE

Vindication of religion by analogy impossible. 296
of the character of God, not attempted in this treatise. 299, 300

Way of salvation for the helpless [186
Will of God, as absolute or conditional. 261
World, wickedness of. 238

PAGE

Worship, mode of, a matter of pure revelation. 195
Writers
on the atonement. . . . . [242
Christian sacraments. . . . . . . [195
miracles. . . . . [264, 268
necessity of revelation. . . . . . [187
prophecy. . . . . [277–285
Scripture difficulties . . . . [215
undesigned coincidences. . . . [266

THE END.

www.ingramcontent.com/pod-product-compliance
Lightning Source LLC
LaVergne TN
LVHW010149110826
845151LV00002B/470

* 9 7 8 1 4 2 5 5 3 8 0 2 6 *